MCSE

TESTPREP

Windows 95
70-64 Exam

New Riders

MCSE TestPrep: Windows 95 70-64 Exam

International Standard Book Number: 0-7897-1609-7

Library of Congress Catalog No.: 98-84506

01 00 99 98   4 3 2 1

Interpretation of the printing code: the rightmost double-digit number is the year of the book's printing; the rightmost single-digit number, the number of the book's printing. For example, a printing code of 98-1 shows that the first printing of the book occurred in 1998.

Screen reproductions in this book were created by using Collage Plus from Inner Media, Inc., Hollis, NH.

Executive Editor
Mary Foote

Acquisitions Editor
Nancy Maragioglio

Development Editor
Ami Frank

Managing Editor
Sarah Kearns

Project Editor
Mike La Bonne

Copy Editors
Audra McFarland
San Dee Philips
Molly Schaller

Indexer
Larry Sweazy

Technical Editors
Walter Glenn
Alain Guilbault

Production Team
Jeanne Clark
John Etchison
Christy M. Lemasters
Heather Stephenson

About the Authors

David Panagrosso is a Microsoft Certified Solution Developer and Microsoft Certified Product Specialist. He is employed as a senior systems engineer for Linc Systems Corporation, a client/server consulting firm in the northeast. He has over 12 years of experience in systems development and training, and his specialties include Microsoft Visual Basic and SQL Server. David has a BS in computer science and an MBA in operations management from Rensselaer Polytechnic Institute in Troy, NY. He can be reached at **dpanagrosso@lincsys.com**. David worked on Chapters 2, 6, and 7.

Danny E. Partain has been involved with NetWare since 1989. He is the MIS manager for Fox 5 - WAGA-TV in Atlanta, GA. He is also a member of the adjunct faculty at Gwinnett Technical Institute in the Business Information Sciences department. Danny teaches the following courses: Introduction to Networking (NetWare) and Advanced Networking (NetWare). On March 30, 1998, he received an award for "Combined Performance Rating Winter 1998," from Gwinnett Technical Institute. He is a Certified NetWare Engineer (CNE), IntraNetWare CNE, and a Microsoft Certified Product Specialist (MCPS) for Windows 95. He is a graduate of Southern Polytechnic State University and Gwinnett Technical Institute. He is a member of NetWare Users International and 3COM groups. Danny worked on Chapters 1 and 4.

R. Andrew Brice currently works as a senior instructor for ProSoft I-Net Solutions in Austin, Texas. His certifications include Novell CNA and CNE, as well as the Microsoft Certified Trainer and Microsoft Certified Systems Engineer in both Windows NT 3.51 and 4.0. Since 1991, he has been a consultant in network design and support to small and large organizations, including Fortune 1000 companies. Over the past three years, he has included training in both Novell and Microsoft technical curriculums. He credits his accomplishments to the love and support provided by both his wife, Susan, and his daughter, Katie. He can be reached at **andrewb@flash.net**. Andrew worked on Chapter 5.

Cory Woodrow has been a consultant and trainer in the field of networking for over five years. He has worked for a variety of public and private corporations including the Canadian federal government and the Praxis Training Institute. Cory is an MCSE and CNA. He worked on Chapter 3.

Dale Holmes is an MCSE and a CNE. He also has a certificate from George Washington University in UNIX Systems and C programming. He has been an Enterprise consultant for the past five years, and has performed many widescale deployments of Windows 95 and Windows NT. He is currently working for Tek Systems, Inc., and living in Baltimore, MD, with his wife, Emma, and his dog, Roxanne. He can be reached at **sysguru@yahoo.com**. Dale did the practice exams at the end of the book.

Dedications

From **David Panangrosso**: I dedicate my portion of this book to Ellen, for playing volleyball in the right place at the right time. Also, to Stoli for helping me wake up in the morning and getting me off to work.

From **Danny Partain**: I dedicate my portion of this book to the memory of my father, Joe Partain.

From **Andrew Brice**: I dedicate my portion of this book to my brother, Kevin. He has been a tremendous inspiration to me, both personally and professionally, as my mentor and my hero.

From **Cory Woodrow**: To Kathy.

Acknowledgments

From David Panagrosso: I thank New Riders for giving me the opportunity to work on this book, and all the employees of Linc Systems for sharing their knowledge.

From Danny Partain: To my wife, Dorothy, for all of her support and encouragement in helping me to complete this project.

From Cory Woodrow: I thank everyone who helped me to get where I am today, including Joe D., Laura E., Benjamin C., Joan M., and many more. I must also give thanks to Kathy, who has supported me and helped me in more ways than I can imagine. Finally, thanks to Papa. You will always be remembered. Rest in peace.

We'd Like to Hear from You!

As part of our continuing effort to produce books of the highest possible quality, MCP would like to hear your comments. To stay competitive, we really want you, as a computer book reader and user, to let us know what you like or dislike most about this book or other Macmillan products.

You can mail comments, ideas, or suggestions for improving future editions to the following address below or email us at **certification@mcp.com**. The address of our Internet site is **http://www.mcp.com** (World Wide Web).

Thanks in advance—your comments help us to continue publishing the best books available on computer topics in today's market.

> **Although we cannot provide general technical support, we're happy to help you resolve problems you encounter related to our books, disks, or other products. If you need such assistance, please contact our Tech Support department at 800-545-5914 ext. 3833.**

Contents at a Glance

Table of Contents

Introduction

The *MCSE TestPrep* series is written as a study aid for people preparing for Microsoft Certification Exams. The series is intended to help reinforce and clarify information with which the student is already familiar. This series is not intended to be a single source for student preparation, but rather as a review of information and a set of practice tests to help increase the likelihood of success when taking the actual exam. The best way to think of this book is as a workbook—mark it up, highlight, scribble things out, and try again.

Who Should Read This Book

The Windows 95 book in the *MCSE TestPrep* series is specifically intended to help students prepare for Microsoft's Implementing and Supporting Microsoft Windows 95 (#70-64) exam, one of the core tests required in the MCSE program.

How This Book Helps You

In addition to presenting a summary of information relevant to each of the exam objectives, this book provides a wealth of review questions similar to those you will encounter in the actual exam. This book is designed to help you make the most of your study time by presenting concise summaries of information that you need to understand to succeed on the exam. The practice problems at the end of each objective help reinforce what you have learned. Each answer is explained in detail in the Answers and Explanations section following the practice problems. Also, key words are noted for that section. The practice exam at the conclusion of each chapter will help you determine if you have mastered the facts. In addition to the practice tests at the end of each chapter, the book contains two full-length practice exams.

How to Use This Book

This book is intended to be used in two ways: First, as a review. The material in each section is the bare-bones outline of the basics you need to know for each objective. Second, you should use this book as a test of your knowledge. There are so many questions and practice problems, complete with explanations and answers, you should have no problem testing your comprehension of any given area.

After you have taken the practice tests and feel confident in the material on which you were tested, you are ready to schedule your exam. Use this book for a final quick review just before taking the test to make sure that all the important concepts are set in your mind.

What the Windows 95 Exam (#70-64) Covers

The Implementing and Supporting Windows 95 exam (#70-064) measures your ability to implement, administer, and troubleshoot computer systems that run Windows 95, and your ability to provide technical support to users of Windows 95. It covers the six main topic areas represented by the conceptual groupings of the test objectives. The exam objectives are listed by topic area in the following sections.

Planning

- Develop an appropriate implementation model for specific requirements. Considerations include choosing a workgroup configuration or joining an existing domain.

- Develop a security strategy. Strategies include system policies, profiles, and file and print sharing.

Installation and Configuration

- Install Windows 95. Installations include

    Automated Windows Setup

    New

    Upgrade

    Uninstall

    Dual boot combination with Microsoft Windows NT

- Install and configure the network components of a client computer and server.

- Install and configure network protocols. Protocols include

    NetBEUI

    IPX/SPX

    TCP/IP

    Data Link Control (DLC)

    PPTP/VPN

- Install and configure hardware devices. Hardware devices include modems and printers.

- Configure system services. Services include Browser.

- Install and configure backup hardware and software. Hardware and software include tape drives and the backup application.

Configuring and Managing Resource Access

- Assign permissions for shared folders. Methods include passwords, user permissions, and group permissions.

- Create, share, and monitor resources. Resources include

    Remote

    Network printers

    Shared fax/modem

    Unimodem/V

- Set up user environments by using profiles and system policies.

- Back up data and restore data.

- Manage hard disks. Tasks include disk compression and partitioning.

- Establish application environments for Microsoft MS-DOS applications.

Integration and Interoperabilty

- Configure a Windows 95 computer as a client in a Windows NT network.

- Configure a Windows 95 computer as a client in a NetWare network.

- Configure a Windows 95 computer to access the Internet.

- Configure a client computer to use Dial-Up Networking for remote access.

Monitoring and Optimization

- Monitor system performance. Tools include Net Watcher and System Monitor.

- Tune and optimize the system. Tools include

    Disk Defragmenter

    ScanDisk

    Compression Utility

Troubleshooting

- Diagnose and resolve installation failures.

- Diagnose and resolve boot process failures.

- Diagnose and resolve connectivity problems. Tools include

    WinIPCfg

    Net Watcher

    Troubleshooting Wizards

- Diagnose and resolve printing problems.

- Diagnose and resolve file-system problems.

- Diagnose and resolve resource-access problems.

- Diagnose and resolve hardware-device and device-driver problems. Tools include MSD and Add/Remove Hardware Wizard.

- Perform direct modification of the registry as appropriate by using Regedit.

The Implementing and Supporting Microsoft Windows 95 Certification Exam uses these categories to measure your ability to implement, administer, and troubleshoot information systems that incorporate Windows 95. Before taking this exam, you should be proficient in the job skills discussed in the following sections.

Hardware and Software Recommended for Preparation

The Windows 95 TestPrep is meant to help you review concepts with which you already have training and hands-on experience. To make the most of the review, you need to have as much background and experience as possible. The best way to do this is to combine studying with working on real networks using the products on which you will be tested. This section gives you a description of the minimum computer requirements you will need to build a solid practice environment.

Computers

The minimum computer requirement to ensure you can study everything on which you'll be tested is one or more workstations running Windows 95, Windows NT Workstation, and two or more servers running Windows NT Server, all connected by a network.

Workstations: Windows 95 and Windows NT

- Computer on the Microsoft Hardware Compatibility List

- 486DX 33MHz (Pentium recommended)

- 16MB of RAM (32MB recommended)

- 200MB (or larger) hard disk

- 3.5-inch 1.44MB floppy drive

- VGA (or Super VGA) video adapter

- VGA (or Super VGA) monitor

- Mouse or equivalent pointing device

- Two-speed (or faster) CD-ROM drive

- Network Interface Card (NIC)

- Presence on an existing network, or use of a hub to create a test network

- Microsoft Windows 95

Servers: Windows NT Server

- Two computers on the Microsoft Hardware Compatibility List

- 486DX2 66MHz (or better)

- 32MB of RAM (64 recommended)

- 340MB (or larger) hard disk

- 3.5-inch 1.44MB floppy drive

- VGA (or Super VGA) video adapter

- VGA (or Super VGA) monitor

- Mouse or equivalent pointing device

- Two-speed (or faster) CD-ROM drive

- Network Interface Card (NIC)

- Presence on an existing network, or use of a hub to create a test network

- Microsoft Windows NT Server

Thank you for choosing *MCSE TestPrep: Windows 95 70-64 Exam*! We're sure you'll find it a valuable study aid. For more contextual study aids, please check your bookstore for the *MCSE Training Guide: Windows 95*, published by New Riders Publishing, or the *MCSE Teach Yourself Windows 95 in 14 Days*, published by Sams Publishing. Good luck with your exam!

CHAPTER 1

Planning

This chapter helps prepare you for the exam by covering the following objectives:

- Develop an appropriate implementation model for specific requirements in a Microsoft and mixed Microsoft/NetWare environment. Considerations include the following:

    - Choosing a workgroup configuration or joining an existing domain

- Develop a security strategy in a Microsoft and mixed Microsoft/NetWare environment. Strategies include the following:

    - System Policies

    - User Profiles

    - File and Printer Sharing

1.1   Develop an Appropriate Implementation Model for Specific Requirements in a Microsoft and Mixed Microsoft/NetWare Environment

This section will look at the planning that must go into an implementation model of Windows 95 in any organization. The goal of this section is to present you with the different options available to you so that you can make appropriate decisions. The decisions that you make will lead to developing a final implementation model that is right for your particular situation. The implementation model should include the type of network you have, either Microsoft or NetWare. The Windows 95 implementation model has been broken into several small sections that you will be studying:

- Taking an inventory of current equipment and software

- Choosing a Windows 95 version

- Choosing a software distribution method

- Choosing a workgroup configuration or logging on to an existing domain

- Using long filenames
- Assembling a distribution team
- Setting up a test lab
- Conducting a test implementation model
- Documenting the problems and solutions
- Conducting the final implementation model

1.1.1 Taking a Current Inventory

Before any other planning for the installation, you will have to take a thorough inventory of all hardware and software that your organization is currently using. From this you will cull any items that are excessively old or otherwise incompatible with Windows 95. You will also be able to determine what upgrades are necessary. You are able to get a copy of the Windows 95 Hardware Compatibility List (HCL) from Microsoft's Web site. For the same reason, the software currently installed on the system should be identified, and a list of software can then be built, detailing items that should be replaced or upgraded. This process helps to determine applications that might be incompatible with Windows 95. Microsoft also provides a software compatibility list.

1.1.2 Choosing a Version of Windows 95

Microsoft has two official versions of Windows 95: the retail version (full or upgrade) and OSR2 (Original Equipment Manufacturer Service Release Two). OSR2 is available only with the shipment of new computers. Some of the reasons why you might want to consider OSR2 are as follows:

- Support for large hard drive partitions (larger than 2GB) in the form of FAT32
- System Agent task scheduler (also available in the Windows 95 Plus Pack)
- DriveSpace 3 disk compression (also available in the Windows 95 Plus Pack)
- Includes drivers for versions of Windows 95: the retail version (Full or Upgrade) and OSR2 newer hardware, without having to supply driver disks
- Comes pre-loaded, so there is less installation work to perform

Some of the reasons why you might want to use the retail version are as follows:

- Upgrade existing copies of Windows.
- Dual boot with DOS 6.*x* and Windows 3.1 or Windows for Workgroups 3.11.
- Does not support FAT32. FAT32 is optional when using OSR2.
- Offers more compatibility with older software and hardware. OSR2 might not work with all.

Some of the most important features of OSR2, with the exception of FAT32, are available as options for the retail version of Windows 95. Many are available in the form of the Windows 95 Plus Pack or from Microsoft's Web site at `http://www.microsoft.com/windows95`.

1.1.3 Installing and Distributing the Software

There are several options that you might want to consider when installing and distributing software. The three most important are Push installations with packages such as Microsoft's System Management Server (SMS), Pull or Automatic installation, and Disk Images. Push and Pull installations both run a standard scripted installation of Windows 95, which is the cleanest (and most recommended) way of deploying Windows 95.

Push installs are initiated at a remote server and sent to the workstation through a logon script or other application. If you are using a network management package such as SMS, the server actually moves your source files to a location of your choice. SMS then sends the installation command to the workstation. The workstation then starts the installation of Windows 95 by using a setup information (*.INF) file that ships with SMS or one that you have created yourself.

Pull installations also use a setup INF file that you have created, but the installation is initiated at the client workstation and pulled down from the server. You can use Netsetup, which comes with Windows 95. This utility enables you to place Windows 95 on a server for setup to desktop systems. This is different than copying files to installation. You can also customize the setup INF file for your organization.

Windows 95 uses an URL, so a drive mapping to a NetWare volume does not have to be the same at each NetWare client for setup. The NetWare drive mappings need to point to the same location on the NetWare server.

Disk Images offer advantages over the previous two methods. The entire hard drive can be configured with multiple applications after the Windows 95 installation has been completed. This fully configured hard drive can now be copied to a single file through a special application. The process is then reversed to copy the contents of the file back to a hard drive. The destination hard drive should be in a computer that is identical in hardware configuration to the original, or source, computer. Microsoft does not fully support or recommend this method of installation of Windows 95. For more information about this process, see the "Binary image copying of Microsoft Operating Systems" White Paper 1.9 from Microsoft.

Scripts (*.INF) are clean, but often several different scripts are required to get Windows 95 and all applications installed. Images are easier to install but are not as clean, because they are hardware-specific.

1.1.4 Choosing a Workgroup Configuration or Logging on to Existing Domain

When configuring a workgroup name for Windows 95, you should take some care in choosing the name. If the name is different from the workgroup names used by any servers on your network, then you will not be able to browse network resources without knowing the names of the servers you want to visit. The term *server* refers to any computer on your network that shares resources. This could be a NetWare server, but also it encompasses Windows for Workgroups, Windows 95, and Windows NT. If you decide to make your workgroup name the same as your domain name, then your computer will appear to have joined the domain in the Network

Neighborhood. The benefit from this is seeing the domain servers as soon as you open the Network Neighborhood (see Figure 1.1), which makes navigating your server's unmapped drives much easier.

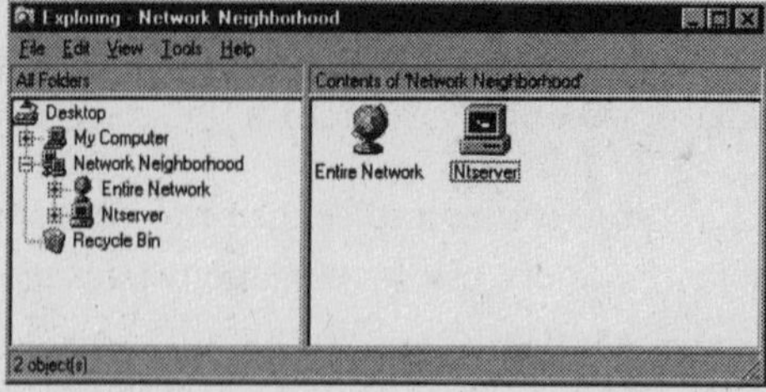

Figure 1.1   When you open the Network Neighborhood, you will see the contents of your current workgroup.

> **Windows 95 can only be a part of a workgroup on your network. The only operating system that can be a part of a Windows NT domain is Windows NT. If you set a Windows 95 workgroup name to a Windows NT domain name currently in use, both computers will share a list of resources. The Windows 95 computers will also appear listed in Windows NT administration tools, such as Server Manager. This appearance is an illusion; the Windows 95 computers are not actually a part of the domain.**

If you choose a name for your workgroup that is different from your domain name, then you will have a shorter server list in that domain, but you will have to locate those servers through the Entire Network icon of the Network Neighborhood (see Figure 1.2).

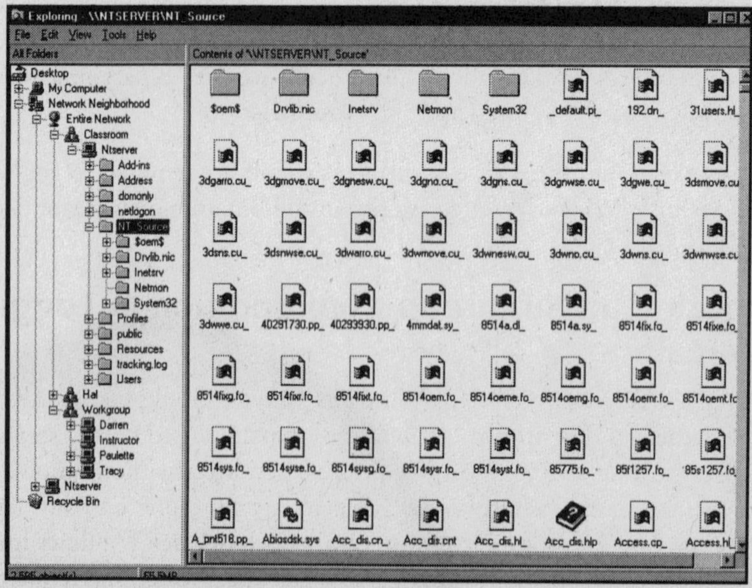

Figure 1.2   When browsing for a domain, you might have to take a long trip to your server.

If you choose a workgroup name that differs from your domain name, then at least one computer in that workgroup must have File and Printer Sharing installed. By installing File and Printer Sharing, you ensure that the computer will maintain a list of servers in the workgroup, as well as a list of other workgroups or domains that exist on the network. If you do not have this list, you will receive an "Unable to Browse the Network" error message when attempting to access the Entire Network icon of the Network Neighborhood.

1.1.5 Preparing to Support Long Filenames

Windows 95 supports filenames up to 255 characters. For the computers that are not running Windows 95, your filenames will have to conform to other standards. Some of your NetWare servers might not support long filenames. You will have to add long-filenames support to your NetWare volumes to store files with longer file names.

1.1.6 Assembling a Distribution Team

Having other people with you as you implement Windows 95 will make the whole process move more smoothly. Choose people who can represent a number of departments or areas; this enables your implementation model to address many of the concerns that are held in each of the departments.

By choosing people from each department, you will be aware of how the departments operate and how Windows 95 will affect both the way each department operates and the applications individuals within each department use.

1.1.7 Setting Up a Test Lab

After taking an inventory, steps should be taken to get a representative sample of the various pieces of hardware and software that are in use on the network. The computers in the test lab will be used to develop the installation script files (*.INF), as well as the installation procedure.

Windows 95 is compatible with a very wide range of hardware, but there are often times when certain pieces of hardware will not function properly together. Occasionally, you will find information about incompatibilities listed in the installation documentation or the Web site for the hardware. You might also need updated drivers for the hardware before it will work properly with Windows 95. The importance of the test lab is like that of the distribution team. By choosing wisely, you will limit the number of surprises that will occur during the actual deployment.

1.1.8 Conducting a Test Implementation Model

After performing thorough testing of software and hardware, you are ready to conduct a test or pilot implementation model. This test should be limited in scope so problems can be given a proper amount of attention and time. A test implementation model might be made up of only one department or even just a handful of people in a department.

The test implementation model provides a shakedown test of the installation procedure you developed through testing. This also enables you to see what changes should be made to the installation procedure to keep problems from arising at the time of the entire installation. Because the number of computers in the test implementation has been kept relatively small, you may be able to revert them back to their original state if problems occur.

1.1.9   Documenting the Problems and Solutions

Documentation is one of the keys to a successful implementation model. Any problems you have should be documented and added to a database. This database can be referred to and updated during the implementation model. Document the steps required to perform the setup of each computer so that your distribution team will not have to perform ad hoc installs.

1.1.10   Conducting the Final Implementation Model

You should plan to perform upgrades in synchronization with a training schedule for the users. The training should cover the changes to their operating system, as well as any changes to the applications they use. Windows 95 enables users to be more productive, but initially productivity will drop during the orientation phase. By delivering timely training, this drop in productivity will be minimized.

The final implementation model should be scheduled to convert users in a logical order. This order should be determined by how one upgraded user will affect the users who have not been upgraded. You might decide that upgrading by branch or department makes the most sense in your situation. You might also decide that because sections of two departments communicate regularly, they should be upgraded at the same time. If you have to upgrade a number of branches, you will likely upgrade them one at a time; but you might start with the head office, because people in the head office need to communicate with all other branches.

Whatever order in which you decide to implement the upgrades, you should educate all of the users, upgraded or not, on how the temporary mixed environment will affect the way they work. Throughout this whole process, you should refer to the deployment database for solutions to previous problems, as well as posting new problems and solutions.

Your deployment plan covers compatibility and logistics, but you have not yet created a secure network. The next major section prepares you to develop a security strategy.

1.1.11   Exercises

Exercise 1: Upgrade to Windows 95

In this exercise you will decide which equipment must be upgraded from the following scenario. List the equipment and give an explanation as to why or why not this equipment should be upgraded for Windows 95.

Scenario: You are going to upgrade your office systems to Windows 95. Your office has 30 Personal Computers in three departments. Of the 30 Personal Computers:

   10 are 386, 33MHz machines with 2MB of RAM and 40MB hard disk.

   7 are 486, 33MHz machines with 4MB of RAM and 110MB hard disk.

   3 are 286, 10MHz machines and 20MB hard disk.

   5 are Pentium, 90MHz with 8MB and 540MB hard disk.

   5 are Pentium, 166MHz with 16MB of RAM and 1.2GB hard disk.

Your office has decided to keep cost at a minimum. Therefore you cannot replace equipment that is 386 and above.

Answer to Exercise 1

3 286 PCs. This equipment is incompatible with Windows 95 and should be replaced with up-to-date equipment. A recommendation of Pentium 166MHz (minimum) with 16MB of RAM and 2.1GB hard drive space.

10 386 PCs. This equipment is compatible with Windows 95, but requires a RAM upgrade to 16MB, if possible, or 4MB minimum. It also requires an upgrade to a larger-than-40MB hard disk. The minimum space required for a complete installation requires 50MB of hard drive space.

7 486 PCs. This equipment is compatible with Windows 95. The system has minimum requirements, but a RAM upgrade would help performance.

10 Pentiums. This equipment is compatible with Windows 95 and would not require an update.

Exercise 2: Steps for an Implementation Model

In this exercise, list the steps of an Implementation Model in progressive order.

Answer to Exercise 2

1. Take an inventory of current equipment and software

2. Choose a Windows 95 version

3. Choose a software distribution method

4. Choose a workgroup configuration or log on to existing domain

5. Use long filenames

6. Assemble a distribution team

7. Set up a test lab

8. Conduct a test implementation model

9. Document the problems and solutions

10. Conduct the final implementation model

1.1.12 Practice Problems

1. To know if existing hardware will work with Windows 95, which of the following must you check?

   A. Hardware Checklist

   B. Hardware Compatibility List

   C. Hardware Component List

   D. Hardware Characteristic List

2. What is the version of Microsoft Windows 95 available only on new computers?

   A. OSR2

   B. ORS2

   C. OR25

   D. OS2R

3. What gives Windows 95 the capability to support large hard drive partitions?

   A. LPD

   B. NTFS

   C. FAT32

   D. NPFS

4. Which of the following cannot be dual booted in Windows 95?

   A. DOS 6.*x*

   B. Windows 3.1

   C. Windows 3.11

   D. Windows 3.0

5. If a user wants to add options to his retail version of Windows 95 that comes with OSR2, where would the user find these options on Microsoft's Web site?

   A. `http://www.microsoft.com/windows`

   B. `http://www.microsoft.com/windows95`

   C. `http://www.microsoft.com/win 95`

   D. `http://www.microsoft.com/windows 95`

6. What is the file extension used with setup information files?

   A. INF

   B. IFN

   C. INB

   D. ISF

7. Which of the following does Microsoft not recommend as an option for the installation of Windows 95?

   A. Push

   B. Pull

   C. Disk Images

   D. Upgrade

8. How many characters does Windows 95 support in long filenames?

   A. 55

   B. 255

   C. 155

   D. 355

9. You are a network administrator implementing Windows 95 on the workstations on the network. What is the name of the Microsoft server application that enables you to automate installations on the network?

   A. SSI

   B. SMS

   C. SDS

   D. SMI

10. What is the installation process which allows installation from a remote server and is sent to a workstation through a logon script?

A. Push

B. Pull

C. Automatic

D. Disk Images

11. A user asks which operating system can be part of a Windows NT domain. What is the correct answer ?

    A. Windows 95 and Windows NT

    B. Windows NT

    C. Windows NT and Windows 3.11

    D. Windows NT and DOS 6.*x*

12. What happens when you make a workgroup name the same as your domain name?

    A. An error message is displayed saying the workgroup does not exist.

    B. Your workstation is the only system you can see in the Network Neighborhood.

    C. Your workstation appears to have joined the domain in the Network Neighborhood.

    D. An error message is displayed saying the domain does not exist.

13. You are developing an Implementation Model for upgrading to Windows 95. Which of the following does not need to be considered as part of the Implementation Model?

    A. Setting up a test lab

    B. Taking an inventory of current equipment and software

    C. Checking power sources

    D. Assembling a distribution team

14. You are considering which version of Windows 95 to implement. You think the OSR2 version would have advantages in your environment. Which of the following is the reason why you want to choose OSR2?

    A. DriveSpace 2

    B. DriveSpace 3

    C. DoubleSpace 3

    D. DoubleSpace 2

15. Your workgroup name is different than your domain name. Also, you do not have File and Printer Sharing installed in the workgroup. What is the message you receive when you try to access the entire network in Network Neighborhood?

    A. File and Printer Sharing has not been installed

    B. No domain exists in the network

    C. You must specify a domain name

    D. Unable to browse the network

16. You have finished your deployment plans. Which of the following steps should you do next?

    A. Document the problems and solutions

    B. Set up a test lab

    C. Assemble an implementation team

    D. Develop a security strategy

17. What is the final step in the Implementation Model?

    A. Set up a test lab

    B. Take a hardware and software inventory

    C. Conduct the Final Implementation Model

    D. Assemble an implementation team

18. Microsoft has published a White Paper for the Disk Images installation process. What is the title of this White Paper?

A. Disk Images on Microsoft Operating Systems

B. Binary image copying of Microsoft Operating Systems

C. On-demand installation with Microsoft Operating Systems

D. Disk Images copying on Microsoft Operating Systems

19. You are assembling your distribution team. What is the advantage of choosing people from each department?

   A. You have more people to help with installation.

   B. You get to know the users.

   C. You will know how Windows 95 will affect the way each department operates.

   D. You manage the installation process remotely.

20. Why is it important to keep a test implementation of Windows small?

   A. To get a feel for the time it will take to implement Windows 95.

   B. To see if users will be able to use Windows 95.

   C. To get the users accustom to Windows 95.

   D. If there is a problem you will be able to revert the workstations back to their original state.

1.1.13 Answers and Explanations

1. **B** Microsoft publishes what is called a Hardware Compatibility List (HCL). HCL can be retrieved from Microsoft's Web page.

2. **A** OSR2 stands for Original Equipment Manufacturer Service Release 2. OSR2 version is installed on new computers.

3. **C** The OSR2 version of Windows 95 comes with support for large hard drive partitions using FAT32.

4. **D** Windows 95 can dual boot with Windows 3.1, DOS 6.*x* and Windows 3.11.

5. **B** The location for updates Windows 95 can be found at `http://www.microsoft.com/windows95`. Watch the spelling.

6. **A** All Windows 95 setup information files have an extension of INF.

7. **C** Disk Images is not recommended by Microsoft because it requires an exact duplicate of the system from which the Disk Images were created.

8. **B** Windows 95 supports long filenames up to 255 characters.

9. **B** The System Management Server from Microsoft moves source files to a location you specify.

10. **A** Push runs a standard scripted installation from the server to the workstation.

11. **B** The only operating system which can be part of a Windows NT domain is Windows NT.

12. **C** You will be able to see the domain servers when you open Network Neighborhood.

13. **C** Hopefully this issue would have already been resolved in an existing computing environment.

14. **B** DriveSpace 3 is the latest version of this utility for disk compression and can be found on the Windows 95 Plus Pack.

15. **D** If you do not have at least one workstation in a workgroup with File and Printer Sharing enabled, you will not be able to see any other workstations or servers on the network.

16. **D** Your deployment model should have covered all the steps in this objective. The next phase would be the beginning of a security strategy.

17. **C**   Conducting the Final Implementation
     Model is the final step and should be done
     in a logical order.

18. **B**   Microsoft does not recommend Disk
     Images on Windows 95 and has released
     White Paper 1.9 on this issue.

19. **C**   You will see how the departments
     operate and how the Windows 95 installa-
     tion will affect the departments. You will be
     able to isolate individual problems on a
     departmental basis.

20. **D**   If there are problems found in the test
     lab, you can revert a small number of
     machines back to their original state. This
     would not be a large disruption to business
     operations.

1.1.14   Key Words and Definitions

Distribution team   The people you assemble in order to implement Windows 95
on all systems in an organization.

Implementation model   The guidelines you configure for implementing
Windows 95.

OSR2   The Original Equipment Manufacturer Service Release 2 version of Windows
95. OSR2 comes installed on new computers.

Server   Refers to any computer on the
network that shares resources.

1.2   Develop a Security Strategy in a Microsoft and Mixed Microsoft/NetWare Environment

There are components of the Windows 95 operating system that behave as double-edged swords, in that they offer indispensable benefits but also unwanted problems. Windows 95 has several components that you will find indispensable, but offer definite security problems for users and LAN administrators. Windows 95 clients on a NetWare network can appear as servers on the network. Setting up File and Printer Sharing in a NetWare environment should be done under the supervision of the LAN administrators. Access to files on a Windows 95 client can be a security problem if it is not controlled. There are also utilities that we would rely on heavily if we only knew that they existed. These are the components that you will consider in this section. They include the following:

- File and Printer Sharing

- System Policies

- User Profiles

- Remote Registry Editing and System Monitoring

- Remote Administration

1.2.1   File and Printer Sharing

File and Printer Sharing services can represent a major security problem on your network, and this is something you must consider before conducting your installations.

There are many LAN administrators who flinch at the mention of "Personal File and Printer Sharing." The reason they flinch is almost exclusively because it takes control away from the central security, which is usually the administrator. This section elaborates on the purpose and use of File and Printer services, as well as the differences in sharing methods between the two services that Microsoft supplies.

Files are kept safe, and information is kept hidden most effectively, if the files reside on a central server where a central security authority can control access to them. With the files in this central location, administrators can control who has access and the level of access each person has. On the point of safe files, most sites have implemented procedures to regularly back up the contents of the servers, daily or less often.

When files are kept on local hard drives, security is compromised. By ignoring the network logon dialog box, you will gain access to all local files with total control, unless some type of local security has been implemented. Local files are also usually not part of a regular and systematic backup procedure. If security and safety does not convince you to keep files on a central server, then enabling users to share local files with others increases the risk to the files.

When you use NTFS in Windows NT, local files and directories can be protected with user-level security. Windows 95 can only use FAT and cannot be protected in the same manner.

When network users have access to files, or are allowed to share files with other network users, they will usually accomplish sharing through Microsoft's File and Printer Sharing for Microsoft Networks. It is also usually implemented with the default system security—Share-level Access Control (see Figure 1.3). With Share-level Access Control, users are asked for either a Read-only password, a Full Access password, or both. Either password can be left blank, which might leave the shared folder open to Full Access with no check in place (see Figure 1.4). This security breach is impossible to control if each user is responsible for his or her own file sharing.

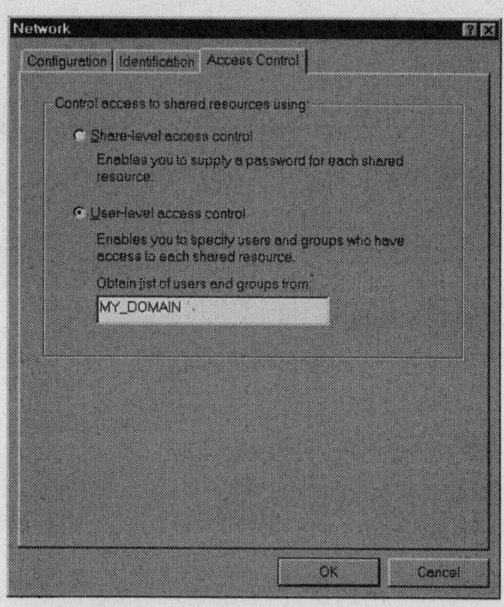

Figure 1.3 When using the File and Printer Sharing for Microsoft Networks, you have two security levels.

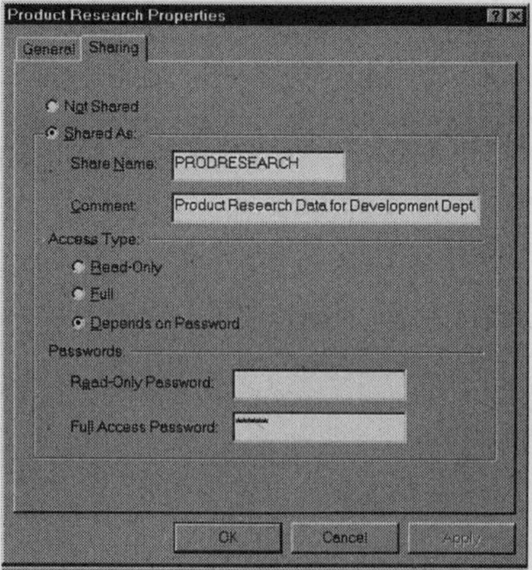

Figure 1.4 When implementing Share-level Access Control, your security is based on one or two passwords.

Rather than implement Share-level Access Control, you might choose to implement the other type of security: User-level Access Control. This method provides substantially better security. You can log on by using a valid username and password on a Windows NT domain, a Windows

NT server, a Windows NT workstation, or a Novell NetWare server (3.*x* or 4.*x*). When you choose User-level Access Security on the Access tab of the Network control panel, you must supply the name of server or domain from which your account originates. This enables you to grant access to your system to users who are registered on a controlled server. It also means that you do not have to distribute a list of passwords to people accessing your computer, because all that they need are their usernames and passwords from the main server.

When using Microsoft's File and Printer Sharing Service for NetWare (see Figure 1.5), the only security option is User-level Access Control, and the security provider must be a Novell NetWare server.

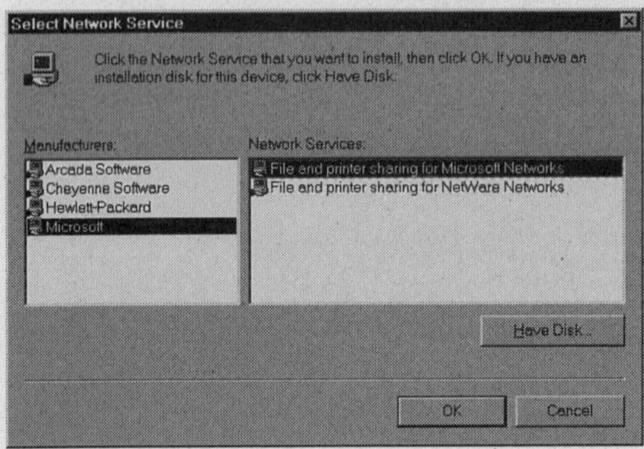

Figure 1.5 File and Printer Services are available for both Microsoft and Novell Networks.

1.2.2 System Policies

A *system policy* is a single file on a server that is processed when users log on to your network. This file contains a list of settings or restrictions that are to be applied to the users at logon. System policies work in conjunction with user profiles (customized settings maintained for each user) to restrict or control access to components of the Windows 95 operating system or to configure an environment for the user. Much of the security of which Windows 95 is capable can be implemented through system policies, which are created with the System Policy Editor. In this section you will do the following:

- Read the installation overview of the System Policy Editor

- Examine the user settings of a policy file

- Examine the computer settings of a policy file

- Create policies for specific users, groups, and computers

- Create policy template files

Installation Overview of the System Policy Editor

The System Policy Editor is not installed as one of the default applications with Windows 95. The application will have to be installed from the ADMIN\APPTOOLS\POLEDIT directory of the Windows 95 CD-ROM. From this location, you are able to install both the System Policy

Editor and group policies on your computer. You have to install the System Policy Editor only on the machine that you will be using to create the system policy. If you plan to assign the policy to users based on the server groups to which they belong, you must install the group policies on every machine on your network.

After the System Policy Editor is installed, you will be able to create a policy file (*.POL). The default policy file that Windows 95 looks for is CONFIG.POL, which is expected to be in one of the following locations:

- Windows NT Domain, in the NetLogon directory of domain controllers, which is
  win_root\SYSTEM32\REPL\IMPORT\SCRIPTS\

- Novell NetWare 3.*x* or 4.*x* server on the SYS volume in the PUBLIC directory

To work with the Policy Editor, select it from the Start menu, under Programs, Accessories, System Tools, System Policy Editor. To create a policy file, select New from the File menu. This will leave you with two icons: DEFAULT USER and DEFAULT COMPUTER (see Figure 1.6). You also have the capability to use the System Policy Editor to edit the local Registry by choosing Open Registry from the File menu. If you open the Registry by mistake, the two icons in the Policy Editor will read LOCAL USER and LOCAL COMPUTER (see Figure 1.7).

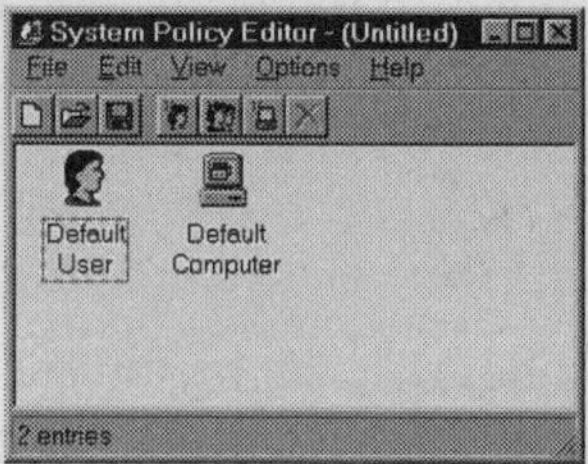

Figure 1.6   System Policy Editor working on a policy file.

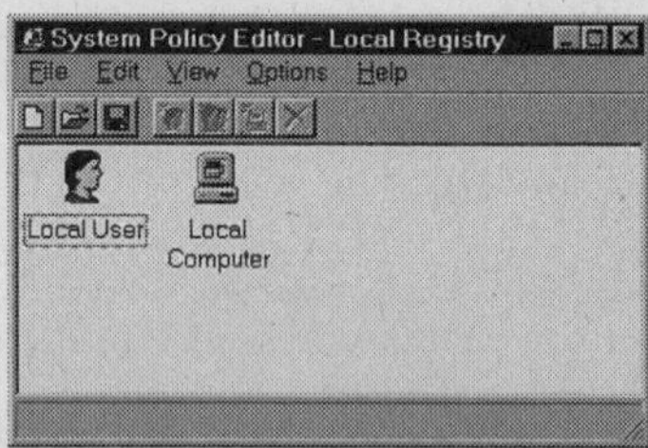

Figure 1.7   System Policy Editor working on a local Registry.

When using the Policy Editor to make a policy file, each check box in the settings windows has three settings: On, Off, and Neutral (see Figure 1.8). When you use the Policy Editor to edit the local Registry, there are only two settings: On and Off.

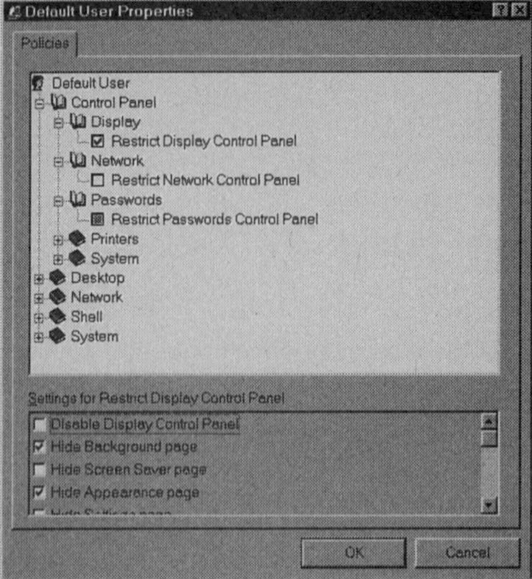

Figure 1.8 Each check box in the Policy Editor has three settings; the gray box is a neutral setting.

Each setting gives you the ability to create the policy file you require. An "on setting" means the policy will be implemented. An "off setting" means the policy will not be implemented. A "neutral setting" means the previous policy will be maintained if one previously existed. The "neutral setting" is represented by a gray check box. The gray check box means two or more policies will be enforced, one after another, such as when group policies are used.

User Settings in the Policy File

The following list examines the settings that can be adjusted or enforced in a system policy. To access this screen, double-click on DEFAULT USER or LOCAL USER in the System Policy Editor (see Figure 1.9). The user settings are applied for each user regardless of the computer they have logged on to, and the changes that are implemented are stored in the user's USER.DAT file. You will next cover the following topics:

- **Control panel settings.** Enables you to disable or restrict sections of certain control panels or disable the entire control panel. You will be able to control the following control panels, which will help you in the following ways:

  - *Display*   Prevents users from changing the current display adapter or the screen resolution.

  - *Network*   Prevents users from changing their workgroup name, which can cause problems when they are browsing the network. This also prevents users from changing the network adapter, protocol, or network client settings.

  - *Passwords*   Prevents users from modifying Remote Administration or user profile settings.

  - *Printers*   Prevents users from modifying printer settings and adding or removing printers.

  - *System*   Prevents users from changing most of the settings in the System control panel, such as the device manager, hardware profiles, and virtual memory settings.

- **Desktop settings.** Does not restrict the desktop, but rather enforces settings for both wallpaper and color schemes.

- **File and Printer Sharing settings.** Enables you to disable the capability to share folders or printers.

- **Windows Explorer Shell settings.** Enables you to control the entire Start menu and to remove from the menu whatever commands you want.

- **Application restrictions.** Enables you to specify additional restrictions on the way in which applications will run on the workstation.

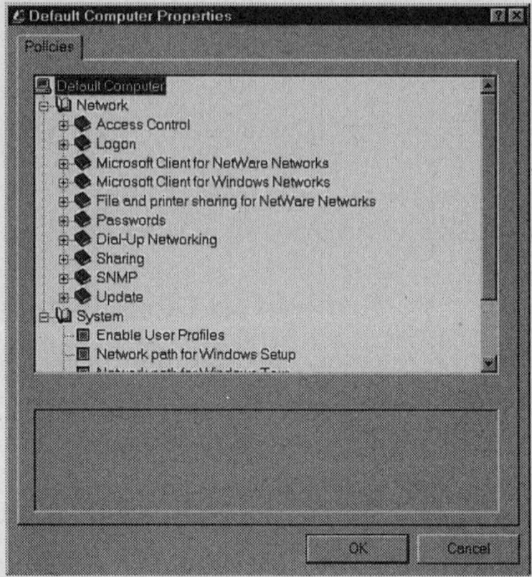

Figure 1.9   Default Computer has settings for Network options and other System restrictions.

Computer Settings in the Policy File

The next list examines the settings that you can adjust or enforce in the computer section of a policy. To access this screen, double-click on DEFAULT COMPUTER or LOCAL COM-PUTER in the System Policy Editor (see Figure 1.9). The computer settings are applied to the computer regardless of the user who has logged on to the computer, and the changes that are implemented are stored in the computer's SYSTEM.DAT file.

- **Network Settings.** Enables you to configure the following settings:

  - *Access Control*   Enables you to configure the type of access control used at the workstation, User-level or Share-level. If you choose User-level, you can specify the name of the security provider.

  - *Logon*   Enables you to specify a logon banner and whether or not the user must log on to gain access to Windows 95.

  - *Microsoft Client for NetWare Networks*   Enables you to configure settings for the NetWare Client, such as the server to which the Client should be logged on.

  - *Microsoft Client for Windows Networks*   Enables you to configure settings for the Microsoft Client, such as which domain should be logged on to.

  - *File and Printer Sharing for NetWare Networks*   Enables you to broadcast your network presence as a Novell NetWare server.

- *Passwords*   Gives you control over how Windows 95 maintains its passwords. This applies both to the Windows password and passwords that are applied to shared resources.

- *Dial-up Networking*   Enables you to disable all dialing connections to the Windows 95 computer.

- *Sharing*   Enables you to disable File and Printer Sharing services on the workstations.

- *SNMP*   Enables you to remotely and automatically disable all of the SNMP settings on the computers on your network, including community names and trap destinations.

- *Update*   Enables you to change the location of the policy file that will be processed for that computer.

- **System settings**   Enables you to enable user profiles, as well as configure RUN and RUN ONCE Registry keys to automatically start up applications when Windows 95 boots.

Creating Policies for Users, Groups, and Computers

When creating a policy file for a server, you have the additional option of adding individual icons for each user or group of users from your server, as well as icons for each computer on your network (see Figure 1.10). To add additional entries to your policy, choose Add User…, Add Computer…, or Add Group… from the Edit menu. If you have configured your system for User-level Access Control, you will be able to browse a list of users, groups, and computers; otherwise, you have to type the name of the user, group, or computer.

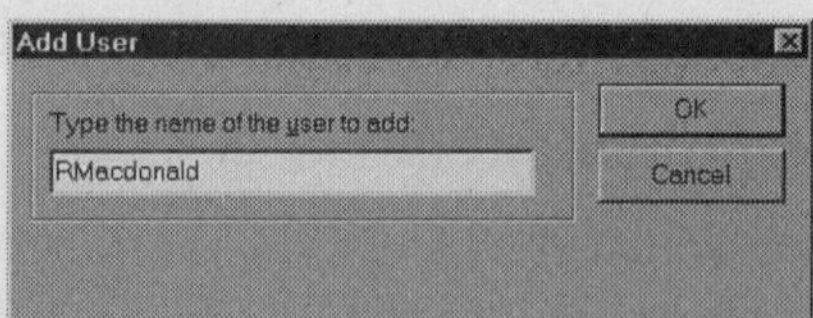

Figure 1.10   Individual policy entries can be created for users or groups from your server, as well as for computers on your network.

When applying the policies, Windows 95 first looks to see if there is an entry for the user logging on, and then applies the changes for the user. If there are no entries for that user, it then checks to see if the user is a member of any the groups that it has entries for. If the user is not a member of any of the groups, then the entry for DEFAULT USER is applied. After applying the user policy, Windows 95 then applies a computer policy. If there is an entry for your current computer name, then it will be applied; otherwise, the entry for DEFAULT COMPUTER is applied.

When working with groups in the Policy Editor, the client computers need to have group policies installed on their computer. The groups listed in the policy file are applied in a particular order, which can be seen by choosing Group Priority… from the Options menu (see Figure 1.11). The policy entries are applied for each group that the user is a member of, starting from the bottom of the list and working up. This means that if any of the entries conflict with one other, the entry that is higher in the list takes precedence.

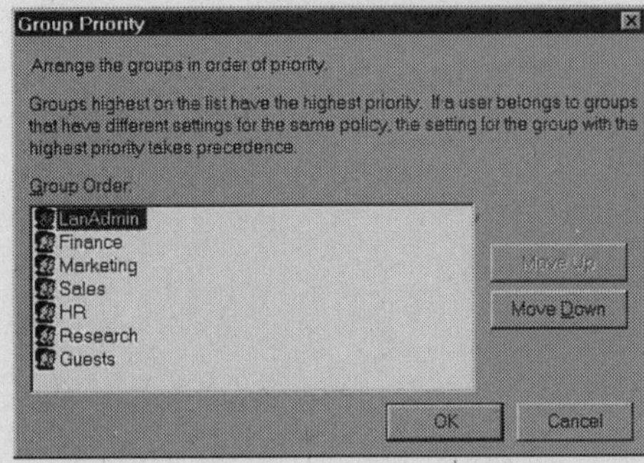

Figure 1.11   Groups are processed from the bottom up, making the items higher in the list override
          lower settings.

Policy Template Files

The Policy Editor is an alternative shell to enable editing of the Windows 95 Registry. It does not
know anything about the structure or form of the Registry. Everything that it displays and
changes is a result of the policy template file that is in use. The default template file is
C:\WINDOWS\INF\ADMIN.ADM. To change the template file, choose Template… from the
Options menu. The template file is a text file with a particular structure. As follows is an excerpt
of the default ADMIN.ADM file that ships with Windows 95, and Figure 1.12 shows the results
of this section of the template:

```
...
CLASS USER


CATEGORY !!ControlPanel
        CATEGORY !!CPL_Display
                POLICY !!CPL_Display_Restrict
                KEYNAME
Software\Microsoft\Windows\CurrentVersion\Policies\System
                PART !!CPL_Display_Disable CHECKBOX
                VALUENAME NoDispCPL
                END PART


                PART !!CPL_Display_HideBkgnd CHECKBOX
                VALUENAME NoDispBackgroundPage
                END PART


                PART !!CPL_Display_HideScrsav CHECKBOX
                VALUENAME NoDispScrSavPage
                END PART


                PART !!CPL_Display_HideAppearance CHECKBOX
                VALUENAME NoDispAppearancePage
                END PART


                PART !!CPL_Display_HideSettings CHECKBOX
                VALUENAME NoDispSettingsPage
                END PART
```

```
                    END POLICY
         END CATEGORY     ; Display

  ...

  END CATEGORY      ; Control Panel

  ...

  [strings]
  System="System"

  ...

  ControlPanel="Control Panel"
  CPL_Display="Display"
  CPL_Display_Restrict="Restrict Display Control Panel"
  CPL_Display_Disable="Disable Display Control Panel"
  CPL_Display_HideBkgnd="Hide Background page"
  CPL_Display_HideScrsav="Hide Screen Saver page"
  CPL_Display_HideAppearance="Hide Appearance page"
  CPL_Display_HideSettings="Hide Settings page"

  ...
```

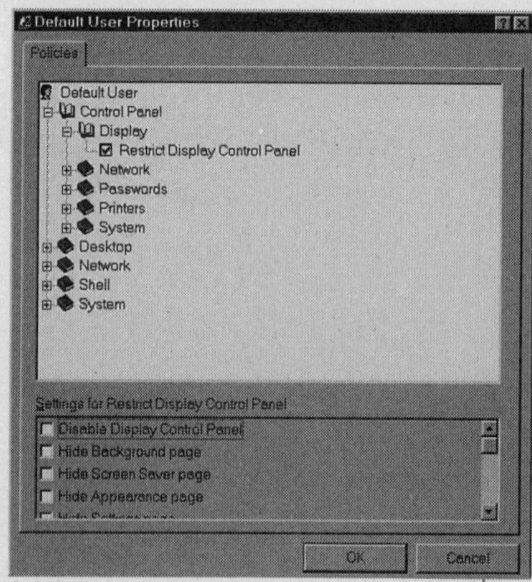

Figure 1.12   The entire structure of the System Policy Editor is based on the contents of the policy template file.

1.2.3   User Profiles

User profiles are customized settings for each user's environment. Until this option is enabled, every person that logs on to the computer uses the same USER.DAT file and shares the same sub-folders in the Windows folder. After turning on this feature, each user gets her own settings or USER.DAT file and her own folder in the Windows folder. If the servers and workstations have all been properly configured, in a network environment, these settings will follow her from computer to computer.

The Basics of User Profiles

To turn user profiles on, you have to choose the User Profiles tab in the Passwords control panel (see Figure 1.13). Switch the option button from All users of this PC use the same preferences and desktop settings to Users can customize their preferences and desktop settings. Windows switches to your personal settings whenever you log on. This enables user profiles after your next reboot. When you reboot, Windows takes your username and creates a directory with your username in the C:\WINDOWS\PROFILES directory (see Figure 1.14).

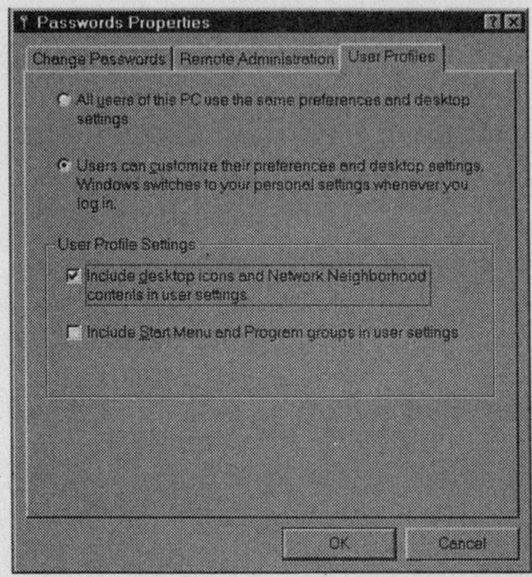

Figure 1.13   Use the Passwords control panel to enable user profiles.

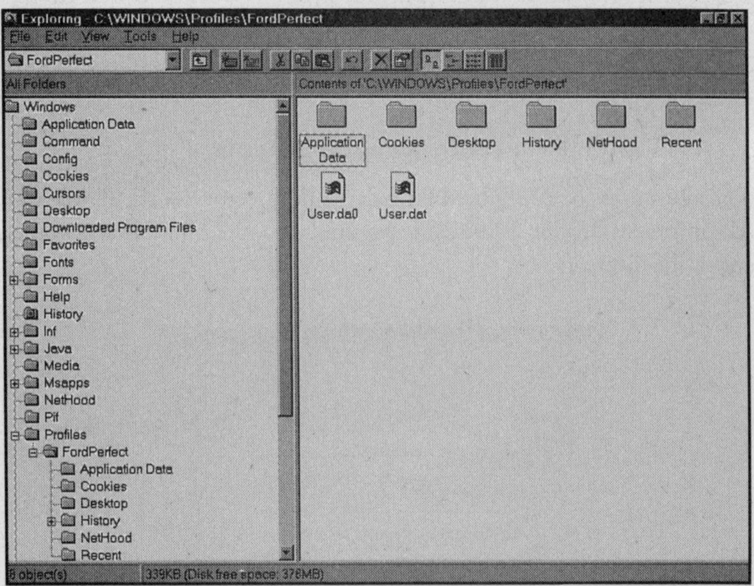

Figure 1.14   Windows 95 creates a directory for each user in the Profiles directory.

By enabling user profiles, Windows now maintains a separate USER.DAT file for each user. The USER.DAT file contains all the personal control panel settings for a user.

By choosing the Include desktop icons and Network Neighborhood contents in user settings check box, you will maintain additional settings for each user. The following folders from the Windows directory will also be duplicated for each user who logs on:

- Desktop

- NetHood

- Recent

By also selecting the Include Start Menu and Program groups in the user settings check box, you will also maintain separate Start menus and Programs folders.

If a local profile becomes corrupt, you can escape the logon dialog box and delete any or all of the profile in the Profile directory. If the entire directory for a user is deleted, then fresh copies of the files and directories will be taken from the Windows directory.

User profiles are vital to security, because system policies enforce their environment changes on the user by modifying each user's profile.

User Profiles on a Network

If you are logging on to a Windows NT domain or a Novell NetWare 3.1*x* or 4.*x* server, your user profile can follow you around the network, if certain conditions are met. The term for the capability of user profiles to follow the user around the network is called roving or roaming profiles.

For Windows NT networks, the following conditions must be met:

- The Windows NT network must be configured as a domain.

- The user's account must be configured for a network directory in the Home Directory section of the User Environment Profile, as shown in Figure 1.15. The user needs at least Change [RWXD] permissions to the directory.

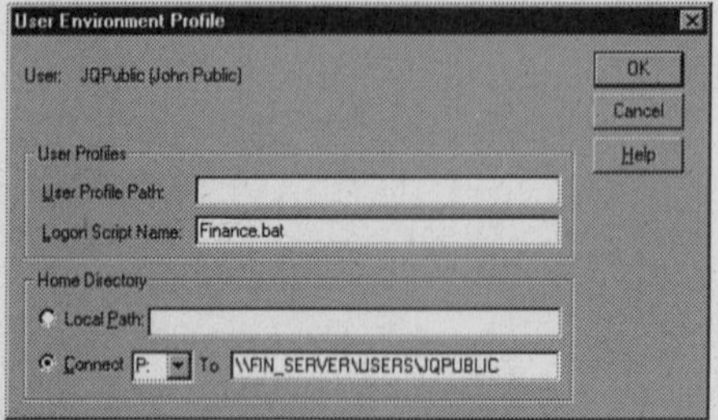

Figure 1.15   Setting a home directory for a user is set with User Manager for domains.

- The client computer must be configured to log on to the Windows NT domain. This is done through the properties of the Client for Microsoft Networks in the Network control panel, as shown in Figure 1.16.

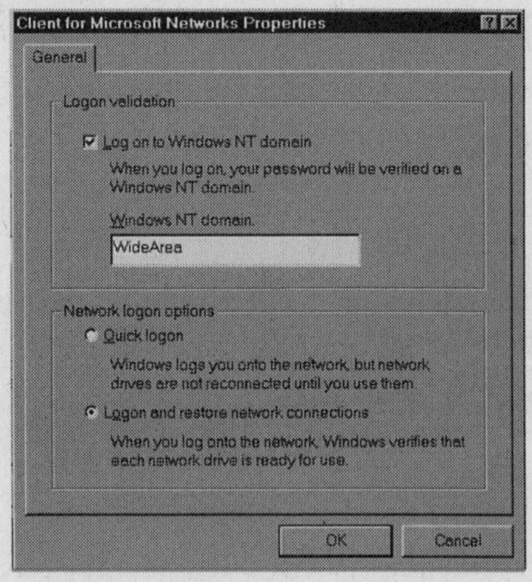

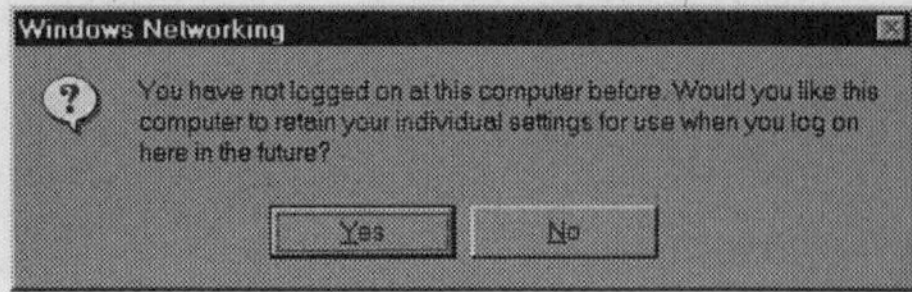

Figure 1.16   Domain logons are enabled in the Network control panel on the client.

- User profiles must be enabled on the User Profiles tab of the Password control panel.

When the prior conditions are met, the user profile will be activated on the next logon. During the logon process, the user will be told that he has not logged on to this computer before and asked if he would like to retain his settings for the future (see Figure 1.17). If the answer is no, use the default files found in the Windows directory; if the answer is yes, these files are copied into the user's Local Profile directory. When the user logs out, the Local Profile directory is copied to the user's directory on the server—this will include any shortcuts that are on the desktop. Windows 95 will not copy the files (except for USER.DAT) as part of the profile. It will move folders but will only copy the contents if they are shortcuts.

Figure 1.17   All new users are prompted to retain settings.

When working with profiles, Windows 95 always checks in the network location to see if you already have a profile created. If it finds one, it copies it down to your Local Profile directory.

If you or your network administrator renames the USER.DAT file to USER.MAN, then any desktop changes that are made will not be saved back to the network copy of your profile. These are referred to as mandatory profiles.

For NetWare 3.1x and NetWare 4.1 servers, the profile is automatically stored in the user's NetWare mail directory. If you are using a NetWare 4.11 server, then a Home directory must be configured in the user's account properties to store the user profile.

1.2.4   Remote Registry Editing and System Monitoring

From the planning side, if you wish to use either of these tools, there are some things you must take into consideration. To perform remote Registry editing, you must meet the following criteria:

- File and Printer Sharing must be installed.

- Remote Administration must be enabled, and the person attempting remote Registry editing must have administration rights.

- The remote Registry editing service must be installed. This can be done through Add, Service in the Network control panel. You must choose the Have Disk… button and specify the path *Windows_95_cd* \ADMIN\NETTOOLS\REMOTREG.

When System Monitor runs, it requires access to Registry key HKEY_DYN_DATA\PERFSTATS and its sub-keys, as shown in Figure 1.18. To perform remote system monitoring, you will require access to the same Registry keys on the remote machine. It is for this reason that all of the requirements for remote Registry editing must also be met for remote system monitoring.

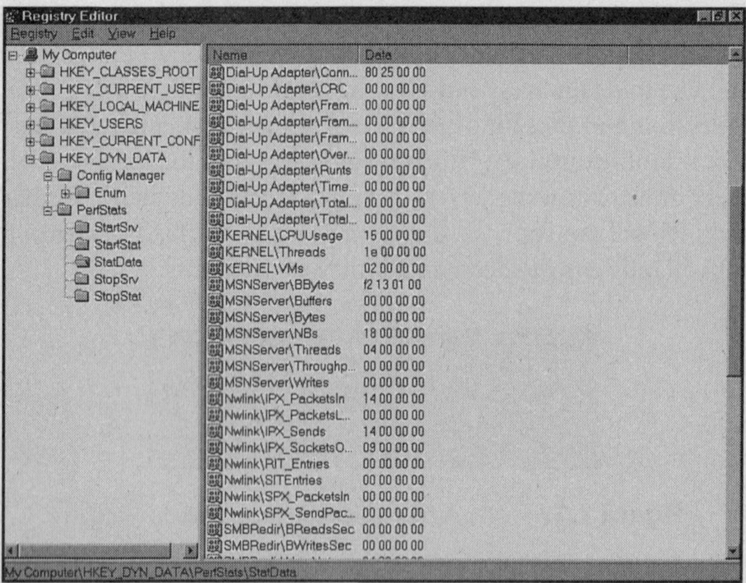

Figure 1.18   System Monitor retrieves its information from the Registry.

The reason this is a planning issue is that it requires that extra services be installed on all machines, and as discussed earlier, the File and Printer Sharing service can be a potential security hole. You do have the option of disabling the sharing controls for all users through a system policy, which helps the situation.

1.2.5   Remote Administration

Remote Administration is enabled in the Passwords control panel. The goal of Remote Administration is to give someone on the network full access to your local file system and to allow remote changes to your File and Printer Sharing settings. This enables a network administrator to control the local shared resources on your computer, as well as update any files that might be corrupted or out-of-date.

Files and Printer Sharing must be installed to implement Remote Administration. When enabling Remote Administration, the settings will look different, depending on the type of access control that you are using. If you are using Share-level Access Control, then the Remote Administration tab has a check box to enable Remote Administration and two text boxes for a password and confirmation. Anyone who knows your password will be able to perform Remote Administration on your computer. If you are using User-level Access Control, then user or group names from your security provider are granted administration rights on your computer (see Figure 1.19).

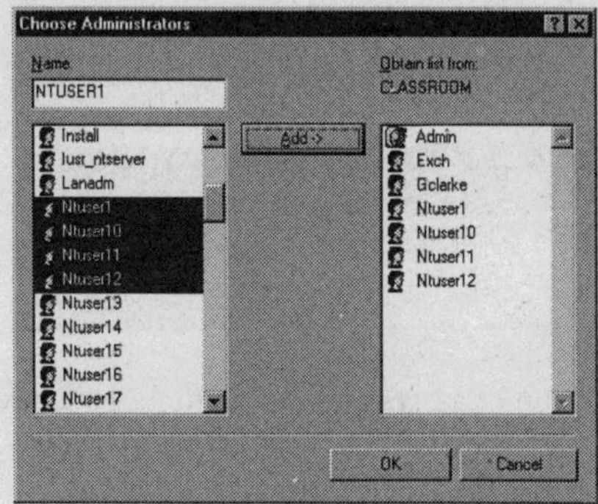

Figure 1.19   Users and groups from your security provider can be assigned administration privileges on your computer.

If you are logging on to a Windows NT domain or a Novell NetWare server, have installed File and Printer Sharing, and are using User-level Access Control, then Remote Administration will be enabled automatically. Remote Administration rights will automatically be granted to Domain Admins, Supervisor, or Admin, depending on the type of security provider you are using. Other users can be granted the right to perform Remote Administration by adding their network account names to the list on the Remote Administration tab of the Passwords control panel.

To perform Remote Administration on a network computer that you have Remote Administration rights on, you can browse the Network Neighborhood for a target computer and get its properties (see Figure 1.20). Choose the Administer button on the Tools tab to gain access to the local file system. You will see all fixed hard drives with dollar signs after the drive letters. These represent the hidden drive shares on the target machine. When Remote Administration is enabled, each fixed drive is automatically shared with Full Control rights for the people who have administration rights. This enables the administrator to navigate the entire directory structure and add, modify, or delete any files that are necessary (see Figure 1.21).

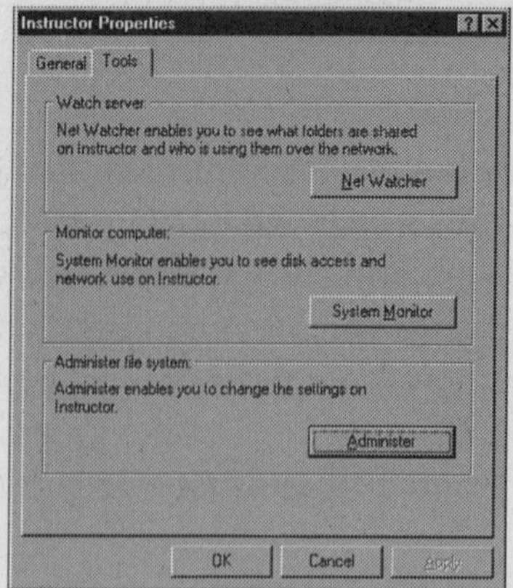

Figure 1.20   Properties of remote computers can give you access to the Remote Administration tools.

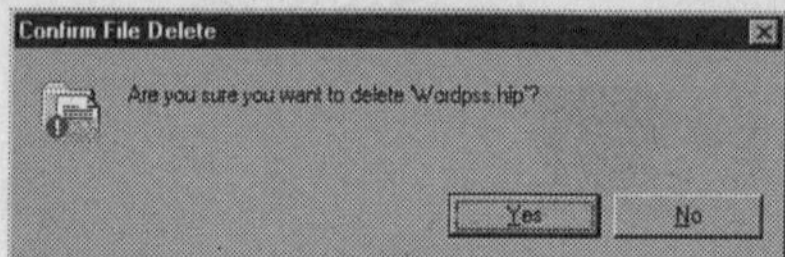

Figure 1.21   Remote Administration of a remote file system gives you full control to the drives on the target computer.

There is one additional share that is not listed when using the Administer button—ADMIN$ (see Figure 1.22)—which is the hidden share for the current Windows directory.

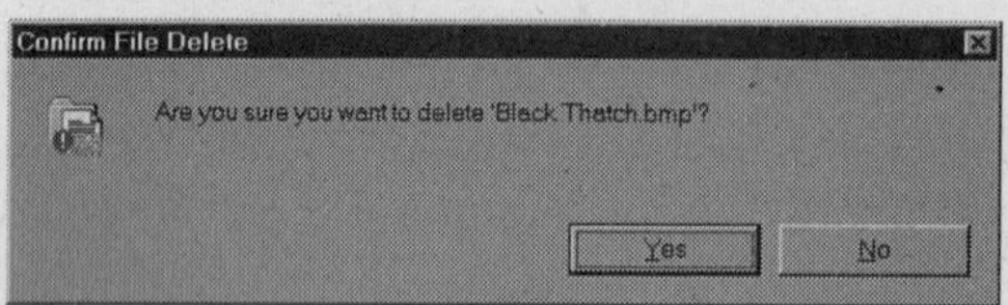

Figure 1.22   The ADMIN$ share is a direct link to the target computer's Windows directory.

In addition to the Administer button, the Tools tab also has buttons to launch System Monitor and Net Watcher. System Monitor enables you to view utilization of system resources, whereas Net Watcher enables you to view and share resources, connected users, and open files; you are also able to modify the shared resources on the target computer. Both System Monitor and Net Watcher require that File and Printer Sharing be installed on the target computer. When File and Printer Sharing has been installed on a computer, care should be taken if giving that computer access to the Internet, which will be the next topic you consider.

1.2.6   Exercises

Exercise 1: Choosing the Appropriate Level of Security

In this exercise, you choose the optimal level of security for a variety of situations. In each of the following cases, select the appropriate level of security: user-level, share-level, or no (no file and printer sharing) security.

1. You are the administrator of a local area network, running against both a Novell NetWare server and a Windows NT server. Users save their work on the NetWare server and also occasionally share resources from their local machine.

2. You are the administrator of a small office network, consisting only of Windows 95 computers, plus some Windows for Workgroups computers that have not been upgraded.

3. You are a member of the Domain Admins in a Windows NT domain. Your users access resources through a wide area network, connecting to UNIX servers and the Internet.

4. You are the administrator of a small Windows NT domain. All resources can be accessed through the Windows NT server. All users save their work on the server through home directories and shares you have created.

5. You are the NetWare supervisor. Your Windows 95 machines all have files and printers to share out.

Answers to Exercise 1

1. User-level security. Share-level security does not provide the level of security offered by user-level security. In addition, the Microsoft Client for NetWare requires user-level security.

2. Share-level security is the only option here. There is neither Windows NT nor NetWare server to act as a security provider.

3. User-level security. Although the Client for Microsoft networks does allow for share-level security, even under Windows NT, use user-level security whenever possible.

4. No file and printer sharing. If all data is accessed through the Windows NT server, it is unnecessary to have File and Printer Services installed.

5. User-level security is required for the Client for NetWare Networks.

Exercise 2: Installing the System Policy Editor

In this exercise, you will install and start the System Policy Editor. The System Policy Editor is located on the Windows 95 CD-ROM in the \ADMIN\APPTOOLS\POLEDIT directory.

1. From the Start menu, choose Settings, and then Control Panel. The Control Panel opens.

2. Double-click on the Add/Remove Programs icon. The Add/Remove Programs Properties sheet appears.

3. Select the Windows Setup tab and choose Have Disk. The Install from Disk dialog box appears.

4. Choose Browse and locate the \ADMIN\APPTOOLS\POLEDIT directory on the Windows 95 CD-ROM. The grouppol.inf and poledit.inf files are displayed.

5. Choose OK twice, select Group Policies and System Policy Editor, and choose Install. The files are copied to the hard drive, and the Start menu is updated.

6. From the Start menu, choose Programs, Accessories, System Tools, System Policy Editor. The System Policy Editor is displayed and you are prompted for the template file to be used.

7. Select ADMIN.ADM as the template to use for creating policies. The System Policy Editor displays a blank window.

8. Close the System Policy Editor.

1.2.7 Practice Problems

1. When enabling user profiles, if you choose Include desktop icons and Network Neighborhood contents, which of the following folders will not be duplicated for each user who logs on?

   A. Briefcase

   B. Nethood

   C. Desktop

   D. Recent

2. The filename for default user profiles is:

   A. USER.BIN

   B. USER.EXE

   C. USER.MDF

   D. USER.DAT

3. When user profiles are created, they are stored in which of the following directories?

   A. C:\PROFILES

   B. C:\WINDOWS\PROFILES

   C. C:\WINDOWS\USERS

   D. C:\USERS

4. What set of permissions are required for a user to have in the home directory of the User Environment Profile on a Windows NT network?

   A. [RWX]

   B. [RXCG]

   C. [RWD]

   D. [RWXD]

5. The location for enabling user profiles can be under which icon in the Control Panel?

   A. System Manager

   B. Network

   C. Passwords

   D. Display

6. Other than Microsoft's File and Printer Sharing for Microsoft Networks, what is another way to implement File and Printer Sharing?

   A. Administration-level Access Control

   B. Group-level Access Control

   C. Share-level Access Control

   D. User-level Access Control

7. What is the only security option available when using Microsoft's File and Printer Sharing for NetWare?

   A. Group-level Access Control

   B. Supervisor-level Access Control

   C. Share-level Access Control

   D. User-level Access Control

8. What is the single file on a server processed referred to when users log on to a network?

   A. Windows 95 policy

   B. System policy

   C. Network policy

   D. Administration policy

9. What sets up a customized environment maintained for each user?

   A. User profiles

   B. User policies

   C. Group policies

   D. Group profiles

10. The System Policy Editor is not installed by default. Where can the System Policy Editor be found on the Windows 95 CD-ROM?

    A. ADMIN\APPTOOLS\POLEDIT

    B. ADMIN\TOOLS\POLEDIT

    C. ADMIN\APPTOOLS\POLICY

    D. ADMIN\ADMINTOOLS\POLEDIT

11. What is the name of the Windows 95
    default policy file?

    A. CONFIG.INF

    B. CONFIG.DAT

    C. CONFIG.POL

    D. CONFIG.SYS

12. Where does Windows 95 store the default
    policy file for a Novell NetWare network?

    A. SYS:SYSTEM

    B. SYS:LOGIN

    C. SYS:ETC

    D. SYS:PUBLIC

13. What condition must be met on a
    Windows NT network in order for a user
    profile to follow the user around a net-
    work?

    A. The user must be part of a global
       group.

    B. The Windows NT network must be
       configured as a workgroup.

    C. The user must be part of a local
       group.

    D. The Windows NT network must be
       configured as a domain.

14. You are developing a security strategy fro
    you network. Which of the following is not
    an item in your security strategy for
    Windows 95?

    A. Group policies

    B. User policies

    C. System policies

    D. File and Printer Sharing

15. Which of the following is considered to
    provide better security than Share-level
    Access Control?

    A. Workstation-level Access Control

    B. Network-level Access Control

    C. User-level Access Control

    D. Group-level Access Control

16. Where does Windows 95 look for the
    CONFIG.POL file in a Windows NT
    domain?

    A. *win_root*\SYSTEM32\EXPORT\SCRIPTS\

    B. *win_root*\SYSTEM32\IMPORT\SCRIPTS\

    C. *win_root*\SYSTEM\REPL\IMPORT\SCRIPTS\

    D. *win_root*\SYSTEM23\RPL\IMPORT\SCRIP\

17. You are using the System Policy Editor to
    create a new policy file. What two options
    are available?

    A. LOCAL USER and DEFAULT
       COMPUTER

    B. LOCAL USER and LOCAL COM-
       PUTER

    C. DEFAULT USER and LOCAL
       COMPUTER

    D. DEFAULT USER and DEFAULT
       COMPUTER

18. Where are the changes stored when you
    make changes to the computer settings in
    the System Policy Editor?

    A. SYSTEM.INI

    B. COMPUTER.DAT

    C. SYSTEM.DAT

    D. COMPUTER.INI

19. A new user logs on to a Windows 95
    workstation. This user does not belong to a
    group and no policy has been set for this
    user. What policy entry does Windows 95
    apply for this user?

    A. DEFAULT COMPUTER

    B. LOCAL USER

    C. DEFAULT USER

    D. LOCAL COMPUTER

20. Which of the following is the default template file used by the System Policy Editor?

    A. ADMIN.ADM

    B. ADMIN.DAT

    C. ADMIN.INI

    D. ADMIN.BIN

1.2.8   Answers and Explanations

1. **A**   The Briefcase folder is user specific and is controlled by the user.

2. **D**   Until user profiles are established, everyone logging on to Windows 95 uses USER.DAT.

3. **B**   A directory for each user profile is created in the C:\WINDOWS\PROFILES directory.

4. **D**   The user needs Read, Write, Execute, and Delete permissions to maintain the user's profiles.

5. **C**   Under the Passwords icon is a tab for user profiles.

6. **C**   The default system security is Share-level Access Control.

7. **D**   The security provider must be a Novell NetWare server with User-level Access Control.

8. **B**   The system policy file contains the settings and restriction applied to users at log on.

9. **A**   User profiles are used in conjunction with system policies to configure a working environment for the user.

10. **A**   ADMIN\APPTOOLS\POLEDIT, from this location you can install both the System Policy Editor and group policies.

11. **C**   The default policy file Windows 95 looks for is called CONFIG.POL.

12. **D**   Windows 95 looks for the CONFIG.POL on a NetWare network on the SYS: volume in the Public directory.

13. **D**   The NT network must be configured as a domain. Also the user account must exist in the Home Directory section of the User Environment Profile.

14. **A**   The three components to consider for security strategy are user policies, system policies, and File and Printer Sharing.

15. **C**   You must have a valid username and password with User-level Access Control.

16. **B**   The CONFIG.POL file is located in the NetLogOn directory of domain controllers. The directory is *win_root*\SYSTEM32\REPL\IMPORT\SCRIPTS\.

17. **D**   The two options you have are DEFAULT USER and DEFAULT COMPUTER. You can edit the Registry from LOCAL USER and LOCAL COMPUTER.

18. **C**   The SYSTEM.DAT file contains the changes made to computer settings and applies to the system no matter who is logged on.

19. **C**   When a user does not have a profile set up and is not a member of a group, then Windows 95 uses DEFAULT USER.

20. **A**   ADMIN.ADM is located in the C:\WINDOWS\INF directory and is the default template file.

1.2.9   Key Words and Definitions

DEFAULT COMPUTER   An icon in the System Policy Editor that shows the computer settings applied to the computer regardless of the user who has logged on to the computer, and the changes that are implemented, are stored in the computer's SYSTEM.DAT file.

DEFAULT USER An icon in the System Policy Editor that shows the user settings for each user regardless of the computer they logged on to, and the changes that are implemented, are stored in the user's USER.DAT file.

File and Printer Sharing Microsoft network users have access to, or are allowed to share, files with other network users. This is accomplished through File and Printer Sharing.

Remote Administration The goal of Remote Administration is to give someone on the network full access to the local file system and to allow remote changes to File and Printer Sharing settings.

System Monitor The Tools tab has buttons to launch System Monitor which enables you to view utilization of the system resources.

System policies A single file on a server that is processed when users log on to the network. This file contains a list of setting or restrictions that apply to the users at logon.

System Policy Editor Much of the security that Windows 95 is capable of is implemented through System policies, which are created by System Policy Editor.

User profiles These profiles are customized settings for each user's environment. When this feature is turned on, each user gets his own settings and his own folder in the Windows folder.

Practice Exam: Planning

1. If you are accessing a user accounts list stored on a Novell NetWare server, then which level of security would be used to base the access rights to shared resources?

   A. Windows 95 access control

   B. Windows 95 logon security

   C. Share-level security

   D. User-level security

2. Which level of security would be used to base the access rights to shared resources on the Windows 95 computer on a password-assigned basis?

   A. Windows 95 access control

   B. Windows 95 logon security

   C. Share-level security

   D. User-level security

3. You have just recently enabled user profiles on your network. You decide to use roving mandatory user profiles and place the appropriate USER.DAT file in the NETLOGON directory of your Windows NT server. You note, however, that when you log on to a Windows 95 computer that has user profiles enabled, your profile information is not downloaded to the workstation.

   In this scenario, what step must you take to correct this problem and complete your implementation of user profiles?

   A. Rename the USER.DAT file to USER.MAN.

   B. Share the NETLOGON directory as EVERYONE read access.

   C. Rename the USER.DAT file to USER.MAN and place the file in the user's home directory.

   D. Rename the USER.DAT file to USER.MAN and place the file in the user's mail user_id directory.

4. You have installed Windows 95 on several computers in your environment. These computers cannot see one another, although they can see the Windows NT and NetWare servers. What do you suspect is the problem?

   A. They do not have permission to see one another.

   B. System policies restrict them from seeing their workgroup.

   C. They do not have File and Printer Sharing activated.

   D. The Browse list has not yet been built.

5. You and a colleague are using system policies for your Windows 95 users. The policies do not seem to be working. However, you think they are being saved in the wrong location. Where on a NetWare server are logon scripts saved?

A. User's home directories

B. User's mail user_id

C. SYS:PUBLIC

D. SYS:LOGON

6. Of the following, what is the best method you can use to change the level of security from share-level to user-level?

   A. Through REGEDIT

   B. Through Control Panel, Passwords

   C. Through Control Panel, Systems

   D. Through Control Panel, Network

7. Where does Windows 95 Setup store your Windows for Workgroups settings during an installation procedure?

   A. C:\temp

   B. C:\windows\temp

   C. Registry

   D. SYSTEM.INI

8. You are trying to install Windows 95 from Windows 3.0, but you are continually unsuccessful. What do you suspect is the problem?

   A. Your hardware is not compatible with Windows 95.

   B. Your installation media is faulty.

   C. Your hardware probably has IRQ conflicts that must be resolved before installing Windows 95.

   D. Windows 95 Setup cannot be run from Windows 3.0.

9. In Windows 95, which of the following is the default access security level?

   A. Group-level

   B. Share-level

   C. User-level

   D. Access-level

10. When new users log on to a Windows 95 computer that has user profiles enabled, a copy of what profile is loaded for the new user?

    A. DEFAULT

    B. SYSTEM

    C. USER.DAT

    D. USER.MAN

11. You log on to two Windows 95 computers. You have implemented roving user profiles on your Windows NT Server network. You make different changes to the settings on both computers you are currently logged into. You then log out of both Windows 95 computers. Which user profile will be downloaded to the workstation the next time you log on to the network?

   A. The profile contained on the server in the NETLOGON directory

   B. The profile with the most recent time stamp

   C. Your original user profile

   D. The default profile

12. When users log on to workstations on your network, you would like to present a message at logon regarding the privacy of your computer systems. Using the System Policy Editor, where would you go to accomplish this task?

   A. Default User

   B. Default Group

   C. Default Computer

   D. Default Policy

13. When Remote Administration is enabled on a Windows 95 computer, two special shared directories are created. What are those two special shares?

   A. ADMIN

   B. IPC

   C. ADMIN$

   D. IPC$

14. You need to be able to provide user restrictions for both individuals and groups in your network. Which policy will provide the required restrictions to both the users and the groups?

   A. System policies

   B. Mandatory user profiles

   C. User profiles

   D. Mandatory user policies

15. From the list below, which of the systems support long filenames? Select all that apply.

   A. OS/2

   B. Windows 95

   C. Windows NT

   D. MS-DOS

16. A user asks how she can modify her user profile. She is running a Windows 95 computer that is not connected to a network. What are the general steps needed to modify her user profile?

    Study each scenario carefully and decide what solution would best answer this question.

    A. Make sure the Users Can Customize Their Preferences and Desktop Settings option, which can be enabled on the User Profiles tab of the Passwords properties sheet, is selected.

       Next, advise the user to make any changes to the desktop, Start menu, and program groups.

       Shut down and reboot the system.

       After logging on, the new changes appear and are part of the user profile for that user.

    B. Make sure the Users Can Customize Their Preferences and Desktop Settings option, which can be enabled on the User Profiles tab of the Security properties sheet, is selected.

       Next, advise the user to make any changes to the desktop, Start menu, and program groups.

       Shut down and reboot the system.

       After logging in, the new changes appear and are part of the user profile for that user.

    C. Make sure the Users Cannot Customize Their Preferences and Desktop Settings option, which can be enabled on the User Profiles tab of the Passwords properties sheet, is selected.

       Next, advise the user to make changes to the desktop, Start menu, and program groups.

       Shut down and reboot the system.

       After logging on, the new changes appear and are part of the user profile for that user.

    D. Make sure the Users Can Customize Their Preferences and Desktop Settings option, which can be enabled on the User Profiles tab of the Passwords Properties sheet, is selected.

       Next, advise the user to make changes to the desktop, Start menu, and program groups.

       Shut down and reboot the system.

       After logging on, the new changes appear and are part of the user profile for that user.

    The answers are similar except for the first step. What scenario best answers the question?

Practice Exam Answers and Explanations

1. **D** Novell networks requires user-level security to access resources on a network.

2. **C** Windows 95 requires share-level security to share resources on a Windows 95 computer.

3. **C** The file must have the .MAN extension and be located in his home directory.

4. **C** Windows 95 computers will not show up in the Network Neighborhood unless File and Printer Sharing has been activated.

5. **C** System policies are saved on the NetWare server in SYS:PUBLIC.

6. **D** Access control is accomplished through Control Panel, Network.

7. **C** Settings are stored in the Windows 95 Registry.

8. **D** Windows 95 Setup cannot be run from Windows 3.0.

9. **B**   By default, share-level security is enabled and is used on peer-to-peer networks and server-based networks.

10. **A**   The default is used for new users and any changes made to the settings will remain for that particular user in the future.

11. **B**   The last settings saved to the profile override all other profile settings.

12. **C**   The Default Computer properties sheet contains the option Logon, Logon Banner.

13. **C, D**   When Remote Administration is enabled on a computer, two special shared directories are created: ADMIN$ gives administrators access to the file system on the remote computer. IPC$ provides an interprocess communication (IPC) channel between the two computers.

14. **A**   System policies enforce computer-specific, user-specific, or group-specific Registry entries.

15. **A, B, C**   OS/2, Windows 95, and Windows NT support long filenames.

16. **A**   The user's profile will be stored locally under *systemroot*\Profiles and will be available whenever the user logs on to that specific workstation.

CHAPTER 2

Installation and Configuration, Part 1: Windows 95

This chapter will help you prepare for the exam by covering the following objectives.

- Install Windows 95. Installation options include:
  - Automated Windows Setup
  - New
  - Upgrade
  - Uninstall
  - Dual boot combination with Microsoft Windows NT
- Install and configure hardware devices, including modems and printers.
- Install and configure backup hardware and software, including tape drives and the Backup application.

2.1 Installing Windows 95

In this section, we will explore some of the considerations you will have to make when installing the Windows 95 operating system. We will look at the issues involved with installing Windows 95 on a clean, newly formatted hard drive, as well as upgrading from an earlier operating system. Some other topics that will be covered include uninstalling Windows 95 and creating a dual-boot with Windows NT.

2.1.1 General Considerations

Before beginning a Windows 95 installation, you should be aware of the installation options available to you. You can choose from four types of installation, as outlined in Table 2.1.

Table 2.1   Types of Windows 95 Installation

Type	Description
Typical	Recommended for most desktop users, this type installs the most common options, requires minimal user interaction, and allows the user to choose the Windows directory and whether or not to create a startup disk.
Portable	The best solution for portable (notebook) computers, this type installs Briefcase and software that supports direct cable connections for exchanging files.
Compact	Recommended for computers with limited disk space, Compact installs the minimum number of files required, and no optional components are selected.
Custom	Recommended for advanced users, this type allows the user to choose which optional accessories and network components are installed.

A consideration to make when determining the type of Windows 95 installation is the amount of hard disk space required. Table 2.2 lists the average amounts of space required for each type of installation. These numbers reflect the basic installation of each type, without any additional components included.

Table 2.2   Approximate Disk Space Requirements for Windows 95

Installation Base	Typical	Portable	Compact	Custom
New installation	47MB	47MB	44MB	48MB
MS-DOS upgrade	55MB	55MB	45MB	55MB
Windows 3.*x* upgrade	40MB	40MB	38MB	40MB
Windows for Workgroups 3.*x* upgrade	40MB	40MB	38MB	40MB

The Windows Setup program offers several switches that can be used to alter processing during installation. Table 2.3 lists those switches and their meanings.

Table 2.3   Windows 95 Setup Switches

Switch	Purpose
/?	Provides syntax help.
/c	Doesn't load SmartDrive disk cache.
/d	Doesn't use the existing version of Windows in early part of setup, which is useful if the existing Windows might be corrupt.
/in	Bypasses the network setup module.
/im	Bypasses the check for the minimum amount of required conventional memory.

Switch	Purpose
/id	Bypasses the check for the minimum amount of required hard disk space.
/iq	Doesn't run ScanDisk when installing from MS-DOS.
/is	Doesn't run the ScanDisk quick check.
/ih	Runs ScanDisk in the foreground so you can see the results.
/l	Loads the Logitech mouse driver.
/nostart	Loads the minimal Windows 3.*x* files required to run Setup, and then exits without starting the setup procedure.
/IW	Bypasses the license agreement, which is useful for automating setup.
/t:tempdir	Specifies the directory in which Windows setup will place temporary files.

In most cases, you will never need to use these override switches for Windows 95 installations. But you still should be aware of them and know what they can do for you.

Another thing to consider when you're installing from Windows 95 is the media from which you are installing. You can install in the conventional way—from floppy disks or a CD-ROM—or you can install across a network.

Installing from Floppy Disks

The least favorable media to use for installing Windows 95 is probably the floppy disk. An installation of Windows 95 will require approximately 14 disks (depending on options and type of installation). Because disk I/O is slower with floppy drives than with a CD-ROM, you will find that it takes a considerable amount of time to install from disks.

Another disadvantage to installing from disks is that the disks don't include all the files and utilities that come packaged on the CD-ROM. Items such as the Windows 95 online help are omitted from the floppy disk version because of size limitations.

Microsoft used a special disk format when creating the installation disks. The first disk is in a standard format, but the subsequent disks are formatted with *DMF*, Distribution Media Format. This format allows Microsoft to put more information onto a floppy disk (approximately 1.68MB). Unfortunately, you cannot make backups of these disks by using conventional means such as COPY or DISKCOPY.

Installing from CD-ROM

Installing Windows 95 from CD-ROM eliminates the process of swapping disks in and out of a floppy drive. Because a CD-ROM drive usually reads data much more quickly, files are copied to the hard drive a lot faster than they are with floppy disks.

In addition to the speed, a major advantage of using the CD-ROM version of Setup is that it includes additional tools. The CD-ROM has the Windows 95 online help files, as well as the Windows 95 Resource Kit help file. It also includes additional administrative tools not available on the floppy disks.

Installing Over a Network

A third option for Windows 95 installation is to install over a network. To use this option, you would place all the required setup files on a network server that can be accessed by all the clients who will be installing Windows 95.

The setup files cannot be copied from the CD-ROM or floppy disks to a network drive. To move the files to the network, you will have to run the NETSETUP program. NETSETUP must be run from a computer with Windows 95 already installed, and it must be run with the CD-ROM version of the installation. Once NETSETUP runs, you will have a server-based version of the setup media.

2.1.2   Automated Windows Setup

If you have to install Windows 95 on a number of machines, you most likely don't want to spend all your time swapping floppy disks in and out of drives while Setup is running. There are several ways in which you can simplify the installation process and reduce the amount of user intervention that is required. As you just learned, one way to simplify the installation process is to install from over a network. Another method is to use *batch scripting* to remove some of the manual effort of the setup process.

Batch scripting can be used with any of the installation media—floppy disks, CD-ROM, or network Setup files. These scripts can be created with the BATCH.EXE utility. With this utility, you can specify various options and parameters required by the setup process. You can select the custom components that you want to install, as well as other general and network features. BATCH.EXE creates a script file (.INF) for you to use when you run Setup. Then, to run Setup with a batch script, you specify the INF filename as a command switch, with a slash (/) as the leading character. The batch script reduces the amount of user interaction required during the setup process by handling some of the input that Windows 95 requires. Depending on the complexity of your installation requirements, most or all of the needed user intervention in the setup process can be eliminated.

Some other options for automating setup include:

- Use a login script to run a custom setup script, which activates when each user logs on to the file server.

- Use the System Management Server to distribute a mandatory Windows 95 Installation Package that runs Setup by using a custom setup script.

- Use a network management software distribution package, such as Norton Administrator for Networks (NAN), to install Windows 95 by automatically running Setup by using a custom setup script.

- Use Network Client Administrator in Windows NT 4.0 Server to create a network startup disk that points to an installation share.

With the first option (using login scripts) and the last option (using the Network Client Administrator), installation of Windows 95 uses a "pull" method. This means that the setup process is initialized on the client. With the second option (using SMS) and the third option (using a distribution package), installation is "pushed" onto a client. "Pushed" means that the setup process is controlled by a server instead of being requested by the client.

2.1.3 New Installations

The Windows 95 installation process is modular. The Windows 95 Setup program steps through this process, running only those modules that are either requested or needed. For example, the hardware detection phase identifies specific components on the computer, and the Windows 95 Setup program runs only those installation modules that match. Some of the modules used by the Windows 95 Setup program are standard wizards, such as those for setting up network components, modems, printers, and display monitors.

Windows 95 installation consists of four logical phases:

- Startup and information gathering
- Hardware detection
- File copy
- Final system configuration

Installation from the System Perspective

From the workstation perspective, the Windows 95 Setup program performs a series of steps when installing Windows 95. The first few steps depend on where the Setup program starts. Whether the setup begins in DOS mode or Windows mode, the Windows 95 Setup program ends up running Windows in protected mode. This merge in the Windows 95 installation process occurs just before the hardware detection phase.

The Windows 95 Setup program automatically performs 12 steps during installation. You will not be aware that these steps are occurring. However, in case you should need to troubleshoot any problems, you should understand the sequence. These are the 12 steps of installation:

1. ScanDisk checks the integrity of your hard drive.

2. The Windows 95 Setup program searches the local hard drives for a previous version of Windows 3.1 or better. If one is found, the Windows 95 Setup program suggests that the user start the existing version of Windows and then run Setup.

3. Setup checks to confirm that the computer is capable of running Windows 95 (checking the processor, amount of RAM memory, amount of disk space, and MS-DOS version).

4. The Windows 95 Setup program checks for extended memory (XMS) and installs an XMS provider if none is present. If disk caching is not running, Setup automatically loads SmartDrive.

5. Certain terminate and stay resident (TSR) programs and device drivers can cause problems with the Windows 95 installation. If any known troublemakers are found, they are either closed or unloaded. Before continuing, Setup will prompt you to close any processes that it cannot close.

6. From DOS, the Windows 95 Setup program installs a minimal Windows 3.*x* environment and starts it with a shell=setup.exe command, running in protected mode.

From Windows, the Windows 95 Setup program switches to protected mode. At this point, a Windows graphical user interface appears. It is here that a safe recovery screen would appear if Windows 95 Setup detected a failed installation attempt.

7. Setup gathers certain user information such as where to install Windows 95, configuration type, username, and company name.

   Setup examines the computer for all attached hardware devices and then creates the Registry entries that will contain the hardware configuration information for the computer.

8. The Windows 95 Setup program requests user input of what components to install, how to configure the network, identification information, and whether to create a Windows 95 startup disk. The user must provide missing information.

9. Setup copies the required files onto the computer's hard drive, according to where the Windows 95 Setup program was instructed to install them.

10. After copying all files, Setup modifies the boot records. This is where the computer is changed from its previous operating system to Windows 95.

11. Windows 95 restarts the computer.

12. Several programs run when Windows 95 boots for the first time. These include the Plug and Play hardware configuration wizard (if any of these hardware devices exist). Other programs perform final system configuration tasks: setting up control panel, migrating existing program group settings, adding programs to the Start menu, creating Windows Help, applying MS-DOS program settings, and setting the time zone. A final reboot might be required to finalize any newly installed Plug and Play hardware devices.

Installation from the User Perspective

Much of the Windows 95 installation process is automatic. Microsoft uses a Setup Wizard to guide the installation, prompting for information and requesting some decisions throughout the entire process. This section covers the typical interaction that takes place during the Windows 95 installation.

As soon as you start the Windows 95 Setup program, a dialog box indicates the running of a routine system check. During this earliest phase, Setup copies several files to the local computer, and ScanDisk checks the integrity of the hard disk. If this phase is successful, another dialog box appears as the Setup Wizard gets ready.

The license agreement appears next. To continue with the installation, you must agree to the licensing terms. If you do not agree to the licensing terms, the Windows 95 Setup program terminates.

If the hard drive does not contain a copy of the old software, you can insert a disk to verify qualification for the upgrade. Usually this does not happen because a previous qualifying version of software is already on the hard drive.

Once loaded, the Setup Wizard divides the remaining activity in the Windows 95 installation into the following three stages:

- **Gathering user and computer information.** Information must be provided to the Windows 95 Setup program from either a script or direct input. This phase includes the hardware detection that's done when analyzing your computer.

- **Copying Windows 95 files.** The Windows 95 Setup program copies files to the computer that are required based on the hardware configuration and the program components you have chosen to install.

- **Restarting the computer and finishing Setup.** Windows 95 starts up and completes the final settings needed to run properly.

The Setup Wizard's initial screen and the steps it follows to complete the Windows 95 installation reinforce this perspective. This initial screen appears during each of the three stages of the process, displaying the current stage highlighted in bold type with a small triangular arrow pointing to it. This allows you to follow along in the Windows 95 installation process.

Gathering Information

The first part of the Windows 95 installation process gathers information about the computer. If a previous installation of Windows 3.1*x* or Windows for Workgroups 3.*x* exists, the Windows 95 Setup program asks you to confirm the directory where Windows 95 is to be installed. If you choose to install Windows 95 in a new directory, you might need to reinstall some Windows-based applications because Windows 95 will not be able to migrate your old program settings to the new environment.

The Windows 95 Setup program asks you to select the type of setup (typical, custom, and so on) you want. The default selection is typical.

Whatever setup option you choose, you will supply user information. Windows 95 uses this information to identify both the username and company. This information will show up in the Windows 95 Help About dialog boxes and the FAX configuration dialog box. The username is also truncated and used to populate the computer name and description fields on the computer identification screen later in the Setup process. You must type a response and then verify it for Setup to continue.

Next, Windows 95 Setup requests a product serial number. The product ID number is on your Windows 95 floppy disks, the CD-ROM jacket, or your Certificate of Authenticity. You must type a response and then verify it for Setup to continue. The serial number dialog box might not appear if you are installing Windows 95 from the network, depending on the license agreement at your site.

Analyzing Your Computer

After you enter the user information, the Windows 95 Setup program prepares to analyze your computer. This is the hardware detection phase. Setup searches automatically for all the basic system components, such as disk drives and controllers, display devices, pointing devices, and keyboards. The detection process involves a series of approaches for detecting these hardware devices.

The first approach determines whether the computer is already running Windows 95. If so, Setup identifies any Plug and Play components.

The second approach is *safe detection mode*. This involves methodically searching the computer for software clues that can indicate the presence of certain devices. Setup checks the CONFIG.SYS, AUTOEXEC.BAT, and all initialization (INI) files, as well as memory locations for installed drivers. If these safe methods suggest the presence of a device, Setup configures the device.

If any devices are not identified during this safe detection, Setup prompts you for the existence of certain classes of devices, including the following:

- CD-ROM drives (proprietary cards)
- Sound, MIDI, or video capture cards
- Network adapters
- SCSI devices

The third approach involves interactive query routines to spot any additional devices. This process of examining specific memory locations, testing values and return codes, and actively probing for devices can cause the computer to lock up during hardware detection. If the computer should fail during this detection process, turn the machine off and restart the Windows 95 Setup program. The Setup Failure and Recovery process will continue from this point, avoiding the trouble area.

Give Windows 95 hardware detection a chance to work. Just because the computer "locks up" during the detection phase does not mean that Windows 95 will be unable to detect the hardware. You might have to turn the machine off two or three times before Setup is able to detect all the hardware. However, patience during this phase of setup will pay dividends during later setup and configuration.

The hardware detection process can take several minutes. The indicator bar shows the progress of the hardware detection phase. Note that this is also the point at which Windows 95 Setup can stall if hardware detection fails for a particular system component.

Optional Components

After the hardware detection is complete, the Windows 95 Setup program asks whether you want to install a variety of tools that allow you to access various services. Three choices are included in the Windows 95 installation:

- The Microsoft Network
- Microsoft Mail
- Microsoft FAX

If you select any of these three choices, the Microsoft Exchange client application is installed as well. This extra component requires another 4.6MB of hard disk space plus a minimum of 8MB of RAM to operate properly.

You will then be given the chance to change the Windows 95 components that will be installed. The Windows 95 Setup program asks you whether you want to install the common components.

The selected setup option (typical, portable, compact, or custom) governs this phase. As you learned earlier in this chapter, the custom setup option gives you the most control over the Windows 95 installation process. With the custom setup option, you will not even see this screen. However, no matter which setup option you select, you will get a chance to choose from the various components.

Network Connection

The Windows 95 Setup program allows you to specify network components and settings. With a typical installation, this happens automatically if you have a network adapter or choose to install Dial-Up Networking. The Network Wizard allows you to configure these settings.

The Windows 95 Setup program provides appropriate settings based on the hardware and software detection for the network components running when you start Setup. You should accept the default settings unless you know that particular settings need to be changed.

After configuring network components and settings, the Windows 95 Setup program prompts you for a unique identifier for your computer. In the Identification screen, supply a computer name, a workgroup (if you plan to use Microsoft Networks), and an optional computer.

Creating the Startup Disk

A startup disk is a Windows 95 bootable floppy disk that contains utilities you can use to troubleshoot a malfunctioning system. The startup disk loads the operating system and presents an MS-DOS command line. You can create a Windows 95 startup disk during the file copy phase of Windows 95 Setup. You can also create or update a disk after the Windows 95 installation by using the Add/Remove Programs option in the Control Panel.

To create a startup disk, Windows 95 formats the floppy disk in drive A and then copies files to the disk in drive A. The 16 files it copies take up 948KB of space on a 1.44MB floppy disk. Other programs and files also need to be added to support access to CD-ROM drives, the network, or any other special requirements.

For recovery purposes, you might also want to copy the following files into a subdirectory on the startup disk: SYSTEM.DAT, CONFIG.SYS, AUTOEXEC.BAT, WIN.INI, SYSTEM.INI, and any CD-ROM or other device drivers. If you do not place these files in a subdirectory, you'll have to rename them to prevent problems with the startup disk.

After hardware detection is complete and Windows 95 Setup has obtained all required information, the next phase of Setup begins. During this phase, Setup copies the Windows 95 files to the destination drive and directory.

Copying Windows 95 Files

This part of the Windows 95 installation process uses the information previously gathered to start copying all the files it needs. The sources for these files are the Windows 95 Cabinet (CAB) files. Depending on the speed of your computer and installation source, this part can take anywhere from 20 minutes to an hour.

The first group of files that are copied includes those used to create a startup disk. This disk will be useful for troubleshooting problems with Windows 95.

Restarting the Computer

Just before it actually restarts the computer, the Windows 95 Setup program renames existing MS-DOS boot files, copies a new IO.SYS file and MSDOS.SYS file, and modifies the boot records and the boot track to point to the new IO.SYS file.

Up to this point in the Windows 95 installation, your old operating system was still available should the Windows 95 installation fail. The Safe Recovery feature of Windows 95 would allow you to restart the Windows 95 Setup program in your old operating system. But now you are running Windows 95. Beyond this point, if the Windows 95 Setup program should fail, you will need to restart in Windows 95 to complete the installation. In most cases, the remainder of the Windows 95 installation goes smoothly.

The initial boot-up of Windows 95 is called *first-time run* because it is the first time that Windows 95 has been started on this computer. The standard Windows 95 bitmap is displayed, with the lower banner indicating that this is the first startup. This is the third and final stage of the Windows 95 installation.

Windows 95 might prompt you to log on to the computer. The user ID and password are saved in a password list (PWL) file.

Windows 95 sets up the hardware configurations and recognizes any Plug and Play devices.

Finally, Windows 95 asks you to complete several configuration options. These are the run-once options that Windows 95 starts the first time it runs. The run-once options include the following:

- Control Panel configuration

- Programs on the Start Menu configuration

- Windows Help file configuration

- MS-DOS program settings

- Time zone configuration

- Printer configuration

Depending on which options you selected during Setup, the hardware devices you have, or the computer you have, you might need to complete additional run-once options, such as configuration of MIDI devices. When you finish completing all the run-once options, the computer is ready to run Windows 95. Some hardware devices, including PnP-enabled hardware devices, might require another reboot of the computer before they are fully configured.

Setup Failure Detection and Recovery

Hardware and software can cause problems during a Windows 95 installation. Therefore, Microsoft built in mechanisms that enable the Windows 95 Setup program to detect a failure and to recover automatically, which ensures a high percentage of successful Windows 95 installations.

The Windows 95 Setup program maintains a setup log (SETUPLOG.TXT) during the installation and can determine where failures occur. The most likely place for failure is during hardware detection. A detection log (DETLOG.TXT) keeps track of what the Windows 95 Setup program discovers during the hardware detection phase.

If any previous attempt to install Windows 95 has failed, Windows 95 Setup lets you choose whether to use the Safe Recovery feature or to run a full new Setup. If the Safe Recovery dialog box appears when you start the Windows 95 Setup program, you should always select the Use Safe Recovery option. When you select this option, Windows 95 Setup can use various built-in methods to avoid the problems that occurred previously.

You should know these basic Safe Recovery rules in case a failure occurs:

- When you restart, before hardware detection begins, the Windows 95 Setup program uses SETUPLOG.TXT to determine the point of failure. The Windows 95 Setup program then knows what to redo and what it can skip.

- During the hardware detection phase, Windows 95 Setup creates DETCRASH.LOG to keep track of identification efforts. When the Windows 95 Setup program restarts, it finds this file and uses it to determine which detection module was running at the point of failure. In Safe Recovery mode, the Windows 95 Setup program reads the Registry to verify all the devices already detected, and it skips any detection modules up to the point of failure. It also skips any detection modules that caused the failure or any previously logged failure. Safe Recovery then proceeds to the next detection module. When the hardware detection phase finishes, Setup deletes DETCRASH.LOG.

- After the hardware detection phase, Setup assumes that all the necessary hardware information is now stored in the Registry.

The Safe Recovery process depends on what stage of the installation Setup reached before encountering problems. It continues from that point forward, attempting to bypass the problems.

To continue if Windows 95 Setup stops during hardware detection, do the following:

1. Press F3 or click the Cancel button to quit Setup. If the computer does not respond to the Cancel button, restart the computer by turning it off and then back on again. Do not press Ctrl+Alt+Del or hit the Reset button.

2. Run Setup again. The Windows 95 Setup program prompts you to use Safe Recovery to recover the failed Windows 95 installation.

3. Choose Use Safe Recovery (it should be the default), and then click the Next button.

4. Repeat your installation choices. Hardware detection then runs again, but the Windows 95 Setup program skips the portion that caused the initial failure.

5. If the computer stops again during the hardware detection process, repeat this procedure until Setup successfully completes the hardware detection portion of installation.

Your most likely point of failure will occur during the hardware detection phase. Only a limited number of interrupts (IRQs), DMA channels, I/O address assignments, and upper memory space allocations are available. Conflicts are especially common if you add multimedia capability, CD-ROMs, network interface cards, SCSI adapters, or other hardware devices to your computer.

If the Windows 95 Setup program fails after modifying the boot records, you simply restart Windows 95 to complete the installation. There is no need to start the Windows 95 Setup program from the beginning.

2.1.4　Windows 95 Server-Based Setup

The following steps describe the process of a network (or server-based) installation. Use NETSETUP.EXE to install Windows 95 source files on a network server and to prepare for either network installations or shared installations of Windows 95. It is recommended that you run NETSETUP from the CD-ROM.

1. From Computer 1 (with a CD-ROM drive), start Windows 95. On Computer 2, install both DOS and Windows for Workgroups. In this case, the server-based installation can be to either Computer 2, as a network shared drive, or to a Windows NT or Novell NetWare server.

2. Establish an Install directory share with full rights on Computer 2. If you're using a Windows NT server or a NetWare server, be sure to grant sufficient privileges or rights if required.

3. Run NETSETUP from the ADMIN\NETTOOLS\NETSETUP directory on Computer 1 from the Windows 95 CD-ROM. The server-based Setup program can be run only from a computer that is already running Windows 95.

4. The Server Based Setup dialog box appears. Click the Set Path button to specify the server path where the Windows 95 installation files will be installed. Then click OK. If the server path has already been defined, the button name is Change Path.

5. Click Install to start the installation.

6. You will be presented with a series of dialog boxes. These boxes confirm the paths to install from and to. The dialog boxes also specify how the users can install Windows 95 from the server to a local hard drive as a shared copy or user's choice. Choose user's choice for the purposes of this exercise, and then click OK to continue.

7. Click Don't Create Setup Batch Scripts (you will be doing that in the next exercise).

8. Enter the product identification number when prompted. Click OK to continue with the server-based setup.

9. A dialog box appears when the server-based setup is complete. Click OK but do not close the window.

The Windows 95 server-based Setup program is simple and makes it easy to install Windows 95 on a server. With the Windows 95 installation files on a server, installations go much faster.

2.1.5　Upgrade Installations

The upgrade version of Windows 95 requires that Windows 3.*x*, Windows for Workgroups, or OS/2 was installed on your computer previously. The Setup program checks for the existence of these files: WINVER.EXE, USER.EXE, WIN.COM, SYSTEM.INI, and (in Windows for Workgroups only) PROTOCOL.INI. Setup also checks the versions of these files to make sure that they are real. If the Setup program does not find these files, you will be asked to insert the Windows 3.*x* or Windows for Workgroups disk into the floppy drive so that the Setup program can verify the upgrade.

If the Windows 95 Setup program detects an earlier version of Windows on the computer, it gives you the choice of installing Windows 95 in the same directory. This is an important choice. If you decide to install Windows 95 in the same directory as Windows 3.*x* or Windows for Workgroups, you will save a lot of time setting up applications under Windows 95. When you use the same directory as a previous version of Windows, Windows 95 reads through your settings and copies all the information from your program groups into Windows 95. You will not have to reinstall your Windows 3.*x* applications in Windows 95.

Should you decide to install Windows 95 in a directory other than the one used for Windows 3.*x* or Windows for Workgroups, you will have to reinstall your applications under Windows 95 and create groups and icons for those applications. On the other hand, by using a different directory, you preserve your older operating system, whereas if you install to the same directory, you lose access to the earlier installation of Windows.

2.1.6   Uninstalling Windows 95

If you upgrade to Windows 95 from Windows 3.*x* or Windows for Workgroups, you will be presented with an option to Save System Files. Selecting this option causes the Windows 95 Setup program to save the existing MS-DOS– and Windows-based system files and enables you to easily uninstall Windows 95 from the computer, if necessary. These system files require about 6MB of hard disk space.

> **The following steps work properly only if you selected the Save System Files option during the Windows 95 installation. If you didn't choose that option, you need to follow a longer series of steps, as described in Chapter 6, "Monitoring and Optimization" of the *Windows 95 Resource Kit*, in the section "Removing Windows 95 with Your Previous Operating System."**

To remove Windows 95, use the Windows 95 startup disk's Uninstall program (UNINSTAL.EXE). Use the following steps to uninstall Windows 95:

1. Place your Windows 95 startup disk in the floppy drive (or the CD-ROM in the CD-ROM drive).

2. From the Start menu, choose Run. Type **a:\uninstal.exe** and press Enter.

3. In the Windows 95 Uninstall dialog box, click Yes to begin the uninstall process. Windows 95 shuts down, and the uninstall process continues automatically.

4. Your previous configuration will be restored. When you are prompted, remove the Windows 95 startup disk or the CD-ROM from the drive and press Enter to reboot your computer.

2.1.7   Dual Booting with Microsoft Windows NT

Windows 95 has the capability to dual boot with other operating systems. As you learned earlier in this chapter, if you install Windows 95 into a separate directory when upgrading from an older version of Windows, you retain the older operating system and can, therefore, boot to the old version of Windows. Or, as is more likely, you can dual boot with Windows NT.

The file that makes dual booting with Windows NT possible is the Windows 95 version of MSDOS.SYS. In MSDOS.SYS, you have to make sure the entry BootMulti=1 is set properly. If it is set to 1, the ability to run multiple operating systems is enabled. If it is set to 0, dual booting is disabled. To set up a dual boot with Windows NT after Windows 95 has been installed, use the following process:

1. Start up Windows 95.

2. Exit to a command prompt.

3. Switch to the directory holding the Windows NT source files and type **WINNT /w** (this allows Windows NT Setup to run under Windows). Windows NT creates a BOOT.INI file that lists the location of the WINNT directory, the Windows directory, and the default boot operating system.

If Windows NT is already installed, the procedure is a bit more difficult. These are the steps to take:

1. Make sure the Windows NT machine will already dual boot between MS-DOS and Windows NT.

2. Start the computer under MS-DOS.

3. Run Windows 95 setup.

4. If you run MS-DOS from a floppy disk when you install Windows 95, you will have to run the Windows NT Emergency Recovery Disk (ERD) to restart Windows NT.

    If you want to run MS-DOS after you have installed Windows 95 in a dual-boot configuration, you will have to select MS-DOS from the boot menu and then select Previous Version from the Windows 95 menu.

Keep these things in mind when dual booting with Windows NT and Windows 95:

*   Windows 95 can read FAT16 and FAT32 partitions. Windows NT can read FAT16 and NTFS partitions.

*   If your Windows NT machine has an NTFS file system but does not have a FAT partition, you will not be able to dual boot Windows 95.

*   If you have Windows 95 installed and you install Windows NT on the same partition, and in the process you convert your FAT partition to NTFS, Windows 95 will no longer work.

*   It works out best if you have two partitions, one FAT and one NTFS (that way you can take advantage of the strengths of both operating systems).

*   If you want to share applications (such as Microsoft Office), you will have to install it twice in order to affect the appropriate Registry entries for both operating systems. (However, you can install to the same directory as long as you select the same options.)

Make sure you have a good backup before you try any of this! (Refer to the section on Windows 95 Backup for assistance in this area.)

2.1.8   Exercises

Exercise 1: Creating a Batch Setup File

This exercise demonstrates how to use the Batch Setup program (BATCH.EXE) to build a batch script that can be used as part of the Windows 95 Setup process.

1. Make sure that the BATCH.EXE program is installed on your computer. The suggested location is C:\program files\batch. If the program is not installed, you can install it by running the SETUP.EXE on the Windows 95 CD in the \admin\nettools\bsetup directory.

2. Start BATCH.EXE by running it from either the Start menu or the Run dialog box.

3. BATCH.EXE requires that you fill in information about the computer you are using. Click the button that reads Click Here to retrieve settings from the Registry. If any information is missing, fill it in now.

4. Click the Network Options button. This opens a dialog in which you can choose the network settings that will be installed.

5. Select NetBEUI to go along with the other defaults, and then click the OK button.

6. Click the Installation Options button. In the dialog box that appears, you can change various settings for the desktop. Click the Time Zone tab, and then select the proper time zone. Click OK.

7. Click the Optional Components button. In the dialog box that appears, specify the optional components you want to install. Click OK.

8. Click Done. You will now be prompted to specify a filename to which the settings will be saved.

9. In Notepad or WordPad, open the INF file you created. You should be able to find all the settings you selected in the file.

Exercise 2: Adding and Removing Windows 95 Components

This exercise demonstrates how to add or remove Windows 95 components after the installation process is complete. After you run setup, you might find that you need some utilities you didn't install. This exercise walks you through the process of adding a Windows 95 component.

1. To add Windows 95 components, you will need the Windows 95 CD in your CD-ROM drive. If it isn't there already, place the CD in the drive.

2. From the Control Panel, run the Add/Remove Programs icon.

3. When the Add/Remove Programs dialog box appears, click the Windows Setup tab. You will see a list of options with check boxes. If a check box is checked and white, it means you have installed all the components for that item. If the check box is checked but gray, it means you have installed some of the components for that item. If the check box is not checked, you have not installed any of the components for that item.

4. Click on either an item that is unchecked or one that is checked but gray (Accessories, for example). Windows 95 tells you how many components make up that item and how many are installed.

5. Click the Details button to see a list of components for the item you selected.

6. Select an item that is not checked (such as Desktop Management) and click OK.

7. Click OK to begin installation of that new component. Windows 95 installs that component from the CD.

8. When the installation is finished, close the Add/Remove Programs dialog box by clicking OK or Cancel.

2.1.9 Practice Problems

1. A typical installation of Windows 95, without any optional components, requires approximately how much hard disk space?

    A. 10–20MB

    B. 40–60MB

    C. 80–100MB

    D. 100–120MB

2. Which of the following are disadvantages of a shared installation of Windows 95?

    A. You lose your network connection when you shut down.

    B. More space is required on the hard drive for network files.

    C. You cannot log off and log on as another user.

    D. Network performance is degraded.

3. Which program(s) can you use to create custom scripts for automated Windows 95 installation?

    A. NOTEPAD.EXE

    B. BATCH.EXE

    C. SETUP.EXE

    D. SCRIPT.EXE

4. What are the types of Windows 95 installations you can choose from?

    A. Compact

    B. Custom

    C. Typical

    D. Portable

5. How can you create a Windows 95 emergency startup disk?

    A. By manually copying the necessary files to a floppy disk.

    B. By allowing the installation process to create the disk for you.

    C. By formatting a floppy disk and selecting the Copy System Files option.

    D. From the Add/Remove Programs icon in the Control Panel.

6. If you choose to install Windows 95 in the same directory as a previous installation of Windows 3.x, what happens?

    A. A dual boot configuration between the two operating systems is created.

    B. Windows 3.x is replaced, and all settings are lost.

    C. Windows 3.x is replaced, and all settings are copied to the Windows 95 Registry.

    D. An error occurs, halting installation.

7. Windows 95 creates which of the following files during the installation process?

    A. BOOTLOG.TXT

    B. SETUPLOG.TXT

    C. STARTUP.LOG

    D. DETLOG.TXT

8. To install Windows 95 using the upgrade package, which operating system(s) must you already have?

    A. MS-DOS 6.0 or higher

    B. Windows 3.x

    C. OS/2

    D. UNIX

9. Briefcase is a standard feature for which type(s) of Windows installation?

    A. Compact

    B. Custom

    C. Typical

    D. Portable

10. On which type of machine can you run the NETSETUP program?

    A. MS-DOS

    B. Windows 3.*x*

    C. Windows 95

    D. OS/2

11. Which utility runs as part of the Windows 95 installation process?

    A. ScanDisk

    B. Disk Defragmenter

    C. Backup

    D. System Monitor

12. From where can you run the Windows 95 installation program?

    A. CD-ROM

    B. Floppy disk

    C. Across a network

    D. All of the above

13. What must you do before you can install Windows 95 across a network?

    A. Copy the installation CD-ROM to a network drive.

    B. Run NETSETUP to create the network setup files.

    C. Place the Windows 95 CD-ROM in your drive and share that drive with other users.

    D. Run the installation but specify the name of the computer on which you want to install Windows 95.

14. If Windows 95 fails during the hardware detection phase of installation, which file is used to restart the detection phase?

    A. SETUPLOG.TXT

    B. DETLOG.TXT

    C. SETUP.LOG

    D. DETCRASH.LOG

15. No matter what type of Windows 95 installation you select (typical, custom, and so on), you are not limited in the choice of which optional components can be installed. True or false?

    A. True

    B. False

16. What is the most likely point of failure for the Windows 95 Setup program?

    A. Startup and information gathering

    B. File copy

    C. Hardware detection

    D. Final system configuration

17. If you choose to keep Windows 3.*x* and create a dual-boot with Windows 95, what happens to applications installed under Windows 3.*x*?

    A. Applications will be available in either operating system.

    B. Applications will be available only in Windows 3.*x*.

    C. Applications will be moved from Windows 3.*x* and made available only in Windows 95.

    D. The Windows 95 installation resets all Registry settings, so applications have to be reinstalled in both operating systems.

18. The CD-ROM and the floppy disk versions of Windows 95 contain the same files. True or false?

    A. True

    B. False

19. Batch setup scripts can be used in which environments to automate Windows 95 installation?

    A. CD-ROM

    B. Floppy disk

    C. Across a network

    D. All of the above

20. If you are creating a dual boot between Windows 95 and Windows NT, which of the following files contains the necessary dual-boot settings?

    A. MSDOS.SYS

    B. SYSTEM.DAT

    C. SYSTEM.INI

    D. CONFIG.SYS

21. You have installed Windows 95 over a Windows 3.1 operating system, replacing Windows 3.1. When can you uninstall Windows 95 and revert back to a Windows 3.1 operating system?

    A. Anytime you install Windows 95 over Windows 3.1.

    B. When you install Windows 95 and select the Save System Files option.

    C. When you install Windows 95 in a directory other than the one used by Windows 3.1.

    D. Never.

22. What extension is used for batch script files that are needed with Windows 95 automated setup?

    A. .BAT

    B. .SCR

    C. .DAT

    D. .INF

23. When you upgrade from Windows for Workgroups to Windows 95, Windows 95 copies settings from which of the following files?

    A. PROTOCOL.INI

    B. SYSTEM.INI

    C. WIN.INI

    D. WFW.INI

24. If you have to install Windows 95 on a large number of computers, which installation choice is the most efficient?

    A. Custom

    B. Compact

    C. NetSetup

    D. Automated

2.1.10　Answers and Explanations

1. **B**　An installation, without any optional components, takes up between 40MB and 60MB depending on whether you choose typical, custom, portable, or compact.

2. **A, C, D**　Because a shared installation requires the network to run Windows 95, you lose network support when you shut down Windows 95, and network performance is degraded because of the file transfer between client and server. In addition, you cannot log off and log on as a different user. You must completely restart Windows.

3. **A, B**　Custom scripts can be created either manually with an editor such as Notepad or with the BATCH.EXE utility.

4. **A, B, C, D**　When installing Windows 95, you have the choice of a compact, custom, typical, or portable installation.

5. **A, B, D**   A Windows 95 startup disk can be created during installation or from the Add/Remove dialog box in the control panel. It can also be created manually, although that is not recommended.

6. **C**   When you install Windows 95 over an existing copy of Windows 3.*x* or Windows for Workgroups, all settings from the prior operating system are copied to Windows 95.

7. **B, D**   During installation, the SETUPLOG.TXT and DETLOG.TXT files are created. BOOTLOG.TXT is created when Windows 95 starts.

8. **B, C**   To install Windows 95 as an upgrade, you must be using Windows 3.*x*, Windows for Workgroups 3.*x*, or OS/2.

9. **D**   Briefcase is a standard feature of the Portable installation (but it can be selected for any type of setup).

10. **C**   The NETSETUP program can be run only on a computer running Windows 95.

11. **A**   When you install Windows 95, ScanDisk is automatically run to check the integrity of the hard drive.

12. **D**   Windows 95 installation can be run from floppy disks, a CD-ROM, or over a network.

13. **B**   Before you can install Windows 95 from a network, you must run the NETSETUP program that creates the required Windows 95 setup files on a network drive.

14. **D**   If Windows 95 installation fails during the hardware detection phase, the DETCRASH.LOG file is used to restart the process.

15. **A**   All components are available as part of any Windows installation (typical, custom, and so on), but most have to be installed manually after Setup is complete except if you are using the custom setup option.

16. **C**   If Windows 95 installation fails, it is usually during the hardware detection phase.

17. **B**   If you create a dual boot with Windows 3.*x* and Windows 95, you will have to reinstall all your applications under Windows 95.

18. **B**   The CD-ROM version of Windows 95 contains additional files, such as online help, which are not available on the floppy disks.

19. **D**   Batch setup scripts can be run when installing Windows 95 from disk, CD-ROM, or across a network.

20. **A**   Information about a dual boot between Windows 95 and Windows NT is kept in the MSDOS.SYS file.

21. **B**   Selecting the Save System Files option allows you to uninstall Windows 95 and revert to a prior operating system.

22. **D**   Batch script files used in automated Windows 95 installations have the .INF extension.

23. **A, B, C**   When upgrading from Windows for Workgroups, Windows 95 reads settings from PROTOCOL.INI, SYSTEM.INI, and WIN.INI, as well as other system files such as AUTOEXEC.BAT and CONFIG.SYS.

24. **D**   Automated installations can remove much of the required user interaction that takes place during Windows Setup.

2.1.11　Key Words and Definitions

Automated setup   The process of simplifying the installation of Windows 95 on many machines by creating batch scripts that can control the setup process.

Compact setup   Windows 95 installation option that's recommended when disk space is limited. Only the minimum number of required files are installed.

Custom setup   Windows 95 installation option that gives you the greatest flexibility for choosing optional components.

Distribution Media Format (DMF)   A file format used on Windows 95 Setup disks to place more data on each floppy disk. Such disks cannot be copied with standard methods.

NETSETUP   A utility that copies Windows 95 files to a network for the purpose of installing to other computers over the network.

OEM (Original Equipment Manufacturer)   Suppliers or vendors of new computers.

Portable setup   Windows 95 installation option that is recommended for portable computers. Includes Briefcase and additional support for portable computing.

Shared Windows 95   An installation of Windows 95 on a network so that it can be shared by clients to reduce the amount of required hard disk space.

Typical setup   Windows 95 installation option in which the most common options are installed. Recommended for most users of desktop computers.

2.2   Install and Configure Hardware Devices

This section will look at installing and configuring printers locally and on a network under Windows 95. It will then look at the installation and configuration of modems. Finally, it examines the use of modems under Windows 95—how they are used and how they work with dial-up networking.

In addition to mastering the printer and modem objectives covered in this section and tested on the exam, you should also have a good understanding of the printing process under Windows 95 and the features that are available to you.

2.2.1   Installing a Local Printer

There are two ways to install a local printer under Windows 95: using PnP and using the Add Printer Wizard. The first way, using Plug and Play, is the simplest way to install a printer that is PnP-compliant. You only have to connect the printer to the computer, and Windows 95 detects and installs it the next time you start the system. Occasionally, Windows 95 can't find a printer driver for the printer, in which case it prompts you to insert a disk or CD-ROM containing the driver.

The second way of installing a printer is by using the Add Printer Wizard, which can be found in the Printers folder (accessible from the Start menu's Settings option or from the Control Panel). To install a printer using the Add Printer Wizard, use the following procedure:

1. Open the Printers folder.

2. Double-click on the Add Printer Wizard and choose Next. You are asked whether the printer is attached directly to the computer or is accessed from the network.

3. Select Local Printer and choose Next.

4. Select the printer manufacturer from the Manufacturers list and select the printer model from the Printers list. If you do not have an actual local printer, you can select Generic as the manufacturer and choose the Generic / Text Only driver.

5. From the list of available ports, select the port to which the printer is connected. For example, for a parallel port, you might select LPT1:. If you do not have a local printer attached, select FILE:.

6. Choose Next and assign the printer a printer name. You can accept the default name, or you can use a more descriptive name such as LaserJet II in Room 312.

7. If you want print jobs to be sent to this printer by default, choose Yes and then choose Next. Otherwise, choose No and then Next.

8. The Add Printer Wizard then asks you whether you want to print a test page. If you do, the wizard copies the files from the Windows 95 distribution media. If Windows 95 cannot find the files, you are prompted for the path. An icon for the printer is created in the Printers folder.

To configure the printer, see the following section.

2.2.2　Configuring a Printer

After a printer is installed under Windows 95, you can use the Printer folder to manage your system printers. From the folder you can perform any of the following tasks:

- Install a printer
- Share a printer on a network
- Set permissions for accessing a printer
- Connect to a network printer
- Manage printers
- Change printer properties, such as page size

When you need to change settings for a printer, opening the property window for that printer will allow you to configure the necessary settings. To do this, right-click the printer in the Printers folder and select Properties. The different tabs of the properties window give you access to the printer's settings. Table 2.3 outlines the tabs and the properties they contain.

Table 2.3　Printer Dialog Box Tabs

Tab	Properties
General	Printer name, descriptive comments, page separator preferences
Details	Printer driver, port settings, spool settings
Paper	Default paper size, orientation, paper source, number of copies
Graphics	Resolution (dots per inch, or dpi) for the printer, dithering (color blending), intensity (lightness or darkness)
Fonts	Installed font cartridges, TrueType settings, font substitutions
Device	Information specific to the printer (such as the manufacturer), memory
PostScript	PostScript options, output format, header information for print jobs, error information, other advanced options

2.2.3　Windows 95 Network Printing

Windows 95 network printing support includes a number of new features:

- A modular architecture, which allows different print providers for different types of networks
- Point and Print installation, which allows printer drivers to be automatically installed over the network
- The capability to assign network permissions to print queues, which can prevent unauthorized changes to the print queues or print jobs
- Support for different network print servers, including HP JetDirect printers and DEC PrintServer printers

Network Printing Architecture

The modular format of the Windows 95 printing subsystem uses a layered model. The four layers are listed in Table 2.4.

Table 2.4 Network Printing Layers

Layer	Description
API	Passes information from an application to the print router. Windows 95 includes 16- and 32-bit APIs. Functions for opening, writing, and closing print jobs. Manages the print queue.
Router	Passes print requests from the API to the correct Print Provider Interface.
Print Provider Interface (PPI)	Passes information from the router to the print providers.
Providers (32-bit DLL)	Translates requests from the PPI into network or local printer requests. The four print providers in Windows 95 are: Local Printing Print Provider; Microsoft 32-bit Network Print Provider; Microsoft 16-bit Network Print Provider; NetWare Network Print Provider.

Network Printer Setup

To connect to a network printer, you must first install, configure, and share the printer on the network server. For information on installing and configuring the driver on the network server, refer to the preceding sections on local printer installation and configuration.

After the Windows 95 printer driver has been configured on the network print server attached to the printer, the printer must be shared to allow other users to access it. In order for a printer to be shared in Windows 95, the network print server must be running a 32-bit protected-mode client, and a File and Printer Sharing service must be enabled. The following steps demonstrate how to share a network printer:

1. Open the properties sheet for the printer.

2. Select the Sharing tab to display the Sharing configuration settings.

3. Select Shared As, and then enter a share name and an optional descriptive comment for the printer.

4. Grant permissions to access this printer. If share-level permissions are used, you must assign a password to the printer; to access the print queue, users must supply the correct password. If user-level permissions are used, you must add the users who will be granted access to this print queue.

5. Choose OK to share the printer. The printer icon now appears as a hand holding or sharing the printer with others. Remote users with the correct permissions can now access the print queue after setting up the correct printer driver on their computers.

When the printer has been configured and shared on the network print server, a Windows 95 client can be configured to connect to the print server and print to the printer over the network. You can set up this configuration either manually with the Add Printer Wizard or by configuring the network printer for Point and Print setup.

To manually configure a Windows 95 client to print to the network printer using the Add Printer Wizard, perform the following steps:

1. Start the Add Printer Wizard from the Printers folder.

2. In the Printer Type field, select Network Printer and choose Next.

3. Enter the Universal Naming Convention (UNC) path for the network printer, such as \\SARAH\HP4.

4. If you will not be using MS-DOS applications to print to this printer, select No under Do You Print from MS-DOS Based Programs?. To have the printer associated with a printer port, such as LPT1:, you should select Yes for that option. Choose Next.

5. If you specified that you will print to the printer using MS-DOS–based applications, you are prompted to select the desired port from the Capture Printer Port dialog box. Choose OK to continue.

6. Choose Next, and then select the printer manufacturer and model from the Manufacturers and Printers lists, respectively.

7. Enter a descriptive name for the printer.

8. If you want to test your ability to print properly to the network printer, select Send Test Page.

9. Choose Finish to have Windows 95 begin copying the printer driver files to the hard drive if the latest drivers are not already on the hard drive. If Windows 95 cannot find the files, you are prompted to enter the path to the Windows 95 distribution files.

10. An icon for the network printer is created in the Printers folder. If desired, you can drag a copy of this icon to the Desktop to create a shortcut.

To connect to a network printer that is *not* configured for Point and Print setup, a client must know the correct printer driver to use, as well as the share name and the network server name. However, after a network printer has been configured to enable Point and Print setup, the printer driver installation on the client is greatly simplified. The Point and Print printer supplies the client with information such as the UNC path, the printer driver to be used, and other information.

To install the printer drivers for the Point and Print printer on a Windows 95 client, locate the icon for the printer in the Network Neighborhood and drag the it onto the desktop. Alternatively, you can right-click on the network printer icon and select Install.

In addition, if you drag and drop a document onto the network printer icon, the printer driver will be installed on the Windows 95 client if it has not already been installed. If the driver version on the network printer is more recent than the version on the client, the later printer driver version will be copied to the client.

A Point and Print printer can be configured on any of the following servers:

- Windows 95 server

- Windows NT server (including both Windows NT Server and Windows NT Workstation servers)

- NetWare bindery-based server

2.2.4 Modems

A *modem* is a special piece of computer hardware that converts the data from your computer into a signal that can be transmitted through normal telephone lines. This process is called *modulation*. The modem also converts signals from the phone line into data that your computer can understand through a process called *demodulation*. Most modems fall into one of these main categories: internal, external, PCMCIA format (for notebook computers), or portable.

Modems also have a variety of attributes and features, such as error correction, compression, and flow control. The most important attribute, however, is the speed with which the modem can transfer data over the telephone line. This speed is measured in bytes per second (bps, which is commonly referred to as *baud*). As you might guess, faster transfer rates are generally better. As recently as five years ago, 1,200bps was considered standard, and 2,400bps was fast. Currently, however, 28,800bps, 33,600bps, and 56,000bps are standard. However, both the sender and receiver—as well as the physical phone lines—must support 56K in order to reach that speed.

To find out whether Windows 95 supports a modem you have or intend to purchase, look in the Windows 95 Hardware Compatibility List located on the Windows 95 CD-ROM in the \DRIVERS folder. The filename is HCL95.HLP; it is a Windows Help file. You can obtain the most recent version of the Windows 95 Hardware Compatibility List, HCL95.EXE, and the most recent versions of the Windows 95 Driver Library drivers, from the following Web site: `ftp://ftp.microsoft.com/kb/softlib`.

Installing and Configuring Modems

Windows 95 makes installing and configuring your modem a simple process. If you have a modem installed in your computer, for example, the Windows 95 Setup program attempts to detect the modem's brand and speed, and then it installs the proper driver files.

If you want to change your modem or install a new modem while you are running Windows 95, you can install and configure the modem yourself from the Windows 95 Control Panel. You also can reconfigure an existing modem. To display the Modem properties sheet, which you use to add, remove, or modify a modem, use the following steps:

1. From the Start menu, choose Settings, Control Panel.

2. Double-click on the Modems icon to display a general Modems properties sheet.

To reconfigure an existing modem from this sheet, use the following steps:

1. Select the modem and click on the Properties button to display the properties sheet for the selected modem.

2. To change the connection settings for the modem, click the Connection tab on the properties sheet. Some of the connection settings you can change include stop bits, parity, and data bits.

3. Make the desired changes and click OK.

Installing a new modem is just as easy. Follow these steps:

1. Click the Add button on the Modems properties sheet. A Windows 95 wizard guides you through the process of installing the new modem.

2. Specify the manufacturer and name of the modem (in order to install the proper modem drivers).

3. Select the port number and enter other required information. When you finish, click OK.

After installing the new modem, you can, if necessary, change its properties as you did in the preceding procedure.

Examining COM Ports

Modems are configured to transfer data to and from your computer through connections called *COM ports* (communication ports). COM ports are connected to your computer's main motherboard and allow communications devices to pass data into and out of the computer.

The Windows 95 Setup program automatically detects your COM ports and attempts to configure any devices (such as modems) attached to those ports. Alternatively, you can select a specific COM port for your modem from the Connections tab of a modem's properties sheet. Windows 95 attempts to communicate with the COM port and creates the computer files and connections necessary to allow data to flow from the computer to the device.

To manually configure a COM port (without a modem attached), follow these steps:

1. Open the Control Panel and double-click the System icon. Then select the Device Manager tab to see a list of all the computer devices in your computer.

2. Double-click on the COM port you want to configure, and a Communications Port properties sheet with several tabs appears.

3. From this properties sheet, you can configure the port to meet whatever specifications you need. These settings include port settings, device driver setup, and resource allocation information.

4. When you finish, click OK.

You can run the modem diagnostics tool in Windows 95 to identify and solve modem problems by using these steps:

1. Open the Modems properties sheet (Control Panel, Modems, Properties) and click the Diagnostics tab.

2. Click the modem you want to troubleshoot and choose More Info. Windows displays a message letting you know that this process might take a few minutes.

After the Modem Diagnostics tool runs, you see a window with information about your modem, including the port and resources it uses, its highest speed, and the command set configured for it. Note, however, that you cannot run this utility while you are using the modem.

2.2.5 Exercises

Exercise 1: Managing the Printer Queue

This exercise demonstrates how to manage the printer queue by pausing a printer, rearranging print priorities, and canceling print jobs.

1. From the Start menu, select Settings, and then Printers. This opens a folder showing all your installed printers.

2. Double-click on your default printer icon. A dialog box appears, listing all pending print jobs.

3. From the File menu, select the Pause Printing item. This stops all print jobs before they go to the printer.

4. Open an application such as Microsoft Word, Excel, or Notepad, and print several documents. If you toggle back to the printer window, you will see each of the jobs in the list of those waiting to print.

5. After you have printed several documents, you might decide that the priority of the last document should be higher than the first. Click and drag the last document and drop it where the first document appears in the list. The other documents shift downward to make room for the document you dropped at the top.

6. To cancel the print jobs before they go to the printer, first select all the documents. Then open the Documents menu and click Cancel Printing. This removes the print jobs from the printer queue.

7. To restart the printer, click on the File menu and select Pause Printing again. If you click the File menu again, you should see that Pause Printing is no longer checked.

Exercise 2: Enabling the MODEMLOG.TXT and the PPPLOG.TXT Files

This exercise demonstrates how to have Windows create two modem log files, MODEMLOG.TXT and PPPLOG.TXT, so that those log files are available to you in case a modem problem occurs.

1. First you will enable the MODEMLOG.TXT file. Open the Control Panel and double-click the Modems icon. A list of all your modems appears.

2. Select the modem you want and click the Properties button to open the properties dialog box for the modem.

3. From the properties dialog box, click the Connections tab, and then choose Advanced. Then click the Record a Log File check box. This enables the creation of the MODEMLOG.TXT file.

4. Click OK as necessary to close the open dialog boxes.

5. Next you will enable the PPPLOG.TXT file for Dial-Up Networking. From the Control Panel, double-click the Network icon. A list of all your network components appears.

6. Select the Dial-Up Networking component and click the Properties button to display the Dial-Up Networking properties sheet.

7. Click the Advanced tab. Select Record a Log File, and then click Yes to the right of the list.

8. Click OK as necessary to close all the dialog boxes.

9. If you're prompted to restart your computer after installation is complete, put the Windows 95 CD in your CD-ROM drive, and then restart the computer.

2.2.6 Practice Problems

1. The Windows Setup program will check all COM ports to determine whether a modem is installed. True or false?

   A. True

   B. False

2. When does Windows 95 detect a Plug and Play printer?

   A. During installation of Windows 95.

   B. When you connect the printer to a parallel port.

   C. When you start Windows 95.

   D. When you turn the printer on.

3. Which of the following statements are true?

   A. Modulation is the translation of signals from a phone line into data your computer can read.

   B. Modulation is the translation of data from your computer into a signal that can be sent over the phone line.

   C. Demodulation is the translation of data from your computer into signals that can be sent over the phone line.

   D. Demodulation is the translation of signals from a phone line into data your computer can read.

4. What type(s) of modems does Windows 95 *not* support?

   A. Internal

   B. External

   C. PCMCIA

   D. Portable

   E. None of the above, all are supported

5. What information does Windows 95 get from a Plug and Play printer?

   A. Manufacturer and model

   B. Paper size

   C. Amount of memory installed

   D. Font cartridges installed

6. COM ports can be configured without a modem attached. True or false?

   A. True

   B. False

7. Windows 95 always attempts to select a driver for a printer it detects. What happens if Windows 95 doesn't find the driver?

   A. You are given a chance to install the driver from a floppy disk.

   B. You can select any driver that is compatible.

   C. Windows uses a standard driver to give you basic printer capabilities.

   D. The printer cannot be used.

8. Which of the following tasks can you perform from the Printers folder (in the Control Panel)?

   A. Connect to a network printer

   B. Share a printer on a network

   C. Set permissions for the printer

   D. Uninstall a printer

9. Dial-Up Networking supports password encryption. True or false?

   A. True

   B. False

10. Which of the following statements is true about the modem log files MODEMLOG.TXT and PPPLOG.TXT?

    A. MODEMLOG.TXT is enabled by default, and PPPLOG.TXT is disabled by default.

    B. MODEMLOG.TXT is disabled by default, and PPPLOG.TXT is enabled by default.

C. Both files are enabled by default.

D. Both files are disabled by default.

11. In order to be able to change the priority of print jobs, which of the following must be true?

A. Network software must support the feature.

B. User-level security must be in effect.

C. You must have administrator privileges.

D. Share-level security must be in effect.

2.2.7 Answers and Explanations

1. **A** Windows 95 Setup checks all COM ports during installation.

2. **A, C** Windows 95 can detect Plug and Play printers during installation and during startup.

3. **B, D** Modulation is the translation of data from your computer into a signal that can be transmitted over telephone lines, while demodulation is the reverse process.

4. **E** Windows 95 supports internal, external, PCMCIA, and portable modems.

5. **A, C, D** Windows 95 can get the manufacturer, make, memory, and font settings from a Plug and Play printer.

6. **B** COM ports can be configured either with or without a modem attached.

7. **A, B** If Windows cannot find a driver for a printer, you are prompted to insert a disk with the driver, or you are given the opportunity to select from a list of compatible drivers.

8. **A, B, C** From the Printers icon in the Control Panel, you can connect to a network printer, share a printer on a network, set permissions, and change various printer settings.

9. **A** Dial-Up Networking does support password encryption.

10. **D** Both the MODEMLOG.TXT and PPPLOG.TXT files are disabled by default; you must turn them on if you want to use them for troubleshooting modem problems.

11. **A, B, C** In order to be able to change the priority of print jobs, you must have administrator rights, user-level security must be in effect, and the network software must support priority changes.

2.2.8 Key Words and Definitions

COM port Short for communications port, a port connected to the motherboard that allows data to pass into and out of a computer.

Dial-Up Networking A Windows feature that enables you to connect to remote servers using telephone lines.

Enhanced Metafile (EMF) A print format that allows control to return to an application more quickly than does RAW print format.

Extended Capabilities Port (ECP) A feature that allows Windows 95 to use data compression to speed the flow of data to a printer.

Image Color Matching (ICM) A color-matching specification that can determine how a screen image will look when printed.

Minidrivers Printer drivers that are supplied by printer manufacturers (and sometimes Microsoft) that talk directly to printers.

Plug and Play printers Printers that can be automatically configured by Windows 95.

Unidrivers Printer drivers that come with Windows 95 that act as an interface between applications and minidrivers. The two unidrivers are PostScript and non-PostScript.

2.3   Install and Configure Backup Hardware and Software

An important—though often ignored—part of being a responsible computer user is backing up data. You never know when something unexpected is going to happen to the files on your computer. Something as rare as a lightning strike near your home can corrupt files, or a common event such as installing new software could erase important files if the installation program is careless. Having good backups on hand reduces the headaches involved in restoring any data you might lose.

Microsoft provides a Backup utility with Windows 95 that can help you save files to disk or other media so that you can have it on hand in case you need to restore data. This utility also restores information from backups for you if necessary. In this section, you will learn about the Backup utility and backup media.

2.3.1   The Backup Application

The Windows 95 Backup utility is a useful, easy-to-use tool for creating backups of data. By default, Backup is not installed with Windows 95. You can check to see whether it is installed on your computer by opening your Programs group, then Accessories, and then System Tools. If it is not there, it is easy to install using the following steps:

1. Open the Control Panel and double-click the Add/Remove Programs icon.

2. When the Add/Remove Programs dialog box appears, click the Windows Setup tab.

3. You will be presented with a list of Windows 95 components. Select Disk Tools, and then click the Details button.

4. Select Backup, and then click OK to close the open dialog boxes.

5. Windows will most likely prompt you for the installation disks or CD-ROM so it can find the necessary program files. If it does, insert the disk or CD. It then installs the Backup utility for you.

The Backup program creates two types of backups:

- **Full.** Makes backups of all the files you have selected.

- **Incremental.** Backs up only files that have changed since the last full or incremental backup. Uses the date/time stamp of the files to determine which should be backed up.

You probably want to perform a mix of full and incremental backups. Then if you need to restore files, you will restore the full backup first, followed by each of the incremental backups you have made since. If you have a large number of incremental backups, this can be a long process. On the other hand, if you use only full backups, you will need a lot of storage space. It is a good practice to perform a full backup on a weekly basis and perform incremental backups daily if you use your computer heavily.

When you create backups, you can save data on floppy disks, a tape drive, or a network drive. Most likely, you will not want to use floppy disks because of the volume of data you will need to back up. Later in this section, we will discuss backup tape drives.

The Backup utility uses backup sets and file sets to store information about data backups. A *file set* is a list of files that you want to back up. You can save file sets so that you don't have to select those files every time you do a backup. The *backup set* is the actual set of files that were created during the backup, as well as the parameters that were used to create them.

Follow these steps to create a backup:

1. Start the Backup utility and click to place a check mark in or remove a check mark from the box beside the directory or file in the list.

2. Select the files inside the directory you want to back up.

3. Click the Next Step button to choose the destination for the backup.

4. Select your tape device (or network drive or floppy drive).

5. Choose File, Save and give it a name with an .SET extension.

To restore from a backup, follow these steps:

1. Start the Backup utility and select the Restore tab.

2. Choose the Restore From location (tape, floppy disk, or network drive).

3. Select the directories or files you want to restore.

4. Choose Next Step, and then select the destination where you want the files restored.

You need to remember a few other important things about the Backup utility:

- It is possible to perform a comparison between a backup set and the directories from which it was backed up to find any differences between the two.

- LFNs are fully supported.

- It is possible to drag and drop backup sets onto a Backup icon to restore the set.

- During a full system backup, Windows 95 also backs up the Registry by copying it to a temporary file. If you restore the backup set later, the Registry files are merged back into the existing Registry.

- Backup allows the filtering of file types for inclusion or exclusion from a file set.

- MS-DOS 6.2 and Windows 3.1 backup sets cannot be restored using the Windows 95 Backup utility because of incompatibility issues with LFNs in MS-DOS 6.2 and earlier.

2.3.2   Tape Drives

After you have installed Backup, you have to tell it what kind of tape drive you have. This is easily done by selecting Tools, Re-Detect Tape Drive.

The capability to back up to a tape drive is new to the Windows 95 version of Backup (previous MS-DOS versions supported only floppy disk backups). The type of tape media that is supported is called *Quarter-Inch Cartridge* (QIC), and it comes in various specifications. The following tape drive specifications are supported:

- QIC 40, QIC 80, and QIC 3010 tape drives connected through the primary floppy disk controller (various manufacturers)

- QIC 40, QIC 80, and QIC 3010 tape drives connected to a parallel port (Colorado Memory Systems only)

SCSI tape backup units are not supported by Windows 95 Backup.

Windows 95 should be able to detect any supported tape drives automatically. If it cannot detect the tape drive, a message to that effect appears when you start Backup, and a number of trouble-shooting suggestions appear.

2.3.3   Exercises

Exercise 1: Creating a Backup

This exercise demonstrates how to use the Windows 95 Backup utility to create a backup set on floppy disk for several files.

1. Run the Backup utility. From the Start menu, select Programs, Accessories, System Tools, and then Backup. If you don't see Backup in the System Tools menu, it probably wasn't installed on your system. If that's the case, you will have to install it from the Windows 95 CD.

2. When you run Backup, you might get a Welcome dialog box. If so, click OK.

3. The first time you run Backup, you will also get a message saying that a full system backup set has been created. Again, click OK.

4. The Backup program starts. First you will see a list of drives, similar in appearance to Windows Explorer. From here, you select the files you want to back up. Expand the C:\ drive, and then click on the \windows directory. A list of files in that directory appears at the right.

5. Select several small files by clicking the check boxes to the left of them.

6. Click on the Next Step button. Next you have to select a destination for the backup file. Select your floppy drive and place a blank disk in the drive.

7. Click the Start Backup button. You will be prompted for the name of the backup. Give it a name, such as Backup 7-1-98, and click OK.

8. Backup creates the backup set. When it finished running, click OK to close the dialog boxes, and then close the Backup utility.

Exercise 2: Restoring from a Backup

This exercise demonstrates how to use the Backup utility to restore files from a backup set you have created.

1. Start by taking the floppy disk from Exercise 1 (which contains your backup set) and placing it in your floppy drive.

2. Run the Backup utility by selecting Start, Programs, Accessories, System Tools, Backup.

3. Click the Restore tab in the Backup utility.

4. The first thing you need to do this time is select the backup set from which you want to restore. Click on the icon for your floppy drive. Information about the backup set will be displayed on the right side of the screen.

5. Select the backup file and click Next Step. The utility shows you the files that are backed up on the disk.

6. Choose the file(s) you want to restore by clicking on the check boxes to the left of them, and then click the Start Restore button.

7. Restore begins. You might get error messages if the files you are restoring have the same names and date/time stamps as files already on the drive. If so, indicate how you want Restore to deal with each one.

8. When the restore is complete, click OK to close the dialog boxes, and then close the Backup utility.

2.3.4   Practice Problems

1. The Windows 95 Backup utility can be used to create backups of compressed drives. True or false?

    A. True

    B. False

2. To which of the following can a backup of data be written?

    A. Floppy disk

    B. Tape drive

    C. Network drive

    D. All of the above

3. Suppose you run a full backup on Monday and an incremental backup on Tuesday. When you run another incremental backup on Wednesday, what happens?

    A. All files that have changed since the full backup are backed up again.

    B. All files that have changed since the incremental backup are backed up again.

    C. All files are backed up.

    D. An error occurs because you can't run two incremental backups consecutively.

4. Suppose you run a full backup on Monday and incremental backups each day Tuesday through Friday. How would you restore Friday's files if necessary?

    A. By restoring the incremental backups backward from last to first, followed by the full backup.

    B. By restoring the full backup and then the last incremental.

    C. By restoring the full backup and each of the incremental backups in order.

    D. By restoring the incremental backups in order and then restoring the full backup.

5. What is included in a backup set?

    A. Data that has been backed up

    B. Parameters used for the backup

    C. Information about all incremental backups needed to restore a drive

    D. Instructions for restoring data

6. Long filenames are fully supportedby the Backup utility. True or false?

    A. True

    B. False

7. MS-DOS and Windows 3.1 backup sets can be restored using the Windows 95 Backup utility. True or false?

    A. True

    B. False

8. SCSI tape backup units are not supported by the Windows 95 Backup utility. True or false?

    A. True

    B. False

9. If you create a file set for a backup, when would you have to re-create that file set?

    A. Every time you do a full backup.

    B. Every time you do an incremental backup.

    C. Every time you do a full or an incremental backup.

    D. Only when you want to change the files included in the backup set.

10. Which of the following statements are true about Backup?

    A. The Backup utility can provide a comparison between the backup set and the directories from which it was created.

B. You can use drag and drop to drop a backup set onto the Backup icon to do a restore.

C. Backup will not erase the floppy drive or tape to which you are backing up data.

D. You can use filtering to include or exclude file types from a backup set.

11. Which types of tape media can be used with the Backup utility?

 A. QIC 40

 B. QIC 80

 C. QIC 3010

 D. SCSI

12. Where does the Windows 95 Backup utility store the settings used to create a backup?

 A. BACKUP.INI

 B. In the backup set

 C. In the file set

 D. In the system Registry

13. The Windows 95 Backup utility can back up data to a Zip drive. True or false?

 A. True

 B. False

14. You created a backup last week, and now you need to restore that data. The Backup utility will let you restore the files to which of the following locations?

 A. To the same directories on the same machine from which they were backed up.

 B. To a different directory structure on the same machine.

 C. To the same directory structure on a different machine.

 D. To a different directory structure on a different machine.

2.3.5 Answers and Explanations

1. **A** With the Windows 95 Backup utility, you can back up compressed files just as you would uncompressed files.

2. **D** Backed up data can be written to floppy disks, tape, or network drives. However, because of the limited room on a floppy disk, you would most likely use a tape or network drive.

3. **B** An incremental backup backs up only files that have changed since the last backup, whether it was a full or an incremental backup.

4. **C** To restore from both full and incremental backups, you must first restore the full backup and then restore the incremental backups in the order in which they were made.

5. **A, D** Backup sets include data that has been backed up, as well as parameters that were used to create the backup.

6. **A** Long filenames are fully supported by the Windows 95 Backup utility.

7. **B** Because they lacked support for long filenames, backup sets created by MS-DOS and Windows 3.x cannot be used by the Windows 95 Backup utility.

8. **A** The Windows 95 Backup utility does not support SCSI tape units.

9. **D** A file set maintains a list of files that you can use over and over again to back up. You don't have to re-create the file set unless you want to change the files included in the backup.

10. **A, B, D** Backup will erase the floppy disk or tape drive that you are using to create a backup, if desired.

11. **A, B, C** Windows 95 Backup doesn't support SCSI, but it does support QIC (quarter-inch cartridge) 40, 80, and 3010.

12. **B**   When a backup is created, the parameters used to create that backup are stored in the backup set.

13. **A**   The Backup utility can back up data to a Zip drive.

14. **A, B, C, D**   The Backup utility can be used to restore files to either the same directories or different directories on either the same computer or a different computer.

2.3.6   Key Words and Definitions

Backup set   The set of files that have been backed up and the parameters used to choose those files.

Backup utility   A Windows 95 program that allows you to back up and restore data.

File set   A list of files to be backed up into a backup set.

Full backup   A backup of all files specified in a file set.

Incremental backup   A backup of only files that have changed since the last full backup.

Practice Exam: Installation and Configuration, Part 1

1. This is a scenario question. First review the situation, and then review the objectives. Following that is a proposed solution. You must pick the best evaluation of that solution.

   SITUATION:

   At your corporation, you have been tasked with the job of upgrading 100 Windows 3.1 computers to Windows 95. The users of these machines have varying needs. Some have local printers; others use network printers. The majority of the computers are desktops, but some are notebooks. To complicate the effort, some of the users still want access to Windows 3.1.

   PRIMARY OBJECTIVES:

   - Install Windows 95 on all the computers.

   - Leave Windows 3.1 installed for the users who still need it, but replace Windows 3.1 for those who don't.

   SECONDARY OBJECTIVES:

   - Install Windows 95 quickly.

   - Eliminate the need for user intervention in the setup process.

   PROPOSED SOLUTION:

   You run NETSETUP to place all the installation files on a network server. Then you use BATCH.EXE to create an automated script for installing Windows 95. You then send out an email telling your users where to find the SETUP.EXE file and asking them to run it with the batch script.

   EVALUATION OF PROPOSED SOLUTION: Choose the best answer.

   A. The proposed solution meets all objectives.

   B. The proposed solution meets all the primary objectives and most of the secondary objectives.

   C. The proposed solution meets only one of the primary objectives and all the secondary objectives.

   D. The proposed solution meets all of the primary objectives but none of the secondary objectives.

   E. The proposed solution meets none of the primary objectives and only some of secondary objectives.

   F. The proposed solution meets none of the primary objectives and none of the secondary objectives.

2. Which of the following is not a benefit of Point and Print? Choose the best answer.

   A. Printer drivers are automatically copied to and installed on a Windows 95 client.

   B. Printer settings for memory and paper size can be automatically installed on the client.

   C. File and Printer Sharing are no longer required.

   D. All of the above.

3. The Backup and Restore utilities are installed automatically when you run Windows 95 Setup from CD-ROM. True or false?

   A. True

   B. False

4. This is a scenario question. First review the situation, and then review the objectives. Following that is a proposed solution. You must pick the best evaluation of that solution.

   SITUATION:

   You have been asked by a user at work for help installing both Windows 95 and Windows NT on a computer. The user is fairly advanced, and she needs the Windows 95 online help files and the Resource Kit help files. The computer is currently running Windows for Workgroups, but the user no longer has a need for it.

   PRIMARY OBJECTIVES:

   - Set up the computer for a Windows 95/Windows NT dual boot.

   - Provide access in Windows 95 to all the applications that the user currently sees in Windows for Workgroups.

   SECONDARY OBJECTIVES:

   - Install the Windows 95 online help and the Resource Kit help.

   - Install Windows 95 and Windows NT on the same drive.

   PROPOSED SOLUTION:

   You create a setup on the network by running NETSETUP from the Windows 95 CD-ROM. Then, from the network, you install Windows 95 into the same directory as Windows for Workgroups. Finally, you install Windows NT and allow it to create the dual boot for you.

   EVALUATION OF PROPOSED SOLUTION: Choose the best answer.

   A. The proposed solution meets all objectives.

   B. The proposed solution meets all the primary objectives and most of the secondary objectives.

   C. The proposed solution meets only one of the primary objectives and all the secondary objectives.

   D. The proposed solution meets all the primary objectives but none of the secondary objectives.

   E. The proposed solution meets none of the primary objectives and only some of the secondary objectives.

   F. The proposed solution meets none of the primary objectives and none of the secondary objectives.

5. Which of the following statements is true about FAT16, FAT32, and NTFS file systems? Choose the best answer.

   A. Windows 95 and Windows NT can both read all the above formats.

B. Windows 95 can read FAT16 drives, and Windows NT can read all the formats.

C. Windows 95 can read all formats; Windows NT can only read NTFS.

D. Windows 95 can read FAT16 and FAT32; Windows NT can read FAT16 and NTFS.

6. If you are installing a printer on a network server and are using share-level security, what must you do to allow other users to access the printer? Choose the best answer.

A. Assign passwords to the printer and then give those passwords to authorized users.

B. Grant authority to the User IDs of the people who will have access to the printer.

C. Both of the above.

D. None of the above.

7. This is a scenario question. First review the situation, and then review the objectives. Following that is a proposed solution. You must pick the best evaluation of that solution.

SITUATION:

Last week, you upgraded one of your users' machines from Windows 3.1 to Windows 95. Before doing so, you created a full backup of the hard drive using the Windows 3.1 Backup utility. After the installation, the user calls to report that some of the data files that were on the drive before the upgrade are unexplainably gone. Other data files from the same directory are still there, however, and have been modified since the upgrade.

PRIMARY OBJECTIVES:

- Restore the missing files.

- Keep the files that aren't missing (don't replace them with backup copies of the files).

SECONDARY OBJECTIVES:

- Make an incremental backup before doing the restore, just in case something goes wrong.

- Check the directory structure of the drive against the backup to ensure it is the same as it was prior to the upgrade.

PROPOSED SOLUTION:

You run the Windows 95 Backup utility and then do an incremental backup to a new tape. When that is done, you run the Backup utility again, select the files you want to restore from the full backup set, and then restore those files.

EVALUATION OF PROPOSED SOLUTION: Choose the best answer.

A. The proposed solution meets all objectives.

B. The proposed solution meets all the primary objectives and most of the secondary objectives.

C. The proposed solution meets only one of the primary objectives and all the secondary objectives.

D. The proposed solution meets all the primary objectives but none of the secondary objectives.

E. The proposed solution meets none of the primary objectives and only some of the secondary objectives.

F. The proposed solution meets none of the primary objectives and none of the secondary objectives.

8. A full backup makes a copy of the system Registry. What happens when you restore from this backup? Choose the best answer.

A. The backed up Registry replaces the current Registry.

B. The current version of the Registry and the backed up version are merged.

C. The current version of the Registry is kept, and the backed up version is ignored.

D. You are prompted as to whether or not you want to restore the Registry.

9. What is the sequence of steps taken by the setup program to install Windows 95? Choose the best answer.

A. File Copy, Startup and Information Gathering, Hardware Detection, and Final System Configuration

B. File Copy, Hardware Detection, Startup and Information Gathering, and Final System Configuration

C. Startup and Information Gathering, File Copy, Hardware Detection, and Final System Configuration

D. Startup and Information Gathering, Hardware Detection, File Copy, and Final System Configuration

Practice Exam Answers and Explanations

1. **C** The proposed solution can be used to install Windows 95 on many computers quickly and with no user interaction. Windows 95 will handle the detection of printers for you. Unfortunately, because you're eliminating all user interaction, the users won't have the chance to decide where to install Windows 95. If, in your batch script, you decide to install to the same directory containing Windows 3.1, the users will lose the access to Windows 3.1 after Windows 95 is installed. If you choose to install Window 95 to a different directory, all your users will keep the access to Windows 3.1 as well as Windows 95.

2. **C** File and Printer Sharing must be installed in order to use Point and Print.

3. **B** The Backup utility must be installed manually as an option during Windows Setup or later through the Add/Remove Programs icon in the Control Panel.

4. **B** This solution meets all the objectives. When you install Windows 95 into the Windows for Workgroups directory, all the applications are moved for you. The help files that the user needs are available on the CD-ROM version of Windows 95. When you install Windows NT after Windows 95 is in place, Windows NT handles the dual boot for you. Because Windows for Workgroups uses FAT16, Window 95 and Windows NT can be installed to the same drive.

5. **D**   Windows 95 can read either the FAT16 or FAT32 file systems. FAT32 can be used with newer OEM releases of Windows 95. Windows NT can read only FAT16 and NTFS.

6. **A**   With share-level security, you must assign passwords to resources that will be available to other users.

7. **F**   This is a bad solution. Because the computer was upgraded after the full backup was made, you can no longer use the Windows 95 Backup utility to restore the files. Backups created with the Windows 3.1 Backup utility are not compatible with the Windows 95 Backup utility. An alternative solution might be to restore the files to a different Windows 3.1 computer and then copy the files to the Window 95 machine manually.

8. **B**   When you restore the Registry from a full backup, the old and new Registries are merged so that any changes that have been made since the backup are not lost.

9. **D**   The process for Windows 95 Setup is Startup and Information Gathering, Hardware Detection, File Copy, and Final System Configuration.

CHAPTER 3

Installation and Configuration, Part 2: Network Components

This chapter helps prepare you for the exam by covering the following objectives:

- Install and configure of the network components of a client computer and peer server in a Microsoft and mixed Microsoft/NetWare environment.

- Install and configure of network protocols in a Microsoft and mixed Microsoft/NetWare environment. Protocols include the following:

  - NetBIOS Enhanced User Interface (NetBEUI)

  - Internet Packet eXchange/Sequenced Packet eXchange (IPX/SPX)

  - Transmission Control Protocol/Internet Protocol (TCP/IP)

  - Data Link Control (DLC)

  - Point-to-Point Tunneling Protocol/Virtual Private Networks (PPTP/VPN)

- Configure system services. Services include the following:

  - Browser

  - File and Printer Sharing for Microsoft Networks

  - File and Printer Sharing for NetWare Networks

In this chapter, you look at the installation of the four major components of the network subsystem: protocols, adapters, client services, and server services. You will be examining protocols and adapters in depth. There will also be an examination of the computer browser service.

3.1   Installation of Network Components

The first time that you are given access to the installation of network components is during the Windows 95 installation. After the Hardware Detection phase and the choice of additional Windows 95 components (only during a Custom setup), you receive a prompt to complete the network information. The Windows 95 installation will collect that information during two Windows 95 Setup Wizard steps. You will first be prompted for the installation of other network components through the dialog box shown in Figure 3.1. After choosing the proper components, you receive a prompt for the computer and workgroup names. After installation of Windows 95, you may access all these network settings through the Network icon in the Control Panel.

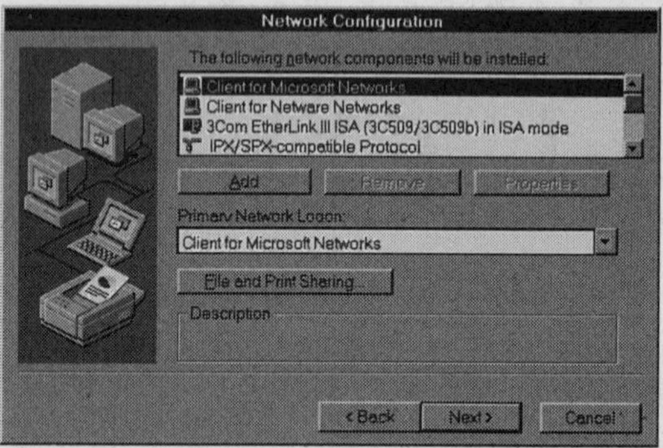

Figure 3.1   All network components can be installed during installation.

Much of the configuration of the network settings will be performed after the initial installation of Windows 95, because of the changing network environment in most workplaces. Because most of the configuration will be accomplished after the installation of Windows 95, this chapter deals with the configuration of the network components through the Network icon in the Control Panel. The Configuration tab of the Network icon in the Control Panel enables you to add, remove, and modify your network components. On this screen, you can modify the following four components:

- Clients
- Adapters
- Protocols
- Services

You may also configure which client will be your Primary Network Logon and enable File and Printer Sharing from the Configuration tab.

3.1.1   Installing Clients

The networking functionality built in to Windows 95 allows a Windows 95 computer to be a client on a wide variety of networks. A Windows 95 client can run multiple network protocols, services, and clients at the same time, and thus can be a client on many different networks at the same time.

Windows 95 includes software to support the following networks:

- Microsoft Windows NT
- Microsoft Windows 95
- Microsoft Windows for Workgroups 3.*x*
- Microsoft LAN Manager
- Novell NetWare version 2.15 and later
- Banyan VINES version 5.52 and later
- DEC Pathworks version 4.1 and later
- SunSoft PC-NFS version 5.0 and later

Microsoft does not include the client files for several 16-bit network clients. These files will have to be installed from the disk supplied from each of the third-party companies. The 16-bit network clients are from Banyan, Novell, DEC, and SunSoft. For most of these clients, Windows 95 does not support installation after the installation of Windows 95. These clients should be installed before the installation of Windows 95. This will not be a problem for any computers upgraded to Windows 95 from either MS-DOS or Windows for Workgroups, because the 16-bit network software will already be installed. This may require the installation of MS-DOS and the network software prior to the installation of Windows 95, if you had been planning to install Windows 95 to a freshly formatted hard drive. If you want to install the client after the installation of Windows 95, you must manually install the client software from the third-party client installation disks.

> **Windows 95 can have only one 16-bit network client installed at a time, but can run multiple 32-bit clients. The 32-bit clients that come with Windows 95 are the Microsoft Client for Windows Networks and Microsoft Client for NetWare Networks.**

Many of the network vendors, whose 16-bit network clients Windows 95 supports, now have 32-bit network clients that can function in conjunction with the network components that ship with Windows 95.

To add a new network client, follow these steps:

1. Open the Network icon in the Control Panel and choose the Configuration tab.
2. Click on the Add button, and then select Client (see Figure 3.2).
3. Click on the Add button.
4. Select the Manufacturer and Client you want to install (see Figure 3.3). If it is an updated or unlisted client, select the Have Disk button and provide the path to the OEMSETUP.INF file and choose the client. Click the OK button.

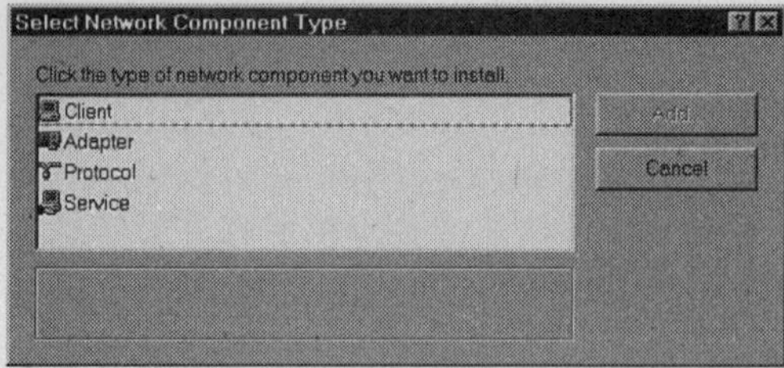

Figure 3.2   This Select Network Component Type dialog box enables you to choose which component
to add.

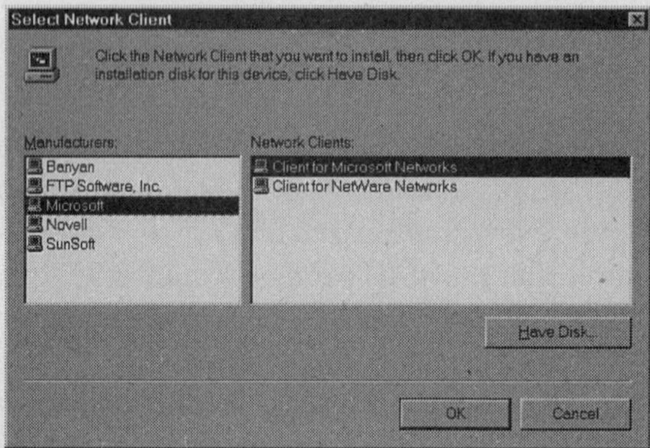

Figure 3.3   The Select Network Client dialog box enables you to choose which type of client you want to
install. Microsoft supplies two 32-bit clients.

5. Click the OK button to close the Network icon in the Control Panel. You may be prompted for the
Windows 95 CD while the client files are copied to your hard drive.

6. At the prompt, restart your computer.

Microsoft Networks

The Client for Microsoft Networks may be used if your network is made up of any of the
following:

- Windows NT

- Windows 95

- Windows for Workgroups

- LAN Manager

To communicate with another computer, both computers must run a proper client for the other
computer, and be using the same network protocol.

NetWare Networks

Windows 95 integrates well into a NetWare network running Novell NetWare version 3.11 or
later. With Windows 95, Microsoft includes the following three options for communicating on a
Novell network:

- Microsoft's 32-bit Client for NetWare Networks

- Novell NetWare Workstation Shell 3.*x* (NETX)

- Novell NetWare Workstation Shell 4.*x* (VLM)

If you choose either of the clients supplied by Novell, you receive a prompt to insert the NETX or VLM client disk from your server client disks that shipped with your original server software. If you install the VLM client, you receive a prompt to manually install the Workstation Shell 4.*x* software after completing the Windows 95 portion of the setup (see Figure 3.4). Windows 95 requires that the VLM client be installed, but will not perform the complete installation from within the Windows 95 client installation. For mixed NetWare 4.*x* (non-bindery mode) and Windows NT environments, Microsoft has a 32-bit Microsoft Service for NetWare Directory Services (NDS) available in Windows 95 Service Pack 1 or by download from `http://www.microsoft.com/windows`.

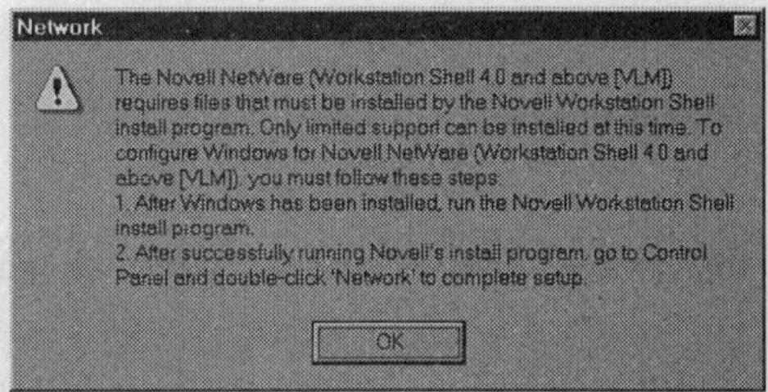

Figure 3.4 To install the VLM client, you must manually run the install the workstation shell.

> **There are some disadvantages or limitations when running Windows 95 on a NetWare network:**
>
> - **Long filenames are not supported natively by NetWare. You must load the OS/2 Name Space (OS2.NAM) NetWare Loadable Module (NLM) in NetWare, which supports 254 characters, or LONG.NAM in IntranetWare 4.11 which supports 255 characters.**
>
> - **If running the real-mode ODI and VLM or NETX real-mode shell, performance may suffer because it (the real-mode NetWare driver) uses RAM that MS-DOS applications could use.**
>
> - **Users of Windows 95 can direct jobs to print queues without capturing a printer port.**
>
> - **Users of Windows 95 can see whichever print queues the bindery or NDS provides them access to use.**

The Client for NetWare Networks can be used to access NetWare servers running NetWare 2.15 and later and NetWare 4.*x* servers using bindery emulation. The Client for NetWare Networks requires the IPX/SPX-compatible protocol, which is installed by default when the client is installed.

Although the 16-bit Novell NetWare clients do not provide all the advantages of the 32-bit client, a 16-bit NETX or VLM client is required if any of the following are used:

- NCP packet signature security (requires VLM).

- NetWare IP protocol (which does not use Microsoft's TCP/IP as it tunnels IPX/SPX through the IP protocol).

- Helper Terminate-and-Stay-Resident (TSR) applications loaded from DOS (such as 3270 emulators).

- Custom Virtual Loadable Modules (VLMs) with functionality not provided by the Windows 95 components, such as Personal NetWare (PNW.VLM).

- Novell utilities, such as NWADMIN or NETADMIN; most of the DOS-based 3.x utilities will still work, such as SYSCON, RCONSOLE, and PCONSOLE.

- NetWare Directory Services (NDSs), although a separate Microsoft Service for NetWare Directory Services (NDS) is now available.

- IPX ODI protocol.

- Monolithic IPX (IPX.COM) or ARCnet protocols.

In addition to the listed clients, Novell has released a 32-bit NetWare client called IntranetWare Client 2.2 for Windows 95, or Client 32. This client has been optimized to communicate with Novell IntranetWare 4.11 servers and NDS. The IntranetWare client can utilize either NDIS (Network Device Interface Specification) network card drivers, which are a cross-industry standard, or ODI (Open Data-Link Interface) network card drivers, which are Novell specific. By using the NDIS drivers, you guarantee compatibility with other network clients.

Banyan VINES

Banyan VINES version 5.52 and later can be used with Windows 95. However, computers running only Banyan VINES cannot use the browser services. For example, Banyan VINES computers are not visible in the Network Neighborhood.

Windows 95 Banyan VINES computers must use NDIS network card drivers rather than monolithic network drivers. This allows the network to be bound to several protocols, or clients.

Banyan now has several 32-bit clients that are designed to work with Windows 95. The latest client from Banyan is the Enterprise Client for Windows 95 Version 8.02.

You will install the updated Banyan client by clicking on the Have Disk button in the Select Network Client dialog box of the Network icon in the Control Panel.

DEC Pathworks

Digital Equipment Corporation (DEC) Pathworks is a LAN Manager–compatible protocol. The Pathworks 4.1, 5.0, and later protocols are included with Windows 95 for use with the Client for Microsoft Networks. Pathworks uses a STARTNET.BAT file called from AUTOEXEC.BAT to load the Pathworks drivers.

Windows 95 Pathworks computers can use the Microsoft NetBEUI, Microsoft TCP/IP, or DEC DECnet protocols. DECnet is not included with Windows 95.

PC-NFS

The SunSoft PC-NFS client and protocol support is included with Windows 95 for use on PC-NFS networks running version 5.0 or later. Computers running only PC-NFS cannot use the browser service, nor are they visible when browsed from other computers.

Sun Microsystems had released a 32-bit version of their PC-NFS client called PC-NFS Pro. This client has now been updated in the form of a new 32-bit client called Solstice Network Client 3.1 Plus.

3.1.2   Installing Adapters

Windows 95 includes drivers for many of the most popular network adapters. Additional network adapter drivers may be supplied by the network adapter vendor for use with Windows 95. Before you can install any other Windows 95 networking components, you must first install a network adapter driver through the Network icon in the Control Panel. If you do not have an actual network card in the computer, you can use the Microsoft Dial-Up Adapter driver along with a compatible modem for network connectivity.

Network adapter card drivers are configured by selecting the adapter in the Network icon in the Control Panel and choosing Properties. If the network card supports the Plug and Play standard, Windows 95 can automatically configure the driver according to information the card provides to the Windows 95 operating system. Otherwise, the card should be configured according to the manufacturer's documentation.

To install a network adapter, follow these steps:

1. Open the Network icon in the Control Panel and choose the Configuration tab.

2. Click the Add button, and then choose Adapter.

3. Click the Add button.

4. Choose the Manufacturer and Adapter you want to install (see Figure 3.5). If it is an updated or unlisted adapter, click the Have Disk button and provide the path to the OEMSETUP.INF file and choose the adapter you want. Click OK.

5. Click the OK button to close the Network control panel. You may be required to specify resource settings (IRQ, IO) for the adapter, and may be prompted for the Windows 95 CD while the adapter files are copied to your hard drive.

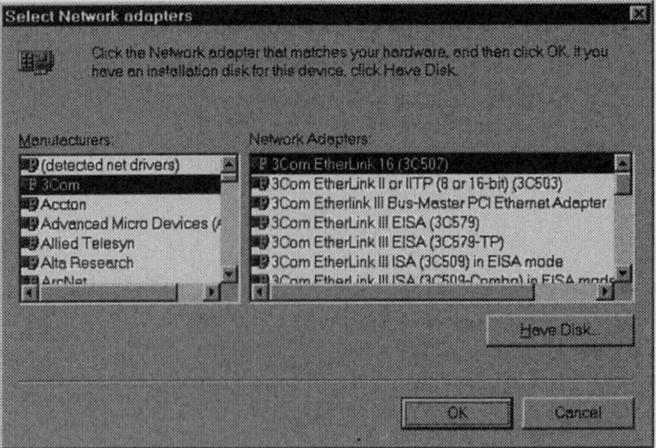

Figure 3.5 Microsoft provides drivers for a wide range of network cards from most major card manufactures.

3.1.3 Installing Protocols

Windows 95 supports many major protocols and ships with four protocols. Some protocols have specific purposes, but others can be chosen by administrators for basic communication on your network. The following protocols ship with the Windows 95 operating system:

- NetBEUI
- IPX/SPX Compatible
- TCP/IP
- Microsoft DLC

These protocols are discussed in depth later in this chapter. If you want to install any protocol other than these four, you need to have software from the manufacturer of the protocol.

To install a network protocol, follow these steps:

1. Open the Network icon in the Control Panel and choose the Configuration tab.

2. Click the Add button and choose Protocol.

3. Click the Add button.

4. Choose the Manufacturer and Protocol you want to install (see Figure 3.6). If it is an updated or unlisted protocol, click the Have Disk button and provide the path to the OEMSETUP.INF file and choose the protocol you want. Click OK.

5. Click the OK button to close the Network icon in the Control Panel. You may be prompted for the Windows 95 CD while the protocol files are copied to your hard drive.

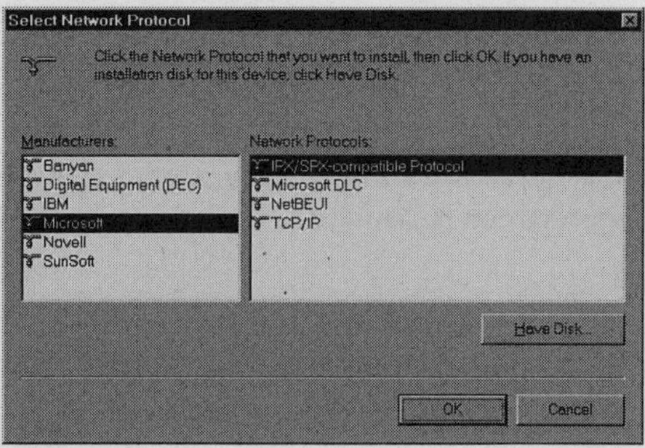

Figure 3.6　Support is included for other protocols, but the only protocols that ship with Windows 95 are found under the Microsoft section.

3.1.4　Installing Services

Services are applications that execute in the background. Services load after Windows 95 boots. They often tend to give additional network functionality in the form of a server application, but can provide other capabilities such as the Hewlett-Packard JetAdmin tool. The most used service is File and Printer Sharing for Microsoft Networks. To install a network service, follow these steps:

1. Open the Network icon in the Control Panel and choose the Configuration tab.

2. Click the Add button and choose Service.

3. Click the Add button.

4. Choose the Manufacturer and Service you want to install (see Figure 3.7). If it is an updated or unlisted service, click the Have Disk button and provide the path to the OEMSETUP.INF file and choose the service you want. Click OK.

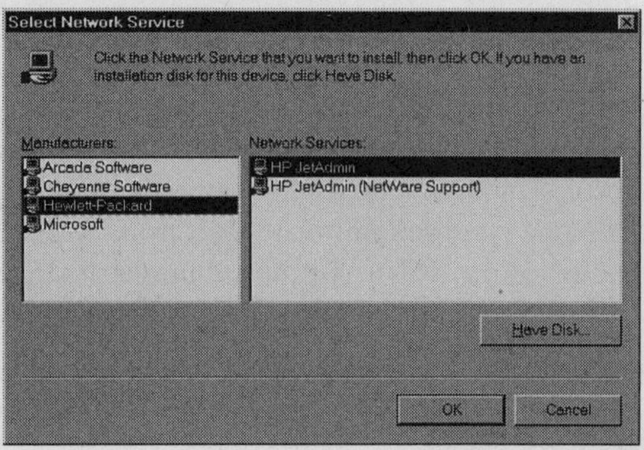

Figure 3.7　Microsoft includes a variety of services from different manufacturers.

5. Click the OK button to close the Network icon in the Control Panel. You may be prompted for the Windows 95 CD while the service files are copied to your hard drive.

> **Services are applications that are automatically started after your network software is loaded and your Logon screen is displayed. You do not have to log on for the services to start.**

Only one file and print sharing service can be installed on a computer at a time. If you install File and Printer Sharing for NetWare Networks, you will receive file and print sharing capabilities for both NetWare and Microsoft networks.

Now that you have examined installing all the network components, it is time to take a look at configuration of network adapters and protocols.

3.1.5 Exercises

Exercise 1: Installing the NetWare Client

In this exercise, you install the NetWare client provided with Windows 95.

1. Choose the Start menu, Settings, Control Panel.

2. Select and Open the Network icon in the Control Panel.

3. Click on the Add button and select Client and Add. Select Microsoft from the manufacturer list and Client for NetWare Networks from the Network Component list. Click OK to close the dialog box.

4. Windows 95 should automatically install the IPX/SPX-compatible protocol for you. Confirm that your Primary Network Logon is still the Client for Microsoft Networks. Click OK to close the Network control panel. Windows 95 then attempts to copy the network software from the original installation media and prompts you to reboot the computer. Reboot.

After rebooting, you should see any NetWare servers on your network in the Network Neighborhood. If they do not appear, Windows 95 may have defaulted to the wrong IPX/SPX frame type. Windows 95 will always try to default the frame type to 802.2. If you are not using 802.2 on your network, you can force Windows 95 to use the same frame type that you are using. To force Windows 95 to a specific frame type, you must choose it from the list for the Frame Type property on the Advanced tab of the IPX/SPX protocol properties in the Network icon in the Control Panel.

3.1.6   Practice Problems

1. Windows 95 includes support for which of the following types of networks? (Choose all that apply.)

   A. Novell NetWare 1.1

   B. Windows NT

   C. Banyan VINES 4.2

   D. DEC Pathworks 4.1

2. How do you start a network service?

   A. Log on

   B. Do nothing

   C. Start -> Programs -> <choose *service*>

   D. Start -> Programs -> NET START

3. Where would you change the name of your computer?

   A. Right-click My Computer -> Properties

   B. Start -> Run -> NETCONFIG.EXE

   C. The Identification tab of the Network icon in the Control Panel

   D. The Identification tab of the System icon in the Control Panel

4. Which of the following protocols are shipped with Windows 95? (Choose all that apply.)

   A. NetBEUI

   B. TCP/IP

   C. AppleTalk

   D. DLC

   E. IPX/SPX

5. Joe did not install or configure any networking settings while performing the Windows 95 install. Where must he do this after installing Windows 95?

   A. System icon in the Control Panel

   B. Network icon in the Control Panel

   C. Start -> Run -> NETCONFIG.EXE

   D. Right-click My Computer -> Properties

6. When do you first have an opportunity to set up networking under Windows 95?

7. How can you edit network service settings in Windows 95? (Choose all that apply.)

   A. Network icon in the Control Panel

   B. System icon in the Control Panel

   C. Start -> Run -> NETCONFIG.EXE

   D. During the installation of Windows 95

8. What will you be prompted for during the two Windows 95 Setup Wizard steps?

9. The _______ Network Logon can be set in the Configuration tab of the Network control panel. (Fill in the blank.)

10. To communicate with another computer, both computers must run a proper ______ for the other computer, and be using the same network ________. (Fill in the blanks.)

3.1.7   Answers and Explanations

1. **B, D**   Windows 95 does not include support for Novell NetWare before version 2.15, or Banyan VINES before version 5.52.

2. **B**   Network services are automatically started when Windows 95 is booted. They do not require you to log on.

3. **C**   You can only change your computer name in the Network icon in the Control Panel.

4. **A, B, D, E**   NetBEUI, TCP/IP, DLC, and IPX/SPX are shipped with Windows 95.

5. **B**   Joe must use the Network icon in the Control Panel to install and configure new network settings.

6. During the installation of Windows 95

7. **A, D**   B only allows you to change the
    resource settings for the network adapter.
    C is not an executable.

8. You will be prompted for the installation of
    other network components, and the
    computer and workgroup names.

9. Primary

10. Client, Protocol

3.1.8   Key Terms and Definitions

Adapter   Network Interface Card.

Client   A networking functionality built
into Windows 95 which allows a Windows
95 computer to be on many different types
networks at the same time.

Namespace   A NetWare server service that
allows NetWare to preserve long filenames.

Protocol   For two computers to communicate, they both must speak the same language. A protocol is a type of language two or
more computers would use to communicate.

Service   Services are applications that
execute in the background. Services load after
Windows 95 boots. They often tend to give
additional network functionality in the form
of a server application.

3.2 Configuration of Network Adapters

Proper configuration of network adapters is required to create and maintain network connectivity, a major concern for most people running Windows 95. Network adapters can have some or all of their settings changed in two locations—either the Network icon in the Control Panel, or the Device Manager. These settings or properties usually include the following:

- Driver type
- Bindings
- Advanced configuration
- Resources

All the settings are accessible through the Network icon in the Control Panel. You can also access the Resources settings for the network card through the Device Manager tab of the System icon in the Control Panel.

If you choose to access the settings on the network card through the Network icon in the Control Panel, you will want to select the installed network card and click on the Properties button.

3.2.1 Choosing a Driver Type

Three driver types can be used: enhanced-mode (32-bit and 16-bit) NDIS, real-mode (16-bit) NDIS, and real-mode (16-bit) ODI drivers.

Whenever they are available, you should use the enhanced-mode (32-bit and 16-bit) NDIS driver because this will load in protected memory, which frees up conventional memory for DOS sessions. If the drivers are 32 bit, they will also give you the added advantage of increased speed.

Sixteen-bit drivers are a second choice. Two versions of 16-bit drivers are available. NDIS is a network driver specification developed by a consortium of Microsoft, Intel, and other vendors in the computer industry. It allows multiple protocols to be used independently on a network card. ODI is a similar network driver specification that was developed by Novell.

3.2.2 Configuring Bindings

Binding involves attaching two items together. The Bindings tab lists the connections to an adapter by various protocols (see Figure 3.8). The Bindings tab will always list the items on the next level up in the Windows 95 network model (discussed later in this chapter). Bindings will list all the protocols that are connected or "bound" to the adapter you are viewing. You can unbind the protocols by clearing the check boxes. To improve the overall speed of your computer's network access, you should unbind all unneeded network protocols. If a protocol is installed on your computer, but not bound to any adapters, you will not actually be using the protocol.

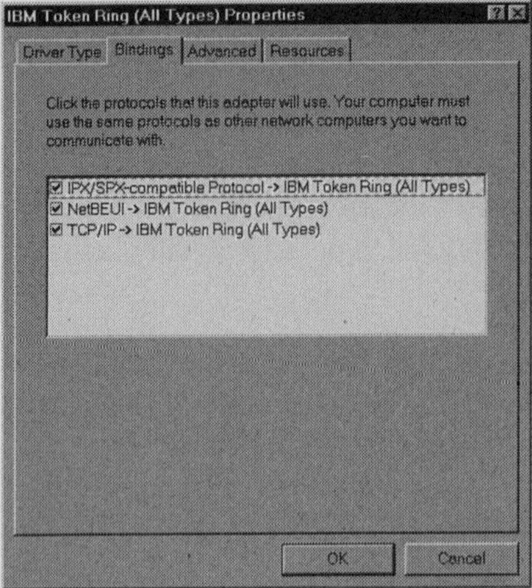

Figure 3.8　By only making necessary bindings, you can decrease the amount of time that it takes for your computer to establish a connection with a server.

3.2.3　Configuring Advanced Settings

The Advanced tab lists a series of advanced settings for the network card (see Figure 3.9). The list of settings varies from one network card driver to another. This tab often includes settings such as the maximum transmission size for network packets, and buffer settings for the network card. You should not change the default values without consulting your network administrator or the card manufacturer to find out how changing the settings will affect your network.

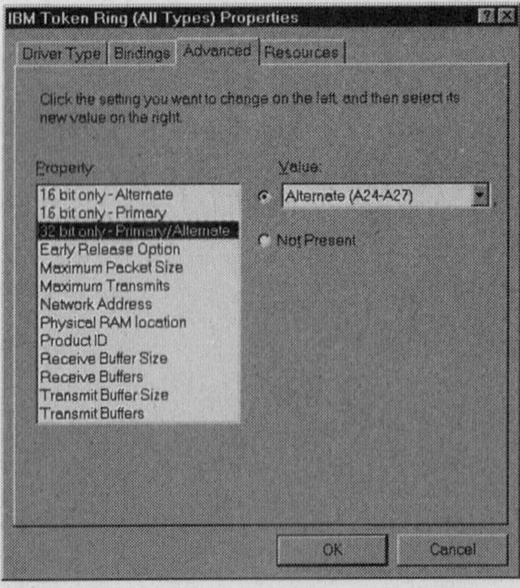

Figure 3.9　Many network adapters have advance settings that can be modified to provide support of specific features of the adapter.

3.2.4　Configuring Resources

Every network card occupies specific hardware resources on a computer. The Resources tab enables you to see—and depending on your network card, change—the resources in use by the

network card (see Figure 3.10). The resources used by the card include the IRQ and Input/
Output (I/O) address.

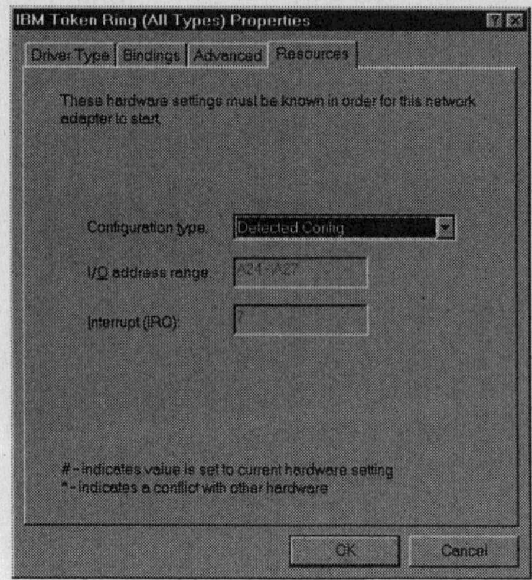

Figure 3.10 Hardware resources that Windows 95 reserves for the adapter may be modified. They may
still have to be modified on the adapter itself.

Changes made to the network card's resources might alter the actual settings on the network card
itself. Not all network cards support these alterations by Windows 95. If you are using a network
card that does not allow Windows 95 to make the modifications to the card's resources, the
settings on the Resources tab will only affect the resources that Windows 95 expects the network
card to have. You will still have to change the settings on the card, using whatever method
suggested by the manufacturer.

3.2.5 Working with Device Manager

If the card does not allow you to change the settings in the Network icon in the Control Panel,
you may be able to change the settings on the Device Manager tab of the System icon in the
Control Panel. Your network card should be located under the Network Adapters section, and
the settings can be changed in the Resources tab of the properties of the card. Not all network
cards can be changed this way.

The use of Device Manager is discussed in depth in Chapter 7, "Troubleshooting."

3.2.6 Installing Plug and Play Cards

If a network interface card is Plug and Play compliant, it can be automatically detected and
configured with Windows 95. Just plug the network card into the appropriate expansion slot and
start Windows 95. The model of the card will be detected, and the appropriate Windows 95
driver will be installed. Windows 95 then assigns an available interrupt request (IRQ) line and
memory or I/O address range to the network card as appropriate and configures the card to use
these settings. The administrator needs only to install the client and protocol software to be used
with the network card.

3.2.7   Installing Legacy Cards

The term *legacy* refers to older cards (not only network cards, but all expansion cards) that are not Plug and Play. Some legacy cards support software configuration for IRQ and I/O addresses, but many in this class only allow configuration changes by changing jumpers or dip switches. Legacy cards do not always have support with 32-bit drivers; 16-bit (possibly real mode) drivers may have to be used.

3.2.8   Dealing with Network Cards Not in Your Windows 95 Distribution

When working with very new network cards, or very old legacy network cards, you may find that the cards are not listed in the default distribution files that ship with Windows 95. Instead of choosing a network card, click the Have Disk button, and then provide the path to the unlisted drivers.

Some Plug and Play cards may require you to supply a path to the drivers if they are not included in the Windows 95 distribution.

3.2.9   Practice Problems

1. Which type of device, in most cases, does not support Plug and Play?

    A.   24× CD-ROM drive

    B.   17-inch Super VGA monitor

    C.   PCI video card

    D.   Legacy network card

2. Where can you change the resource settings for a network interface card? (Choose all that apply.)

    A.   Network icon in the Control Panel

    B.   Start -> Run -> NETCONFIG.EXE

    C.   Device Manager tab of the System icon in the Control Panel

    D.   During installation of Windows 95

3. You install a Plug and Play network card into an appropriate slot and start Windows 95. What further action is necessary to complete the installation of the network card? (Choose all that apply.)

    A.   Insert the driver disk supplied by manufacturer (if required).

    B.   Specify an IRQ (interrupt) for the card.

    C.   Specify an I/O (input/output) port for the card.

    D.   No further action is necessary.

4. What three driver types may be used with Windows 95? (Choose three.)

    A.   Enhanced-mode NDIS

    B.   Enhanced-mode ODI

    C.   Real-mode NDIS

    D.   Real-mode ODI

5. What are the two major advantages of using an enhanced-mode (32- and 16-bit) NDIS driver?

6. _______ involves attaching two items together. (Fill in the blank.)

7. If a network interface card is __________ compliant, it can be automatically detected and configured with Windows 95. (Fill in the blank.)

8. Unlike Plug and Play cards, in many cases, legacy card resource settings are configured using _______ or _______ switches. (Fill in the blanks.)

9. Where must you change the resource settings for an adapter if the adapter does not allow you to change the settings in the Network control panel?

10. To improve the overall speed of your network, you should _______ all unneeded network _________. (Fill in the blanks.)

3.2.10   Answers and Explanations

1. **D**   Most legacy cards (older cards) were produced before the advent of Plug and Play, and therefore cannot take advantage of the technology.

2. **A, C, D**   There is no executable called NETCONFIG.EXE. The resource settings (IRQ, I/O port) may be changed through any of the three other choices.

3. **A**   You will have to supply a driver disk for the network card. If the driver is included with Windows 95, you will most likely be asked for the Windows 95 installation disks/CD.

4. **A, C, D**   The three driver types that may be used are enhanced-mode (32- and 16-bit) NDIS, real-mode (16-bit) NDIS, and real-mode (16-bit) ODI.

5. Enhanced-mode NDIS drivers load into protected memory, which frees up conventional memory and also gives you increased speed.

6. Binding

7. Plug and Play

8. Jumper, Dip

9. In the Device Manager tab of the System control panel

10. Unbind, protocols

3.2.11 Key Terms and Definitions

Binding   A connection between a protocol and a network adapter.

Driver   A program that allows a piece of hardware to communicate with the operating system.

Legacy   Refers to older cards. Usually not Plug and Play. Must be configured manually using jumpers or dip switches.

Plug and Play   A technology that allows a piece of hardware to automatically be detected and configured.

3.3 Configuration of and Differences Between Network Protocols

For two computers to communicate, they both must speak the same language—they must both use the same network transport protocol. The following transport protocols are included with Windows 95:

- Microsoft NetBEUI

- Microsoft IPX/SPX-compatible (NWLINK)

- Microsoft TCP/IP

- Microsoft DLC

- Microsoft PPTP/VPN (included with OSR2 or can be downloaded from WWW.MICROSOFT.COM)

The NetBEUI and IPX/SPX-compatible protocols install by default when a network adapter driver is installed.

If the Windows 95 computer needs to communicate with other computers, it must have the same protocol installed as the other computers.

The following sections highlight the configuration options for each protocol. Refer to the section titled "Installing Protocols" earlier in this chapter for the procedure used to install protocols.

> **Unless you are required to use a third-party protocol to communicate with other computers, use one of the Microsoft protocols to take full advantage of the Windows 95 networking features. As a further consideration, be aware that the third-party protocols provided often require extra components, licenses, and configuration.**

3.3.1 NetBIOS Extended User Interface (NetBEUI)

The NetBIOS Extended User Interface (NetBEUI) protocol is relatively easy to implement because it does not require the configuration of additional network settings for each computer other than the computer name and domain or workgroup name.

The advantages of the NetBEUI protocol include the following:

- Communication is fast on smaller networks.

- Performance is dynamically self-tuned.

- The only configuration required is a NetBIOS computer name and workgroup or domain name.

The disadvantages of the NetBEUI protocol include the following:

- Not routable

- Broadcast based, causing more network traffic

Other than the computer name and workgroup name, only two settings can be changed. You can find these two settings on the Advanced tab of the Protocol to Adapter properties. The two settings are as follows:

- Maximum Sessions identifies the maximum number of network sessions of which your computer is capable of keeping track. These include both inbound and outbound sessions.

- NCBS (Network Control Block Size) identifies the size or number of network control blocks that Windows 95 will use. These blocks are used to transfer or carry NetBIOS information for the NetBEUI protocol.

Because these are the only two configuration settings that may be changed, it makes NetBEUI an easy protocol to configure. Bindings, as with adapters, can be configured for each protocol. Protocols are bound to items on the next layer up in the Windows 95 network model. The next major layer above the protocols includes both clients and services (see Figure 3.11).

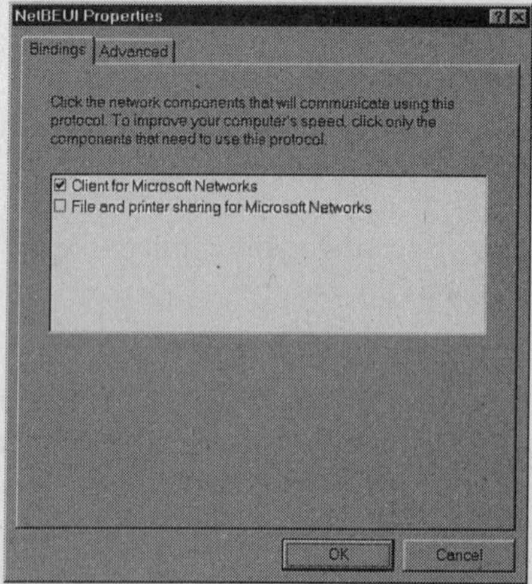

Figure 3.11 NetBEUI bindings enable you to disable clients or services for the protocol.

Bindings are listed on the Bindings tab for any clients or services that can work using NetBEUI. Because the NetWare client requires the IPX/SPX-compatible protocol, it is not listed on the Bindings tab for NetBEUI. As with bindings on the network card, any that are not used should be disabled.

3.3.2   Internet Packet eXchange/Sequential Packet eXchange (IPX/SPX)

The IPX/SPX protocol is a routable network protocol developed by Novell. IPX/SPX is a more complex protocol than NetBEUI. If you have multiple network segments on your network, you will require a routable protocol. The IPX/SPX protocol is required for communication with NetWare servers, and has now become an industry standard protocol (used by many network operating systems). IPX/SPX must be installed if the Client for NetWare Networks is used, although other protocols may also be installed at the same time. If IPX/SPX is used with the Client for Microsoft Networks, the optional NetBIOS support should be enabled.

IPX/SPX has a number of settings that you can adjust on the Advanced tab of the IPX/SPX protocol, including the following:

- Force Even Length Packets is used for compatibility with earlier NetWare Ethernet drivers with monolithic protocol stacks, and on some older IPX routers.

- Frame Type: IPX supports several variations on standard network packets. The different frame specifications are referred to by the term *frame type*. You can only talk to servers or clients that are using the same frame type as you. If a frame type is not specified, Windows 95 will go with the detected frame type or 802.2. You can choose from these other frame types:

    - 802.2

    - 802.3

    - ETHERNET II

    - ETHERNET_SNAP

    - Token_Ring

    - Token_Ring_Snap

- Maximum Connections enables you to set the maximum number of network sessions that Windows 95 will support.

- Maximum Sockets specifies the number of IPX Socket connections that may be made to or from the server. This is excluded from NetBIOS traffic.

- Network Address enables you to change the network, hardware, or MAC address of your network card. This address is the basis of all communication on your network. Not all addresses typed in will be valid, and invalid addresses will prevent you from communicating with other computers on your network. You should change this only with extreme caution.

- Source Routing specifies the cache size to be used with source routing.

With the number of settings that can be modified, and the loss of network connectivity if the settings are configured incorrectly, IPX/SPX is a more difficult protocol to work with on a network than NetBEUI.

NetBIOS is required for Microsoft network clients to communicate with Microsoft servers. NetBIOS is also used to create and maintain lists of servers on the network. By default, IPX/SPX does not use NetBIOS—although you can enable NetBIOS on the NetBIOS tab of the IPX/SPX protocol properties (see Figure 3.12).

3.3.3 Transmission Control Protocol/Internet Protocol (TCP/IP)

Windows 95 comes with the Microsoft 32-bit TCP/IP protocol, related connectivity utilities, and an SNMP client.

To install the TCP/IP protocol on a Windows 95 computer, follow these steps:

1. From the Start menu, choose Settings, Control Panel.

2. Double-click on the Network icon and select the Configuration tab.

3. Click Add to open the Select Network Component Type dialog box.

4. Select Protocol and choose Add to open the Select Network Protocol dialog box.

5. Select Microsoft from the Manufacturers list and TCP/IP from the Network Protocols list.

6. Click OK to return to the Network dialog box.

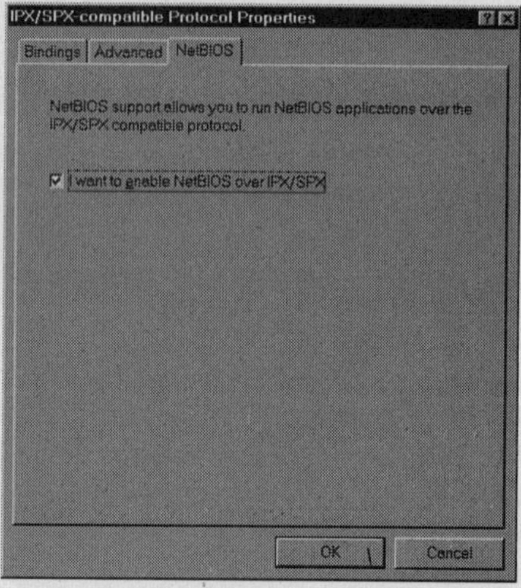

Figure 3.12 You can either enable or disable IPX/SPX-compatible protocol NetBIOS settings.

After installing TCP/IP on a Windows 95 computer, the tabbed TCP/IP Properties dialog box appears. From this dialog box, you can configure the appropriate values. To reconfigure TCP/IP, click the Network icon from the Control Panel to open the Network dialog box again.

To configure TCP/IP for Windows 95, follow these steps:

1. From the Network dialog box Configuration tab, select TCP/IP and click on Properties.

2. From the TCP/IP Properties sheet, select the IP Address tab. Select Obtain an IP Address Automatically if there is a Dynamic Host Configuration Protocol (DHCP) server on the network configured to supply this machine with an IP address. Otherwise, type the IP address and subnet mask in the spaces provided.

An incorrect IP address or subnet mask can cause communication problems with other TCP/IP nodes on the network. If an IP address is the same as another already on the network, it also can cause either machine to hang.

---

3. Each of the other tabs in the TCP/IP Properties sheet contains optional configuration information. For each of these tabs, enter the appropriate values as required. Click OK when you finish to restart the computer and initialize TCP/IP.

The other tabs of the TCP/IP Properties sheet, discussed in the following sections, contain optional TCP/IP configuration parameters.

> It is highly recommended that a default gateway be configured for the Windows 95 client using the Gateway tab. The default gateway can help route TCP/IP messages to remote destinations.

IP Address

Every computer on a TCP/IP network is individually identified by a unique 32-bit address. Currently, this address is written using dotted decimal notation (see Figure 3.13). In addition to the IP address, you also require a subnet mask. The subnet mask is used to determine whether the other people to whom you are contacting are on your network segment or elsewhere.

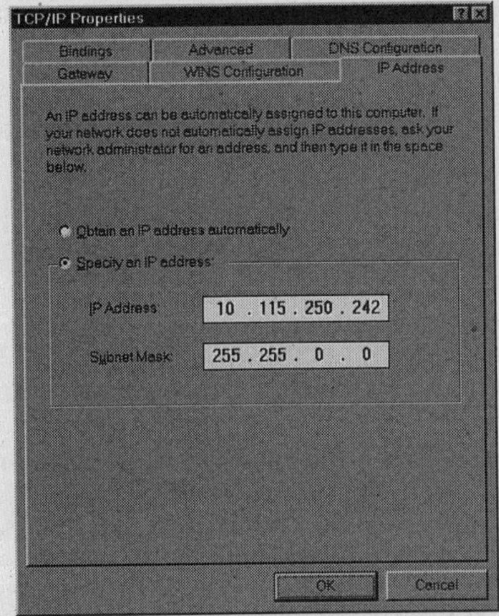

Figure 3.13   Every computer on your network requires a network-specific IP address.

These numbers should be received from your network administrator. If your network administrator has created a server to host Dynamic Host Configuration Protocol (DHCP) service, all you have to do is select Obtain an IP Address Automatically and you will receive complete IP configuration from the server.

Gateway

When the route needed for an IP message to reach a destination is not known, the message is forwarded to the default gateway. The default gateway is a router connected to other TCP/IP network segments. Messages are sent to this gateway when it is not known on which segment the destination is. The Gateway tab contains the IP addresses of default gateways that can be used in the order they appear on the list.

If the subnet mask determines that the address you are trying to reach is remote, your computer will send it to a gateway.

> Only one gateway is used to route messages. If a gateway is unavailable (because of hardware problems, for example), the next gateway on the list is used. If that gateway does not respond, the next gateway is used. A second gateway is never used if the first one is available, even if the destination computer is unavailable, or the message is undeliverable.

WINS Configuration

A Windows Internet Name Service (WINS) server can be used to register and resolve NetBIOS names to IP addresses. If the Windows 95 computer wants to map a drive to the computer name SERVER3 on a remote TCP/IP network, for example, it can query the WINS server to find out the IP address of SERVER3.

Communication using TCP/IP must always use IP addresses; therefore, a WINS server or some other form of NetBIOS name-to-IP-address-resolution must be used if communication using NetBIOS names is required. An alternative to using a WINS server is to use a static LMHOSTS file in the *systemroot* directory, which contains NetBIOS name-to-IP-address mappings. A WINS server is preferred, however, because NetBIOS names can be automatically and dynamically registered with the WINS server, which is much more flexible and accurate than an LMHOSTS file or other method. All the WINS configuration is completed on the WINS tab.

The three choices of WINS configuration for a Windows 95 TCP/IP client are as follows:

- **Enable WINS Resolution.** If WINS resolution is enabled, you must enter the IP address of one or two WINS servers in the appropriate fields. If the primary WINS server is unavailable for some reason, TCP/IP accesses the secondary WINS server if one is configured.

- **Disable WINS Resolution.** If WINS is disabled, an alternative form of NetBIOS name resolution is required to resolve NetBIOS names to computer names for destinations on remote networks.

- **Use DHCP for WINS Resolution.** If DHCP has been enabled in the IP Address tab, you can select the Use DHCP for WINS Resolution option to use the WINS servers specified by the DHCP Server options.

> This last option on the list, Use DHCP for WINS Resolution, does not mean that a DHCP server provides name resolution. The option is used when a DHCP server has been configured to advise the DHCP clients of the IP address(es) of the WINS server(s).

DNS Configuration

The *domain name service* (DNS) provides address resolution for DNS host and domain names. Host names are used with Windows Sockets applications. The host name for a Windows-based computer is often the same as the computer name, but the domain name is usually something like `domain.company.com`. World Wide Web addresses often consist of DNS host names appended to the DNS domain name to form a Fully Qualified Domain Name, such as `www.microsoft.com`, where `www` is the host (computer) name, and `microsoft.com` is the domain name. You configure DNS options on the DNS tab.

To access a computer using a DNS name over TCP/IP, the DNS name must be resolved to an IP address. This can be done using a static HOSTS file in the *systemroot* directory, or by accessing a DNS server. The DNS server contains a database that is distributed over an internetwork. If a DNS server cannot fully resolve a domain name to an IP address, it can pass the request on to another DNS server until the name is found and resolved.

The DNS Server Search Order list in the TCP/IP Properties sheet lists the order in which DNS servers will be queried for DNS name resolution. The Domain Suffix Search Order list shows the order in which domain names can be appended to a host name to try to resolve the resulting Fully Qualified Domain Name. If the Domain Suffix Search Order list contains `acme.com`, and if the host name FRED cannot be resolved, DNS then attempts to resolve the name `fred.acme.com`. If that fails, DNS attempts to resolve the host name with the next suffix on the list.

Advanced TCP/IP Settings

Use the Advanced tab to specify whether you want the TCP/IP protocol to be the default or preferred protocol. The default protocol is the first protocol used when attempting to connect to network resources. If the NetBEUI protocol is installed, it will be the default protocol. If most of the network resources you will be connecting to are using TCP/IP, you can improve performance by setting TCP/IP as the default protocol.

TCP/IP Component Bindings

The Bindings tab shows network components that can use the TCP/IP protocol. If a component has a check mark next to it, it will bind to TCP/IP and can then use the TCP/IP protocol for communication. To improve performance, remove the check marks from any components that do not require TCP/IP.

3.3.4   Data Link Control (DLC)

The other Microsoft-written network protocol included with Windows 95 is Microsoft DLC. This protocol is used only for communicating with certain network interface printers and mainframe systems. DLC is not used for peer-to-peer networking of Windows 95 computers. Due to DLC's limited use, you should consult the documentation for the items you are connecting to with DLC to determine the best settings for items listed on the Advanced configuration tab.

3.3.5   Point-to-Point Tunneling Protocol/Virtual Private Networks (PPTP/VPN)

Point-to-Point Tunneling Protocol is a secure wide area network (WAN) protocol which is starting to receive wide acceptance as a secure protocol over the Internet. PPTP enables you to make secure a connection to your network from a remote location on the Internet. If you will have Internet connectivity on your network, you should consider installing PPTP on both your network servers and remote workstations. The protocol (NDISWAN) is a virtual protocol, and does not actually exist; instead, it is a modified version of TCP/IP that allows for carrying other packets in the data section of the IP packet. This virtual protocol receives a binding with an equally virtual local area network (LAN) adapter—the Microsoft Virtual Private Networking (VPN) adapter (see Figure 3.14).

Figure 3.14   Microsoft Virtual Private Networking adapter is bound to the NDISWAN protocol, and

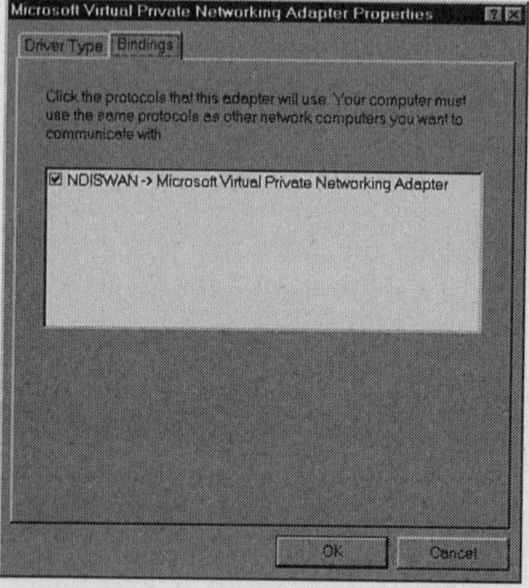

both use TCP/IP for communication.

The Advanced settings tab on the VPN Properties dialog box allows for a log file (similar to the PPP or modem log files) to track and troubleshoot connections to remote servers (see Figure 3.15). The Advanced settings also enable you to identify the physical media over which you will be running the PPTP connection.

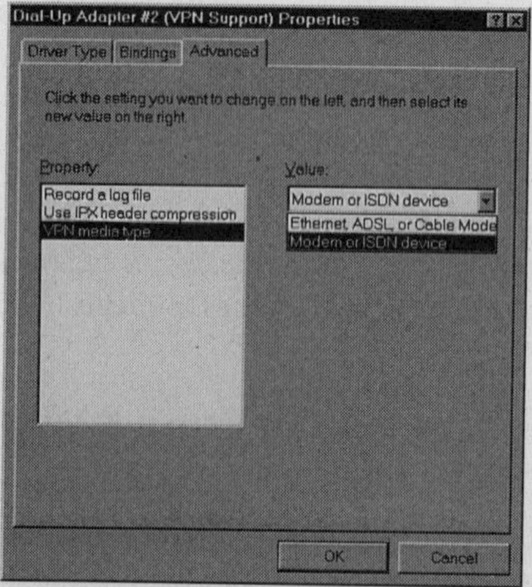

Figure 3.15   Dial-Up Adapter #2 (VPN Support) Advanced Properties enables you to specify the log file creation and PPTP media types.

To effectively use PPTP and VPN, you need some or all of the following components installed (see Figure 3.16):

- Client for Microsoft Networks.

- Optional second client for use on remote LAN.

- Dial-up adapter if making the VPN connection through an Internet service provider (ISP).

- NDISWAN protocol installed for packet encapsulation.

- TCP/IP to act as a transport for the NDISWAN protocol.

- Optional second protocol to be used on the remote LAN. This would include NetBEUI or IPX/SPX if you will not be using TCP/IP on the remote LAN.

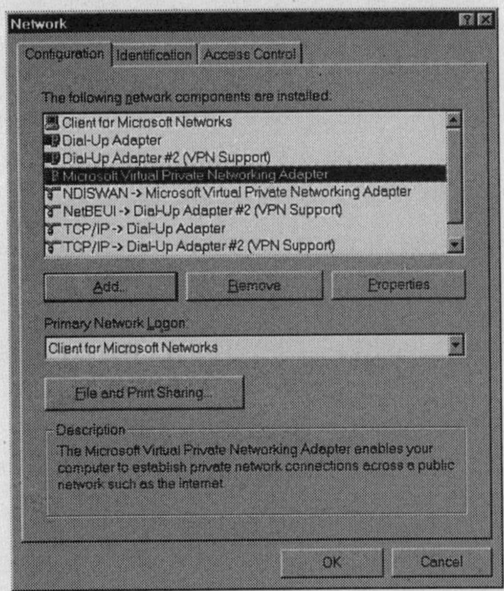

Figure 3.16   All the components that make up a PPTP client configuration.

> **PPTP and VPN are only available if you have applied the WinSock and Dial-Up Networking updates to your installation of Windows 95. Both of the updates are available from Microsoft's Web site at** `http://www.microsoft.com/windows`. **These updates have already been included in OSR2.**

When creating the Dial-Up Networking document to connect to your Remote Access Services server running PPTP, you will not be specifying a modem as a connection device, but the Microsoft VPN adapter instead. This connector will not be dialing a phone number; instead, it will require the IP address of the network adapter on the RAS server.

Before establishing a PPTP connection, you will first establish a connection to a TCP/IP network. This may be a LAN connection or a dial-up connection to an ISP. After that connection is in place, you will open up the PPTP dial-up connection (see Figure 3.17). This connection will have the IP address of the PPTP adapter on the RAS server as the destination. You will dial this virtual call, but it will keep your modem connected. Once dialed, you have all the transactional security that you would have had by dialing the server directly.

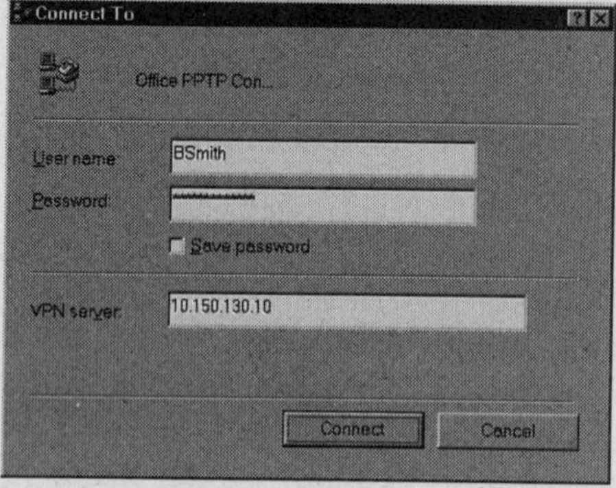

Figure 3.17   The dial-up connection leaves previous connections open.

3.3.6   Exercise

Exercise 1: Installing Network Components

This exercise takes you through the installation of several network components. You install two network adapters, two protocols, and configure your computer name.

1.   Boot Windows 95 on your computer.

2.   At the Windows 95 logon, log on as usual.

3.   Choose the Start menu, Settings, Control Panel.

4.   Click on the Network icon in the Control Panel.

5.   The Network control panel should have opened on the Configuration tab. If you have a Plug and Play card that has its drivers included in Windows 95, you will already have the following items loaded:

   - Client for Microsoft Networks

   - Client for Netware Networks

   - *Your network card*

   - NetBEUI

   - IPX/SPX-compatible protocol

   If you have all these listed items, go to step 8.

6.   To add your network card, click the Add button and select Adapter. Click the Add button again. (Check the documentation that came with your network card to see whether your card requires any special setup to work with Windows 95.)

7.   Locate the manufacturer of your network card in the Manufacturer list and the card model or type in the Network Device list. When a network card is added, by default Windows installs all the software on the preceding list.

8. Select the Client for Netware Networks and click the Remove button. Select IPX/SPX Compatible protocol and click Remove.

9. If Windows 95 did not install all the client software for you. Click the Add button and select protocol and Add. Choose the NetBEUI protocol by Microsoft and then click the OK button. Then click the Add button again and select Client and Add. Choose the Client for Microsoft Networks and then click the OK button.

10. Click the Add button, Adapter, and Add. Select the Dial-up Adapter from Microsoft and then click the OK button. The Dial-up Adapter is used by Dial-Up Networking as a modem interface. Click the Add button, Protocol, and Add. Select Microsoft's TCP/IP and click on OK. This sets up TCP/IP and the dial-up adapter for dialing to a TCP/IP network, such as the Internet.

11. Select the Identification tab of the Network control panel. It should have, unless changed during the installation, your name for the computer name and part of your company name as the workgroup name. Give you computer a single-word name with fewer than 15 letters. Set your workgroup name to match the domain name of your Windows NT Server. Click the OK button to close this window.

12. Close the Network control panel by clicking on the OK button. Windows 95 then attempts to copy the network software from the original installation media and prompts you to reboot the computer. Reboot.

After rebooting, you should receive no error messages from Windows 95 regarding your network card. If you receive any error messages, refer to the card manufacturer's documentation to resolve the error.

3.3.7 Practice Problems

1. Which of the following protocols are routable? (Choose all that apply.)

   A. IPX/SPX

   B. NetBEUI

   C. TCP/IP

2. Which frame type is automatically used if no frame type is detected when using Autodetect with IPX/SPX?

   A. 802.1

   B. 802.2

   C. 802.3

   D. Ethernet II

3. Every computer on a TCP/IP network must be assigned a unique IP address comprised of how many bits?

   A. 4

   B. 8

   C. 16

   D. 32

4. What configuration settings are available for the NetBEUI protocol? (Choose all that apply.)

   A. Computer Name

   B. Maximum Sessions

   C. Maximum Sockets

   D. Network Address

5. Which TCP/IP feature will resolve NetBIOS names to IP addresses?

   A. IPS

   B. DHCP

   C. DNS

   D. WINS

6. When is the DLC protocol most widely used? (Choose all that apply.)

   A. Small local area networks (LANs)

   B. Network printing

   C. Wide area networks (WANs)

   D. Connecting to mainframe computers

7. Which of the following items do not have to be unique on a network? (Choose all that apply.)

   A. Computer name

   B. IP address

   C. Workgroup name

8. Which protocols does Windows 95 install by default when installing an adapter? (Choose all that apply.)

   A. NetBEUI

   B. TCP/IP

   C. IPX/SPX

   D. DLC

   E. AppleTalk

9. Which protocol is required for the Client for NetWare Networks?

   A. NetBEUI

   B. TCP/IP

   C. IPX/SPX

   D. DLC

10. What type of adapter do you specify when you are setting up Dial-Up Networking for PPTP?

3.3.8 Answers and Explanations

1. **A, C**   If you have multiple network segments on your network, you will require a routable protocol to communicate between them. IPX/SPX and TCP/IP packets can be routed over multiple segments.

2. **B**   802.2 is used when no other frame type is detected on the network.

3. **D**   A TCP/IP IP address is comprised of 32 bits split up into 4 octets (8 bits each).

4. **A, B**   Only A and B are correct. The only other configurable settings for NetBEUI are Workgroup Name and Network Control Block Size. Maximum Sockets and Network Address are settings for the IPX/SPX protocol.

5. **D**   WINS (Windows Internet Naming Service) will resolve a NetBIOS name into an IP address. This enables the client to use a windows computer name to connect to another computer in a solely TCP/IP network.

6. **B, D**   DLC is most widely used for network printing and connecting to mainframe computers.

7. **C**   A workgroup name must be the same for every computer that is participating in that workgroup. An IP address and computer name must be different from every other computer on that network.

8. **A, C**   TCP/IP is installed by default on Windows NT. DLC is not installed by default. AppleTalk is not shipped with Windows 95.

9. **C**   IPX/SPX is the only required protocol when installing Client for NetWare Networks.

10. A VPN adapter

3.3.9 Key Terms and Definitions

DHCP   Dynamic Host Configuration Protocol. Used to dynamically assign IP addresses and other TCP/IP configuration information to computers.

Frame type   Used with the IPX/SPX protocol. Both the workstation and the server must be using the same frame type to communicate.

Gateway   A device used to pass packets to remote subnets based on their network ID.

NetBIOS   Network Basic Input/Output System.

Subnet mask   A TCP/IP parameter that distinguishes between the network ID and host ID portion of an IP address.

3.4   Configuration of the Computer Browser Service

As mentioned previously, a Windows 95 computer can have more than one network client installed at a time. If a network contains both Windows NT and Novell NetWare servers, for example, the Windows 95 computer can run both the Client for Microsoft Networks and the Client for NetWare Networks. If the passwords are the same for the two networks, the Unified Logon feature of Windows 95 requires that the password be entered only once for both networks. Similarly, if the Windows password is the same as the network password, the password needs to be entered only once. If the passwords are not the same, they need to be entered individually.

> The password list file (PWL) is secured by each user's Windows 95 password. To cut down the number of different passwords a user must track and maintain, some network administrators advocate the use of a blank Windows 95 password. However, the use of a blank Windows 95 password along with password caching can expose your user's network resources to unauthorized use. This author recommends not using a blank Windows 95 password.
>
> The Password List Editor, PWLEDIT, is used to edit a user's password list file. Use it to view the entries and remove specific password entries if problems are encountered using a cached password.
>
> To install this tool on your local hard disk, follow these steps:
>
> 1. Choose the Add/Remove Programs option in the Control Panel.
> 2. Select the Windows Setup tab.
> 3. Click on the Have Disk button.
> 4. Install the ADMIN\APPTOOLS\PWLEDIT directory from a Windows 95 CD-ROM.

Windows 95 also features *unified browsing*—all computers that can be browsed by Windows 95 are displayed together in the Network Neighborhood. NetWare servers appear along with Windows-based computers in the Network Neighborhood, for example, if both the Client for Microsoft Networks and Client for NetWare Networks are installed.

When users access the Network Neighborhood, they are viewing a list of computers on the network known as a *browse list*.

Microsoft and NetWare networks can use NetBIOS to distribute browse lists throughout a domain. The browse list contains all NetBIOS computers and shared resources in the domain; it is compiled by the master browser of the domain.

When the master browser has compiled the browse list, it distributes the list to the backup browsers. When a client requires access to the browse list, it obtains it from a backup browser; thus the master browser does not become overloaded with requests from all the computers.

The decision of which computers are master and backup browsers is determined through browse elections. If a primary domain controller is present, that controller will always be the master browser. Each type of operating system in the network has a different potential to be a browser.

Windows NT computers are more favored to be browsers than Windows 95 computers. If a computer is a preferred browser, it can be elected to be a browser depending on the operating system it is running and whether it has been manually configured to be a preferred browser.

When a network client needs to consult a browse list to browse the network, it contacts one of the backup browsers for a copy of the current browse list. The backup browsers periodically receive updated browse lists from the master browser to make sure the browse lists remain current.

A Windows 95 computer can be configured to maintain or to not maintain browse lists by configuring the File and Printer Sharing service for either Microsoft or NetWare networks.

3.4.1   Configuring Browse Masters

Normally, you let the browser elections automatically determine which computers are the browsers. If you do not want the potential performance load on the Windows 95 computer that can result from browsing, however, you can configure the computer to *never* be a browser. In addition, you can set a particular computer, on which an extra network load would have little effect, to be a preferred browser.

The browser configuration is performed using the properties for the File and Printer Sharing for Microsoft Networks service or the File and Printer Sharing for NetWare Networks service.

Configure Browse Master for Microsoft Networks

To access the browser configuration options for a computer running File and Printer Sharing for Microsoft Networks, follow these steps:

1. Click on the Network icon in the Control Panel and select the File and Printer Sharing for Microsoft Networks service.

2. Choose Properties and select the Browse Master property.

3. Choose one of the following options from the Value drop-down list (see Figure 3.18):

    *   Select *Automatic* as the value to have Windows 95 automatically determine whether the computer is needed as a browse server.

    *   Select *Disabled* as the value to prevent the computer from maintaining browse lists for the network.

    *   To give the computer a higher weighting for the browse elections, select *Enabled* for the value. This computer then will be preferred over other Windows 95 computers that have Automatic set for the Browse Master value for the browse elections.

4. Double-click OK and restart the computer.

Configure Browse Master for NetWare Networks

To access the browser configuration options for a computer running File and Printer Sharing for NetWare Networks, follow these steps:

1. Click on the Network icon in the Control Panel applet and select the File and Printer Sharing for NetWare Networks service.

2. Choose Properties and select the Workgroup Advertising property.

3. Choose one of the following options from the drop-down list (see Figure 3.19):

    - To have Windows 95 automatically determine whether the computer is needed as a browse server, select *Enabled: May Be Master* for the value.

    - To prevent the computer from maintaining browse lists for the network, select *Enabled: Will Not Be Master* for the value.

    - To give the computer a higher weighting for the browse elections, select *Enabled: Preferred Master* for the value. This computer will then be preferred over other Windows 95 computers that have Automatic set for the Browse Master value for the browse elections.

    - To prevent the computer from using the browser service to browse network resources, select *Disabled* for the value.

4. To allow the computer to send SAP broadcasts announcing its presence to real-mode NetWare clients, select the SAP Advertising property and change the value to Enabled.

5. Double-click on OK and restart the computer.

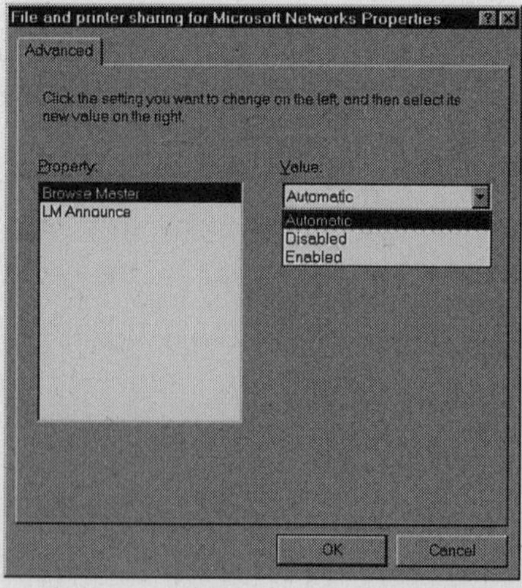

Figure 3.18   Browser options for File and Printer Sharing for Microsoft Networks.

3.4.2   Handling Browser Failures

A number of things can go wrong with the browser operations on a Microsoft network. If you are aware of the problems, it is easy to compensate for them. Table 3.1 lists some of the most common problems and solutions that will get you through the rough parts.

Table 3.1   Diagnosing Browser Problems

Problem	Solution
Computers appear on the browse list, but are not accessible.	When a computer shuts down properly, it notifies the master browser. The master browser removes the computer from the browse list. It may take up to 15 minutes for the master

Problem	Solution
	browser to let the backup browser know that the computer is gone. If a computer is shut down improperly, it has to fail at three of its 12-minute announcements before the master browser removes the computer from the browser list. Wait and it will fix itself, or reboot the master browser.
DOS clients and Windows clients receive different browse lists.	DOS browser clients do not know how to deal with backup browsers. Windows browser clients will always receive their server list from the backup browser. Because the DOS client always gets the list from the master browser, it will be more current than the Windows list. Wait 15 minutes and the lists should be the same.
Windows 95 reports an error when attempting to browse the Network Neighborhood. Network unavailable.	This will happen if there is no master browser for your workgroup. You should either change your workgroup name to match a workgroup that has a master browser or install File and Printer Sharing and configure your workstation to maintain the browse list.
No other workgroups or domains are listed in the Network Neighborhood.	If your master browser has just started up, it will make Workgroup Announcements in addition to the default announcements every 15 minutes. This allows it to show up on other workgroup browse lists; however, it will have to wait until the other servers reach their 15-minute announcement period before it knows about other domains.

Most problems with the browse list will be solved on their own, if you just wait.

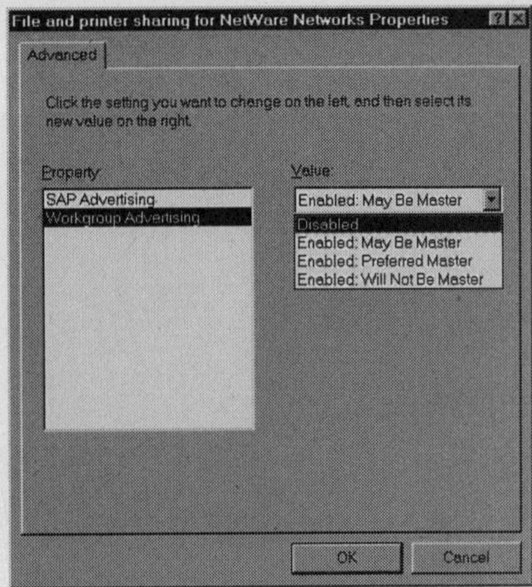

Figure 3.19   Browser options for File and Printer Sharing for NetWare Networks.

3.4.3   Exercise

Exercise 1: Network Browsing with Windows 95

This exercise examines some of the aspects of network browsing with Windows 95.

1. When opening the Network Neighborhood's Entire Network icon, you should see a complete list of domains and workgroups available on your network. This may mean that you only see your domain.

2. You should now change your workgroup name in the Network icon in the Control Panel. If you are not sure how to do this, consult Exercise 3.1, step 11. Change your Workgroup name to "MYGROUP" and reboot.

3. Immediately after rebooting, go to the Network Neighborhood's Entire Network icon. You should see your workgroup only. If you get an error, you are a little too fast.

4. Check the Entire Network icon on the Windows NT Server machine. You should see your workgroup in the list at the server.

5. It may take as long as 15 minutes before the domain shows up on the Windows 95 computer. You have to wait for the next workgroup announcement. The Windows 95 computer (having just been made the master browser) announces immediately, but the domain will not make an announcement until its next scheduled cycle.

3.4.4   Practice Problems

1. You have both the Client for NetWare Networks and Microsoft Networks installed. You are always required to enter two passwords to log on. What must you do so that you only have to type in one password at logon? (Choose all that apply.)

    A. Set your primary logon to Client for Microsoft Networks.

    B. Set your primary logon to Client for NetWare Networks.

    C. Set both passwords so they are exactly the same.

    D. Change your NetWare password to a blank password.

2. What compiles a list of all computers and shared resources in a domain or workgroup?

    A. Backup browser

    B. Master browser

    C. Each computer

    D. Router

3. Organize the following list of operating systems into the order they would place in a browser election to be the master browser.

    A. Windows NT Workstation

    B. Primary domain controller

    C. Windows NT Server

    D. Windows 95 computer

4. Where would you change the browse master settings on a Windows 95 computer?

    A. Network icon in the Control Panel

    B. System icon in the Control Panel

    C. Start -> Run -> NETCONFIG.EXE

    D. In the CONFIG.SYS file under SET MASTERBROWSE=yes/no

5. How many minutes are the intervals at which a master browser will update a backup browser?

6. What problems may be encountered if a user turns off his computer without properly shutting down the computer through Start -> Shutdown?

7. What is the name of the application used to edit a user's password list file?

    A. PASSEDT

    B. PWLEDIT

    C. PWDEDIT

    D. PWEDITOR

8. What must you do to enable browsing on your network?

    A. Change a setting in the Registry

    B. Change a setting in File and Printer Sharing

    C. Do nothing

9. The ________ _____ feature of Windows 95 requires that the password be entered only once for two networks. (Fill in the blank.)

10. When users access the Network Neighborhood, they are viewing a list of computers on the network known as a ______ ____. (Fill in the blank.)

3.4.5   Answers and Explanations

1. **C** A or B would not work. D would only work if the Microsoft password is currently blank. Blank passwords are not recommended, and therefore should not be used. If the two passwords are the same, you will only need to type in the password once.

2. **B** The master browser is responsible for compiling a list of all computers and shared resources. It passes that list periodically to the backup browser(s). The computers on

the network contact the backup browsers for the browse list. A router does not participate in compiling a browse list.

3. **B, C, A, D** A primary domain controller will always be master browser if one is present. The others will be given priority based on their operating system. A Windows NT Server will always win over a Windows NT Workstation, which in turn will always win over a Windows 95 computer if they are all in the same domain and the Windows 95 computers have their workgroup name the same as the domain.

4. **A** The settings to determine whether a Windows 95 computer is preferred to be, will be, or will not be a master browser are set in the Network icon of the Control Panel under File and Print Sharing for Microsoft Networks.

5. **A** Master browser will update a backup browser every 15 minutes.

6. If a computer is shut down improperly, it does not have a chance to notify the master browser. It then must fail at three of its 12-minute announcements before the master browser will remove the computer from the browse list. This will result in the computer being visible in the browse list, even though the computer is not online.

7. **B** PWLEDIT is used to edit a user's password list file. It can be used to view the entries and remove specific password entries if problems are encountered using a cached password.

8. **C** Browsing is automatically enabled. Changes are only required if you do not want a specific computer to participate in the browse list compiling process, or prefer that certain computers do participate.

9. Unified Logon

10. Browse list

3.4.6 Key Terms and Definitions

Backup browser A computer that receives the browse list from the master browser and responds to browse requests from computers on the network.

Browser election Used to determine which computer will become the master browser.

Master browser A computer that keeps a list of all computers, shares, servers, and domains on a network.

Share *Share* as a verb means to allow others to access a resource; as a noun, it is a resource such as a directory or print queue that others can access.

Unified browsing All computers that can be browsed by Windows 95 are displayed together in the Network Neighborhood.

3.5   Installation of the File and Printer Sharing

To set up Windows 95 to use user-level security, you must have at least one Windows NT computer on your network. The Windows NT computer can be either a Windows NT Server, Windows NT Domain Controller, or a Windows NT Workstation. All these computers maintain a list of users that Windows 95 will use when applying access permissions. You also need to have Client for Microsoft Networks enabled.

You now can set up folders and printers to be shared on the Windows 95 client computers. You can share a folder, for example, by opening Explorer in Windows 95, locating the folder you want to share, and right-clicking. Choose Sharing from the context-sensitive menu and set up access rights as explained in Chapter 4, "Configuring and Managing Resource Access."

To enable directories and print queues to be shared with NetWare users, add the File and Printer Sharing for NetWare Networks service in the Network control panel. If the File and Printer Sharing for Microsoft Networks service is already installed, remove that service first.

After File and Printer Sharing for NetWare Networks is installed, enable sharing by choosing the appropriate File and Printer Sharing options from the Network control panel.

> **File and Printer Sharing for NetWare Networks must use the User-level Access Control security model.**

The computer name of the NetWare server that maintains the list of user accounts must be specified in the Access Control tab of the Network control panel.

You can use user-level security when running Windows 95 on a NetWare network and want to have peer services enabled for the Windows 95 clients. The user-level security available with NetWare networks is similar to user-level security with Microsoft networks. When using user-level security with NetWare networks, security authentication requests are handled by using the pass-through security method. This type of security method passes the authentication requests to a NetWare server for authentication.

User-level security on NetWare is used to protect shared network resources by storing a list of users and groups who have access to a network resource. To gain access to a resource, a user must be on the access account list stored on the NetWare server bindery and also have the proper access rights for that resource. Administrators can set up access rights on a per user or per group basis. The rights that can be assigned to a user for a specific resource includes read, write, create, delete, change attribute, directory search, and access control.

Specifying the specific folders and printers to be shared on a client computer is accomplished at a user level. To set up a folder as a shared resource, for example, a user opens Explorer, locates the folder to share, and right-clicks on it. From the context-sensitive menu, the Sharing command is selected and the Sharing tab is filled out. You can learn more about sharing a folder in Chapter 4.

3.5.1   Exercise

Exercise 1: Installing File and Printer Services

In this exercise, you install the File and Print Sharing services for Windows 95.

1. Choose the Start menu, Settings, Control Panel.

2. Select and open the Network control panel.

3. You can install the File and Printer Sharing services for your Primary Network Logon by clicking on the File and Printer Sharing button, placing checks in both check boxes, and then clicking on OK. The two check boxes are I Want to Be Able to Give Others Access to My Files, and I Want to Be Able to Allow Others to Print to My Printer(s).

    The other way to install the File and Print Sharing services is to click on the Add button, choose Services, and then click on Add. Then select Microsoft as a manufacturer and File and Printer Services for Microsoft Networks. Then close the dialog box by clicking on the OK button.

4. Close the Network control panel by clicking the OK button. Windows 95 then attempts to copy the network software from the original installation media and prompts you to reboot the computer. Reboot.

After rebooting, you should see a Sharing option in the context menu when you click on Folders. Exercises in Chapter 4 illustrate the process of sharing and managing shared folders.

3.5.2 Practice Problems

1. Which levels of security are available in Windows 95? (Choose all that apply.)

   A. Workgroup-level

   B. Share-level

   C. Server-level

   D. User-level

2. Joe is running Windows 95 and wants to connect to a share on your Windows 95 computer. Both computers are using the NetBEUI protocol. What must you enable for Joe to connect to your share?

   A. Install File and Printer Sharing for Microsoft Networks.

   B. Install the Microsoft Client for Microsoft Networks.

   C. Install the DLC protocol.

   D. Install user-level security.

3. What must you do to set up a Windows 95 computer so that it can operate as a print server on a NetWare network? (Choose all that apply.)

   A. Install NetBEUI.

   B. Install Client for Microsoft Networks.

   C. Install Client for NetWare Networks.

   D. Set up a user account in the NetWare server.

4. You are installing a NetWare server for use by a Windows 95 workgroup. What must you do to make sure Windows 95 long filenames are preserved on the NetWare server? (Choose all that apply.)

   A. Install the NetWare LONG.NAM namespace option.

   B. Choose long filenames during installation of Client for NetWare Networks.

   C. Install the NetWare OS/2 namespace option.

   D. Do nothing; no further action is required.

5. What must you have installed to enable directories and printers to be shared with NetWare users? (Choose all that apply.)

   A. User-level security

   B. File and Printer Sharing for NetWare Networks

   C. NetBEUI protocol

   D. Computer name of the NetWare server with the list of user accounts

6. To set up user-level security, what must you have at least one of installed on your network? (Choose all that apply.)

   A. Windows 95 computer

   B. Windows NT Workstation

   C. Windows NT Server

   D. Primary domain controller

7. What are the rights that can be assigned to a user for a specific resource for user-level secured NetWare users?

8. Other than a Windows NT–based computer, what must you have enabled to use user-level security in a Microsoft network?

9. File and Printer Sharing for NetWare Networks must use the _____ _____ Access Control model.

10. What service must you remove, if installed, to install File and Printer Sharing for NetWare Networks?

3.5.3   Answers and Explanations

1. **B, D**   The two levels of security available in Windows 95 are share-level and user-level. Share-level security is controlled on a user-by-user basis with no central user database. User-level security requires a user database stored on a central server.

2. **A**   Only File and Printer Sharing for Microsoft Networks is required. Although user-level security would work in this situation, it is not necessary.

3. **B, C**   Both the Client for NetWare Networks and File and Printer Sharing for NetWare must be used to share a printer to NetWare clients.

4. **C**   The NetWare server is responsible for preserving long filenames. The OS/2 namespace and LONG.NAM options on the NetWare server will mimic the Windows 95 long filename format. However, the OS/2 namespace only supports 254 characters; the LONG.NAM supports 255.

5. **A, B, D**   All these are necessary to enable directories and print queues to be shared with NetWare users.

6. **B, C, D**   You must have one of these operating systems installed on your network to use user-level security. All these are capable of maintaining a list of users that Windows 95 will use when applying access permissions.

7. The rights that you can assign to a shared resource that is being accessed by a NetWare user are read, write, create, delete, change attribute, directory search, and access control.

8. Client for Microsoft Networks

9. User-level

10. File and Print Sharing for Microsoft Networks

3.5.4   Key Terms and Definitions

Domain controller   A Windows NT Server that stores and authenticates a list of users. Can be primary or backup.

Server-based   A group of computers that assign rights based on a list of users stored on a central computer.

Share-level security   Access based on rights given to users stored in an account database stored on each computer.

User-level security   Access based on rights given to users stored in a central account database located on a server.

3.6   Supporting Universal Naming Convention (UNC) Path Names

The *Universal Naming Convention* (UNC) is a standardized naming convention for specifying a share name on a particular computer. The computer name is limited to 15 characters, and the share name is usually limited to 12 characters, depending on the network. Share names can be given to a print queue or a directory of files—HP4 or WINAPPS, for example.

The UNC uniquely specifies the path to the share name on a network. The UNC path takes the form of *server_name**resource_name* [*path*]. The UNC path of the printer share HPLJ created on the server ADMIN_EXEC, for example, would be \\ADMIN_EXEC\HPLJ. Figure 3.20 shows the result of typing UNC pathnames at the Run command.

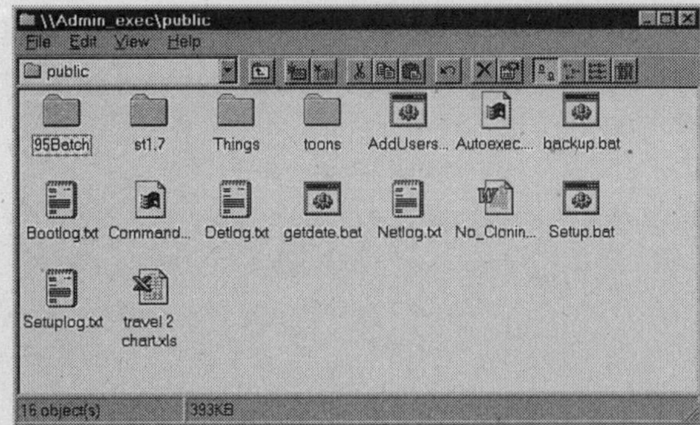

Figure 3.20   UNC pathnames can be used to access resources from within the Windows environment. By typing a UNC path at the Run command, you can access any resource on your network.

UNC pathnames can be used from a command prompt to perform tasks that do not require mapped drive letters (see Figure 3.21). Some executables and commands will require a mapped drive letter to operate correctly, or at all. This will usually be reported as a DOS Error that refers to disk access. If your UNC path has spaces in it, you will have to enclose the entire path in quotation marks; otherwise, Windows will treat the information after the space as parameters for the program before the space.

> **A UNC name does not require a drive-letter assignment. Windows 95 takes full advantage of network connectivity using UNC names, so you can connect to a remote directory or printer share without having to map a drive letter to it. For MS-DOS–based applications that require a drive letter or port to be used, however, you can map a drive letter to a shared directory or a port to a shared printer.**

The UNC can also specify the full path to a file in a subdirectory of a file share. To share the entire C: drive on the computer ADMINEXEC, for example, the share name CDRIVE could be created for the root directory c:\. To specify the directory c:\windows\system using a UNC path with these share names, use \\ADMINEXEC\CDRIVE\windows\system.

> **Add a dollar sign ($) to the end of the share name to prevent a share name from being visible to another computer through a browser, such as Network Neighborhood. The share name CDRIVE$, for example, would not be visible to users browsing the computer ADMINEXEC. Even though it is not visible, they can access it by typing in \\ADMINEXEC\CDRIVE$. This follows the "out of sight, out of mind" rule: If people can't see the shared folder, they will not attempt to access it. You should still take all normal precautions to prevent other people from accessing these files by assigning passwords or access permissions to users.**

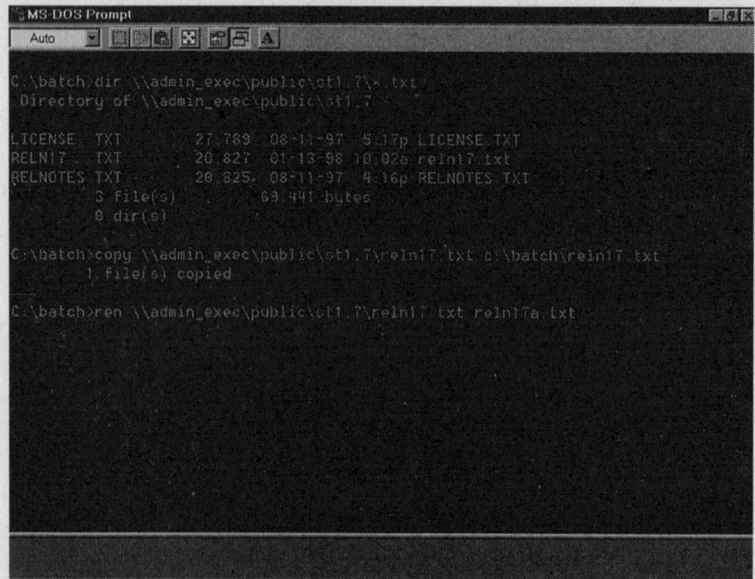

Figure 3.21   UNC pathnames also work from a command prompt. This avoids having to map drive letters to all network resources.

All Windows 95 functions support using a UNC name, including the Run option on the Start menu and the command prompt. NetWare servers, like Windows NT servers, can be accessed through a UNC name. Instead of share name, substitute volume name to access a NetWare server.

> **Share names in Windows 95 can be as long as the involved protocols and user interfaces will allow. NetBIOS names, however, can be only 15 characters long and should not contain embedded blanks. Therefore, when establishing share names on your servers, keep them short. Do not use spaces within the name, and use 15 or fewer total characters so that Windows 95 can view them from within Network Neighborhood when browsing for network resources. Some network printers might even require 14 or fewer characters in total.**

> The actual folder name under Windows NT and Windows 95 can still be a long filename (LFN) of up to 255 characters, only the share name needs to follow the preceding guidelines. Your TOPSECRET$ share can be on a folder named "My Top Secret Projects," for example.

3.6.1   Exercise

Exercise 1: Connecting to a Server and Accessing Resources

In this exercise, you connect to a server and access a resource without mapping a drive letter to the resource. This lab requires that there be files in your Windows NT Server's NETLOGON share. The NETLOGON share is actually *win_root*\SYSTEM32\REPL\IMPORT\SCRIPTS on the NT Server's local hard drive—where *win_root* is the WINDOWS directory, usually WINNT on Windows NT 4.0 Servers.

1. Start Windows 95 and log on to your network. If you cancel the Logon dialog, Windows 95 does not start your network client. This applies even if you are not logging on to a domain.

2. Double-click on the Network Neighborhood icon on your desktop. This should show you all the servers in your domain. If not, select the Entire Network icon and your domain icon within.

3. Double-click on your server. This opens a window listing all the shared resources on the server.

4. Double-click the NETLOGON directory to open it.

5. Close the NETLOGON directory while holding down your Shift key. This closes all the windows back to the desktop.

6. To access the same folder without opening the Network Neighborhood, choose the Run command from the Start menu and type *server_name***NETLOGON**. Then click on OK. The NETLOGON window should appear. Close the window.

7. To see the contents of the NETLOGON windows from a command prompt, open a command prompt, and type the following:

   DIR *server_name*\\NETLOGON

3.6.2 Practice Problems

1. In what situation would you need to put the UNC names in quotation marks when accessing a shared resource through the MS-DOS command prompt?

    A. When you are specifying a printer resource

    B. When you are specifying a NetWare volume

    C. When there is a space in the UNC path

    D. All the time

2. What is the maximum number of characters in a NetBIOS share name?

    A. 8

    B. 15

    C. 32

    D. 255

3. What would the UNC path be for a shared printer named HPLJET, which is located on the server named PLUTO?

    A. \\PLUTO_HPLJET

    B. \PLUTO\HPLJET

    C. //PLUTO/HPLJET

    D. \\PLUTO\HPLJET

4. How many characters can a folder name be in Windows 95?

    A. 15

    B. 32

    C. 254

    D. 255

5. What is the maximum number of characters in a UNC computer name?

    A. 8

    B. 15

C. 254

D. 255

6. Which utilities could you use to share a folder? (Choose all that apply.)

    A. Windows Explorer

    B. Network icon in the Control Panel

    C. DOS prompt using NET.EXE

    D. System icon in the Control Panel

7. You want to hide the shared directory called PRIVATE on your computer named MYCOMP from appearing on the browse list. To do this, what would you name the share?

    A. \\MYCOMP\$PRIVATE

    B. \\MYCOMP\PRIVATE$

    C. \\MYCOMP\PRIVATE#

    D. \\MYCOMP\PRIVATE@

8. In which of the following would you most likely be required to map a drive letter to a share, instead of using the UNC path to the share? (Choose all that apply.)

    A. Accessing a shared resource through a DOS program

    B. Accessing a shared resource through a Windows-based program

    C. Viewing the directory of a shared folder using DIR (in DOS)

    D. Accessing a shared resource through Start -> Run

9. What must you substitute the share name with when accessing a NetWare server using a UNC name?

10. Due to the limitations of NetBIOS, to how many characters should you limit a share name?

3.6.3 Answers and Explanations

1. **C** You need only to enclose the UNC name in quotation marks when there is a space in the UNC path.

2. **B** NetBIOS share names can be only 12 characters long. They also should not contain spaces.

3. **D** The correct format for a UNC path is *server**volume & path*.

4. **D** Using Windows 95 long filenames, a folder can be up to 255 characters in length.

5. **B** A computer name is limited to a maximum of 15 characters

6. **A** Windows Explorer could be used to share a folder. The Network and System icons in the Control Panel cannot be used. NET.EXE can only be used to connect to an existing share

7. **B** Adding a dollar sign ($) to the end of a share name will hide it from view in the browse list. The share will still be accessible to anyone manually typing in **\\\\mycomp\\ private$**.

8. **A** Most DOS programs cannot recognize the UNC naming convention. Windows-based programs, the DOS command DIR, and the Start -> Run command can all use UNC names.

9. Volume name

10. 15 characters or fewer

3.6.4 Key Terms and Definitions

Hidden share A share that has been hidden from view in the browse list by adding a dollar sign ($) to the end of a share name.

Long filename A file or folder that is longer than the 8.3 standard naming convention. Can be up to 255 characters in Windows 95.

UNC Universal Naming Convention. The full name of a resource on the network.

Practice Exam: Installation and Configuration, Part 2: Network Components

1. Which TCP/IP feature will automatically assign an IP address to a computer?

   A. IPS

   B. DHCP

   C. DNS

   D. WINS

2. You can reach a remote computer by using its IP address, but not with its host name. What setting is most likely the problem?

   A. IP address of the WINS server.

   B. Frame type is not the same.

   C. IP address of the DNS server.

   D. Your subnet mask.

3. When setting up PPTP/VPN, what must you specify on the remote workstation?

   A. Phone number of the modem on the RAS server

   B. IP address of the network adapter on the RAS server

   C. Computer name of the RAS server

   D. IP address of the DNS server on the remote network

4. What are the six frame types that you can choose from when setting up IPX/SPX?

5. Windows 95 supports share-level and user-level security. You want to set up Windows 95 on 10 workstations on a network to share printer and file resources, but you want to make sure pass-through authentication is used to validate users who access these resources. Which type of security must you set up?

6. You receive a call while stationed at the company help desk. The caller says she is trying to save her long filenames to the NetWare server, but the server does not support them. What do you have to do to enable NetWare to support long filenames?

7. UNC is supported by Windows 95. What does UNC mean? What two items make up a UNC? Does UNC require a drive-letter assignment?

8. What are the three major advantages of the NetBEUI protocol?

9. What are the four major Networking components you can add, remove, and modify through the Network control panel?

10. What is the purpose of the subnet mask?

11. What is the purpose of the LMHOSTS file, and where is it located?

12. What is the function of the default gateway?

13. What is the function of a DHCP server?

14. Joe, Sally, and Jack are in a three-user workgroup. Sally can communicate with Joe and Jack, but Joe and Jack cannot communicate with each other. You examine the network settings and find that Joe and Sally are using NetBEUI, and Jack and Sally are using IPX/SPX.

PRIMARY OBJECTIVE:

- Change the network settings so that all three computers can communicate with one another.

SECONDARY OBJECTIVES:

- Maintain the speed of the network by not creating unnecessary traffic.

- Make sure that all the users can view a browse list.

PROPOSED SOLUTION:

Tell Joe to add IPX/SPX protocol.

EVALUATION OF PROPOSED SOLUTION:

Choose the best answer

A. The proposed solution satisfies the primary objective and both of the secondary objectives.

B. The proposed solution satisfies the primary objective and only one of the secondary objectives.

C. The proposed solution satisfies the primary objective and none of the secondary objectives.

D. The proposed solution does not satisfy any objectives.

15. One of the employees has decided to change the TCP/IP settings of his computer. After having changed most settings, he finds that he cannot communicate with the network, and calls you for help. He tells you that he does not know what the old numbers were.

PRIMARY OBJECTIVE:

- The computer must be able to communicate with the network again.

SECONDARY OBJECTIVES:

- The computer must be able to use NetBIOS names to communicate.

- The computer must be able to communicate with other remote subnets.

PROPOSED SOLUTION:

Supply him with new numbers for him to change his IP address, subnet mask, WINS server address, and the IP address of the default gateway.

EVALUATION OF PROPOSED SOLUTION:

Choose the best answer.

A. The proposed solution satisfies the primary objective and both of the secondary objectives.

B. The proposed solution satisfies the primary objective and only one of the secondary objectives.

C. The proposed solution satisfies the primary objective and none of the secondary objectives.

D. The proposed solution does not satisfy any objectives.

16. John finds that after setting up his computer, he cannot communicate with the rest of the four-computer workgroup using NetBIOS names. The network uses DHCP. There is no WINS server.

PRIMARY OBJECTIVE:

- John must be able to use NetBIOS names to communicate.

SECONDARY OBJECTIVE:

- There is no money in the budget for more hardware, so don't spend anything.

PROPOSED SOLUTION:

Tell Joe to enable the Use DHCP for WINS Configuration setting in the WINS tab of the TCP/IP Properties in the Network control panel.

EVALUATION OF PROPOSED SOLUTION:

Choose the best answer.

A. The proposed solution satisfies the primary objective and the secondary objective.

B. The proposed solution satisfies the primary objective and not the secondary objective.

C. The proposed solution does not satisfy the primary objective and does satisfy the secondary objective.

D. The proposed solution does not satisfy any objectives.

17. Joe just installed a new computer and configured the network adapter card with only the default protocols. He finds that he cannot communicate with, or browse to, any other computers. He discovers that the network is running TCP/IP.

PRIMARY OBJECTIVE:

- Change the network settings so that he can communicate with the rest of the network.

SECONDARY OBJECTIVES:

- Maintain the speed of the network by not creating unnecessary traffic.

- Joe can use NetBIOS computer names to communicate with other computers.

PROPOSED SOLUTION:

Tell Joe to add the TCP/IP protocol. Provide him with an IP address and subnet mask. Tell him to remove the two existing protocols.

EVALUATION OF PROPOSED SOLUTION:

Choose the best answer.

A. The proposed solution satisfies the primary objective and both of the secondary objectives.

B. The proposed solution satisfies the primary objective and only one of the secondary objectives.

C. The proposed solution satisfies the primary objective and none of the secondary objectives.

D. The proposed solution does not satisfy any objectives.

18. Joe just upgraded his computer, and in a cost-saving effort, he is using the old non–Plug and Play network card from the computer that was replaced. He installed the card in the new computer and installed the network card in the Network control panel with the same settings from the old computer. When he tries to load Windows 95, however, Windows 95 reports an IRQ conflict with the sound card. He must have communication with the network by the end of the day.

PRIMARY OBJECTIVE:

- Joe's computer must be communicating with the network by the end of the day.

SECONDARY OBJECTIVE:

- The sound card must work.

PROPOSED SOLUTION:

Tell Joe to change the IRQ in the Network control panel, under Properties of the Network Card, to an unused IRQ.

EVALUATION OF PROPOSED SOLUTION:

Choose the best answer.

A. The proposed solution satisfies the primary objective and the secondary objective.

B. The proposed solution satisfies the primary objective and not the secondary objective.

C. The proposed solution does not satisfy the primary objective and does satisfy the secondary objective.

D. The proposed solution does not satisfy any objectives.

Practice Exam Answers and Explanations

1. **B** DHCP (Dynamic Host Configuration Protocol) will automatically assign IP addresses to nodes on the network. The client must be configured to do this, and a DHCP server must be available to assign the addresses.

2. **C** A DNS server is responsible for resolving a TCP/IP host name to an IP address. Because you can connect using the IP address, you know it is the host name resolution at fault.

3. **B**   PPTP/VPN works by carrying other packets within the data section of the IP packet. This IP packet is sent through a TCP/IP network to the remote RAS server, and therefore requires the IP address of the RAS server.

4. 802.2, 802.3, ETHERNET II, ETHERNET_SNAP, Token_Ring, and Token_Ring_Snap

5. User-level security

6. Long filenames are not supported by NetWare by default. The OS/2 namespace or LONG.NAM must be installed.

7. UNC stands for Universal Naming Convention. The computer name and share name make up a UNC. No drive-letter assignment is needed.

8. Communication is fast on smaller networks, performance is dynamically self-tuned, and the only configuration required is a NetBIOS computer name and workgroup or domain name.

9. Clients, adapters, protocols, and services

10. The subnet mask is used to determine whether the other computers that you are contacting are on your network segment or elsewhere. It does this by distinguishing which parts of the IP address are the network ID and the host ID.

11. The LMHOSTS file is a static test file that contains NetBIOS name-to-IP-address mappings. It is an alternative to using a WINS server for NetBIOS-IP resolution. It is stored in the *systemroot* (usually C:\WINDOWS) directory.

12. When the route needed for an IP message to reach a destination is not known, the message is forwarded to the default gateway. The default gateway is a router connected to other TCP/IP network segments. Messages are sent to this gateway when it is not known on which segment the destination is.

13. The DHCP (Dynamic Host Configuration Server) is responsible for handing out IP addresses and other TCP/IP addresses such as default gateway, DNS server, and WINS server.

14. **C**   The primary objective of communication is met, but the NetBEUI protocols are not removed, and therefore create extra network traffic. The browse list cannot be viewed when solely using IPX/SPX. Browsing requires NetBIOS and must be enabled in the NetBIOS tab of the IPX/SPX properties.

15. **A**   The proposed solution will get the computer back to normal. It will be able communicate with the network and remote subnets using the default gateway, and will be able to resolve NetBIOS names to IP addresses by using the WINS server.

16. **C**   The secondary objective of not spending money is met. However, the proposed solution does not allow for NetBIOS communication. It will automatically set the WINS configuration using DHCP. This will not work unless there is a WINS server to use. This option does not turn the DHCP server into a WINS server, or let it act as a WINS server in any way.

17. **B**   This solution does meet the primary objective, and enables him to communicate with the other TCP/IP computers. The secondary objective of maintaining network speed is met by unbinding the other unused protocols. The secondary objective of using UNC names is not met because you did not provide him with the IP address of the WINS server or an LMHOSTS file for NetBIOS-to-IP resolution.

18. **D**   The conflict has rendered the sound card useless, along with the network card. Changing the settings in the Control Panel is necessary, but not the only step. Joe must also change the settings on the network card. Usually, this is done by using jumpers or dip switches on the older legacy cards.

CHAPTER 4

Configuring and Managing Resource Access

This chapter helps prepare you for the exam by covering the following objectives:

- Assign access permissions for shared folders. Methods include the following:

    - Passwords

    - User permissions

    - Group permissions

- Create, share, and monitor resources. Resources include the following:

    - Remote file shares

    - Network printers

    - Shared fax modem

    - Unimodem/V

- Set up user environments by using profiles and system policies.

- Back up data and restore data.

- Manage hard disks. Tasks include the following:

    - Disk compression

    - Partitioning

    - Dealing with long filenames

- Establish application environments for Microsoft MS-DOS applications.

4.1   Assign Access Permissions for Shared Folders

The types of assigning access permissions for shared resources include the following:

- Passwords

- User permissions

- Group permissions

4.1.1   Passwords

To enable passwords as a security method, you must enable share-level access control in the Network control panel. This is the default setting for Windows 95. After share-level access control has been enabled, any resource that you wish to present to the network will provide you with an option for typing in a password for the resource (see Figure 4.1). To allow others to access this resource, you must somehow distribute the password to them.

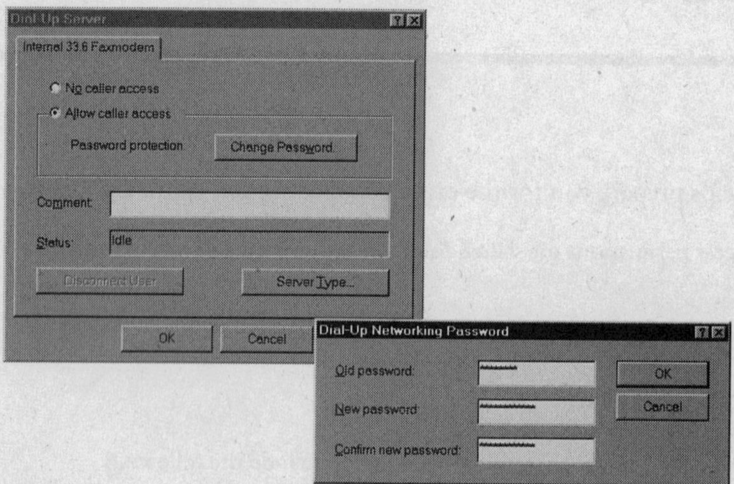

Figure 4.1   When implementing share-level security, passwords are assigned to resources as a method of security.

The major advantage of this method of security is that it requires no other support devices elsewhere on the network. This security method has the following two major flaws, however:

- Distribution of passwords

- Maintaining control of passwords

The first major drawback of this system is the distribution of the passwords after they have been assigned. If you want other people to use this resource, you must have some method of notifying all the potential users.

The second major drawback is having to maintain control of passwords, or rather having to maintain control of access to the resource. Even on a small network, the number of passwords that must be remembered can quickly climb to an unmanageable limit.

User permissions and group permissions may be implemented on your network, offering easier password distribution and greater security.

4.1.2   User Permissions

To implement user permissions, you must enable user-level security on your Windows 95 system. You can share resources with individuals on your network by the user's network name. This requires access to additional network services.

To enable user-level security, open the Network control panel and choose the Access Control tab. When choosing user-level access control, you will have to provide the name of a security provider. The security provider may be any of the following:

- Microsoft Windows NT domain

- Microsoft Windows NT Server

- Microsoft Windows NT Workstation

- Novell NetWare 3.*x* or 4.*x* server

The security provider will be responsible for providing a list of users when you want to share a resource (see Figure 4.2). The security provider will also be responsible for verifying usernames and passwords for Windows 95 when users attempt to access resources.

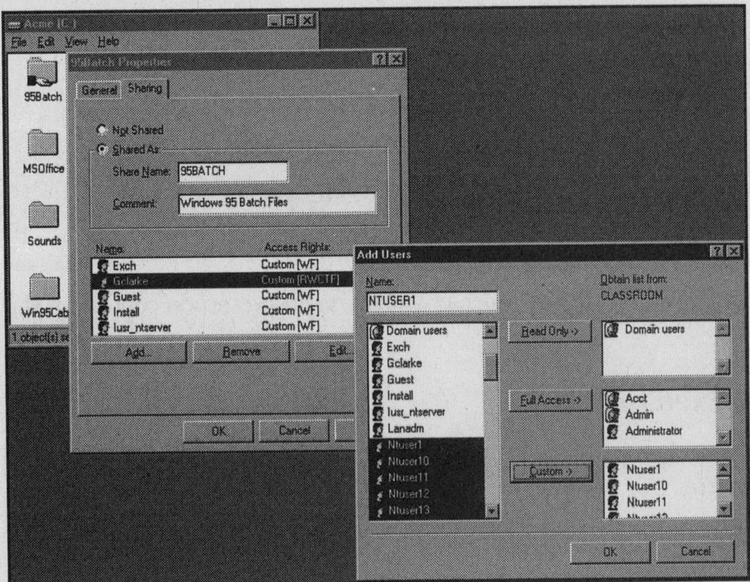

Figure 4.2   The security provider is responsible for supplying a list of users when sharing a resource.

When sharing resources, Windows 95 can provide you with a list of users to which you might grant access. From the list, you can select those users to whom you want to grant access. These users will then need no additional information before being able to access the resource. When users attempt to connect to the resource, their network client will pass their network usernames and passwords to the Windows 95 computer they are connecting to. The Windows 95 computer will then connect to its security provider and verify the client's username and password.

4.1.3   Group Permissions

Implementing group permissions is similar to implementing user permissions. The first step is to enable user-level security on your Windows 95 system. After user-level security has been enabled, you can share information with users on the network based on their group membership on your security provider.

The security providers listed in the "User Permissions" section support the creation of groups of users also. In the same fashion as sharing with users, you can share your resources and assign permissions with groups. The Windows 95 computer will then connect to its security provider and check to see whether the user's name and password are valid, and then check to see which groups the user is a member of. If the user is a member of any groups that have been granted access to the resource, the user will be granted access to the resource.

> When you assign permissions for users to a directory, these permissions are termed *explicit*. Each subdirectory automatically has the same list of permissions applied to it. For the subdirectories, the permissions are *implicit*, or *inherited*.
>
> These explicit and implicit permissions enable you to control access to your directory structure on a folder-by-folder basis.

4.1.4   Exercises

Exercise 1: How to Implement User Permissions

In this exercise, you set up user permissions in Windows 95.

1. Perform the steps necessary to enable user permissions in Windows 95.

2. Choose the correct security provider available in user-level access control for the network you are using.

Answer to Exercise 1

To implement user permissions, you need to enable user-level security on Windows 95. You need to follow these steps:

1. Open the Network control panel.

2. Choose the Access Control tab.

3. When choosing user-level access control, you must provide the name of a security provider from the following choices:

   Microsoft Windows NT domain

   Microsoft Windows NT server

   Microsoft Windows NT workstation

   Novell NetWare 3.*x* or 4.*x* server

4. The security provider is responsible for providing a list of users who wish to share a resource and for verifying usernames and passwords. Windows 95 connects to the security provider and verifies the client's username and password.

Exercise 2: Examining Explicit and Implicit Permissions in a Directory Structure

This exercise examines the explicit and implicit permissions in a directory structure: C:\DATA\MYFILES.

1. List the users' permissions.

2. List the permissions for the subdirectories with read permissions.

Answer to Exercise 2

1. C:\DATA\MYFILES can share the DATA directory with a group of users and grant them read access.

2. The read permission you grant them at this level is explicit.

3. You then do not want the users (with the exception of your user account) to have read access to MYFILES.

4. Initially the MYFILES directory has implicit permissions that are the same as the DATA directory.

5. If you proceed to the Sharing tab of the Folder properties, you can change the permission list, without sharing the folder, thus changing the access to subfolder MYFILES.

When you assign permissions to users to a directory, these permissions are termed explicit. Each subdirectory automatically has the same list of permissions applied to it. For the subdirectories, the permissions are implicit or inherited.

These explicit and implicit permissions enable you to control access to your directory structure on a folder-by-folder basis.

4.1.5 Practice Problems

1. Where do you enable passwords for access to shared folders in Windows 95?

    A. Passwords control panel

    B. Network control panel

    C. Users control panel

    D. System control panel

2. You are wanting to share resources on your Windows 95 system. You have decided to use user-level access control. Which of the following cannot be a security provider for user-level access control?

    A. Windows NT domain

    B. NetWare 3.*x* or 4.*x* server

    C. Windows 95 workgroup

    D. Windows NT server

3. Which of the following information must you provide when configuring user-level access control?

    A. Usernames

    B. Workgroup name

    C. Security provider name

    D. User passwords

4. What is the term for these permissions called when you assign permissions to users for a folder called Data?

    A. Implicit

    B. Inherited

    C. Implied

    D. Explicit

5. From the preceding question, after you have the permissions for Data, you create a subfolder called Private. This folder should contain information that only you can access, yet you realize other users can access it also. Why can other users access this subfolder?

    A. The permissions are implicit to the subfolder.

    B. The permissions are Explicit to the subfolder.

    C. The permissions are implied to the subfolder.

    D. The permissions are implicated to the subfolder.

6. Robert is attaching his Windows 95 computer to another Windows 95 computer using the Microsoft Network. He wants to provide access from one computer to the other so that each computer has access to files and printers on either machine. What must he do to enable this in Windows 95?

    A. Set up user-level security.

    B. Disable File and Printer Sharing for Microsoft Networks.

    C. Set up share-level security.

    D. Enable the Windows 95 Firewall program.

7. A Dial-Up Networking server in your company enables users to access resources remotely. You enable these users to access files on a Windows NT Server. Which of the following should you do to provide the highest level of protection from unauthorized access to these files?

    A. Enable the Windows 95 Firewall program.

    B. Set up share-level security.

    C. Set up user-level security.

    D. Disable Printer Sharing.

8. Windows 95 offers which two levels of access security?

    A. Group-level

    B. User-level

    C. Share-level

    D. Resource-level

9. Which level of security is used by default when Microsoft File and Printer Sharing is installed?

    A. Group-level

    B. User-level

    C. Share-level

    D. Resource-level

10. With which type of security are passwords assigned to resources?

    A. Group-level

    B. User-level

    C. Share-level

    D. Resource-level

11. If no password is assigned a resource in share-level security, what rights will a remote user have to the directory?

    A. Full

    B. Read-only

    C. Depends on which option was specified when the shared directory was created

    D. Modify

12. When creating a shared directory by using share-level security, which three types of access can be granted?

    A. Read

    B. Full

    C. Depends on password

    D. Modify

13. Print queues also can be shared with other network users using which level of security?

    A. Group-level

    B. User-level

    C. Share-level

    D. Resource-level

14. With which level of security can specific user accounts be granted access to a shared directory or printer?

    A. Group-level

    B. User-level

    C. Share-level

    D. Resource-level

15. When running Windows 95 on a NetWare network, what level of security should be implemented?

    A. Share-level

    B. User-level

    C. NDS-level

    D. Bindery-based

16. When using user-level security on a NetWare network, security authentication requests are handled by what method?

    A. Bindery-based

    B. NDS

    C. Passthrough

    D. Mutex

17. What is the primary benefit of using user-level security on a NetWare server in a shared network environment?

    A. Further protection of shared resources

    B. Less stringent passwords

    C. More enforced password changes

    D. Stronger algorithms

18. With a NetWare network, administrators can set up rights based on which two criteria?

    A. Resource

    B. User

    C. Group

    D. Time

19. Your computer is running Windows 95 and you would like to share your printer on the Windows NT network. You only want valid Windows NT users to access the printer. Which access control should you select in the network properties?

    A. Share-level

    B. User-level

    C. Domain-level

    D. Admin-level

20. Your computer has share-level security enabled, and you are switching to user-level security. What must you do to your existing shared folders so that they are accessible to other users after you change security levels?

    A. Nothing

    B. You must remove the shared status of the folders and reshare the folders after you switch to user-level security.

    C. You must reshare the folders after you switch to user-level security.

    D. You must change the attributes of the folders.

4.1.6 Answers and Explanations

1. **B** You enable passwords for access to shared folders under the Access Control tab in the Network control panel.

2. **C** Windows 95 workgroup. The other security provider available to you is Windows NT Workstation.

3. **C** The security provider will be responsible for verifying usernames and passwords for Windows 95.

4. **D** The term is explicit because the permissions are made at the folder and nowhere else.

5. **A** Their permissions are considered to be implicit to the subfolder if they are explicit to the folder.

6. **C** Share-level security allows other Windows 95 systems to access shared resources on a Windows 95 network.

7. **C** The Windows NT server is the security provider, so user-level access would be required.

8. **B, C** Windows 95 enables you to leverage security access to users by using either share-level or user-level security.

9. **C** Share-level security is used by default when File and Printer Sharing for Microsoft Networks is installed.

10. **C** With share-level security, passwords are assigned to each share to permit access to a directory or printer share. To access the share, a user must supply the correct password.

11. **C** If no password is used, any user will have full or read-only access to the directory, depending on which option was specified when the shared directory was created.

12. **A, B, C** When creating a shared directory using share-level security, one of three types of access can be granted: read, full, or depends on password.

13. **C** Print queues can be shared with other network users using share-level security.

14. **B** With user-level security, specific user accounts or group accounts can be granted access to a shared directory or printer.

15. **B** User-level security is available when you are running Windows 95 on a NetWare network.

16. **C** When you are using user-level security with NetWare networks, security authentication requests are handled using the passthrough security method. This type of security method passes the authentication requests to a NetWare server for authentication.

17. **A**   User-level security on NetWare is used
     to protect shared network resources by
     storing a list of users and groups who have
     access to a network resource. To gain access
     to a resource, a user must be on the access
     account list stored on the NetWare server
     bindery and then have the proper access
     rights for that resource.

18. **B, C**   Administrators can set up access
     rights on a per-user or per-group basis.

19. **B**   User-level security enables the user to
     select valid users from the Windows NT
     domain. The name of the domain of which
     the users are members must be the security
     provider.

20. **C**   Share-level security and user-level
     security have different access configurations
     to shared resources.

4.1.7 Key Terms and Definitions

Share-level access control   The user assigns
a password to a specific resource in share-level
access control. Depending on the password
used, a user may have read-only or full
control.

User-level access control   In user-level
access control, specific users are given rights
to a specific resource. A network server
(NetWare or Microsoft) is required as a
security provider, which provides a list of
authorized users.

User-level security   Security based on rights
assigned to a specific user.

4.2   Create, Share, and Monitor Resources

Several types of resources on your Windows 95 computer can be shared with other people on your network. Although these are local resources (on your computer) to you, to other people on your network they will be remote resources (on the network). Most resources are monitored with different tools, depending on the resource.

Before sharing folders or printers, you must enable the File and Printer Sharing services on your Windows 95 computer. Because each resource is different, you will now examine how to create, share, and monitor each resource.

4.2.1   Remote File Shares

You can employ three basic methods to create a new directory or folder on your computer. Two methods use the graphic Windows environment, and one uses the DOS command prompt. In the Windows 95 GUI, open the folder where you wish to create your new folder and either choose File, New, Folder from the menus, or right-click in a white area of the folder and choose New, Folder. The folder name will be selected. To give the folder a new name, you must type the name and press the Enter key to save it. If you create a new folder from a command prompt, you have a choice of two commands that do the same thing: MKDIR, and the shorter MD.

> **When using Windows Explorer to work with folders, menus at the top of the window are context-sensitive. They will change depending on which folder is selected in the left-hand, or navigation, frame of the Explorer window. When creating new folders, the folder will be created inside the folder selected in the navigation frame.**

You can share a created folder by viewing the shared folder properties, through any of the following methods:

- Select the folder and choose Sharing from the File menu.

- Right-click the folder and choose Sharing from the context menu.

- Select the folder and choose Properties from the File menu. Then select the Sharing tab.

- Right-click the folder and choose Properties from the context menu. Then select the Sharing tab.

The Sharing tab enables you to assign a share name for the folder. This name may differ from the actual name of the folder. Depending on the type of access control that has been implemented on your system, you will either be asked to provide a password for the resource, or to provide a list of users that will be allowed access to the resource.

To enable you to see who is currently connected to your shared folders, Microsoft provides Net Watcher with Windows 95. Net Watcher can provide you with information about who is currently connected to your computer, and what they are connected to (see Figure 4.3). The View by Connections option enables you to disconnect users by selecting Disconnect User from the

Administer menu. Net Watcher can also provide you with a list of shared folders, and can tell who is connected to each one. The last feature of Net Watcher is to allow you to Share, Stop Sharing, or Modify the properties of Shared Folders.

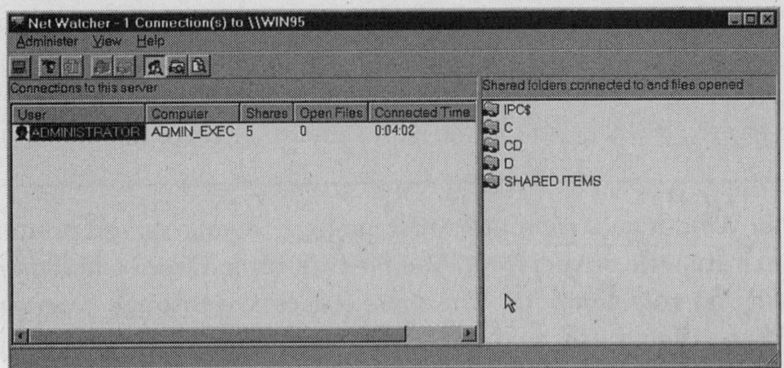

Figure 4.3　Net Watcher enables you to view users and see the shared folders to which they are connected.

4.2.2　Network Printers

Shared printers are like shared directories on Windows 95 computers.

The easiest way to install a printer in Windows 95 is to plug it in and reboot. Windows 95 scans the printer port at every boot, and if the printer can provide enough information to Windows 95, Windows 95 automatically installs the printer driver for the printer. If the printer is not identified by Windows 95, you can manually add the printer by following these steps:

1. Choose Printers from Settings in the Start menu.

2. From the Printers folder, open the Add Printer icon.

3. Choose Local Printer and select the Next button.

4. Choose your printer from the list provided, which includes most printer manufacturers and types. If your printer model is not listed, you can click the Have Disk button and locate the OEMSETUP.INF or equivalent INF file for your new printer driver. Click the Next button to continue the installation.

5. Choose the printer port that you want to use. Click the Next button.

6. Choose a name for your printer. This name will be the default name used when the printer is shared, but does not have to be the name used to share the printer. Choose whether you want Windows 95 to use this printer as the default Windows printer. Click the Next button to continue.

7. Windows 95 will then finish the installation of the printer and ask you whether the test page printed properly.

After the printer is installed, it may be shared by doing any of the following:

- Select the printer and choose Sharing from the File menu.

- Right-click the printer and choose Sharing from the context menu.

- Select the printer and choose Properties from the File menu. Then select the Sharing tab.

- Right-click the printer and choose Properties from the context menu. Then select the Sharing tab.

When the Share Printer window opens, it will look like one of the two shared folders windows (for user-level or share-level access control), with the exception that it is geared to sharing printers. You will still have the option of adding users or groups from the server to grant them access, or to assign a password to the printer. In this window, you can also assign a share or network name for your printer; it will default to the local name you gave to it.

> When other Windows 95 computers first connect to your shared printer, they are required to install the drivers for it. The files are copied from a hidden read-only shared folder on your computer. The share is accessed through *server_name*\ PRINTERS$ and is your *win_root*\SYSTEM folder.

Management of the printer is done through its icon in the Printers folder. When you open the Printer icon, it will list all the jobs that have been spooled and are waiting to be printed on the printer. You have the option of changing the order of the print jobs, pausing them, or canceling them.

Settings in the Printer properties sheets also affect printing performance. To view the properties of your printer, right-click the printer and select Properties. The Details properties page has the Spool Settings button. Table 4.1 summarizes the options that can be configured in the Spool Settings dialog box, as shown in Figure 4.4.

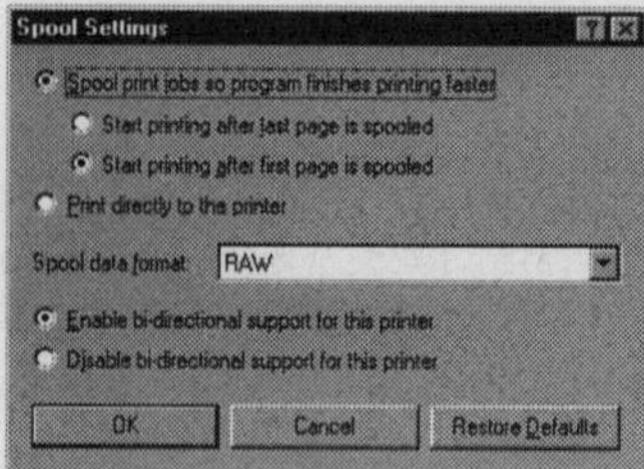

Figure 4.4   Proper spool settings can greatly improve the performance on your computer.

Table 4.1   Printer Spool Settings

Item	Description
Spool print jobs so program finishes printing faster	If you disable print spooling, you will find that your printer takes longer to print.
Start printing after the last page is spooled	If you choose this setting, the total print time may be increased.
Start printing after the first page is spooled	If this option is chosen, a large print job will tie up the printer after the first page is spooled, until it is finished printing.

Item	Description
Spool data format	If your network is composed of only Windows 95 computers, you might want to implement Enhanced Metafile (EMF) spooling. It takes less time for the application to generate this file than it takes to generate a RAW file.

4.2.3   Shared Fax Modem

Fax modems and separate phone lines are rare for users in offices. Even though they are rare, however, people have come to rely on having this service at their desktops. Even though you can share a fax modem, this is not being used as widely as with printers.

Setting Up Fax Services

To use Fax services, you must set up Microsoft Exchange. You can launch Microsoft Exchange by selecting it from Program in the Start menu, or using the Inbox icon on the desktop.

To set up Fax services, follow these steps:

1. Open the Add\Remove Programs control panel, and select the Windows Setup tab.

2. Ensure there is a check mark in front of Microsoft Fax, and then click the OK button to close the Control Panel. You may be prompted for the Windows 95 CD-ROM, as well as to reboot your computer.

3. Choose Start, Programs, Accessories, Fax, Compose New Fax. The first time you run the Compose New Fax application, it runs the Inbox Setup Wizard to configure the Fax services.

4. Select your fax device. You will be presented a list of installed fax modems.

5. Configure your preferences for answering the phone for incoming faxes.

6. Type your personal information into the Fax setup. This information will be used for your Fax cover pages.

7. Choose the Default Dialing location for the Fax services. A check box enables you to bypass this dialog box on all future faxes.

8. The next dialog box prompts you for a list of recipients for the new fax.

9. You can choose from a list of cover pages on the computer. You can use the Options button to schedule the fax to be sent at a future time.

10. You can now fill in the Subject for the fax, and the actual message of the fax (see Figure 4.5). After this dialog box, you can attach other files from your hard drive to be sent with your fax (as additional pages).

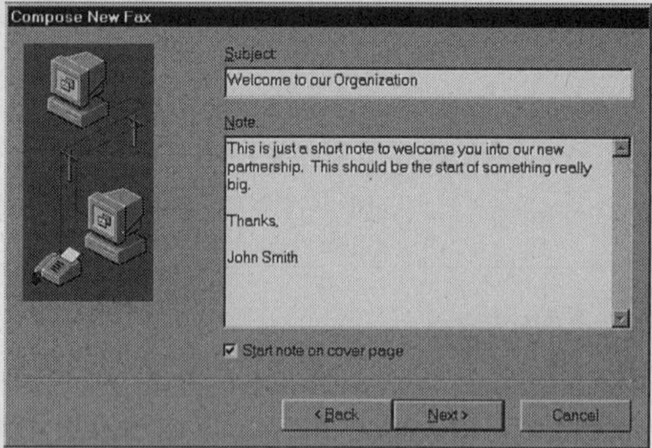

Figure 4.5 Your cover page message and subject lines are collected and inserted into the appropriate fields.

Sharing the Fax Service

To share your Fax service, follow these steps:

1. Right-click the Inbox icon on your desktop and choose Properties, or open the Inbox and choose Services from the Tools menu.

2. Choose the Microsoft Fax service and click the Properties button. Select the Modem tab to configure sharing.

3. Place a check mark in the box in front of Let Other People on the Network Use my Modem to Send Faxes (see Figure 4.6). You receive a prompt for a drive that will host the shared Fax service.

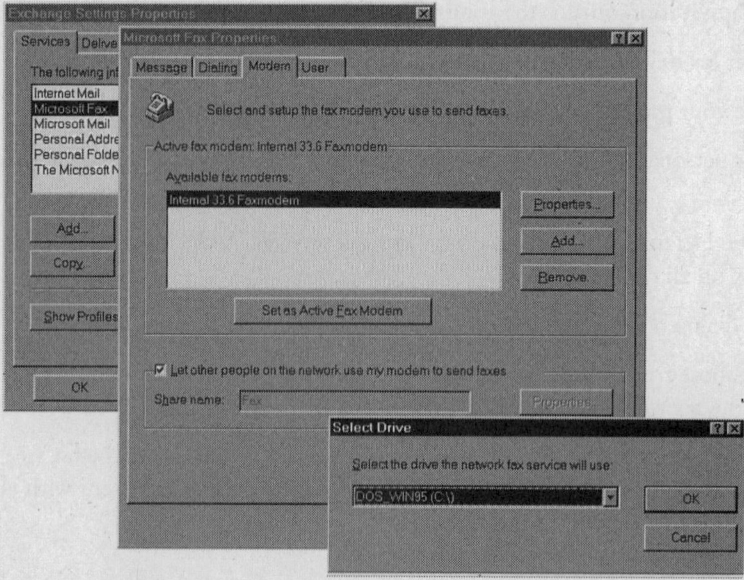

Figure 4.6 Sharing a fax modem is extremely easy.

4. The next dialog box that appears is the same as the Share options under the Properties button. Like the other two resources, if user-level access control has been set, you have the option of assigning access to a list of users.

5. Other users can now connect to the shared Fax service by setting up an additional fax modem and selecting Network Fax Server. You then type in the UNC path to the Fax service on the server (see Figure 4.7).

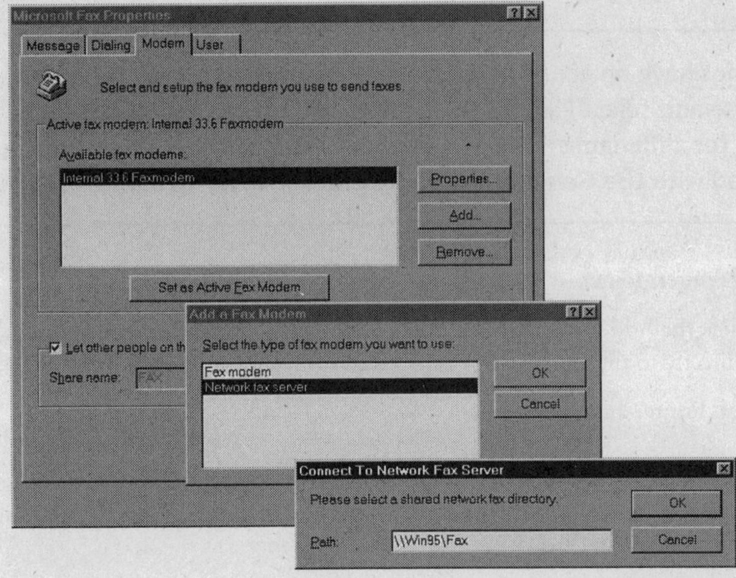

Figure 4.7 Attaching to a shared fax is a matter of adding it to the list of network Fax servers, and knowing the name of the Fax server and the share.

Monitoring Fax Services

You can see the fax activity in Microsoft Exchange. Any faxes that have had a send attempt show up in the Sent Items folder. If there was a problem sending any of the faxes, you will see messages from System Administrator in your Inbox. When you are reading the error message, a button enables you to Send Again. This is the only tool available to you to see what type of activity has taken place on your fax modem.

4.2.4 Unimodem/V Devices

The Unimodem/V driver allows for shared Fax services to operate over your network. Unimodem itself is short for Universal Modem and refers to the basic modem driver components that Microsoft provides with the Windows 95 operating system. Unimodem/V (Unimodem/Voice) supports the following items:

- **Unimodem/V Telephony Service Provider (TSP) and VxD.** The upgraded drivers.

- **Operator Agent.** A phone answering agent that supports routing a call after answer to the appropriate user.

- **Wave driver.** Support for some modems' WAV tables.

- **Wave wrapper.** The basic WAV support for all other modems.

4.2.5   Exercises

Exercise 1: Adding a Local Printer with the Add Printer Wizard

This exercise demonstrates how to use the Add Printer Wizard to install a locally attached printer.

> **If you do not have an actual printer attached to your computer, you can still perform this exercise and select FILE: as the port to print to. When you print to FILE:, you are prompted for a filename and path to which to save the output. Printing to FILE: is usually used with the Generic/Text Only printer driver to create text output in a file.**

1. Open the Printers folder.

2. Double-click the Add Printer Wizard and choose Next. You are asked whether the printer is attached directly to the computer or is accessed from the network.

3. Select Local Printer and click Next.

4. Select the printer manufacturer from the Manufacturers list.

5. Select the printer model from the Printers list. If you do not have an actual local printer, you can select the Generic/Text Only driver after selecting Generic as the manufacturer.

6. From the list of Available Ports, select the port to which the printer is connected. For a parallel port, for example, you may need to select LPT1:. If you do not have a local printer attached, select FILE:.

7. Click Next and assign the printer a printer name. You can accept the default name, or you can use a more descriptive name.

8. If you want print jobs to be sent to this printer by default, choose Yes and then click Next. Otherwise, choose No and then click Next.

9. The Add Printer Wizard asks whether you want to print a new page, and then copies the files from the Windows 95 distribution media. If Windows 95 cannot find these files, you are prompted for the path.

10. An icon for the printer is created in the Printers folder.

Exercise 2: Sending Faxes Using a Shared-Network Fax Modem

In this exercise, you configure Exchange so that you can share your fax with other users on a network. For this exercise to work, you should have a working network with Windows 95 installed, as well as File and Printer Sharing enabled on the computer that has the shared fax. You also need a fax modem installed and working on this computer.

1. Choose Tools, Services in the Exchange Client. The Services dialog box appears.

2. Select Microsoft Fax from the list of services and choose Properties. The Microsoft Fax Properties sheet appears.

3. Select the Modem tab.

4. Select the Let Other People on the Network Use My Modem to Send Faxes check box and click OK.

5. Choose the Properties button next to the share name to display the Shared Fax Directory dialog box. By default, the directory is C:\NetFax, the share name is FAX, and all users have full control permissions to the C:\NetFax directory.

6. Click OK. By default, the local fax modem is shared on the network with the share name FAX under the current computer name.

7. From another computer on the network, start the Exchange Client and add the Microsoft Fax service. The Microsoft Fax service appears in the list of services under the Service option of the Tools menu.

8. Select Microsoft Fax from the list of services and choose Properties. You are prompted as to whether you want to configure your name, fax number, and fax modem to use.

9. Choose Yes. The Microsoft Fax Properties sheet appears.

10. Enter your name and return fax number and any optional information in the User tab.

11. Select the Modem tab and choose Add. The Add a Fax Modem dialog box appears.

12. Select Network Fax Server and click OK. The Connect to Network Fax Server dialog box appears.

13. Enter the UNC path to the FAX share you created on the other computer. For example, enter **\\TESTPC\\FAX**. The fax server appears in the list of available fax modems.

14. Select the network fax and choose Set as Active Fax Modems. The fax server is set to the active fax modem.

15. Configure any additional properties you desire, double-click OK, and exit and restart the Exchange Client. The Exchange Client is ready to send faxes to the fax server.

16. Choose Compose, New Fax. The Compose New Fax Wizard appears.

17. Specify Default Location in the I'm Dialing From field. Click Next. The next Compose New Fax Wizard screen appears.

18. Type the name and fax number of the recipient and choose the Add to List button. The recipient name appears in the Recipient list.

19. Choose Next, specify whether you want a cover sheet, choose Next, specify a subject or note for the fax if desired, and click Next again. The Add File option appears.

20. If you are sending the message to another fax modem, you can attach an electronic document in binary format, which can be detached by the recipient if the receiving fax modem and software support binary attachments. Click on Next when done, and choose Finish to send the fax. The fax is generated and sent.

To find out whether you did this exercise correctly, you can go to your Inbox to check for a message from the System Administrator to see whether there was an error in sending the fax. If not, you were successful.

4.2.6   Practice Problems

1. Which services must you enable before you can share folders or printers on your Windows 95 system?

   A. Usernames

   B. Passwords

   C. Folder and Print Sharing

   D. File and Printer Sharing

2. Which is the command to create a new folder from the DOS prompt?

   A. MC

   B. MCD

   C. MD

   D. CD

3. Which Windows 95 utility enables you to see who is currently connected to your computer?

   A. Net Searcher

   B. Network Neighborhood

   C. Explorer

   D. Net Watcher

4. From the preceding question, which menu in this utility enables you to disconnect users from your system?

   A. User Maintenance

   B. Administer

   C. Tools

   D. View

5. Which option of Add Printer do you choose from when you connect a new printer to your Windows 95 system printer port?

   A. Local Printer

   B. New Printer

   C. Select Printer

   D. Configure Printer

6. If the new printer you are installing is not listed as a printer model selection, what is the name of the file you must provide to Windows 95 to continue installation?

   A. PRINTER.INF

   B. WIN95.INF

   C. OEMSETUP.INF

   D. SETUP.INF

7. What is the name of the tab in Properties you select to share a printer?

   A. Users

   B. Sharing

   C. Details

   D. General

8. As you instruct a user on how to configure a peer-to-peer network with five Windows 95 computers connected together, you use the term *Windows 95 server* several times. After you finish, he asks you what a Windows 95 server is. What do you tell him?

   A. A computer that is the primary domain controller on the LAN

   B. A computer running Windows 95 that has the Enable Windows 95 Server Registry option turned on

   C. A Windows 95 computer that has the File and Printer Sharing Service enabled

   D. A computer running Windows 95 that performs as an application and database server for the LAN

9. For non-PostScript printing, Windows 95 can create an EMF file. An end user asks why he should keep EMF turned on. You tell him that the major benefit of Enhanced Metafile Spooling is _______.

   A. Faster return-to-application time

   B. Better control of print queues

C. Better support for color printing

D. Shorter time in the print queue

10. You are manning the company help desk and receive a call from a user who is trying to use a shared fax modem. The fax modem is on another workstation to which he is connected. The network connection is working correctly; however, he cannot access the fax modem. Pick two reasons why this may be happening.

A. The shared fax modem is out of paper.

B. The user does not have the correct password to access the shared fax modem.

C. The computer on which the shared fax modem resides is not running Exchange.

D. The phone line is busy.

11. You want to optimize all printers connected to your Windows 95 computers. From what you know about Windows 95 printer support, what is the main factor in ensuring print performance?

A. Spool settings

B. Driver compatibility

C. Queue management

D. Font management

12. To enable people to install printer drivers from your Windows 95 system using Point and Print, you need to

A. Copy the files to C:\ and create a share called PRINTERS.

B. Copy the files to C:\WINDOWS and create a share called DRIVERS.

C. Copy the files to C:\WINDOWS\PRINTERS and create a share called PRINTERS$.

D. Just share the printer: The share PRINTER$ is automatically created where the files are located.

13. A Windows 95 system is set up as a print server. Jason wants to connect to the shared printer from his Windows 95 system. The printer drivers on the server are newer than the driver he has installed on his computer. What should he do?

A. Remove his printer first, and then install the newer drivers from the print server.

B. Upgrade his print drivers before trying to connect to the shared printer.

C. Allow the newer files to be copied to his computer from the print server.

D. Refuse to copy the files to his computer because there may be a virus on the print server.

14. How do you remove a print job that someone else has sent to a network printer?

A. Pause the printer and purge the print queue.

B. Select the job in the queue and press Delete.

C. You cannot remove it. Only the creator or a print manager can remove someone else's print jobs.

D. Power off the printer and then power it back on.

15. When can you pause a network printer?

A. When you are a normal user

B. When you are the administrator

C. When you are viewing the print queue

D. When the printer is in your office

16. What is the default access that users have to the shared fax directory?

A. Full

B. Read-only

C. Depends on password

D. Write-only

17. You send a print job to the printer and you have EMF enabled. At what stage does Windows 95 return control to the application that issued the print job?

    A. After the EMF file is created

    B. As soon as the GDI receives the print job

    C. When the printer receives the print job

    D. None of the above

18. Julie uses Net Watcher to view connections to her local computer. She wants to see the users connected to her computer. Which toolbar button does she click to do this?

    A. View Users

    B. Show Connected Users

    C. View Connected Users

    D. Show Users

19. What are three compelling reasons to set up a dedicated fax modem workstation on which all users in a company can send and receive fax messages?

    A. To eliminate the expense of equipping every machine with a fax modem

    B. To eliminate the expense of installing additional phone lines

    C. To avoid the trouble of installing Microsoft Fax on each computer

    D. For easier backup of faxes, because all messages are stored on a single computer

20. For users on a network to send and receive fax messages on a shared fax modem, which two requirements must be met?

A. The Automatic Routing option should be set so that messages are automatically forwarded to the appropriate user on the network.

B. On the computer with the Shared Fax mode, Exchange must be running at all times.

C. Microsoft Fax must be running at all times.

D. The Let Other People on the Network Use My Modem to Send Faxes option should be set on the computer with the fax modem.

4.2.7 Answers and Explanations

1. **D** File and Printer Sharing must be enabled from the Network control panel.

2. **C** You use the MD command or you can also use the MKDIR command.

3. **D** Net Watcher utility enables you to see who is currently connected to your computer and can also provide a list of shared folders.

4. **B** The Administer menu enables you to disconnect users when you use the View by Connections option.

5. **A** You have two options at this point: Local Printer or Network Printer.

6. **C** OEMSETUP.INF is the file required to continue the installation of a new printer Windows 95 does not recognize.

7. **B** Use the Sharing tab to begin Sharing a Printer.

8. **C** With File and Printer Sharing enabled, the Windows 95 system appears as a server to other systems on the network.

9. **A** EMF is faster than RAW printing because it sends a graphic file to the printer.

10. **B, C**   Microsoft Exchange must be running on the system with a shared fax, and users must supply a correct password to access it.

11. **A**   Configuring spool settings will affect how fast your printer prints on your Windows 95 system.

12. **D**   The files are copied to the SYSTEM folder and the PRINTER$ share is created automatically when a printer is installed and shared.

13. **C**   Windows 95, recognizing that Jason's driver files are older, prompts him to upgrade his files at that time.

14. **C**   Only a print manager or administrator can manage another person's print jobs.

15. **B**   The administrator can manage a network printer.

16. **A**   By default, all users have full control permissions to the shared fax directory.

17. **B**   As soon as the GDI portion of the Windows 95 Kernel receives the print job, control is returned to the application.

18. **D**   The Show Users option in Net Watcher enables you to see who is connected to your system.

19. **A, B, D**   The advantages to having a dedicated fax modem workstation are that you do not have to install fax modems and additional phone lines for each computer, and you can back up all users' fax messages simultaneously.

20. **B, D**   Because Exchange is in charge of sending and receiving fax messages, it must be running at all times. You enable fax sharing with the Let Other People on the Network Use My Modem to Send Faxes option, located on the Modem tab of the Microsoft Fax Properties sheet.

4.2.8   Key Terms and Definitions

Enhanced Metafile (EMF)   A graphic file that is a representation of the print output for the application.

Fax modem   A device attached to a computer that can send and receive text and images through telephone lines. The fax modem offers the functionality of a fax machine, but all documents are electronic.

File and Printer Sharing   A service that enables a Windows 95 machine to share resources on a network.

Graphical user interface (GUI)   A generic term in the context of how an operating system is displayed.

Local resources   Resources available on your computer.

Net Watcher   Windows 95 provides Net Watcher as a tool to see who is currently connected to your shared folders. The Net Watcher provides information about who is currently connected to your computer and to what folder.

Remote resources   Resources available to other users through the network.

Unimodem   Unimodem stands for Universal modem and refers to the basic modem driver components that Microsoft provides with Windows 95.

Unimodem/V   Unimodem/V stands for Unimodem/Voice, which is a driver that allows for shared Fax servers to operate over your network.

4.3   Set Up User Environments by User Profiles and System Policies

User profiles enable users to keep personalized settings on a computer. If the computer is accessed by multiple users, each user may have his own settings saved. These settings include items such as the following:

- Wallpaper and desktop settings

- Mouse tracking speed and button settings

- Desktop icons

- Start menu icons

- Application settings such as Microsoft Office 97

In a network environment, these settings may roam with the user (roaming user profiles).

The Registry in Windows 95 is stored in two files on your local hard drive: USER.DAT and SYSTEM.DAT. SYSTEM.DAT stores all the hardware-specific information about your computer, and USER.DAT stores all the user-specific information for the computer. If you create a generic USER.DAT file on one computer, you can move that file to all other computers in your organization. Users can still make modifications to their settings, which is beneficial because it places all users at the same starting point. User profiles will maintain individual USER.DAT files for each user on your computer.

User profiles are enabled through the User Profiles tab of the Password control panel. To enable user profiles, the proper choice is Users Can Customize Their Preferences and Desktop Settings. This option alone will keep a separate USER.DAT file for each user that logs on to the computer. The USER.DAT file for each user is initially copied from the USER.DAT file in the Windows directory. Two additional settings can be included in each user profile: Include Desktop Icons and Network Neighborhood Contents in User Settings, and Include Start Menu and Program Groups in User Settings.

When working in a network environment, user profiles are copied to and from your servers as you log on and log off. These profiles are referred to as roaming user profiles. The following criteria must be met to implement roaming user profiles:

- For Windows NT networks, your Windows 95 computer must be configured to Log On to Windows NT Domain. This is configured in the Client for Microsoft Networks, on the Configuration tab of the Network control panel.

- Your Windows NT domain controller must have a home directory configured for the user to be stored on a server.

The Windows 95 user profile will automatically be copied from the local hard drive to the user's home directory when the user logs off. When the user logs on, profile existence is checked in the following order:

1. If there is a server copy, it is copied to the local hard drive;

2. If there is not a server copy, the local copy is used;

3. If there is not a local copy, a new copy is created from the default files in the Windows directory. This new local profile will be copied to the server when the user logs off.

If you are implementing user profiles on a Novell NetWare network, the user profile is stored in the user's NetWare Mail directory. This is a directory in the SYS:MAIL directory.

System policies can be used to create and enforce a custom environment for users. It allows restrictions to be set on system usage, such as Control Panels.

System policies enable you to modify the USER.DAT and SYSTEM.DAT files on a destination computer automatically when the user logs on to the network. If you wish to create a new policy configuration file for your server, you must use the System Policy Editor. To install the System Policy Editor, follow these steps:

1. Click on the Start button and choose Settings, Control Panel.

2. Open the Add\Remove Programs control panel.

3. Select the Windows Setup tab, and click the Have Disk button.

4. Select the following path from the Windows 95 CD:
   Windows_95_CD\ADMIN\APPTOOLS\POLEDIT directory.

5. Select the check boxes for both the System Policy Editor and Group Policies, and then click the Install button.

You only have to install the System Policy Editor on the machine you will be using to create the system policy. If you plan to assign the policy to users based on which server groups they belong to, you must install the group policies on every machine on your network.

You can install the group policy files on any computer by following these steps on each workstation that requires them:

1. Click the Start button and choose Settings, Control Panel.

2. Open the Add\Remove Programs control panel.

3. Select the Windows Setup tab, and click the Have Disk button.

4. Select the following path from the Windows 95 CD:
   Windows_95_CD\ADMIN\APPTOOLS\POLEDIT directory.

5. Select the check box for Group Policies, and click the Install button.

With group policies installed, your computer will import policy settings from the configuration file based on the server groups to which you belong.

Depending on the type of network you are working on, Windows 95 expects the policy configuration file to be in certain locations. The locations are as follows:

- Windows NT Domain, in the NetLogon directory of domain controllers, which is *win_root*\SYSTEM32\REPL\IMPORT\SCRIPTS\.

- Novell NetWare 3.*x* or 4.*x* server, on the SYS volume in the PUBLIC directory.

> **By default, the name of the configuration file is CONFIG.POL. If you are creating policy files to be used with Windows NT 4.0 as well, the Windows NT default policy filename would be NTCONFIG.POL. You can use other filenames as long as the local computer is set up to find the other filenames.**

To launch the System Policy Editor, choose it from the Start menu under Programs, Accessories, System Tools. It opens with a blank window. To create a new policy file, choose New from the File menu. If you are working on a policy file, you should have at least two icons visible: Default User and Default Computer.

When working with the Policy Editor to make a policy file, you will notice that each check box in the Settings windows has three states: on (checked), off (clear), and neutral (gray).

> **The three states of the check boxes in the System Policy Editor (checked, clear, and gray) can be interpreted this way:**
>
> > *Checked* **is a value that you are setting to the On position. This turns the setting on for all computers processing this policy.**
> >
> > *Clear* **is a value that you are setting to the Off position. This turns the setting off for all computers processing this policy.**
> >
> > *Gray* **is a value that you are leaving alone. These values are neutral, and will not change the settings. This is the default for all values in a Default User and Default Computer.**

4.3.1 Changing the User Settings in the Policy File

This section examines the user settings that may be adjusted or enforced in a system policy. To access this screen, double-click Default User in the System Policy Editor. The user settings are applied for each user regardless of which computer they have logged on to, and the changes that are implemented are stored in the user's USER.DAT file.

Control Panel Settings

The Control Panel settings enable you to control or restrict access to most of the Control Panel applets.

You can apply restrictions to the following Control Panel applets:

- Display

- Network

- Passwords
- Printers
- System

Restricting the Display Control Panel

The restrictions for the Display control panel are as follows:

- **Disable Display Control Panel.** Disables all access to the Display control panel.
- **Hide Background Page.** Removes the Background tab from the Display control panel.
- **Hide Screen Saver Page.** Removes the Screen Saver tab from the Display control panel.
- **Hide Appearance Page.** Removes the Appearance tab from the Display control panel.
- **Hide Settings Page.** Removes the Settings tab from the Display control panel.

Restricting the Network Control Panel

The following settings enable you to modify the restrictions to the Network control panel:

- **Disable Network Control Panel.** Prevents all access to the Network control panel.
- **Hide Identification Page.** Hides the Identification properties of the Network control panel.
- **Hide Access Control Page.** Hides the Access Control (user-level versus share-level) properties of the Network control panel.

Restricting the Passwords Control Panel

For most users, some access to the Passwords control panel is required. You can, however, apply the following list of restrictions:

- **Disable Passwords Control Panel.** Prevents all access to the Passwords control panel.
- **Hide Change Passwords Page.** Hides the Change Passwords properties of the Passwords control panel.
- **Hide Remote Administration Page.** Hides the Remote Administration properties of the Passwords control panel.
- **Hide User Profiles Page.** Hides the Profiles properties of the Passwords control panel.

Restricting Printer Configuration

You can place the following restrictions on printers:

- **Hide General And Details Pages.** Hides the General and Details properties for the Printer icons in the Printers folder.
- **Disable Deletion Of Printers.** Prevents the deletion of installed printers.
- **Disable Addition Of Printers.** Prevents the installation of printers.

Restricting the System Control Panel

You can apply the following restrictions to the System control panel:

- **Hide Device Manager Page.** Hides the Device Manager properties from the System control panel.

- **Hide Hardware Profiles Page.** Hides the Hardware Profiles properties from the System control panel.

- **Hide File System Button.** Hides the File System button from the Performance properties in the System control panel.

- **Hide Virtual Memory Button.** Hides the Virtual Memory button from the Performance properties in the System control panel.

These are all of the settings that you can change in the Control Panel section of the policy file.

Desktop Settings

The security-side desktop settings are fairly low. The settings that may be enforced are as follows:

- Wallpaper name

- Tile wallpaper

- Color scheme

If the Display control panel has been restricted, users cannot change any of these settings.

File and Printer Sharing Settings

File and printer sharing is necessary on workstations to make remote administration possible. The following two policy entries enable you to leave the service installed, but they remove all the controls from the users.

- Disable File Sharing Controls

- Disable Printer Sharing Controls

Windows Explorer Shell Settings

Windows Explorer is the default shell used by Windows 95. A *shell* is the program that sets up the working environment for applications and other services to run. In Windows 3.1, for example, the shell was referred to as Program Manager. Policy Editor provides several security features regarding Windows Explorer, which can be found in the form of custom folders and shell restrictions.

You can find the settings for both of these security features in the following lists. These are the custom folders that you can configure:

- **Custom Programs Folder.** Enables you to specify an alternative location for a folder that has the contents of the Programs directory. The folder can be stored locally on the workstation, or can be located on a network drive and accessed through a UNC path such as this:

```
Error! Bookmark not defined.
```

- **Custom Desktop Icons.** Enables you to specify an alternative location for a folder that has the contents of the Desktop directory.

- **Hide Start Menu Subfolders.** Enables you to hide the default Start menu folders.

- **Custom Startup Folder.** Enables you to specify an alternative location for a folder that has the contents of the Startup directory.

- **Custom Network Neighborhood.** Enables you to specify an alternative location for a folder that has the contents of the Network Neighborhood.

- **Custom Start Menu.** Enables you to specify an alternative location for a folder that has the contents of the Start Menu directory.

In addition to the custom folders, you can apply several restrictions to the users' desktop shells. The various restrictions are as follows:

- **Remove Run Command.** Removes the Run command from the Start menu, which will help to prevent users from running executables that you have not provided shortcuts for in the Start menu.

- **Remove Folders From Settings On Start Menu.** Hides the Printers and Control Panel folders in the Settings folder in the Start menu.

- **Remove Taskbar From Settings On Start Menu.** Hides Taskbar in the Settings folder in the Start menu.

- **Remove Find Command.** Removes the Find command from the Start menu.

- **Hide Drives In My Computer.** Removes all drive icons from My Computer.

- **Hide Network Neighborhood.** Removes the Network Neighborhood from the desktop.

  - If you choose to leave the Network Neighborhood on the desktop, you may choose to hide the Entire Network icon to prevent network browsing outside of the current workgroup.

  - If you choose to leave the Network Neighborhood on the desktop, you may choose to hide the current workgroup contents. This forces browsing resources through the Entire Network icon.

- **Hide All Items On Desktop.** Removes all icons from the desktop, both user- and OS-created icons.

- **Disable Shut Down Command.** Removes the Shutdown command from the Start menu.

- **Don't Save Settings At Exit.** Prevents desktop changes from being saved when users are exiting Windows.

With the desktop shell settings dealt with, it is time to focus on additional restrictions that apply to other applications.

System Restrictions

System restrictions are in place to disallow the user from getting away from the Windows 95 graphical user interface (GUI), and away from the controlled environment (see Figure 4.8). If a user is allowed to close the Windows 95 GUI, none of the policy changes that you have implemented will have any effect on the user. The system restrictions are not limited to the shell itself, but rather to the operating system:

- **Disable Registry Editing Tools.**

- **Only Run Allowed Windows Applications.** Allows only the applications listed under the Show dialog box to be run on the system.

- **Disable MS-DOS Prompt.**

- **Disable Single-Mode MS-DOS Applications.**

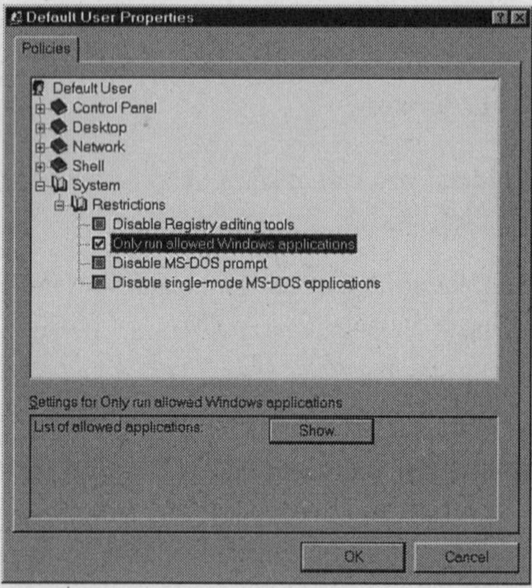

Figure 4.8   System restrictions are aimed at controlling the applications that are executed.

These are all the user settings that can be modified based on Microsoft's default template. You will now look at the sections of the template file that can be used to modify computer settings.

4.3.2   Changing Computer Settings in the Policy File

To access computer settings in policies files, double-click Default Computer or Local Computer in the System Policy Editor (see Figure 4.9). The computer settings are applied to the computer regardless of which user has logged on to the computer, and the changes that are implemented are stored in the computer's SYSTEM.DAT file. Use the Default Computer in the System Policy Editor when you are creating a new system policy.

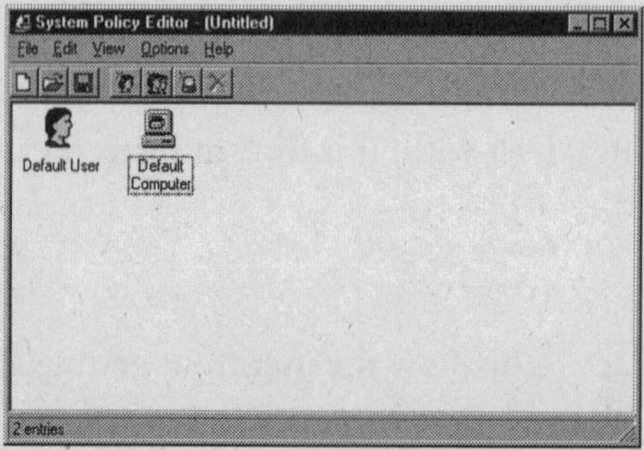

Figure 4.9   Initial policy files start with settings for Default Computer and Default User.

Configuring General Network Settings

The Network Settings section of the computer policy covers configuration options for most of the network interface of Windows 95. The first section deals with network settings that only have a single configuration option:

- **Access Control.** Enables you to specify user-level access control. When checked, it enables user-level access control with security provider list in options section.

- **File And Printer Sharing For NetWare Networks.** Enables you to disable SAP advertising. This will stop the Server Advertising Protocol from being used for File and Printer Sharing for NetWare Networks.

- **Dial-Up Networking.** Enables you to disable Dial-In. This stops Dial-up Server from working on this computer.

Configuring Logon Settings

The Logon section enables you to set additional warnings and security on Windows 95. This is done through these two settings:

- **Logon Banner.** Enables you to set an option that causes a logon banner to display before the Logon dialog box appears.

- **Require Validation By Network For Windows Access.** Forces users to have their usernames and passwords validated before they can gain access to the Windows 95 desktop.

Configuring the Microsoft Client for NetWare Networks

You can make several configuration changes to the Microsoft Client for NetWare Networks. These configurations are as follows:

- **Preferred Server.** Specifies the name of your preferred NetWare server or the server where your user account resides.

- **Support Long Filenames.** Enables Windows 95 to determine what to do when working with long filenames on your network. This option defines which level of support for long filenames that your Novell NetWare server supports. A value of 0 means that there is no support for long filenames on NetWare servers. A value of 1 means that there is support on NetWare servers version 3.12 and higher. A value of 2 means that there is support if the NetWare server supports long filenames.

- **Search Mode.** Enables you to set the NetWare Search mode to a valid binary value between 0 and 7.

- **Disable Automatic NetWare Logon.** Prevents Windows 95 from using the credentials of the Primary Network Logon to authenticate the user on the NetWare network.

Configuring the Microsoft Client for Windows Networks

You can make many configuration changes to the Microsoft Client for Windows Networks. These configurations are as follows:

- **Log On To Windows NT.** Enables the domain logon for Windows NT Networks.

- **Display Domain Logon Validation.** Displays a message that notifies the user if he is logged on to the domain.

- **Disable Caching Of Domain Password.**

- **Workgroup.** Specifies the workgroup name for the computer.

- **Alternative Workgroup.** Specifies a workgroup name to use for network browsing.

Configuring Password Settings

The following changes alter the way that Windows 95 works with passwords:

- **Hide Share Passwords With Asterisks.** Applies to the passwords listed in the Sharing tab of folder properties. The default value is on or `hidden`.

- **Disable Password Caching.** Disables the caching of network and other passwords in the local password list file.

- **Require Alphanumeric Windows Password.** Forces users to choose Windows passwords that are a combination of letters and numbers.

- **Minimum Windows Password Length.** Sets a minimum length for the Windows password.

Configuring Sharing Settings

The Sharing settings apply to all file and printer sharing on the computer. The options are as follows:

- **Disable File Sharing.** Enables you to turn off File Sharing.

- **Disable Printer Sharing.** Enables you to turn off Printer Sharing.

Configuring Simple Network Management Protocol Settings

Windows 95's SNMP service can be configured through the following settings:

- **Communities.** Enables you to specify the SNMP community names that will be used by this computer.

- **Permitted Managers.** Enables you to specify IP or IPX addresses of computers that will be allowed to make SNMP queries to this computer.

- **Traps For Public Community.** Specifies the IP or IPX address of the computer that you will be sending public traps to.

- **Internet MIB.** Stores the computer's contact name and location as specified in the Internet MIB standards.

Configuring Update Settings

The options for Update settings are as follows:

- **Remote Update.** Sets the method of update for future downloads of the system policy.

- **Update Mode.** Can be either Automatic (for policies in the default location) or Manual (for policies stored in an alternative location).

- **Path For Manual Update.** Requires a UNC path to the alternative location for the policy file.

- **Display Error Message.** Enables the display of an error message if the policy is not available.

- **Load-Balance.** Allows Windows 95 to process policy files from the backup domain controller on a Windows NT network.

System Settings

System settings enable you to configure a few basic options for Windows 95 (see Figure 4.10). The settings are as follows:

- **Enable User Profiles.** Allows you to enable user profiles.

- **Network Path For Windows Setup.** Enables you to specify a UNC path to the network location of the Windows 95 Setup program.

- **Network Path For Windows Tour.**

- **Run.** Specifies a list of applications to run after the Windows shell loads. The applications are executed in order of value name.

- **Run Once.** Specifies a list of applications to run before the Windows shell loads.

- **Run Services.** Specifies the list of applications to execute as services to startup when Windows 95 loads.

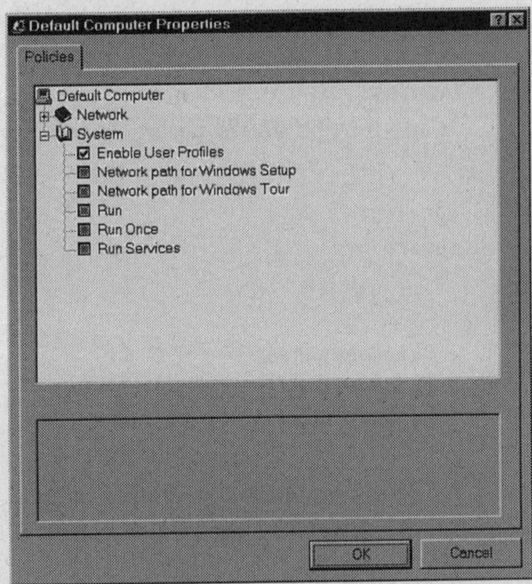

Figure 4.10 System settings enable you to configure startup commands to Windows 95.

4.3.3   Creating Policies for Users, Groups, and Computers

When you are creating a policy file for a server, you have the additional option of adding individual icons for each user or group of users from your server, as well as icons for each computer on your network. To add additional entries to your policy, choose Add User, Add Computer, or Add Group from the Edit menu.

Windows 95 follows a particular order when reading the policy file:

1.   Windows 95 checks for entries to see whether the user is a member of any of the groups.

2. Windows 95 then checks to see whether there is an entry for the user logging on. If there is an entry for the user, it then applies the changes for that user.

3. If there are no entries for that user or no groups processed, the entry for Default User is applied.

4. After applying the user policy, Windows 95 then applies a computer policy.

5. If there is an entry for your current computer name, it is applied. Otherwise, the entry for Default Computer is applied.

4.3.4   Using Policy Template Files

The Policy Editor may be used as a second type of Registry editor, but everything it knows about the Registry comes from the policy template file. The default template file is c:\WINDOWS\INF\ADMIN.ADM. You can change the template by choosing Template from the Options menu. The template file is a text file with a particular structure. Following is a list and description of the keywords and their uses within a policy file:

- CLASS is the largest section in the policy files. It must be either User or Machine.

- !!, or two exclamation marks, defines the next word as a variable or string that must be defined in the [STRINGS] section at the end of the policy file.

  Strings are defined with the following structure:

  ```
  StringName="String value"
  ```

- CATEGORY and END CATEGORY enclose each category in the Policy Editor structure. These will be the expanding branches of the file and may be nested within each other as follows:

  ```
  CATEGORY !!CategoryOne
          CATEGORY !!CategoryTwo
          CATEGORY !!CategoryThree

          ...
          ...

          END CATEGORY ; CategoryThree
      END CATEGORY   ; CategoryTwo
  END CATEGORY       ; CategoryOne
  ```

- KEYNAME indicates where in the Registry the changes should be made. Each category will contain a KEYNAME or Registry key path that would start immediately after HKEY_LOCAL_MACHINE or HKEY_CURRENT_USER. For example:

  ```
  KEYNAME System\CurrentControlSet\Services\Control\FileSystem
  ```

- POLICY is used to define the check boxes that will be displayed.

- VALUENAME is the name of the Registry value that you want to change. VALUENAME will always be contained within a PART.

- PART defines individual items that will be displayed in the Settings section of the Policy Editor, at the bottom of the window. An example of a PART statement is

  ```
  PART !!CPL_Display_Disable CHECKBOX
      VALUENAME NoDispCPL
  END PART
  ```

PARTS can be any of the following types:

- TEXT for display text. An example of this type is

  ```
  PART !!NetworkTourPath_TIP TEXT END PART
  ```

- NUMERIC for values to be written to the Registry as REG_DWORD types. An example of this type is

  ```
  PART !!SearchMode1 NUMERIC
        VALUENAME SearchMode
        MIN 0 MAX 7 DEFAULT 0
        END PART
  ```

- DROPDOWNLIST for list boxes and values. An example of this would be

  ```
  PART !!MyPolicy DROPDOWNLIST
      VALUENAME ValueToBeChanged
        ITEMLIST
          NAME "One" VALUE NUMERIC 1
          NAME "Two" VALUE NUMERIC 2
          NAME "Three" VALUE NUMERIC 3
          NAME "Four" VALUE NUMERIC 4
        END ITEMLIST
      END PART
  ```

- COMBOBOX for list boxes that have a text field that can be overridden. The suggestions in the drop-down list would have the following format:

  ```
  SUGGESTIONS
          Red Yellow Pink "Royal Blue"
  END SUGGESTIONS
  ```

- EDITTEXT for string data that is to be written to the Registry with a type of REG_SZ.

- REQUIRED may be added to make data entry mandatory.

- EXPANDABLETEXT for string data that will include replaceable strings such as %SYSTEMROOT%, and is stored in the Registry with a type of REG_EXPAND_SZ.

- CHECKBOX for values that will be set to 0 or 1. An example of this is

  ```
  PART !!DomainLogonConfirmation CHECKBOX
        KEYNAME Network\Logon
        VALUENAME DomainLogonMessage
      END PART
  ```

PARTS may also contain the following values:

- MAXLEN is used to set a maximum length to strings that are typed.

- MIN and MAX are used to set boundaries on NUMERIC datatypes.

- DEFAULT is used to a default value for text or numeric datatypes.

- DEFCHECKED causes check boxes to be initially checked.

- VALUEON and VALUEOFF are similar to CHECKBOX, but are used when ON and OFF values are not 1 and 0. An example of this is

```
POLICY !!HideDrives
     VALUENAME "NoDrives"
     VALUEON NUMERIC 67108863          ; low 26 bits on (1 bit per drive)
END POLICY
```

- ACTIONLISTON and ACTIONLISTOFF are used to display alternating action lists if a check box is on or off.

4.3.5 Exercises

Exercise 1: Creating User Profiles

This exercise demonstrates how to enable individual users to maintain user profiles.

1. From the Start menu, choose Settings, Control Panel. The Control Panel opens.

2. Double-click the Passwords icon. The Passwords Properties dialog box appears.

3. Select the User Profiles tab. By default, the All Users of This PC Use the Same Preferences and Desktop Settings option is selected.

4. Select the following options:

   Users Can Customize Their Preferences and Desktop settings.

   Include Desktop Icons and Network Neighborhood Contents in User Settings.

   Include Start Menu and Program Groups in User Settings.

   Click OK. You are prompted to restart the computer.

5. Click OK to restart the computer.

6. Log on with the username TESTPROFILE and type **password** for the password. You will be prompted to verify the password by typing it again.

> Do not press Enter after typing the username without first typing a password. If you do, the password will be blank, and you will not see the User Logon screen again when you next log on. If a blank password is used with a username, that user is automatically logged on, and a different username cannot be used. To fix this situation, use the Passwords control panel to change the password to something other than blank.

7. Confirm the password by typing it again. A message appears asking whether you want to save the settings for the user in a user profile.

8. Choose Yes to save the sessions settings in a user profile. The default desktop is displayed.

9. Right-click the desktop and select Properties from the context-sensitive menu. The Display Properties sheet appears.

10. Select a different wallpaper for the desktop and click OK. The new wallpaper is displayed.

11. Choose Shut Down from the Start menu. The Shut Down Windows dialog box opens.

12. Select Close All Programs and Log on as a Different User?. Then click Yes. All programs close, and the Enter Windows Password logon screen appears.

13. Log on with a different username. The original default wallpaper or pattern appears on the desktop.

14. Log off and log back on with the TESTPROFILE username. The wallpaper that was selected for that profile appears on the desktop.

15. Log off and then log on with your normal username. The original settings are displayed.

16. Start the Explorer and open the Windows 95 folder and the Profiles subfolder. The Profiles folder contains a subfolder for each of the profiles that have been created on the computer.

17. Examine the contents of each folder in the Profiles folder. You will notice a USER.DAT file that was created for each profile. In addition, there may be Start Menu, NetHood, Desktop, and Recent folders for each profile, depending on which options were chosen in the User Profiles tab of the Passwords control panel applet.

Exercise 2: Creating a System Policy

In this exercise, you create a simple system policy and set up a system so that the policy overwrites the previous Registry setting for the specified workstation.

1. Start the System Policy Editor. The System Policy Editor appears, and you are prompted for the name of the template file to be used.

2. Locate the *systemroot*\\INF\\ADMIN.ADM file and click OK. The ADMIN.ADM template is loaded, and a blank System Policy window appears.

The INF directory is a hidden directory. To see this directory, choose Options from the Explorer View menu. On the View tab, select Show All Files.

---

3. Choose File, New File. The Default User and Default Computer icons appear.

4. Double-click the Default Computer icon. The Default Computer Properties sheet appears.

5. Click on the plus sign next to Network. The Network policy subkeys appear.

6. Click on the plus sign next to Logon. The Network Logon Policy settings appear.

7. Click on the check box next to Logon Banner until a check mark appears in the box. The Caption and Text fields appear.

8. Type **System Policies Test** in the Caption field and **Welcome** in the Text field. Then click OK. The Default User and Default Computer icons are again displayed.

9. Choose File, Save As and save the filename as CONFIG.POL in the *systemroot* directory.

10. This file now has to be copied to one of two locations. If you are using a Windows NT domain, the file must go into the NETLOGON directory of the server. If you are using a Novell NetWare server, the file should be placed in the SYS:PUBLIC directory.

> **The policy that you create will affect all users that are logging on to your server. If you are using a production server, create a computer entry in the policy file by using Add Computer from the Edit menu. Name this entry with your computer's name.**

11. Choose Shutdown from the Start menu, and select Close All Programs and Log On As A Different User. Then repeat this step. The first logon changes the HKEY_LOCAL_MACHINE section of the Registry. This will not be visible until the second logon; changes to HKEY_CURRENT_USER take effect immediately.

12. Log on to the computer. The logon banner specified in CONFIG.POL appears during logon.

13. Edit the policy file to reverse the Logon Banner options and resave it to your server location.

14. Choose Shutdown from the Start menu, and select Close All Programs and Log On As A Different User. Then repeat this step.

15. The logon banner should not appear during your second logon.

16. Delete the policy file from the server.

4.3.6 Practice Problems

1. As system administrator, you set up each user's computer so that a user cannot start an MS-DOS prompt from within Windows 95. How can this be done?

   A. Use the System Policy Editor. Open the Default User Properties sheet, click System, click Restrictions, and select the Disable MS-DOS Prompt check box.

   B. Use the System Policy Editor. Open the Default User Properties sheet, click System, click Restrictions, and deselect the Enable MS-DOS Prompt check box.

   C. Use the System Policy Editor. Open the Default User Properties sheet, click System, and select the MS-DOS Prompt check box.

   D. Use the System Policy Editor. Open the Default User Properties sheet, click System, click Restrictions, and select the Disable Single-Mode MS-DOS Applications check box.

2. For a PowerPoint presentation in front of the help desk staff, you create a slide with a bullet point describing the Windows 95 System Policy feature. What would be the appropriate ending to the sentence: A Windows 95 system policy ______.

   A. Assigns priorities to applications accessing memory

   B. Assigns priorities to users

   C. Enables an administrator to set various Windows 95 Registry entries

   D. Is a summary of configuration details

3. On the same PowerPoint slide as in the preceding question, you place another bullet point explaining what the primary purpose of a Windows 95 system policy is. From the following list, choose the correct answer for this statement: The primary purpose of a Windows 95 system policy is to ______.

   A. Limit the ability of users to customize their environments

   B. Increase the ability of users to customize their environments

   C. Make the system run more efficiently

   D. Make the system more adaptable

4. Brenda modifies her user profile so that each time she starts Windows 95, a shortcut to her finance spreadsheet displays on the desktop. Which of the following cannot be done by setting user profiles?

   A. Display specific applications in the Start menu.

   B. Customize desktop settings, such as colors and wallpaper.

   C. Install an application for a specific user only.

   D. Display recently used documents in the Start menu Documents folder.

5. Mitch administers a Windows NT network that has several Windows 95 workstations attached to the server. He stores user profiles for all workstations on the server to be downloaded during bootup time. The user profiles can be updated by the users. To ensure that each profile is available from the server, where are they stored on the server?

   A. User's home directory

   B. User's C:\WINDOWS directory

   C. Any directory on the server to which the user has read permission

   D. None of the above

6. A user complains that the settings she made to her desktop are not saved each time she logs on to the network and starts Windows 95. You have her computer set up to download a user profile from the server and enable her to save changes to it. What might be one of the causes for her settings not being saved properly?

   A. Her version of Windows 95 needs updated.

   B. Her workstation's time is not synchronized with the server's time.

   C. She does not have the Remote Administration feature enabled.

   D. All the above.

7. In a training class you conduct for system administrators, you are asked why the Registry comprises two files. From the following list, what is the best answer to this question?

   A. Makes editing configuration settings safer.

   B. Separates user and system information so that system policies and user profiles can be created.

   C. Allows dynamic information from the hardware tree to be updated while user settings are idle.

   D. Enables a user to copy his USER.DAT from a floppy disk to a laptop and maintain the same look and feel as his desktop computer.

8. In which file does Windows 95 store specific user profile information?

   A. SYSTEM.DAT

   B. CONFIG.POL

   C. USER.BAK

   D. USER.DAT

9. You are storing user profiles on a Windows NT server. You want to enable users to access the same desktop settings anywhere on the network; however, you do not want users to have the ability to change the settings from session to session. Where must you store the user profile information on the Windows NT server, and by what name should the file be named?

   A. NETLOGON directory, USER.DAT

   B. NETLOGON directory, SER.MAN

   C. User's home directory, USER.MAN

   D. User's home directory, USER.DAT

10. As a network administrator, you choose to implement roving user profiles using Windows 95 and Novell NetWare. Where should you place the user profiles on the NetWare server?

   A. SYS:SYSTEM

   B. SYS:PUBLIC

   C. User's home directory

   D. Mail user_id directory

11. The computers on your network are configured with a 16-bit network client. What must you do so that the users of these computers can use system policies?

   A. Enable system policies on each of the workstations individually.

   B. Each of the workstations must have user-level security enabled to use system policies when using a 16-bit network client.

   C. Each workstation must be upgraded to a 32-bit network client before the users can use system polices.

   D. These workstations can use system policies without changes.

12. What would be the result of implementing system policies and not enabling user profiles on each of the target workstations?

    A. None of the system policy will be implemented at the workstation.

    B. Only their user settings will be written to the Registry of the workstation.

    C. Only the computer-specific settings will be written to the Registry of the workstation.

    D. The system policy will be downloaded and written to the Registry as normal. User profiles need only be enabled for use with user profiles and mandatory user profiles.

13. Which of the following files may be edited with a text editor to define system polices?

    A. SYSTEM.DAT

    B. USER.DAT

    C. CONFIG.POL

    D. ADMIN.ADM

14. Jack asks you to define the System Policy Editor and tell why it is useful. Name two System Policy Editor features that help you administer Windows 95 workstations.

    A. It enables you to edit the Registry without using the Registry Editor.

    B. It enables you to set default settings on a user's group or user's computer using a template file.

    C. It enables you to edit the Registry with the Registry Editor.

    D. It enables you to set only user-related settings.

15. You have implemented system policies on your network; however, a number of computers do not reflect the policy settings that you have instituted. Which best describes the reason that the computers in question do not reflect the changes?

    A. User profiles are not enabled on the computers.

    B. The computers have not been restarted since the policy file was instituted.

    C. The users of the computers already have a user profile defined.

    D. The system policy was already in effect on those computers.

16. A user logs on while the server that contains the user's profile is offline. The user continues to log on and make changes to the user profile contained on the local workstation. Later that afternoon, the server is brought back online and the user logs off and back on. After logging on, which user profile will be used on the local workstation?

    A. The default profile contained on the local workstation.

    B. The user profile contained on the server.

    C. The user profile on the local workstation will be loaded and, upon logging off, the profile information on the server will then be updated to reflect the changes made to the workstation.

    D. The user will log on using the most current user profile.

17. You have implemented user profiles on your server, but your server has had a hard disk failure, causing your backup of the user profile files to be unreadable. You are unable to restore the user profiles of the users on your network. What is the best way to recover the user profiles?

    A. You must re-create user profiles and put them in place for the users.

B. You should create a generic user profile and backdate the files to when your users log on. Their local user profile information will be copied to the server at logoff.

C. You decide to copy local copies of your users' profiles from their workstations to the server.

D. You must use the default profile.

18. Similar to configuring user profiles, to use system policies your workstation must have _______ for policy settings to be established.

A. User profiles enabled

B. A computer account on the domain

C. Local user profiles

D. User-level security

19. The Windows 95 System Policy Editor can be opened in one of two modes. Select the modes that apply.

A. User mode

B. Policy File mode

C. Computer mode

D. Registry mode

20. Kim wants to install the Policy Editor on several machines. On which directory on the Windows 95 CD can the System Policy Editor be found?

A. \ADMIN\NETTOOLS\POLEDIT directory

B. \ADMIN\APPTOOLS\POLEDIT directory

C. \ADMIN\APPTOOLS\SYSEDIT directory

D. \ADMIN\TOOLS\POLEDIT directory

4.3.7 Answers and Explanations

1. **A** Selecting Disable MS-DOS Prompt prevents access to the MS-DOS prompt.

2. **C** System policies will automatically edit the Registry on the computers that process the policy.

3. **A** System policies both automatically configure an environment for users and prevent them from customizing many of the components of their environment.

4. **C** User profiles will allow users to maintain their personal settings, such as wallpaper settings, as well as maintaining custom Start menu settings.

5. **A** User profiles are stored in the user's home directory on Windows NT networks.

6. **B** Windows 95 checks the date stamp on the user profile and treats all profiles that were created in the future as invalid, and ignores them.

7. **B** Keeping the files separate allows for an easier implementation of user profiles (just replacing the USER.DAT file) and system policies.

8. **D** USER.DAT is the component of the Registry that contains user information.

9. **C** In Windows NT, a user's profile is pulled from his home directory. The .man extension prevents changes from being written to his profile.

10. **D** In NetWare, a user's profile is pulled from his mail user_id directory.

11. **C** System policies require the 32-bit network client.

12. **C** User profiles must be enabled on the workstation for user- and group-specific policies to be downloaded to the Registry.

13. **D** ADMIN.ADM is a text file. All others must be edited with the Policy Editor or the Registry Editor.

14. **A, B** Using the Register Editor is always a last resort to changing a system's settings. Default settings on a group of users' computers will make administration easier because they represent a consistent environment.

15. **B** The user must at least log off and log back on for the policies to be downloaded and enforced.

16. **C** The date and time on the workstation were more current, so that profile was used. When logging off, the workstation profile overwrote the information on the server.

17. **B** Creating this backdated profile will enable the profile on the user's workstation to overwrite the profile on the server.

18. **A** Profiles must be manually turned on.

19. **B, D** Both modes are possible ways of opening the System Policy Editor.

20. **B** \ADMIN\APPTOOLS\POLEDIT directory contains the file to set up the System Policy Editor.

4.3.8 Key Terms and Definitions

Dial-Up Networking A service used for remote access to network services such as File and Printer Sharing, electronic mail, scheduling, and SQL database access.

Long filenames Windows 95 allows up to 255 characters in a filename, and 258 characters maximum for both the path and the filename.

Registry A database in which Windows 95 stores configuration information for hardware and software. The Registry in Windows 95 is stored in two files, USER.DAT and SYSTEM.DAT.

Simple Mail Transfer Protocol (SMTP) An ASCII message format commonly used for mail sent on the Internet.

System policies Files used to control a user's environment and restrict privileges based on users, groups, or computers.

System Policy Editor Use the System Policy Editor to create system policy users, groups of users, and computers.

SYSTEM.DAT One of two files that make up the Registry. This is the Registry file that contains the hardware- and computer-specific settings for a workstation. By default, this file is located in the Windows SYSTEM directory. SYSTEM.DAT contains machine-specific data.

User profile A profile that enables users to keep personalized settings on a computer. If the computer is used by multiple users, each user can have her own settings.

USER.DAT The file that contains user configuration settings used to implement user profiles either locally or on a network. This is one of the two files of the Registry.

4.4   Back Up Data and Restore Data

Windows 95 includes a Backup utility that enables users to make a copy of the data on their hard drives and store it on alternative media. If you have installed the Backup utility, it will be located in the Start menu under Programs, Accessories, System Tools, Backup (see Figure 4.11).

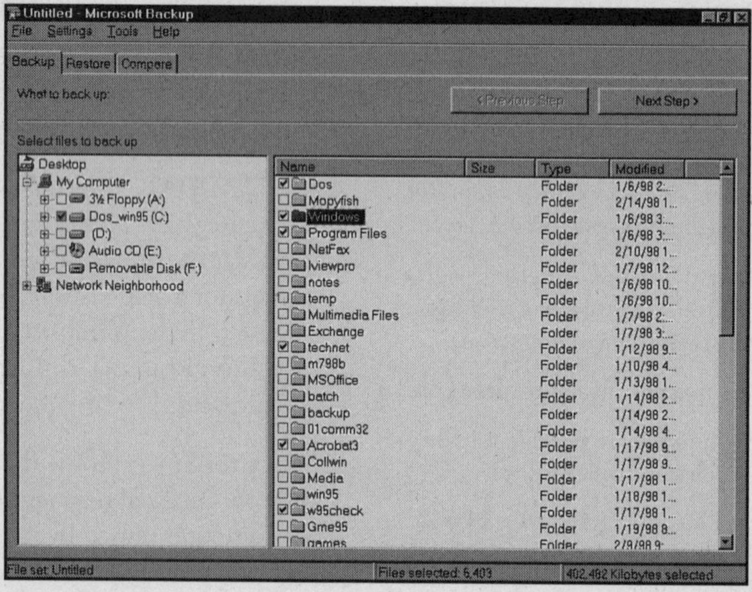

Figure 4.11   The Backup utility provided with Windows 95 is capable of maintaining complete backups of your system.

4.4.1   Learning the Different Backup Destinations

The Windows 95 Backup program supports four backup methods:

- Back up to a tape drive

- Back up to floppy disks

- Back up to hard drive

- Back up to a network location

Back Up to Tape

The capability to back up to a tape drive is new to the Windows 95 version of Backup. The type of tape media that is supported is called Quarter-Inch Cartridge (QIC) and it comes in various specifications. The supported tape-drive specifications are as follows:

- QIC 40, QIC 80, and QIC 3010 tape drives connected through the primary floppy disk controller.

- QIC 40, QIC 80, and QIC 3010 tape drives connected to a parallel port.

> SCSI tape backup units are not supported by Windows 95 Backup.

Windows 95 should be able to detect any supported tape drives automatically. If it cannot detect the tape drive, a message appears upon starting Backup, and a number of troubleshooting suggestions are listed.

Back Up to Floppy Disks

Floppy disks are the standard backup destination for both the MS-DOS and Windows 3.1 versions of Backup. Files are transferred from the local hard drive to a number of floppy disks.

Back Up to Hard Drive

If you have a second hard drive in your computer, a folder on this drive can be a backup destination. The destination could be on the same drive, but this does not give you any safety if the drive seizes or becomes corrupted. This method also eliminates the need for dozens of floppy disks.

Back Up to a Network Location

This backup destination enables the user to back up files to a remote location on the network. Backing up to a remote network location can be useful if, for example, a network administrator wants all users to back up their files to one central location on the network to simplify the administrator's management tasks. If you are going to use a network location, ensure that you have received permission from your network administrator.

4.4.2   Learning the Backup Types

Files can be backed up in two ways: by a full backup and by an incremental backup. In a full backup scenario, all selected files are backed up. An incremental backup copies only those files that have changed since the last backup (full or incremental). Files required to be backed up are determined by the time/date stamp on the file.

An example of a full backup is your complete hard disk, including the operating system. An incremental backup would back up only files with the archive bit turned on.

4.4.3   Learning the Backup Sets and File Sets

A backup set is a collection of files that have been backed up. A backup set is created during each backup procedure and contains not only the actual files, but also the parameters that were set for the backup (for example, which file types to include in the backup). A file set is a list of files you want to back up. You can save file sets so that you don't have to reselect the files for backup every time you perform the backup.

4.4.4   Other Features of Windows 95 Backup

Windows 95 Backup contains a number of additional features, including the following:

- It is possible to perform a comparison between a backup set and the directories from which it was backed up to determine any differences between the two.

- LFNs are fully supported.

- It is possible to drag and drop backup sets onto a Backup icon to restore the set, or to double-click the Backup Set icon to start the backup procedure.

- During a full system backup, Windows 95 also backs up the Registry by copying it to a temporary file. When the backup set is restored, the Registry files are merged back into the existing Registry.

- Backup allows the filtering of file types for inclusion or exclusion from a file set.

> MS-DOS 6.2 and Windows 3.1 backup sets cannot be restored using the Windows 95 Backup utility, due to incompatibility issues with LFNs in MS-DOS 6.2 and earlier.

4.4.5   Restoring Files from Backup

To restore files on your computer, you first launch the backup application. Choose the Restore tab, and locate your backup file (*.QIC). The Next Step button brings you to a screen that enables you to select the individual files you want to restore. To select a file or folder to restore, place a check mark in front of the file or folder. To start the restore procedure, press the Start Restore button.

4.4.6   Exercises

Exercise 1: Using the Windows 95 Backup Utility

This exercise demonstrates the use of the Windows 95 Backup utility. Please ensure that you have at least 6MB of free space on your C: drive to complete this exercise.

1. Right-click the My Computer icon and choose Explore. The Exploring window appears.

2. From the list of drives, right-click C: and choose Properties. The Properties sheet for the C: drive appears.

3. Click the Tools tab. From this tab, you can run ScanDisk, Backup, or the Disk Defragmenter.

4. Click on the Backup Now button. The Microsoft Backup screen appears.

5. Click on the plus sign next to the C: drive. The tree expands to show the subdirectories of C:.

6. Click on the plus sign next to the Windows subdirectory. The tree expands to show the subdirectories of Windows.

7. Click on the plus sign next to the Media subdirectory. The tree expands to show the files in the Media subdirectory.

8. Click on the check box next to Media. Note that all the files in the Media subdirectory now are marked for backup.

9. Having selected the files for backup, choose the Next Step button. You are prompted for a backup destination.

10. Click on the A: drive icon. This selects the root of A: as the destination directory.

11. Click on the Start Backup button. You are prompted for a backup set name.

12. Type **TEST** and press Enter. A status screen appears, showing the progress of the backup.

13. Click OK when the backup is complete. You are returned to the main Backup window.

14. Click on the Restore tab. You are prompted to select a backup set to restore.

15. Click on the icon for the A: drive. The TEST backup set is displayed in the root of A: .

16. Double-click the TEST backup set. You are prompted to select the files you want to restore.

17. Click three times in the check box next to TEST to select all files in the backup set.

18. Choose Settings, Options. The Settings - Options dialog box appears.

19. Click on the Restore tab, verify that Overwrite Files is selected under Advanced Options, and click OK. You are returned to the main Backup window.

20. Click on the Start Restore button. A status screen shows the progress of the restore procedure.

21. When the restore is complete, double-click OK to return to the main Backup window.

Exercise 2: Restore Files from Backup

This exercise shows the steps necessary to restore files on your computer using Backup.

1. Launch the backup application.

2. Choose the Restore tab.

3. Locate your backup file (.QIC).

4. The Next Step button brings you to a screen that enables you to select the files you want to restore.

5. Place a check mark in front of the file or folder.

6. To start the restore procedure, press the Start Restore button.

The backup utility is located in the Start Menu under Programs, Accessories, System Tools, then Backup.

4.4.7   Practice Problems

1. As system administrator, you draft a purchase order to acquire tape backup devices. Windows 95 supports QIC tape systems, but not universally. Which of the following tape backup systems is not supported by Windows 95?

   A. QIC 3010 through parallel port

   B. QIC 3010 through floppy disk controller

   C. QIC 3010 through SCSI port

   D. QIC 80 through floppy disk controller

2. As the system administrator, you want to protect your users' data and enable for restoration from a central location. How can you accomplish this?

   A. Instruct your users to back up to a predetermined network location.

   B. Ask your users to email their most recent backup sets to you.

   C. Visit all of your users' workstations and back up their drives to floppy disks.

   D. Back up your users' hard drives to CD-ROM.

3. A backup set that includes only files that have changed since the last full backup is called what?

   A. A partial backup

   B. An incremental backup

   C. An incomplete backup

   D. An archive backup

4. Cindy is concerned that she will not be able to reproduce certain data files if she should have a hard drive failure. Which disk-management tool would you recommend to her?

   A. Disk Defragmenter

   B. ScanDisk

   C. DriveSpace

   D. Backup

5. Why can't Windows 95 Backup restore MS-DOS backup sets?

   A. Windows 95 Backup cannot mount MS-DOS drives.

   B. There are incompatibility issues with long filenames in MS-DOS drives.

   C. Windows 95 and MS-DOS use different file allocation tables.

   D. MS-DOS backup sets do not contain the Windows 95 Registry.

6. You find that you often back up the same files each time you run Windows 95 Backup. How can you avoid selecting the individual files each time you run Backup?

   A. Save the list of files in a file set.

   B. Save the list of files in a text file, and specify that text file on Backup's command line.

   C. Run Backup from a batch file.

   D. You must reselect the files each time you run Backup.

7. What information is contained in every backup set, in addition to the files that were backed up?

   A. The patch to the Windows 95 Backup program

   B. The Windows 95 Registry

   C. The parameters that were set for the backup session

   D. The name of the last full backup set

8. Agnes is running Windows 95 Backup. She wants to select an appropriate backup destination. Which of the following can she choose?

   A. Windows NT Server share

   B. Novell NetWare volume

   C. A 1.44MB floppy drive

   D. SCSI tape backup unit

9. Which is *not* a feature of Windows 95 Backup?

   A. LFNs are fully supported.

   B. Backup sets can be compared to source directories to determine differences.

   C. Backup sets can be dragged and dropped onto a Backup icon to perform a restore operation.

   D. Backup sets can be used by MS-DOS 6.2 Backup utility.

10. Lori wants to know what will happen to her Registry files when she restores from a full backup. What do you tell her?

   A. The backup copies of the Registry files will be merged into the existing Registry.

   B. The current Registry files will be overwritten by those from the backup set.

   C. The date/time stamps on the Registry files will be compared, and she will be prompted to select the ones she wants to use.

   D. Nothing will happen to her Registry files.

11. Sean runs incremental backups on his system twice a week. Why would he do this?

   A. He wants to conserve space on his backup media.

   B. He has only floppy disks as backup media.

   C. He does not want to spend time backing up files that have not changed since the last full backup.

   D. He wants to maintain an archive of his personal data.

12. How can a Windows 95 user maximize available disk space?

   A. Run the Disk Defragmenter

   B. Run the DriveSpace utility

   C. Select all BMP files

   D. Create a RAM drive

13. Danny is worried about losing his data files because of hardware failure. What can he do to prevent this?

   A. Run DriveSpace

   B. Run ScanDisk

   C. Run Disk Defragmenter

   D. Run Backup

14. Which of the following contains parameters for a backup session?

   A. Registry set

   B. File set

   C. Backup set

   D. Time/date stamp

15. How does Windows 95 Backup restore the Registry?

   A. It uses filtering to determine which entries should be restored.

   B. It merges the backed up Registry into the existing Registry.

   C. It replaces the existing Registry with the backed up Registry.

   D. It cannot restore the Registry.

4

16. Brandon receives an error message when he tries to back up to his SCSI tape drive. How can you explain this?

    A. SCSI tape backup units are not supported by Windows 95 Backup.

    B. His tape drive must be using the wrong SCSI ID.

    C. He should reinstall Windows 95 backup.

    D. He must first format the tape he intends to use as a backup destination.

17. What is *not* a new feature on Windows 95 Backup?

    A. It is possible to perform a comparison between a backup set and the directories from which it was backed up to in order to determine any differences between the two.

    B. LFNs are not supported.

    C. During a full system backup, Windows 95 also backs up the Registry by copying it to a temporary file.

    D. Backup allows the filtering of file types for inclusion or exclusion from a file set.

18. Ralph is setting up a backup schedule to back up several of his machines. What is the name of the utility included with Windows 95 that Ralph can use to back up his data?

    A. CONFIG.SYS

    B. BACKUP.EXE

    C. BACKUP.SYS

    D. BACKUP.INI

4.4.8 Answers and Explanations

1. **C** QIC 3010 SCSI drives are the only tape drives supported.

2. **A** Backing up to a predetermined network location allows for data protection and restoration from a central location.

3. **B** Incremental backups contain only files that have changed since the last full backup.

4. **D** She should run Backup to make a copy of her files that can be restored if the hard drive fails.

5. **B** Windows 95 Backup is not compatible with the MS-DOS Backup program.

6. **A** A file set is a reusable list of files you want backed up.

7. **C** A backup set contains the parameters in effect for that backup session, as well as the data files that were backed up.

8. **A, B, C** Network locations and floppy disks are valid backup locations. Windows 95 Backup does not support SCSI tape drives.

9. **D** Windows 95 Backup is not compatible with the MS-DOS Backup program.

10. **A** When it restores from a full backup, Windows 95 Backup merges the old Registry files into the existing Registry.

11. **A, C, D** Incremental backups allow for archiving of data files while saving time and conserving backup media space by only backing up files that have changed since the last full backup.

12. **B** The Drive Space utility compresses data on disk, thereby making more space available.

13. **D** Backup will create copies of his data files that can be restored in the event of data loss caused by hardware failure.

14. **C** A backup set contains the parameters in effect for that backup session, as well as the data files that were backed up.

15. **B** When restoring Registry files, Windows 95 Backup merges the old Registry files into the existing Registry.

16. **A** Windows 95 Backup does not support SCSI tape devices.

17. **B** In Windows 95, long filenames are fully supported.

18. **B** BACKUP.EXE is the utility included with Windows 95 that backs up Ralph's data.

4.4.9 Key Terms and Definitions

Backup set A backed-up copy of data files along with the preferences that were set up for that backup session.

Full backup All selected files are backed up.

Incremental backup Only files that have changed since the last backup are copied.

Restore The process of retrieving files from a backup set and copying them back to their original location.

4.5   Managing Hard Disks

This section discusses some of the basic items that you can use to manage your hard disks. This section specifically covers the following:

- Disk compression

- Partitioning

- Long filenames

These topics cover disk management, not disk maintenance. Disk management pertains to ScanDisk and Disk Defragmenter. Disk management concerns are with how files are stored on the disk.

4.5.1   Disk Compression

Windows 95 implements a form of disk compression known as on-the-fly compression. On-the-fly compression is so named because the compression/decompression process occurs automatically in the background and is transparent to the user. On-the-fly compression is the process of intercepting normal MS-DOS read/write calls and compressing the data before writing it to the hard disk.

Disk compression, as implemented in Windows 95 (and in the versions released with MS-DOS 6.*x*), consists of two processes. The first, called *token conversion*, replaces repetitive patterns that occur in a given piece of data with a token, which takes up less space.

The second, called *sector allocation granularity*, involves changing the way data is stored on a hard drive by circumventing the often large amounts of wasted space created under a normal FAT file system.

DoubleSpace and DriveSpace Structure

The first time Microsoft included disk compression with MS-DOS was in version 6.0. Microsoft called their disk compression DoubleSpace. It was later re-released as DriveSpace in version 6.2 of MS-DOS, with some changes to the compression routines and with a new feature: the capability to uncompress a drive.

After disk compression is installed and the files are initially compressed, the files are stored in the compressed volume file (CVF), which is actually a large hidden file that sits on the physical C: drive. When the system boots up, however, the CVF is assigned the drive letter *C*. The physical C: drive, which now contains only a few files because everything else is in a compressed state inside the CVF, is assigned a higher drive letter, typically *H*. This higher-lettered drive is called a host drive and, by default, is hidden from normal view. The process of switching the drive letters and making the CVF available for viewing in MS-DOS and Windows is called *mounting*.

Advantages of Windows 95 Disk Compression

The main advantages to using Windows 95 disk compression are as follows:

- Disk compression is implemented with 32-bit code for better performance.

- It does not use any conventional memory.

- It is integrated with the operating system for ease of use and better performance.

> When a floppy is compressed, the DriveSpace drivers load only when the floppy disk is in the drive. In general, the DriveSpace drivers load only when compressed media (hard drive or floppy disk) is detected.

Further Notes on Windows 95 Disk Compression

The following information should be noted whenever a user is considering Windows 95 disk compression:

- Windows 95 is compatible with many third-party compression software programs such as Stacker versions 2.*x*, 3.*x*, and 4.*x*, and with all versions of SuperStor, another disk compression utility.

- The maximum size of a compressed volume is 512MB when using DriveSpace 2.0, which comes with Windows 95. If you use Microsoft Plus! or have Windows 95 OSR2, which includes DriveSpace 3.0, the maximum size of a compressed volume is 2GB. This size refers to the compressed size.

- The average compression ratio of a compressed volume is 2:1 (using DriveSpace 2.0, which comes with Windows 95). If you use Microsoft Plus! or OSR2, you can take advantage of DriveSpace 3.0; this improves the average compression ratio to approximately 2.4:1.

4.5.2 Partitioning

The Windows 95 partitioning utility is FDISK.EXE, as shown in Figure 4.12.

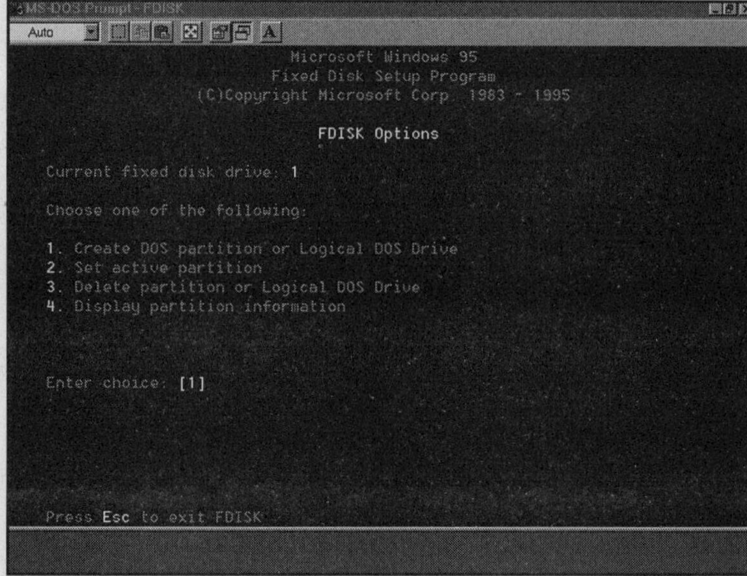

Figure 4.12 The partitioning utility creates and deletes partitions.

The Windows 95 partitioning utility, FDISK.EXE, is used to create and delete partitions. With drives over 540MB with OSR2, you have the option of enabling Large Drive Support. This will enable you to have partitions larger than 512MB formatted with FAT32. Table 4.2 details the differences between FAT16 and FAT32.

Table 4.2   Comparison Between FAT16 and FAT32

Description	FAT16	FAT32
Maximum partition size	2GB	2TB
Cluster size on a 2GB partition	32KB	4KB
Support for DriveSpace compression	Yes	No

> In addition to these differences, once installed, the only operating system that can read FAT32 partitions is Windows 95 OSR2. The only way to remove a FAT32 partition is to delete it and create a new partition.

FDISK knows how to identify primary partitions that are FAT16, FAT32, and OS/2's HPFS. FDISK will identify NTFS partitions as HPFS. Windows 95 cannot read information off either NTFS or HPFS partitions. You will be able to delete either of these partitions (NTFS or HPFS) by choosing option 3—Delete Partition or Logical Drive—from the FDISK main menu, and then choosing to delete the non-DOS partition.

4.5.3   Understanding File System Support

This section looks at the Installable File System architecture.

With the Windows 95 modular design, generic features of Windows 95 subsystems such as networking, printing, and communications are implemented into a universal component (for example, the Universal Printer Driver). Functions specific to a type or brand of hardware/software are implemented in a type-specific driver.

Microsoft also uses a modular architecture for the Windows 95 file systems; all I/O requests are first handled by a universal file system manager.

> The Windows 95 file systems are known as *installable* file systems because they can be loaded into and removed from the system memory as needed.

File operations are handled by the Installable File System (IFS) components of Windows 95. These components include the following:

- IFS Manager
- File system drivers
- I/O Supervisor

- Volume Tracker

- Type-specific drivers

- Port drivers

IFS Manager

The IFS Manager is responsible for analyzing incoming I/O requests from applications and other processes and determining which file system driver can fulfill requests most effectively. The important thing to note is that the file system driver does not need to know how to communicate with applications or other processes directly; it only needs to know how to communicate with the IFS Manager.

File System Drivers

The file system drivers enable I/O requests to be sent to and from the installed file systems. Windows 95 includes support for the following file systems:

- 32-bit Virtual-FAT (VFAT)

- 32-bit CD-ROM file system (CDFS)

- 32-bit network redirectors

- 16-bit FAT

The VFAT file system driver (FSD) is the primary FSD for the system and cannot be disabled. It is responsible for all local hard disk I/O requests (including SCSI). This FSD gives Windows 95 a fully 32-bit virtualized MS-DOS FAT file system. Like all FSDs, VFAT supports long filenames.

> **VFAT is used only for hard drives that have the 32-bit disk access components installed. If a drive is accessed through real-mode drivers, the drive is accessed through MS-DOS Compatibility mode and will not take advantage of the 32-bit VFAT.**

In the case of SCSI drives, after the TSD for hard drives determines that a given I/O request is intended for a SCSI drive, a number of sublayers come into play. The TSD passes the request to one of two SCSI translators: for hard drives or for CD-ROM drives. The translator is responsible for translating generic I/O commands into commands that the SCSI bus can understand—these are known as *SCSI Command Descriptor Blocks*.

Because data on a CD-ROM is stored and accessed in a different way than data on a hard drive, a separate FSD for CD-ROM file access is required. CDFS passes on the CD-ROM I/O request to a specific device driver based on one of four possible CD-ROM configurations:

- IDE CD-ROM.

- SCSI CD-ROM.

- Proprietary CD-ROM controller.

- Real-mode CD-ROM drivers specified in CONFIG.SYS or AUTOEXEC.BAT. All CD-ROM drives that do not fall in the preceding categories are supported using MS-DOS–based drivers specified in CONFIG.SYS or AUTOEXEC.BAT. The CD-ROM drive is said to be operating in MS-DOS Compatibility mode.

> **Any hard drive or CD-ROM drive running in MS-DOS Compatibility mode cannot take advantage of protected-mode caching. The MS-DOS disk cache, SmartDrive, must be used instead.**

Windows 95 includes support for the 16-bit FAT file system, which was used in MS-DOS and Windows 3.1. These operating systems used 16-bit, real-mode code to manage the 16-bit FAT. Under Windows 95, protected-mode drivers can be used to access the 16-bit FAT.

I/O Supervisor

The I/O Supervisor is responsible for overseeing all local I/O requests (as opposed to network-based requests). When the IFS Manager has determined that a given I/O request can be fulfilled on the local computer, it passes on the request to the I/O Supervisor.

Volume Tracker

The Volume Tracker component is responsible for identifying and monitoring removable media, such as CD-ROMs, floppy disks, and removable hard drives. It must ensure that the correct type of media is present and that the media is not removed or inserted at the wrong time.

Type-Specific Drivers

Type-specific drivers (TSDs) are drivers intermediate to the I/O Supervisor and the physical device drivers (port drivers) that communicate with the hardware. TSDs are responsible for all functions associated with a particular type of hardware, such as CD-ROMs, floppy drives, or hard disks.

Port Drivers

Port drivers, the last in the chain of command, are responsible for translating logical I/O requests (for example, "Put this data on the CD-ROM") into physical requests (for example, "Put these bytes on track 9, section 5 of the CD-ROM").

4.5.4   Long Filenames

Windows 95 supports long filenames. You should also be aware of the following in relation to long filenames:

- Rules for the construction of long and short filenames

- Long filename data structure

- Issues with long filenames

- Adding long filename support for Novell NetWare

Windows 95 has built-in support for descriptive filenames up to 255 characters, including blank spaces. The path for a file may have up to a total of 260 characters. If both the path and the filename are specified, however, the total is still only 260 characters. To remain backward-compatible with Windows 3.1 and DOS applications, however, Windows 95 also automatically generates an 8.3 format short filename (known as the *alias*) for each LFN. The algorithm for the autogeneration of this short filename is as follows:

1. Remove any characters illegal in an MS-DOS filename, such as spaces.

2. For the eight-character name, take the first six remaining characters of the LFN and add a tilde character (~) and an incremental number beginning with 1.

> **The number is added to ensure unique short filenames. It is possible, for example, that two files named November Sales Forecast and November Marketing Report would both auto-generate the character name Novemb~. To differentiate them, one would be named Novemb~1; the other would be named Novemb~2. If more than nine similar files exist, the first five characters are used, then a tilde (~), and then a two-digit number.**

3. To create the three-character extension, take the first three remaining characters after the last period. If the long filename contains no period, the extension is omitted.

> **Long filenames preserve the case of characters, but are not case sensitive. When you copy long filenames to floppy disks, they are preserved. Also, 8.3 filenames are not case sensitive and they do not preserve the case of characters.**

Table 4.3 shows how sample long filenames convert to short filenames. Each of the files shown in the table are assumed to be saved to the same folder and created in the order shown.

Table 4.3   Converted Long Filenames to Short Filenames

Long Filename	Converted Short Filename
Fiscal Report Quarter 1.XLS	FISCAL~1.XLS
Fiscal Report Quarter 2.XLS	FISCAL~2.XLS
Fiscal Report Quarter 4.XLS	FISCAL~3.XLS
Employee Benefits 1997.DOC	EMPLOY~1.DOC
Employee Benefits 1998.DOC	EMPLOY~2.DOC
Taxes.Mdb	TAXES.MDB

Rules for the Construction of Long and Short Filenames

The following rules are applied when creating a long filename and when generating a short filename alias:

- The symbols \ / : * ? " < > | are illegal in both long and short filenames.

- The symbols + , ; = [ ] are permitted in a long filename, but not in a short filename alias.

- Lowercase characters in a long filename are converted to uppercase in a short filename alias.

Long Filename Data Structure

In a standard FAT-based operating system, the root directory of a hard disk can contain a maximum of 512 directory entries. Under MS-DOS, each file or subdirectory typically takes up an entry. In the case of long filenames, however, each requires a minimum of two directory entries: one for the alias and one for every 13 characters of the long filename.

> **This requirement for additional directory entries is especially important to remember when dealing with LFNs in the root directory because the MS-DOS limit of 512 entries in the root directory still applies.**

Issues with Long Filenames

Long filename issues to keep in mind include the following:

- LFNs are active only when Windows 95 is running. LFNs are not visible when Command Prompt Only is selected from the Boot menu (however, LFNs are visible from a DOS prompt inside Windows 95).

- When specifying LFNs with embedded spaces, it is necessary to enclose the name in double quotation marks, such as "MARKETING BUDGET WORKSHEET".

- If you do not add an extension to a file when you create it, the application you are using may automatically add an extension to the file. Filenames enclosed with double quotation marks will not usually have the extension added.

- Windows 95 can read LFNs from an NTFS volume, but only at a remote location (across a network).

- Windows 95 can read LFNs from a NetWare server, but only at a remote location (across a network). The NetWare server needs to be running OS/2 Name Space to store LFNs using HPFS rules (not Windows rules) for the naming of the 8.3 alias.

Adding Long Filename Support for Novell NetWare

When you run Windows 95 on a Novell NetWare volume, you must install a module called OS2.NAM (the OS/2 Name Space feature) to activate long filenames. NetWare does not support long filenames by itself. To install the OS/2 Name Space feature, type the following at the file server console:

```
LOAD OS/2
ADD NAME SPACE OS/2 TO VOLUME volume_name
```

In the preceding command, the `volume_name` parameter should be replaced by the name of the volume on which you want Name Space to be added. You also need to add the following to the STARTUP.NCF configuration file:

```
LOAD OS/2
```

> Novell NetWare 3.1*x*, 4.0, and 4.1 use OS/2 name space for the support of long filenames, which only actually supports 254 characters. With the introduction of IntranetWare 4.11, the name of the support file is now LONG.NLM. It supports filenames up to 255 characters in length.

4.5.5   Exercises

Exercise 1: Creating and Using Long Filenames

This exercise illustrates the creation and use of long filenames in Windows 95. Perform the following steps:

1. Choose Start, Programs, MS-DOS Prompt. A DOS window appears.

2. Type **C:** and press Enter to switch to the C: drive.

3. Type **CD ** and press Enter to switch to the root of the C: drive.

4. Type **MD\LFNTEMP** and press Enter. A directory called LFNTEMP is created.

5. Type **CD\LFNTEMP** and press Enter. The current directory changes to LFNTEMP.

6. Type **DIR > "Directory Listing"** and press Enter to save the directory listing to a file. You are returned to a command prompt (note the quotation marks around the filename).

7. Type **DIR** and press Enter. Note that the alias for the file that was created is listed on the left, whereas the LFN is on the right.

8. Type **DIR > "Directory Listing 2"** and press Enter. You are returned to a command prompt.

9. Type **DIR** and press Enter. Note how the alias has been auto-numbered sequentially, and yet the full name is preserved on the right.

10. Type **DIR >*DIRLIST** and press Enter. You receive a `File creation error` message because the * is illegal.

11. Shut down Windows 95. You are in MS-DOS mode (no LFN support).

12. Type **CD\LFNTEMP** and press Enter. The current directory changes to LFNTEMP.

13. Type **DIR** and press Enter. Note that LFNs no longer are displayed in the directory.

14. Type **COPY DIRECT~1 C:** and press Enter. The file that was created earlier is copied to the root of C:.

15. Restart Windows 95 by typing **EXIT** and pressing Enter.

16. When Windows 95 is open, open a DOS window and type **CD** and press Enter. Then type **DIR** and press Enter. Note that the file that was copied to the root no longer has an LFN associated with it (only the alias remains).

Exercise 2: Using Windows 95 Disk Compression

This exercise illustrates how disk compression can be used in Windows 95. Note that due to the considerable amount of time involved in compressing an entire hard drive, the exercise focuses on compressing a floppy disk. This exercise requires a formatted floppy disk with at least 512KB of free space.

1. Choose Start, Programs, Accessories, System Tools, and then click DriveSpace. The DriveSpace menu appears.

2. Select the A: drive and choose Drive, Compress. A window appears, showing the free/used space before and after compression (estimated).

3. Choose the Start button. The drive is checked for errors, and a status bar shows the progress of the compression procedure.

4. When the procedure is complete, choose Close. You are returned to the main DriveSpace window. (Note that the A: drive now shows as compressed, and there is now a host H: drive for the A: drive.)

4.5.6   Practice Problems

1. Third-party developers can create file systems that extend the capabilities of Windows 95. A key feature of Windows 95 that will allow this and will let Windows 95 adapt easily to future technological developments is its ________.

   A. Preemptive multitasking

   B. VCACHE cache subsystem

   C. Modular design

   D. Peer-to-peer networking support

2. You are responsible for teaching users about the Windows 95 Installable File System (IFS). You create a diagram to display the different components of it. Which three of the following are components of the IFS?

   A. I/O Supervisor

   B. VFAT file system driver

   C. TSD Supervisor

   D. CDFS file system driver

3. On a diagram showing the IFS, you point out the role for each of the components. One of these components is responsible for the insertion and removal of media. Which one?

   A. Drive Controller

   B. IFS Manager

   C. System Driver Supervisor

   D. Volume Tracker

4. Jennifer is using an older version of Windows and wants to know whether she can use an older CD-ROM drive with Windows 95. You tell her yes. However, you tell her that a drive that is accessed through ________ cannot take advantage of the 32-bit VFAT.

   A. Protected-mode drivers

   B. Real-mode drivers

   C. Virtual device drivers

   D. Network redirector file system drivers

5. VCACHE is an upgrade to SmartDrive and is used for read-ahead and lazy-write (or write-behind) caching. VCACHE is used by all Windows 95 file system drivers except ________ file system drivers.

   A. CDFS

   B. VFAT

   C. Network redirector

   D. SCSI

6. Betsy saves her files under Windows 95 in long filename format. She asks you to explain how Windows 95 will save the file as a short filename. You tell her, for example, that the autogenerated alias for the long filename "The Departmental Budget.wks" is ________.

   A. THEDEPAR.~1

   B. THEDEP~1.WKS

   C. THEDEP~1

   D. BUDGET~1.WKS

7. A client asks how he can fit more data on his existing hard drive without adding another hard drive or storing files on a network. What Windows 95 disk utility should he use to compress the data on his hard drive?

   A. DoubleSpace

   B. DriveSpace

   C. Disk Defragmenter

   D. ScanDisk

8. When John runs Disk Compression under Windows 95, he calls asking you how files are compressed. You tell him which two of the following are ways in which disk compression maximizes disk space?

   A. Cluster conversion

   B. Token conversion

    C.   ASCII collapse

    D.   Sector allocation conversion

9. Your company runs Windows 95 with a NetWare server, but you experience problems with the long filename support. A help desk administrator tells you to install a specific feature under NetWare to enable long filename support. What is this feature?

    A.   Install OS/2 on the server.

    B.   Run an NLM released by Microsoft.

    C.   Install OS/2 Name Space.

    D.   NetWare cannot support Windows 95 long filenames.

10. Susie creates a file named Budget For Department. She wants to rename the file to Budget For Marketing Team. Which of the following commands can she use at the command prompt and retain the long filename?

    A.   Type **RENAME Budget For Department TO Budget For Marketing Team**.

    B.   Type **RENAME Budget For Department Budget For Marketing Team**.

    C.   Type **REN Budget For Department Budget For Marketing Team**.

    D.   Type **RENAME "Budget For Department" "Budget For Marketing Team"**.

11. You are assigned a new department to administer. This department has a mixture of computers, including many MS-DOS and Windows 3.1 computers and some Windows 95 computers. Because this department shares files a great deal and the file naming conventions must remain consistent, you instruct your Windows 95 users to use short filenames at all times. To guarantee that these users do not create LFNs, you disable this feature using which Registry change? You make this change in the `HKEY_LOCAL_MACHINE\System\CurrentControlSet\control\FileSystem`.

    A.   Set the Registry value `LongFileNames=` to `01`.

    B.   Set the Registry value `Win31FileSystem=` to `01`.

    C.   Set the Registry value `Win31FileSystem=` to `Yes`

    D.   Set the Registry value `ShortFileNames=` to `Yes`.

    E.   None of the above. This cannot be done with Windows 95.

12. You receive a help desk call from a Windows 95 user who cannot save his file to the hard disk. He is trying to save the file with the name "Invoices>$200 Dollars.XLS". What could be causing the trouble?

    A.   A read-only filename INVOIC~1.XLS is on the hard disk.

    B.   The > character is an illegal character in a filename.

    C.   The $ character is an illegal character in a filename.

    D.   Spaces are not allowed in long filenames.

13. Joyce has created a file called Data.June.Sales.DOC. What will the auto-generated 8.3 format short filename be?

    A.   DATA.JU~1.DOC

    B.   DATAJU~1.SAL

    C.   DATAJU~1.DOC

    D.   DATAJU~1.NES

14. How many directory entries are used by the file named "This is a very long file name. DOC"?

    A. 33

    B. 4

    C. 2

    D. 3

15. The 8.3 format short filename that Windows 95 autogenerates for a file with a long filename is known as what?

    A. Synonym

    B. Algorithm

    C. Alias

    D. Name space

16. Windows 95 implements which form of disk compression?

    A. On-the-fly compression

    B. Read/write compression

    C. Token conversion

    D. LIZ compression

17. Rhone wants to compress his 1.5GB hard drive into one compressed volume. Which of the following should he use?

    A. DriveSpace 2.0

    B. DriveSpace 3.0

    C. DoubleSpace

    D. Stacker

18. Which is *not* a benefit of DriveSpace compression?

    A. DriveSpace is integrated into the operating system.

    B. DriveSpace uses no conventional memory.

    C. DriveSpace uses all 32-bit code.

    D. DriveSpace drivers stay loaded at all times.

19. Karen uses DriveSpace 2.0 to compress her hard disk. She wants to know where her files have been stored. What do you tell her?

    A. They are stored in a hidden file called a compressed volume file (CVF).

    B. They have been moved to another disk, called a CFI disk.

    C. They have been moved to H: drive.

    D. They have been replaced by tokens.

20. What is the maximum size of a compressed volume using DriveSpace 2.0?

    A. 2.0GB

    B. 512KB

    C. 512MB

    D. 1.44MB

4.5.7 Answers and Explanations

1. **C** Windows 95 is extensible because it is modular.

2. **A, B, D** The TSD Supervisor is not part of the IFS.

3. **D** The Volume Tracker tracks removable media.

4. **B** Only 32-bit, protected-mode drivers can take advantage of the 32-bit VFAT.

5. **A** CDFS maintains a separate cache to increase the performance of the CD-ROM.

6. **B** Windows 95 uses the first six valid characters, adds a tilde (~) and a number, and then applies the extension for the file.

7. **B** DriveSpace is the compression program included in Windows 95.

8. **B, D**   Token conversion and sector allocation conversion are the two ways that space is saved.

9. **C**   Installing OS/2 name space enables you to store filenames up to 254 characters in length.

10. **D**   When working with long filenames from the command prompt, place the full path for a file inside quotation marks.

11. **E**   Even though the Registry exists, this feature does not work.

12. **B**   The > character is illegal in both long and short filenames.

13. **C**   Only one period is permitted in 8.3 format filenames. The extension for an autogenerated alias will be the first three characters after the last period in the long filename. All other periods in the long filename are stripped out.

14. **B**   There are 33 characters in the filename. The file will require one entry for the characters 1 through 13, one entry for characters 14 through 26, one entry for characters 27 through 33, and one entry for the alias—for a total of four directory entries.

15. **C**   An alias is another name for a file with a long filename. Windows 95 autogenerates aliases in 8.3 format for compatibility with applications that do not support long filenames.

16. **A**   DriveSpace performs compression on-the-fly, transparently and in the background.

17. **B**   The maximum size of a compressed volume with DriveSpace 2.0 is 512MB. Included with Microsoft Plus! is DriveSpace 3.0. DriveSpace 3.0 can compress volumes up to 2GB.

18. **D**   DriveSpace drivers are loaded only when compressed media is detected and mounted.

19. **A**   A CVF is a single file that contains the data files that have been compressed by DriveSpace.

20. **C**   Under DriveSpace 2.0, a compressed drive cannot exceed 512MB. With DriveSpace 3.0, the maximum size of a compressed volume is 2GB.

4.5.8   Key Terms and Definitions

Compressed volume file (CVF)   The CVF contains the contents of a compressed drive.

DriveSpace   Compresses the data on the computer's hard disk to make more space on the disk.

FAT32   The file system provided by OEMs through the OSR2 release of Windows 95. Accessible only through Windows 95 OSR2.

FDISK   A utility used to create and delete partitions, mark drives as active, and retrieve disk configuration information.

File system drivers (FSD)   Enable I/O requests to be sent to and from installed file systems.

IFS Manager   The IFS Manager is responsible for analyzing incoming I/O requests from applications and other processors and determining which file system driver can fulfill requests more effectively.

Installable File System (IFS)   A file system with which the operating system may work.

On-the-fly disk compression   The process of disk compression which replaces repetitive patterns that in a given piece of data with a token take up less space.

Sector allocation granularity   This process of disk compression involves changing the way data is stored on a hard drive by circumventing the often large amounts of wasted space created under a normal FAT file system.

4.6 Establishing Application Environments for Microsoft MS-DOS Applications

This section reviews the following topics:

- Virtual Memory Manager
- Processor pings
- Virtual machines
- Configuring MS-DOS PIFs

4.6.1 Virtual Memory Manager

Windows 95 uses two types of memory: physical and virtual memory. Most users are familiar with the amount of RAM, or physical memory, on the computer itself. The minimum requirement for RAM on a computer running Windows 95 is 4MB. The recommended amount of RAM is at least 8MB. You can overcome hardware memory limitations through the use of virtual memory.

The Windows 95 operating system uses a flat memory model, which leverages off the Intel 386 or greater processor's capability to handle 32-bit addresses. This flat memory model provides a logical address space range of up to 4GB. Virtual memory bridges the gap between physical memory and logical memory.

The 4GB of addressable space used as virtual memory under the flat memory model is implemented through the use of RAM and a swap file. The Windows 95 operating system performs memory management, called demand paging, whereby code and data are moved in 4KB pages between physical memory and the temporary Windows 95 swap file on the hard drive. The Virtual Memory Manager controls paging and maintains a page table. The page table tells which pages are swapped to the hard drive, which remain in RAM, and to which system process or application they belong.

Both 32-bit Windows and MS-DOS–based programs are allocated private virtual memory address space. All 16-bit Windows-based programs share a single, common virtual memory address space. Figure 4.13 shows how Windows 95 allocates the 4GB of virtual memory to each address space. Each process is allocated a unique virtual address space of 4GB. The upper 2GB is shared with the system, whereas the lower 2GB is private to the application.

The virtual memory is allocated as follows:

- **0–640KB.** If not used for a virtual DOS machine (VDM), this memory is made available for any real-mode device drivers and terminate-and-stay-resident (TSR) programs.

- **0–1MB.** In a VDM, this memory range is allocated for the execution of MS-DOS programs. If 16-bit Windows applications are run, then they run in this space in the system VM.

- **1–4MB.** Normally, this memory range is unused. Windows 95 does not use this space, nor do Windows 32-bit applications. If this memory is needed by 16-bit Windows applications, it is available.

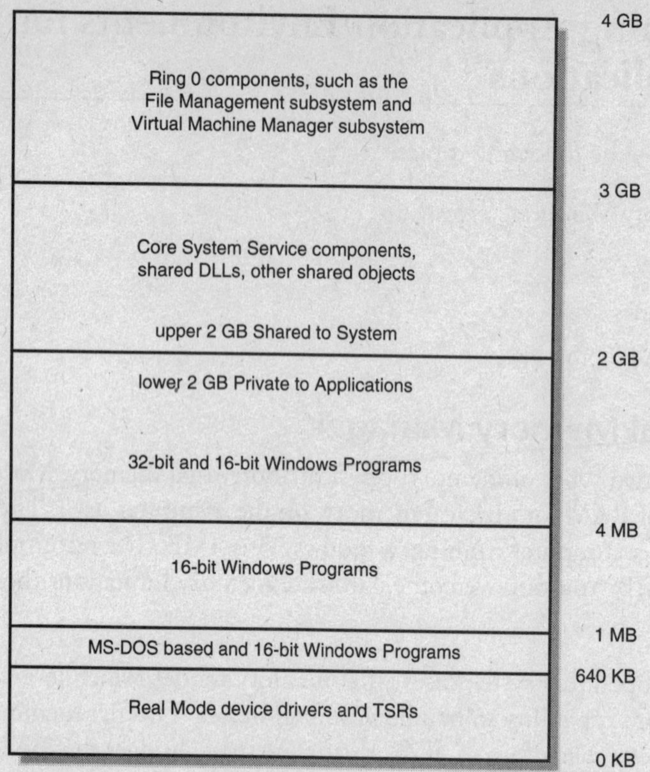

Figure 4.13   Virtual memory address space allocation.

- **2MB–2GB.** This memory range is allocated for use by 32-bit Windows applications and some 16-bit Windows applications. Each Windows 32-bit application has its own address space, whereas Windows 16-bit applications all share a common address space.

- **2GB–3GB.** This memory range is allocated to run all Core System Service components, shared DLLs, and other shared objects. Those components are available to all applications.

- **3GB–4GB.** This memory range is reserved for all Ring 0 components, such as the File Management subsystem and the VMM subsystem. Any VxDs are loaded in this address space.

By default, Windows 95 uses a dynamic swap file, which shrinks and grows based on the needs of the operating system and the available hard disk space. A permanent swap file has little benefit in Windows 95.

4.6.2   Processor Rings

Windows 95 uses an Intel 386 or better processor to support multiple privilege levels for executable code. This means that programs may run at one of four privilege levels. Privileges refer to how the program is allowed to interact with other programs, either at the same privilege level or at a different privilege level. Of the four levels, or "rings," in the Intel 386 protection model, Windows 95 uses Rings 0 and 3. These rings provide different levels of protection and privileges. The lower the ring number, the higher the levels of protection and privileges.

Components of Windows 95 are divided between Ring 0 and Ring 3 code. Each ring offers a different level of system protection. The Ring 0 code is protected by the Intel processor architecture and consists of all the low-level operating system services, such as the File Management subsystem and the Virtual Machine Manager subsystem. The Ring 3 code runs the system VM and any virtual DOS machines.

Ring 0 components are protected by the processor architecture. These Ring 0 components are the core elements of Windows 95. They can run all privileged operations, including direct communication with the hardware components. They have access to the entire operating system. All the low-level Windows 95 core components run in Ring 0.

Ring 3 components have no processor protection; the operating system must provide protection for Ring 3 components. Applications and noncritical system services of Windows 95 components run on Ring 3.

Ring 3 hosts the virtual machines (VMs) in which MS-DOS, Windows 16-bit, and Windows 32-bit applications execute. The MS-DOS applications all run in separate VMs, known as virtual DOS machines (VDMs). All Windows applications, whether Windows 16-bit or 32-bit, execute in the system VM. The system VM allows multiple concurrent applications to run. Whereas all Windows 32-bit applications are isolated in private address spaces, all the active Windows 16-bit applications share a single, common address space. These applications are managed by the Virtual Machine Manager (VMM) in Ring 0. The central components of the Windows graphical environment also run as system services. These include Kernel, GDI, and User.

Ring 0 hosts both the VMM subsystem and the File Management subsystem. The VMM subsystem provides the resources needed for each application and system process running on the computer, including memory management and task scheduling. Virtual Device Drivers (VxDs) are 32-bit, protected-mode drivers that manage a system resource, such as a hardware device or installed software. They allow more than one application to use the resource at the same time. The File Management subsystem features an Installable File System Manager, which supports multiple file systems, such as VFAT, CDFS, and network redirectors. The Installable File System Manager also supports an open file system architecture. The Block I/O subsystems are responsible for the interaction with the physical storage devices.

Much of the code within Windows 95 is either new 32-bit code or Windows 3.*x* code rewritten as 32-bit code. Windows 95, however, is not completely a 32-bit operating system. Windows 95 strikes a balance between three requirements: delivering compatibility with existing applications and drivers, and decreasing the size of the operating system to run on 4MB of RAM. To provide this balance, Windows 95 uses a combination of both 32-bit and 16-bit code.

Three sets of files constitute the Windows 95 system service. These are the Kernel, Graphics Device Interface (GDI), and User Interface files.

- The Kernel files (KRNL386.EXE and KERNEL32.DLL) provide base operating system functions, including file I/O services, virtual memory management, application management, and task scheduling.

- The GDI files (GDI.EXE and GDI32.DLL) control the graphics operations that create images on the system display and other devices, such as printers.

- The User Interface files (USER.EXE and USER32.DLL) create and maintain windows onscreen and carry out all requests to create, move, size, or remove a window. The User Interface files also handle requests regarding the icons and other components of the user interface.

Most of the system services provided by the operating system Kernel are provided as 32-bit code. Roughly half of all GDI calls are handled in the 32-bit code. The 16-bit code for GDI contains most of the drawing routines. Much of the window management User code still remains 16-bit to maintain Windows 16-bit application compatibility.

The Thunk layer makes reference to the term *thunking*. This special term describes how 16-bit code components communicate with their 32-bit code component counterparts. The thunking process translates memory addresses between 32-bit calls and 16-bit calls.

4.6.3   Virtual Machines

All applications and dynamic link library (DLL) programs run in Ring 3. They execute in a virtual machine (VM), which looks like a separate computer from the application's perspective. A VM is an environment created by Windows 95 to simulate a complete computer, with all the resources available to a physical computer. The Virtual Machine Manager (VMM) creates and maintains the virtual machine environments and provides each application the system resources needed to run the system.

The Virtual Machine Manager, in addition to creating and maintaining virtual machines, provides several key services:

- **Memory management.** Controls the 4GB of addressable virtual memory, paging from RAM to the hard disk, and performs memory address translation.

- **Task scheduling and multitasking.** Allocates system resources and time to the applications and other processes running on the computer.

- **MS-DOS mode support.** For MS-DOS applications that need exclusive access to system resources. This special mode of Windows 95 operations should not be confused with the VDM. It is a separate and exclusive MS-DOS operating environment.

4.6.4   Understanding MS-DOS Program Information Files (PIFs)

A Program Information File (PIF) contains settings for establishing an MS-DOS environment for your MS-DOS application. This environment includes settings such as the amount of RAM that the application will have available to it. MS-DOS applications are 16-bit applications designed to work with MS-DOS version 6.*x* or earlier. Because these applications have no understanding of multitasking environments, simulating an MS-DOS environment is necessary for them to function properly. Windows 95 includes a number of improvements over Windows 3.*x* or Windows for Workgroups 3.*x* in handling MS-DOS applications:

- The capability to run in a window in most cases

- Better access to system resources due to the new 32-bit structure of the system resource stacks

- Improved support for sound devices

- Improved memory protection schemes that enable you to isolate the MS-DOS system area to prevent its corruption by misbehaving MS-DOS programs

- Support for scalable TrueType fonts in MS-DOS windows

- The capability to customize individual MS-DOS VMs with environment variables run from a batch file

The following additional information should be noted when using MS-DOS applications in Windows 95:

- Each MS-DOS application that is executed is assigned its own VM, with separate virtualized device access and addressable memory space.

- The memory space created for an MS-DOS application mirrors that of a standalone DOS environment, with 640KB of conventional memory, 384KB of upper memory, and whatever extended or expanded memory is specified in the configuration settings of the MS-DOS session.

- Each MS-DOS application run under Windows 95 can execute only one thread at a time because MS-DOS does not support multithreading.

- Each MS-DOS application has its own separate message queue to receive keyboard and mouse input.

- The APPS.INF file also contains configuration parameters for MS-DOS applications that are known to require them.

MS-DOS applications can be run in one of three modes:

- In an MS-DOS VM

- In MS-DOS mode after shutting down the Windows 95 GUI

- In MS-DOS mode outside of Windows 95, using parameters that have been customized for the application

By default, if Windows 95 detects that the application should be run in MS-DOS mode, it shuts down the Windows 95 GUI and runs the application in an environment similar to that if Command Prompt Only were selected from the Boot menu. However, the options on the shortcut Properties sheet for the MS-DOS application can be set to force the application to always run in MS-DOS mode or in a customized MS-DOS mode.

If the application does not require or is not configured to use MS-DOS mode, it will run in an MS-DOS VM.

MS-DOS Virtual Machine

MS-DOS VM mode should be used whenever possible, because the application can then take advantage of 32-bit, protected-mode driver support, preemptive multitasking, increased conventional memory, and other Windows 95 enhancements. By default, all MS-DOS applications are set to run in an MS-DOS VM, whether they are executed by double-clicking on the application from the Explorer or by typing the name of the file from a DOS prompt within Windows 95. If

Windows 95 detects that the application must have exclusive use of the system resources and must run in MS-DOS mode, however, you are prompted to have Windows 95 automatically shut down the system and run the application in MS-DOS mode. Most applications should be able to function without incident in a VM. If an application functions, but not as well as it should, you can alter the configuration of the MS-DOS environment for that application.

Modifying PIF Settings

You can modify numerous settings to facilitate the operation of MS-DOS programs. These settings can be configured by getting the properties of the application itself or by getting the properties of a shortcut to an application (see Figure 4.14). The settings are grouped into the following tabs on the Properties sheet for the MS-DOS application:

- Program tab

- Font tab

- Memory tab

- Screen tab

- Misc tab

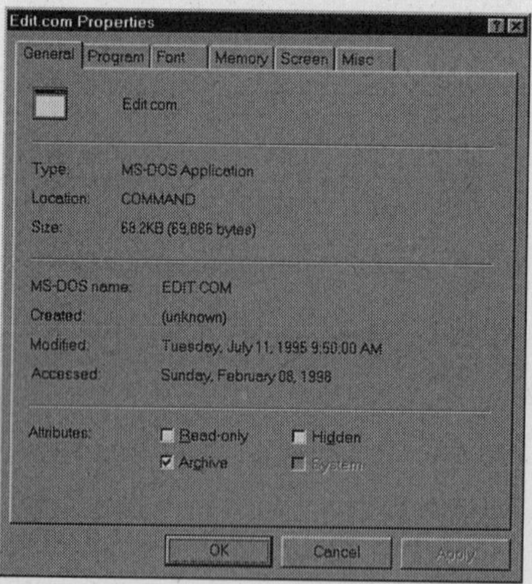

Figure 4.14 Properties of an application enable you to change the way the application will execute.

The actual file extension on shortcuts to MS-DOS applications is .PIF, unlike other shortcuts in Windows 95 which have the extension .LNK. Each shortcut or PIF for an MS-DOS application may have its own settings.

Program Tab

The Program tab includes settings defining the location of files used to run the application, as well as some other settings. The Advanced button of the Program tab is used to force the application to run in MS-DOS mode.

Font Tab

The parameters on this tab enable you to specify whether you want to use TrueType fonts, bitmap fonts, or both to display characters in the MS-DOS session.

If you leave the font size set to Auto, it will be adjusted each time you resize the window of the MS-DOS application.

Memory Tab

You can use the Memory tab to specify what type and quantity of memory the program needs access to in order to function. The four supported types are as follows:

- Conventional
- Expanded (EMS)
- Extended (XMS)
- DOS protected mode (DPMI)

By default, Windows 95 automatically allocates the memory the application needs when the application first requests it during operation. However, some applications function better if a fixed amount is allocated to them from the beginning. If the application queries the system for the amount of free memory before launching, it will fail to launch.

The Initial Environment setting is used to specify additional environment memory for variables and other MS-DOS settings.

Screen Tab

You can use the Screen tab to control how the application is displayed and how it uses video memory.

The settings of the Screen tab include the following:

- Usage
- Display Toolbar
- Restore Settings on Startup
- Fast ROM Emulation
- Dynamic Memory Allocation

Misc Tab

The Misc tab contains other miscellaneous uncategorized settings for the application.

The following list describes the parameters of the Misc tab:

- Allow Screen Saver Box
- Always Suspend

- Idle Sensitivity
- Quick Edit
- Exclusive Mode
- Warn If Still Active
- Fast Pasting
- Windows Shortcut Keys

4.6.5   Determining When to Run Applications in MS-DOS Mode

Some MS-DOS applications cannot run in an MS-DOS VM for one of several reasons:

- The application requires direct access to the hardware, which is not permitted in a multitasking environment because of potential device conflicts (this is the most common reason).

- The application has incompatible memory requirements. The application does not like the way Windows 95 manages the 640KB of conventional memory for the application (as a section of all the available memory), and wants to see the actual memory below 640KB being used.

- The application's install program checks to see whether Windows is running and will not continue if Windows is detected.

- The application has video problems (usually with MS-DOS games) and does not want to draw the screen properly, either in a window or running full screen.

If any of these situations applies to the application, you must run the application in MS-DOS mode. You can configure MS-DOS mode by using the Advanced button on the Program tab of an MS-DOS PIF, as shown in Figure 4.15.

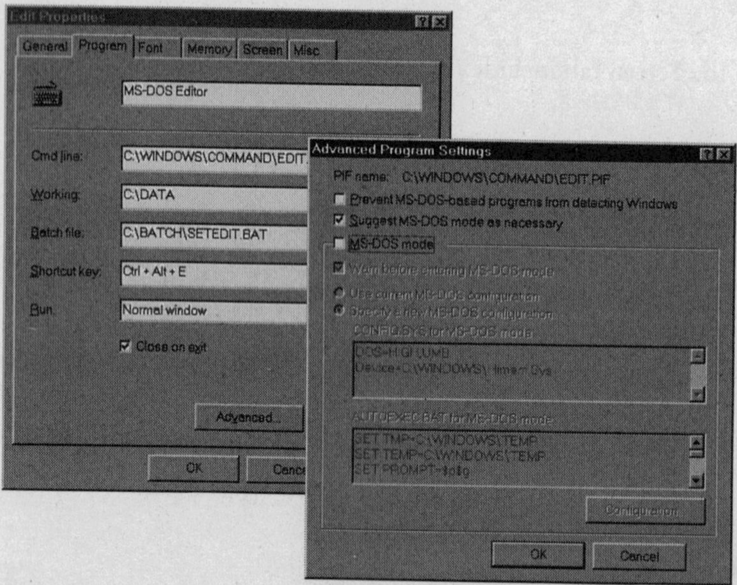

Figure 4.15   By default, MS-DOS is suggested based on the contents of *APPS*.INF.

Prior to using MS-DOS mode, you may want to attempt using the Prevent MS-DOS Based Programs From Detecting Windows option. With this option enabled, some applications that do not desire to run within the Windows environment, will execute.

In MS-DOS mode, Windows 95 unloads itself from memory, leaving the computer in a single-tasking MS-DOS type of environment. All protected-mode support and drivers are removed, permitting the application to use only the CONFIG.SYS and AUTOEXEC.BAT parameters that were in effect at boot time before Windows 95 loaded. If the application needs a more particular configuration than that provided by default in the normal CONFIG.SYS and AUTOEXEC.BAT, you can create a customized MS-DOS environment for each application.

4.6.6 Customized MS-DOS Mode

If the application in question requires specific configuration parameters that differ significantly from those needed by most MS-DOS applications, you can create a customized CONFIG.SYS and AUTOEXEC.BAT that will be swapped with the standard versions of these files when you double-click the application (see Figure 4.16). For the settings in these customized files to take effect, Windows 95 must reboot the computer.

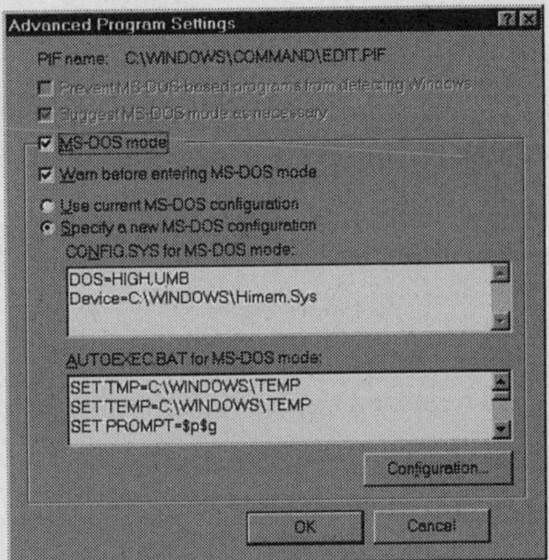

Figure 4.16 Custom configuration files require the reboot of your computer.

When Windows 95 restarts the computer, it uses the customized configuration files and inserts a special command into the CONFIG.SYS. The command reads DOS=SINGLE and indicates that this CONFIG.SYS and AUTOEXEC.BAT are to be used only once and that the system should return to the normal versions of these files when this application terminates.

Microsoft has provided a helper window to aid with the creation of custom configuration files. This option is enabled by choosing the Configuration button in the Advanced PIF settings (see Figure 4.17). It only allows for the four options; but Expanded Memory, Disk Cache, and Direct Disk Access are the three most common items that people will need to add to their configurations. DOSKEY is a very useful option, but not usually required.

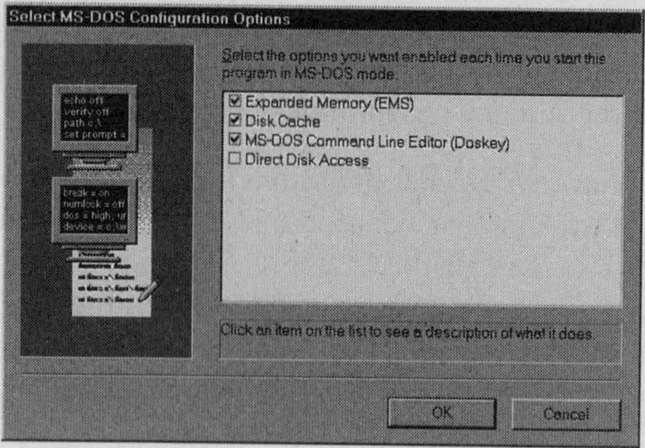

Figure 4.17　Creating Custom configuration files is easier with the helper that Windows 95 provides.

4.6.7　Exercises

Exercise 1: Counting Virtual Machines

To illustrate the point about how Windows 95 manages virtual machines, follow this exercise to count the number of virtual machines running on your Windows 95 computer.

1. From your computer, start Windows 95.

2. If you installed Windows 95 on your computer with the Typical Setup option, the System Monitor program might not be installed, because it is an optional component.

   To determine whether the System Monitor utility program is installed, from the Start menu choose Programs, Accessories, System Tools, System Monitor. If System Monitor is not available, you must add it to your computer by following these steps:

   a. From the Start menu, choose Settings, Control Panel. From the Control Panel program group, choose the Add/Remove Programs icon.

   b. Click on the Windows Setup tab, double-click Accessories, and add a check mark to the System Monitor check box. Press Enter or click OK. Press Enter or click OK again to install the System Monitor.

3. From the Start menu, choose Programs, Accessories, System Tools, System Monitor. The System Monitor utility program displays key system information in either a line chart, bar chart, or numeric chart format.

4. Any items previously selected are displayed when the System Monitor utility program starts. When you run the System Monitor utility program for the first time, the Kernel Processor Usage (%) appears in a line chart.

5. You must remove all current items to run this exercise. Highlight any items you want to remove, and then from the Edit menu choose Remove Item.

6. Click Edit, Add Item to open the Add Item dialog box. From the Category list, click Kernel to display the list of Kernel items.

7. Choose Virtual Machines from the Item list. If you need an explanation of each item, choose Explain to see that this shows the number of virtual machines present in the system. Press Enter or click OK to add the item Virtual Machines as a selection.

8. Choose View, Numeric Charts to obtain the number of virtual machines that currently are active. Normally this value is 1, because the Windows 95 computer has just been started. It could be higher.

9. Open some Windows program applications or the Windows Explorer. Has the number of virtual machines changed? The number of active virtual machines should not change when Windows programs are started.

10. Start an MS-DOS command prompt by choosing Start, Run to open the Run dialog box; or choose Start, Programs, MS-DOS Prompt. Has the number of virtual machines changed? It should change, because each MS-DOS application will start another virtual machine.

11. Start another MS-DOS command prompt, and then a third. What happens to the count of virtual machines after you start each new MS-DOS command prompt? Each time another MS-DOS command prompt is started, the number of virtual machines should increase by a count of 1. If the initial count was 1, then starting three MS-DOS command prompts increases the number to 4.

12. Close all three MS-DOS command prompts. How many virtual machines are currently active? The count of virtual machines should be back down to 1, or the starting number in step 8.

    Based on what you know about virtual machines, explain why the count changes during the exercise.

    All the Windows 16-bit and 32-bit applications run in a single system virtual machine. But each MS-DOS application runs in its own virtual DOS machine. Opening a new MS-DOS command prompt causes the virtual machine count to increase by one.

13. When you finish viewing the System Monitor utility information, close the System Monitor.

Exercise 2: Configuring MS-DOS Applications

This exercise demonstrates how to configure the various MS-DOS modes for a given application.

1. Right-click the My Computer icon and choose Explore. The Exploring window appears.

2. Click on the plus sign next to the C: drive. Subdirectories of the C: drive appear.

3. Click on the plus sign next to the Windows subdirectory. The tree expands to show the subdirectories of Windows.

4. Right-click the COMMAND file in the right panel and choose Properties. The COMMAND.COM Properties sheet appears.

5. Click on the Memory tab. The list of configurable memory settings appears.

6. Set the XMS memory parameter to 4096 and click OK. You return to the Explorer window.

7. Double-click the COMMAND file. An MS-DOS window appears.

8. Type **MEM** and press Enter from the command prompt. Note that the free XMS reads as 4096KB.

9. Type **EXIT** and press Enter. You return to the Explorer window.

10. Go back to the Properties sheet of the COMMAND file and change the XMS memory parameter to 16384KB, click OK, and double-click the COMMAND file again. An MS-DOS window appears.

11. Type **MEM** and press Enter. Note that the free XMS memory now reads 16384KB.

> **Even if the amount of memory you assign exceeds the physical RAM of the computer, the parameter will be accepted. The additional memory comes from the paging file system.**

12. Type **EXIT** and press Enter. You return to the Explorer window.

13. Reset the XMS memory parameter to its original setting of Auto and click OK. You return to the Explorer window.

14. Click on the Command folder. The files in the Command folder appear in the right panel of the Explorer window.

15. Right-click the EDIT file and choose Properties. The Properties sheet for the EDIT file appears.

16. Click on the Program tab, and then click the Advanced button. The Advanced Program Settings window appears.

17. Select the MS-DOS Mode check box to enable use of standard MS-DOS mode support for this program. Some of the options below MS-DOS mode parameter become available.

18. Verify that Use Current MS-DOS Configuration is selected and click OK. You return to the Properties sheet, and all other settings are disabled, because this file will now inherit all default MS-DOS settings.

19. Double-click the EDIT file and click Yes to continue. Windows 95 is unloaded, and the EDIT file is executed.

20. Choose File, Open (or press Alt+F, O) to open a file for editing, type **\CONFIG.SYS** as the filename, and press Enter. The CONFIG.SYS file appears.

21. Note the contents of the file and press Alt+F, X to exit the program. Windows 95 restarts automatically.

22. When Windows 95 has restarted, go back to the Advanced Settings tab and choose to specify a new MS-DOS configuration. The CONFIG.SYS and AUTOEXEC.BAT for MS-DOS mode are now available and have default settings already in place.

23. Click on the Configuration button. A wizard appears that helps you select which options you want to be active in your MS-DOS environment.

24. Verify that Expanded Memory is deselected and that Disk Cache is selected; click OK three times to close all Properties sheets. You return to the Explorer window.

25. Double-click the EDIT file again and choose Yes to continue. The system restarts, and the EDIT program is executed.

26. Choose File, Open to open a file for editing. Type **\CONFIG.SYS** as the filename, and press Enter. The CONFIG.SYS file appears for editing (note that DOS=SINGLE has been added to the file).

27. Choose File, Open to open a file for editing, type **\AUTOEXEC.BAT** as the filename, and press Enter. The AUTOEXEC.BAT file appears for editing (note that a SmartDrive command has been added).

28. Choose File, Exit (or press Alt+F, X) to exit the program, and then press any key. The system restarts, and Windows 95 loads normally.

29. Go back to the Properties sheet of the EDIT file and disable MS-DOS mode.

4.6.8   Practice Problems

1. The ring architecture of Intel 386 processes provide different levels of protection and privileges. Windows 95 executes in which two of the following rings of the Intel 386 protection model? Select the two best answers:

   A. Ring 0

   B. Ring 1

   C. Ring 2

   D. Ring 3

2. Windows 95 is an advanced operating system that takes advantage of the Intel ring architecture. To understand how Windows 95 uses the ring architecture, you need to understand the rings themselves. Which one of the following rings of the Intel 386 protection model offers the most privileges, including direct communication with the hardware components?

   A. Ring 0

   B. Ring 1

   C. Ring 2

   D. Ring 3

3. You are asked to present an overview of the Windows 95 system architecture, including rings. You draw a diagram that points out each ring and its protection level. Which of the following rings of the Intel 386 protection model offers no processor protection, but instead needs the operating system to provide processor protection?

   A. Ring 0

   B. Ring 1

   C. Ring 2

   D. Ring 3

4. On the diagram you create for the presentation in question 3, you need to point out where applications run. In which of the following rings of the Intel 386 protection model do the MS-DOS, Windows 16-bit, and Windows 32-bit applications run?

   A. Ring 0

   B. Ring 1

   C. Ring 2

   D. Ring 3

5. Within its system services, Windows 95 uses a combination of 32-bit and 16-bit code to run applications. In which of the following rings of the Intel 386 protection model do the system services run?

   A. Ring 0

   B. Ring 1

   C. Ring 2

   D. Ring 3

6. Windows 95 runs applications in virtual machines. The Virtual Machine Manager is used to manage these applications. In which of the following rings of the Intel 386 protection model does the Virtual Machine Manager run?

   A. Ring 0

   B. Ring 1

   C. Ring 2

   D. Ring 3

7. Scott runs several applications simultaneously on his Windows 95 computer. Which of the following applications do not run in separate, private, virtual machines?

   A. Windows 32-bit

   B. Windows 16-bit

   C. MS-DOS

   D. All the above

8. The Virtual Machine Manager provides several services, including memory management, task scheduling, and DOS-mode support. Every time you open an MS-DOS application, the count of the number of virtual machines running under Windows 95 _______.

   A. Decreases by two

   B. Decreases by one

   C. Stays the same

   D. Increases by one

9. Windows 95 uses two types of memory: physical and virtual. Virtual memory is comprised of which two of the following components? Select the two best answers:

   A. ROM

   B. RAM

   C. VMM

   D. A swap file

10. You are migrating to Windows 95 and will be upgrading many of your applications to 32-bit applications designed to run under Windows 95. You know that Windows 95 runs 32-bit applications differently than Windows 3.1 applications (16-bit applications). Every Windows 95 application is executed from within a specialized container called _______.

    A. An application box

    B. A virtual partition

    C. A task space

    D. A virtual machine

11. Jeff is upgrading to Windows 95 and wants to be sure his existing computer can run Windows 95. The Windows 95 multitasking feature requires an Intel processor to perform in two types of modes. Which two of the following are operating modes for Intel processors?

   A. Enhanced mode

   B. Protected mode

   C. Fault mode

   D. Real mode

12. The Windows 95 protected-mode feature has the capability to regulate the behavior of the multitasking process in two ways. One way is through graduated levels of processor privilege, commonly called rings. In the Intel ring protection scheme, Ring _______ allows complete control of the processor.

    A. 1

    B. 0

    C. 3

    D. 4

13. Typically, applications running under Windows 95 do so at a specific ring level. The operating system runs at a specific ring level as well. This way applications do not have access to critical system functions. Which of the following is true about rings?

    A. Most Windows 95 applications run in Ring 3.

    B. Most operating system components run in Ring 3.

    C. Windows 95 uses all Intel rings.

    D. Windows 95 uses only Rings 1, 2, and 3.

14. Donna is considering upgrading from Windows 3.x to Windows 95. She is not sure how to justify the upgrade based on application support, because Windows 3.x, like Windows 95, supports multitasking. You explain the differences between how 16-bit applications and 32-bit applications support multitasking. You tell her that WIN16 applications use _______ multitasking.

A. Fault-tolerant

B. Preemptive

C. Cooperative

D. Real-mode

15. It's important for your users to understand how 16-bit applications are handled by Windows 95. Which of the following is true?

A. WIN16 applications do not access the Registry.

B. WIN16 applications do not use the system VM.

C. WIN16 applications support multithreading.

D. Each WIN16 application has its own message queue.

16. Kimberly has several MS-DOS applications she runs under Windows 95. She wants to optimize the way they run under Windows 95, as well as run 32-bit applications simultaneously with her DOS applications. If possible, you advise her it is best to run MS-DOS applications in ________.

A. MS-DOS mode

B. Customized MS-DOS mode

C. A WIN16 VM

D. An MS-DOS VM

17. A user calls you while you are manning a help desk. He asks how his MS-DOS program and Windows 95 will work together in MS-DOS mode. You tell him that in MS-DOS mode Windows 95 ________.

A. Unloads itself from memory

B. Remains in memory

C. Runs the application in protected mode

D. Can multithread multiple DOS sessions

18. You are a systems administrator in a company that migrated to Windows 95. Many users still use MS-DOS applications and must run them under Windows. Because of some compatibility problems with the older DOS applications, you customize the DOS-mode applications. What command is added to the CONFIG.SYS when you run a customized MS-DOS-mode application?

A. DOS=Custom

B. MODE=DOSCUST

C. DOS=CMODE

D. DOS=SINGLE

19. Windows 95 provides compatibility with many of today's existing computers. Before installing Windows 95 on a computer, make sure it has a processor that can run it. What is the lowest Intel processor recommended to run Windows 95?

A. 80286

B. 80386SX

C. 80386DX

D. 80486

20. Gladys uses a computer at work that runs Windows 95. Her computer at home does not have Windows 95 installed yet. She asks you how much RAM she needs in her computer to install Windows 95. What is the minimum amount of RAM required for Windows 95?

A. 2MB

B. 4MB

C. 8MB

D. 16MB

4.6.9 Answers and Explanations

1. **A, D** Windows 95 executes programs in Ring 0 and Ring 3.

2. **A** Ring 0 is the only processor ring that has direct access to hardware; Ring 3 processes must go through Ring 0 to get to the hardware.

3. **D** Ring 0 has application processing protection built in, but Ring 3 requires the OS to provide protection.

4. **D** All applications run in Ring 3; Ring 0 is reserved for the OS.

5. **D** Most system services are applications, and would therefore run in Ring 3.

6. **A** Ring 0 supports the Kernel, system drivers, and manager applications.

7. **B** 16-bit Windows applications are the only applications that share a memory address space; they do this for backward compatibility.

8. **D** Each MS-DOS application runs in its own virtual machine.

9. **B, D** Physical memory is RAM and virtual memory is space on your hard drive in the form of a swap file.

10. **D** All 16-bit Windows applications and 32-bit Windows applications share a common virtual machine.

11. **B, D** The Intel processor may run in protected mode or real mode. Windows 95 would use real mode prior to the GUI starting up.

12. **B** Ring 0 is the only ring that allows direct access to hardware.

13. **A** Most Windows 95 applications run in Ring 3; Ring 0 is usually reserved for OS functions.

14. **C** Windows 95 uses preemptive multitasking, which provides better scheduling of processor time than the cooperative multitasking used by 16-bit applications.

15. **A** 16-bit applications store their settings in INI files; only 32-bit applications will use the Registry.

16. **D** To multitask MS-DOS applications and Windows applications, you will run the MS-DOS applications in an MS-DOS virtual machine.

17. **A** When running applications in MS-DOS mode, Windows 95 is removed from memory.

18. **D** DOS=SINGLE is added to the CONFIG.SYS file when running an MS-DOS application with custom CONFIG.SYS or AUTOEXEC.BAT settings.

19. **C** Microsoft recommends a minimum of 80386DX processor for Windows 95; however, you realize performance improvements with a faster processor.

20. **B** Microsoft specifies at least 4MB of RAM for Windows 95; however, performance improves with 8MB of RAM.

4.6.10 Key Words and Definitions

MS-DOS mode An environment in which the Windows 95 GUI unloads itself from memory and grants a single MS-DOS application exclusive use of system resources.

Program Information File (PIF) The PIF contains settings for establishing an MS-DOS environment for your MS-DOS applications.

System virtual machine   The virtual machine in which all 16-bit and 32-bit Windows applications run. The 16-bit applications share a common address space within the system virtual machine, and 32-bit applications each maintain separate address space.

Virtual DOS machines (VDM)   The virtual machine created for each MS-DOS application running. Each MS-DOS application executed creates another VDM.

Virtual machine (VM)   Applications in Windows 95 are designed to be run in a virtual machine that provides the application access to memory, resources, and the use of hardware-using virtual drivers.

Virtual Machine Manager (VMM)   The VMM subsystem provides the resources needed for each application and system process running on the computer, including memory management and task scheduling.

Virtual memory   A combination of physical RAM and hard disk space that provides more memory than is actually installed on the computer.

Practice Exam: Configuring and Managing Resource Access

1. Your security provider is NetWare. You must use user-level security under NetWare. What is user-level security?

   A. Access to resources is based on the users' accounts.

   B. Access to resources is based on passwords.

   C. Access to resources is based on passthrough authentication.

   D. Access to resources is restricted to users identified through the Share As dialog box.

2. Participating in a Windows NT domain enables a Windows 95 computer to use which level of security?

   A. Group-level

   B. User-level

   C. Share-level

   D. Resource-level

3. Workgroups must use which level of security in a Windows 95–only network?

   A. Group-level

   B. User-level

   C. Share-level

   D. Resource-level

4. In the absence of Windows NT Server, user-level security can be implemented using which of the following? (Choose all that apply)

   A. NetWare server

   B. Windows NT Workstation

   C. Windows 95 PLUS! Pack

   D. Windows for Workgroups

5. What must be running on each client to have user-level security working in a Windows NT environment with Windows 95 clients?

   A. Client for Microsoft

   B. Client for NetWare Networks

   C. File and Printer Sharing for Microsoft Networks

   D. File and Printer Sharing for NetWare Networks

6. To create a shared folder on a remote computer using the Net Watcher administration tool, you would select which of the following choices to initiate the process of creating the shared resources?

   A. Select the Administer menu, and then select Add Shared Folder.

   B. Select Administer menu, and then select Add Shared Local Resource.

   C. You must connect to the computer prior to creating shares on the remote computer.

   D. After connecting to the remote computer, you should select the Administer menu and then select Add Shared Folder.

7. After connecting to a remote computer using the Net Watcher administration tool, you want to view the shares on that computer. What must you select to view the current shares on the target remote computer?

   A. Click on the Show Shared Folders button to see the names of the shared folders on the selected computer.

   B. Click on the Show Shared Resources button to see the names of the shared folders on the selected computer.

   C. Click on the Shared Folders button to see the names of the shared folders on the selected computer.

D. None of the above will display the shared resources on the remote computer.

8. A coworker who is using Windows 3.1 wants to use EMF spooling to speed up his work by reducing printer time. He copies the printer files from you and places them in the proper directory on his computer, but there is no difference. Why not?

A. The printer needs to be restarted after the files have been copied.

B. The computer needs to be restarted after the files have been copied to the right directory.

C. Windows 3.1 does not support EMF spooling.

D. He does not have the proper rights to upgrade his printer.

9. Approximately how much longer does printing take without EMF spooling?

A. Three times as long

B. Twice as long

C. One-third the time

D. Half the time

10. As the system administrator, you need to configure Exchange to send and receive mail in Microsoft Mail. Which three of the following actions must you take?

A. Create a Workgroup Postoffice on a Windows 95 computer running the Microsoft Mail workstation edition.

B. Create a mailbox for each member of the Workgroup Postoffice.

C. Make the requisite Exchange folder: Inbox, Outbox, Sent Items, and Deleted Items.

D. Configure the Exchange Client with the Microsoft Mail service.

11. When you are creating a Workgroup Postoffice, it is important that you take which two of the following steps?

A. Give all Postoffice members full-control access to the Workgroup Postoffice directory.

B. Assign the same password to all Postoffice members when share-level security is used.

C. Give all Postoffice members read-only access to the Workgroup Postoffice directory.

D. Have each Postoffice member choose a unique password when share-level security is used.

12. Before Annette can use her modem to send a fax with Exchange, which tree of the following items does she need?

A. Installed Microsoft Fax software

B. The Microsoft Fax Information Service added to her profile

C. A fax profile

D. A fax modem configured for the Windows 95 client

13. You have implemented roving user profiles on your network, but your users are complaining that when they log on to other Windows 95 computers, they do not get their user profile information. What could be the cause of this problem?

A. User profiles are not enabled on the computers they are accessing.

B. The users in question are not members of your Windows NT domain and cannot access information on the Windows NT Server.

C. The network users do not have rights to the NETLOGON directory located on the Windows NT Server.

D. The users have accidentally deleted their profile information.

14. Setting up automatic downloading of system policies from a Windows NT Server requires that you place the CONFIG.POL file in which shared location on the NT server?

    A. NETLOGON

    B. SYS:PUBLIC

    C. C$ SHARE

    D. EXPORT/SCRIPTS

15. The company for which you work is implementing Windows 95. Your job is to configure a user desktop environment that limits access to the configuration of the computer, reduces administration, and provides a more efficient workspace. This environment would best be served by instituting which of the following?

    A. Installing the Remote Registry service to enable centralized administration of Windows 95 computers

    B. Implementing mandatory user profiles

    C. Implementing system policies

    D. Implementing user profiles

16. You want to enable support for long filenames on volume VOL1 on your Novell NetWare file server. Which three steps must you perform?

    A. Type **LOAD OS2** at the server console.

    B. Type **ADD NAME SPACE OS2 TO VOLUME VOL1** at the server console.

    C. Add the command **LOAD OS2** to the server STARTUP.NCF file.

    D. Add the command **ADD OS2 NAME SPACE** to the server STARTUP.NCF file.

17. When are the DriveSpace drivers loaded into memory?

    A. Whenever compressed media is detected and mounted

    B. At system startup

    C. When the user runs DriveSpace from the START button

    D. When Microsoft Plus! is installed

18. How long can the total path and filename be under Windows 95?

    A. 255 characters

    B. 260 characters

    C. 256 characters

    D. 256 bytes

19. If a long filename contains no period, how is the alias extension formed?

    A. The alias will have no extension.

    B. The last three characters of the filename will be the extension.

    C. The extension will consist of a tilde character and an incremental numeric character.

    D. The extension will default to .doc.

20. What is the best drive compression ratio, using DriveSpace 2.0?

    A. 5:1

    B. 3:1

    C. 2:1

    D. 2.5:1

21. What is the process of assigning a drive letter and making a CFV visible?

    A. Mounting

    B. Matching

    C. Compression

    D. Allocation

22. Which is not available on the Properties sheet for an MS-DOS application?

    A. Program tab

B. Display tab

C. Memory tab

D. Screen tab

23. How much conventional memory is allocated to an MS-DOS application VM?

    A. 640KB

    B. 64KB

    C. 384KB

    D. 1,024KB

24. Jeff is running a Windows 16-bit application, two Windows 32-bit applications, and three MS-DOS applications. How many VMs are currently in use?

    A. 1

    B. 2

    C. 3

    D. 4

25. This is a scenario question. First you must review the situation, and then review the objectives. Following that is a proposed solution. You must pick the best evaluation of that solution.

SITUATION:

You are setting up a Windows 95 network of 25 systems. Four of the systems will be sharing resources with the other systems on the network. One system will be sharing a printer. Two systems will be sharing two applications and printers. One system will be sharing files, applications, printer, and modem.

Ten users will not have access to the last system's files (three DIR) and three applications. Share-level access has been enabled for the resources.

MAJOR OBJECTIVES:

The objective is to distribute the correct passwords to the correct users and to control the number of passwords you will have to configure.

PROPOSED SOLUTION:

Based on this scenario, discuss how many passwords are required, and how you will distribute the passwords to the users who require them.

EVALUATION OF PROPOSED SOLUTION:

Choose the most correct answer:

A. Twelve passwords, and tell each user verbally which passwords to use for resources.

B. Thirteen passwords, and distribute email to the groups who have access to their respected resources.

C. Five passwords: one for printers, one for the modem, one for the shared applications for all, one for the files for 15 users, and one for shared applications for 15 users. Then send email to the groups who have access to their respected resources.

D. One password for all resources.

26. This is a scenario question. First you must review the situation, and then review the objectives. Following that is a proposed solution. You must pick the best evaluation of that solution.

SITUATION:

You have set up a network with Windows 95 workstations connected to a Windows NT Server. You have configured the users to have roaming profiles. This works for the network because most users are not at the same workstation everyday. For the first two weeks, the new network is up and running and there are no problems. Then one Monday morning you get two calls from different users saying that when they log on the network, all they have on their screen is the taskbar, and there are no application programs. You get a call from a third user with the same problem.

MAJOR OBJECTIVE:

Solve the problem before you get any more calls.

PROPOSED SOLUTION:

Which of the following is the best diagnostic to solve the problem?

EVALUATION OF PROPOSED SOLUTION:

Choose the most correct answer:

    A. Check to see whether the users' profiles have been deleted or changed.

    B. Scan for viruses on the network.

    C. Check to see whether the workstations are connecting to the network.

    D. Check the time and date on the workstations.

27. This is a scenario question. First you must review the situation, and then review the objectives. You must pick the best evaluation of that solution.

SITUATION:

You are setting up Windows 95 workstations to be part of a NetWare 3.1x network. When the users enter their usernames and passwords, in the View Network Neighborhood they only see an icon for the entire network. When they click this icon, nothing happens.

MAJOR OBJECTIVE:

Because users cannot access their network resources, they get quite upset.

EVALUATION OF PROPOSED SOLUTION:

Choose the most correct answer:

    A. Return to using Novell's VLM Client. The users will have to log on before Windows 95 GUI starts.

    B. Install Novell's 32-bit client for Windows 95.

    C. Re-install Microsoft's Client for NetWare.

    D. Specify the preferred server under Properties in the Microsoft Client for NetWare.

28. This is a scenario question. First you must review the situation, and then review the objectives. You must pick the best evaluation of that solution.

SITUATION:

You are planning on installing disk compression a 750MB hard disk. You need to get the best results possible on the disk compression.

MAJOR OBJECTIVES:

From the requirements, choose the best solution.

EVALUATION OF PROPOSED SOLUTION:

Choose the most correct answer:

    A. Stacker Version 2.x

    B. SuperStor Version 3.0

    C. DriveSpace Version 2.0

    D. DriveSpace Version 3.0

29. Judy calls you from marketing and tells you she just created a file in Microsoft Excel 95 and saved it as a long filename called "Marketing Budget.XLS". She copies the file to her laptop, which also runs Windows 95, but the version of Excel on the laptop was released prior to Windows 95. She says she cannot find the "Marketing Budget.XLS" file. What is one possible short filename you tell her to look for?

    A. MARKET~1.XLS

    B. MARKET~1.EXE

    C. MARKET.1~.XSL

    D. MARBUD~1.XLS

30. Cindy runs an MS-DOS–based application under Windows 95. She wants to take advantage of the Windows 95 32-bit, protected-mode driver support, preemptive multitasking, and increased conventional memory. In which mode should Cindy try to run her MS-DOS application in order to use these features?

    A. MS-DOS mode

    B. MS-DOS Virtual Machine mode

    C. MS-DOS CONFIG mode

    D. MS-DOS Command mode

Practice Exam Answers and Explanations

1. **A** User-level security is based on a user's logon account to access resources.

2. **B** When a Windows 95 computer participates in a domain, it can use user-level security to share and access resources on a per-user account basis.

3. **C** Workgroups must use share-level security, because the clients do not access a central Windows NT or NetWare accounts database.

4. **A, B** To set up Windows 95 to use Windows NT user-level security, you must have Windows 95 running on a Windows NT server, such as a Windows NT Server domain or a Windows NT Workstation server, or use a NetWare server.

5. **A** You must have Client for Microsoft Networks enabled.

6. **D** You must be connected to the remote computer before you can add shared folders.

7. **A** The Show Shared Folders button shows the folders and their descriptions, if any.

8. **C** EMF spooling was developed for Windows 95 and Windows NT, not for Windows 3.1.

9. **B** Printing takes approximately twice as long when you are not using EMF.

10. **A, B, D** The system administrator must set up the Workgroup Postoffice and all the mailboxes before configuring Exchange for Microsoft Mail. The Exchange folders are created automatically.

11. **A, B** Because the Workgroup Postoffice directory (WPGO0000) is a temporary storage area for all sent messages, it must be shared with full-control access. With share-level security, the same password is assigned to all Postoffice members.

12. **A, B, D** Before Annette can send a fax in Exchange, she needs to install Microsoft Fax, add Microsoft Fax to her existing profile, and make sure that her modem is configured.

13. **A** Profiles have not been enabled under Control Panel, Passwords, User Profiles.

14. **A** The NETLOGON is the default directory from which the CONFIG.POL file is copied to the workstation.

15. **C** System policies enable the greatest control of the users' environment from the administration side.

16. **A, B, C** Steps A and B enable long filename support on the NetWare volume. Step C ensures that the necessary support file (OS2.nlm) is loaded each time the server is booted.

17. **A** DriveSpace drivers are not loaded automatically at system startup unless compressed media is detected and mounted at that time.

18. **B** The total path and filename in Windows 95 is limited to 260 characters.

19. **A** If a long filename does not contain a period, Windows 95 will not add an extension to the autogenerated alias.

20. **C** DriveSpace 2.0 achieves a compression ratio of 2:1.

21. **A** Assigning a drive letter and making a compressed volume file visible is called mounting.

22. **B** Configuration of display properties for an MS-DOS application is done from the Screen tab of the Application Shortcut icon's Properties sheet.

23. **A** The initial VM environment for MS-DOS applications is allocated 640KB of conventional memory and 384KB of upper memory.

24. **D** Each DOS application requires a separate VM, and the Windows 32-bit and 16-bit applications share a common VM.

25. **B** Even though users have to remember five passwords, it is the most secure answer for the network.

26. **D** If the time and date are out of sync on the workstations, roaming profile will not follow a user to a workstation whose time and date are set earlier than another workstation the user was logged on.

27. **D** Specifying the preferred server would be the easiest to do because the users are not attaching to the correct server which contains their usernames and passwords.

28. **D** DriveSpace 3.0 gives you a compression ration of 2.4:1. You will have to get Microsoft Plus! or OSR2 version of Windows 95. This software also enables you to compress larger than 512MB.

29. **A** MARKET~1.XLS is the short filename. The first six valid characters followed by ~ and an incremental number.

30. **B** MS-DOS Virtual Machine mode. If she runs the application in MS-DOS mode, she will lose 32-bit, protected-mode driver support, preemptive multitasking, and increased conventional memory.

CHAPTER 5

Integration and Interoperability

This chapter helps you prepare for the exam by covering the following objectives:

- Configure a Windows 95 computer as a client in a Windows NT network.

- Configure a Windows 95 computer as a client in a NetWare network.

- Configure a Windows 95 computer to access the Internet.

- Configure a client to use Dial-Up Networking for remote access in a Microsoft and mixed Microsoft/NetWare environment.

5.1 Configuring a Windows 95 Computer as a Client in a Windows NT Network

The Windows 95 modular architecture allows concurrent communications with several different networks using multiple protocols. A Windows 95 computer can have concurrent connections to a NetBEUI-based Windows NT network, an IPX/SPX NetWare network, and the TCP/IP-based Internet.

5.1.1 Network Providers

Windows 95 uses a modular network provider interface to allow multiple simultaneous networks. Each network provider interface uses the service provider interface to access the multiple provider router, where features common to all networks are located.

The network provider interface allows users to access shared disk resources using the particular network's native server name syntax. If you want to access a Microsoft Networks (SMB) compatible shared resource, the UNC format *computer_name**share_name* is recognized. In addition, Windows 95 can correctly interpret the NetWare server syntax *server_name/volume name:directory*. The Windows 95 user interface and Net command also support UNC names for connecting to NetWare resources.

5.1.2 Microsoft Network Redirector

VREDIR.VXD is the redirector for the Client for Microsoft Networks. It reformats the data into Server Messenger Block (SMB) packets as it passes through to the appropriate transport protocol.

5.1.3 NetWare Redirector

NWREDIR.VXD is the redirector for the Microsoft Client for NetWare Networks. It reformats the data into NetWare Core Protocol (NCP) packets as it passes through to the IPX/SPX-compatible transport protocol.

5.1.4 Peer Resource Sharing

At this layer of the networking model, Windows 95 provides two peer resource sharing server services:

- File and Printer Sharing for Microsoft Networks supports SMB file sharing among resources.

- File and Printer Sharing for NetWare Networks supports NCP resource sharing.

5.1.5 Transport Protocols

Windows 95 includes support for NetBEUI, IPX/SPX-compatible, and TCP/IP transport protocols. All three protocols interact with the network adapter driver and network adapter hardware through the Network Device Interface Specification (NDIS) interface.

NetBEUI

NetBEUI, the NetBIOS framing protocol, is a protocol designed to have low resource overhead that features automatic configuration and installation. NetBEUI is designed for small LANs and supports only certain Microsoft-based clients. NetBEUI isn't routable. The NetBEUI module is NETBEUI.VXD.

IPX/SPX-Compatible Protocol

The IPX/SPX-compatible protocol from Novell allows Windows 95 to communicate over an IPX network. Novell NetWare servers and other IPX routers can be used to transfer packets across LANs to access other IPX devices.

The Microsoft IPX/SPX-compatible protocol uses the 32-bit client to access the NetWare environment. Although the NetWare 16-bit client is available, it is recommended that you use the Microsoft 32-bit client for NetWare Networks over the 16-bit client.

TCP/IP

Transmission Control Protocol/Internet Protocol is a standard routable protocol for wide area networks, UNIX-based networks, and the Internet. The Windows 95 implementation of TCP/IP supports Windows Sockets or NetBIOS over TCP/IP (NetBT) connections.

5.1.6 Network Adapter Drivers

Normally, adapter drivers are provided by the NIC manufacturer. But Windows 95 does provide a large selection of drivers for many common NICs.

All Windows 95 network adapter drivers and protocol settings are configured using the Network Settings icon found in the Control Panel instead of by editing text configuration files as was common in Windows 3.*x*. Windows 95 stores these settings in the Registry.

5.1.7   NDIS

Microsoft networking protocols communicate with network interface card (NIC) drivers using the Network Driver Interface Specification (NDIS). The NDIS interface layer provides basic services common to all networking protocols and provides a standard interface to which NIC adapter drivers can be written. The transport protocol uses the NDIS specification to send raw data packets over a network device and to receive notification of incoming packets received by the NIC. Windows 95 supports versions 2.*x* and 3.1 NDIS protocol and adapter drivers.

NDIS allows a single adapter driver to be used for multiple protocols, eliminating the need to rewrite an adapter driver for each possible transport protocol and separate the transport protocols from the physical network media. NDIS 3.1 also incorporates Plug and Play features. This allows Plug and Play network adapters, such as PCMCIA network cards for laptops, to be inserted or swapped while the computer is running. If such an event occurs, the NDIS 3.1 protocols and drivers can automatically add or remove themselves from memory.

5.1.8   Workgroups and Domains

If you're installing Windows 95 in a Windows NT environment, one of the first decisions to make is whether to join an existing domain or to establish or join a workgroup. Windows 95 offers the user the unique ability to be a member of a separate workgroup in the browse list yet still log on and be a member of a domain. It is important to remember that Windows 95, unlike a Windows NT machine, does not create a computer account in the NT domain.

The two main administrative architecture types of a Windows NT network are workgroups and domains.

Workgroups are used for small groups in which there is no centralized security or server. In a workgroup, each user is in full control of shared network resources on her workstation. The lack of centralized resources makes enforcement of security regulations very difficult.

Domains are used in complex environments to centralize security and administration. A domain requires at least one central server running Windows NT Server that serves as the domain controller and manages the security database. The domain model allows relatively easy, centralized administration by a few specialists. Security regulations can be set from the central server to force users to operate within policy constraints.

5.1.9   Universal Naming Convention (UNC)

Microsoft's Universal Naming Convention (UNC) is a standardized nomenclature for specifying a share name on a particular computer. The NetBIOS computer name is limited to 15 characters, and the share name is usually limited to 15 characters. Share names can be given to a print queue or a shared directory of files.

The UNC uniquely specifies the path to the share name on a network. The UNC path takes the form of *computer_name**share_name* [*optional path*]. For example, the UNC path of the printer share LaserJet created on the server Server1 would be \\Server1\LaserJet.

> **A UNC name does not require a drive-letter assignment. Windows 95 takes full advantage of network connectivity using UNC names so that you can connect to a remote directory or printer share without having to map a drive letter to it.**

The UNC also can specify the full path to a file in a subdirectory of a file share. For example, a file named directions.txt located in the Sample folder on the computer named Simon is represented as \\Simon\Sample\directions.txt.

All Windows 95 functions support using a UNC name, including the Run option on the Start menu and the command prompt. NetWare servers, like Windows NT servers, can be accessed through a UNC name. Instead of share name, however, substitute a volume name to access a NetWare server.

> **When establishing share names on your servers, keep them short, do not use spaces within the name, and use 15 or fewer total characters so Windows 95 can display them within Network Neighborhood when users are browsing for network resources.**

5.1.10 Browsing Services

The Windows 95 browsing service reduces network traffic by maintaining a central list of all active servers in a workgroup. This list is kept current by having all active servers send a status message to a single computer, the master browser, on a regular basis. The master browser server updates the list as servers join and leave the local network section.

In a Windows NT network, the Primary Domain Controller (PDC) serves as the Domain Master Browser, collecting browse lists from the local master browsers. This centralized collection of browse lists allows an enterprise-wide browsable network.

If no master browser is present for a workgroup, the first workstation that attempts to access a browse list sends out an election request to the remaining servers in the workgroup. This election request invokes a comparison of all the remaining servers to determine which is most suitable to be the new master browser.

If the Browse Master parameter is set to Automatic (the default), the Windows 95 computer can participate as a master browser. If the Browse Master parameter is set to Enable, the workstation will attempt to become a master browser. This might be desirable for a little-used computer that is always left on. If the Browse Master parameter is set to Disable, the Windows 95 computer will never serve as master or backup browser. Remember that at least one computer in the workgroup must serve as master browser.

5.1.11   Configuring File and Printer Sharing

Once you have your network set up, you'll want to share files or resources from your Windows 95 workstation. Depending on your network, you might want to assign passwords to each share, or you might want to use the account database on a server to assign permissions. The first task is to install a service to allow sharing.

Windows 95 supports two types of network share security:

- Share-level

- User-level

Only one of these can be configured on a Windows 95 computer at a time (see Figure 5.1).

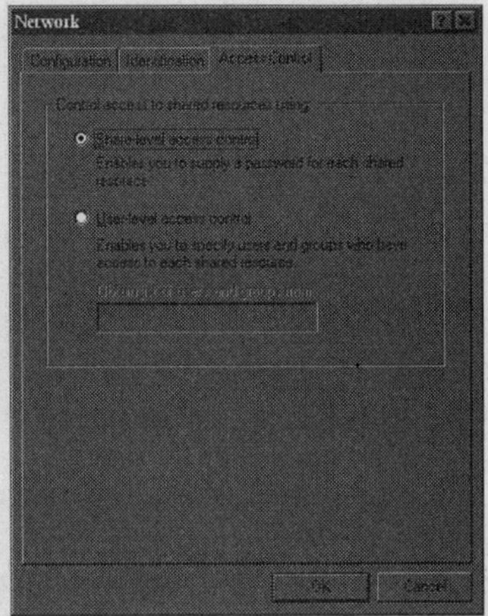

Figure 5.1   The Access Control tab in the Network properties sheet.

Share-Level Security

Share-level security is easy to implement and maintain because access to a resource is determined by a password assigned to the resource. Anyone with access to your network who has the password can use the resource. Share-level security offers three levels of password protection:

- **Read-Only.** Allows users access to a shared directory but prevents them from changing the contents.

- **Full.** Allows users to read and alter files.

- **Depends on Password.** Allows the type of access to be determined by the user's password. Different users can be given different passwords depending on their access needs.

> Share-level security is not supported if Windows 95 is configured to use File and Printer Sharing for NetWare Networks. When you're planning to integrate a Windows 95 computer into a NetWare network, keep in mind that an account database on a NetWare server will have to be made available to the Windows 95 user.

User-Level Security

User-level security requires a user database to reference logon attempts. Because Windows 95 doesn't have a user database, a server running Windows NT Workstation or Windows NT Server must be available. The name of the Windows NT computer or the domain name must be configured in the Access Control tab of the Network properties sheet accessible through the Control Panel (see Figure 5.2).

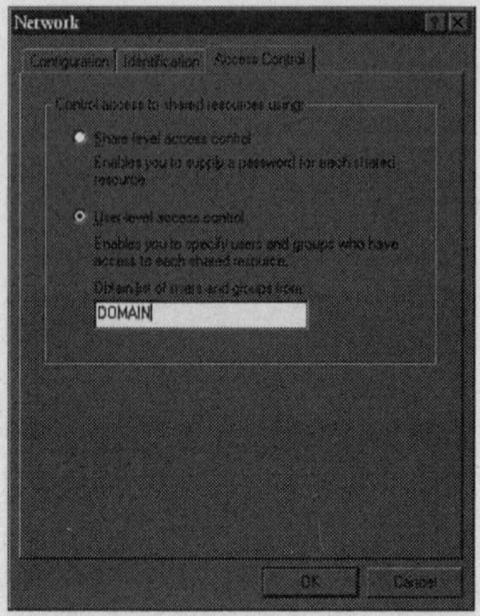

Figure 5.2   Configuring a Windows 95 computer to use a Windows NT server for user-level security.

When Windows 95 processes a request for access to a shared resource, the request is redirected over the network to the specified Windows NT machine that contains a user database. When sharing a file or resource, the Windows 95 administrator has three user-level options:

- **Read-Only.** Allows users to access a shared directory but prevents them from editing files or changing contents.

- **Full Access.** Allows users to view and edit files.

- **Custom.** Is a specialized combination of individual privileges.

If you choose Custom access, you can create an access level to a folder that consists of a combination of the following permissions:

- Read Files

- Write Files

- Create Files and Folders

- Delete Files

- Change File Attributes

- List Files

- Change Access Control

5.1.12   Exercises

Exercise 1: Install Client for Microsoft Networks

In this exercise you will install the Client for Microsoft Networks, which enables you to connect to a Windows NT domain:

1. Click Start, Settings, Control Panel, and then the Network icon to display the Network properties sheet.

2. Click the Add button. This opens the Select Network Component Type dialog box.

3. Select Client and click the Add button.

4. In the Manufacturers list, select Microsoft. From the list of Network Clients, select Client for Microsoft Networks.

5. Click OK. Client for Microsoft Networks is added to your installed network components. You're returned to the Network properties sheet.

6. Click OK, and the system updates itself. It might prompt you for the location of required files.

7. Restart Windows 95.

Exercise 2: Install File and Printer Sharing for Microsoft Networks

1. Click Start, Settings, Control Panel, and then the Network icon to display the Network properties sheet.

2. Click the Add button. This opens the Select Network Component Type dialog box (see Figure 5.3).

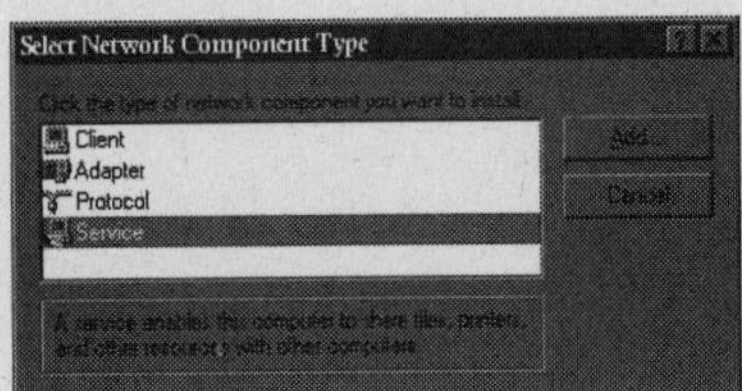

Figure 5.3   The Select Network Component Type dialog box.

3. Select Service and click the Add button.

4. In the Manufacturers list, select Microsoft. From the list of Network Services, select File and Printer Sharing for Microsoft Networks (see Figure 5.4).

5. Click OK. File and Printer Sharing for Microsoft Networks is added to your installed network components. You're returned to the Network properties sheet.

6. Click OK, and the system updates itself. It might prompt you for the location of required files.

7. Restart Windows 95.

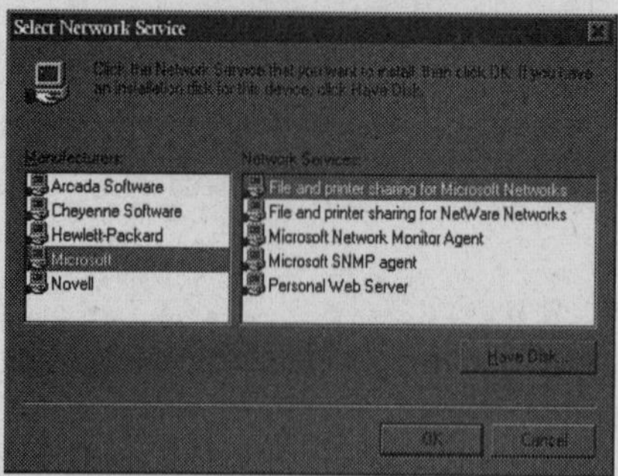

Figure 5.4   The Select Network Service dialog box.

5.1.13   Practice Problems

1. Which of the following are valid NetBIOS names?

   A. Computer One

   B. ComputerOne

   C. Computer 1

   D. Computer1

2. What are the options for share-level security?

   A. Read – Password Protected

   B. Write – Password Protected

   C. Full – Password Protected

   D. No Access

3. You are the administrator of a Windows NT network. A user contacts you and requests help connecting to a printer located on the network. What steps would you use to guide the user?

   A. Click Start, Run, and then type *//computer_name/printer_name*.

   B. Click Start, Settings, Printers, Add Printer, Network, and then type *//computer_name/share_name*.

   C. Click Start, Control Panel, Printers, Add Printer, Network, and then type *//computer_name/printer_name*.

   D. Click Start, Settings, Printers, Add Printer, Network, and then type *\\computer_name\share_name*.

   E. Click Start, Settings, Printers, Add Printer, Network, and then type *\\computer_name\printer_name*.

4. **Required Result:** Log on to a Windows NT domain.

   Option One: Connect to a network shared folder.

   Option Two: Share a folder so that members of the domain can read the files it contains.

   Action: Install and configure Client for Microsoft Networks to log on to Windows NT Domain. Install File and Printer Sharing for NetWare Networks.

   Evaluation: Which of the following statements is true of the suggested action?

   A. It fulfills the required result and all options.

   B. It fulfills the required result and option one only.

   C. It fulfills the required result and option two only.

   D. It fulfills the required result only.

   E. None of the above.

5. When installing TCP/IP, it is recommended that a default gateway be configured for the Windows 95 client. What steps must be taken to achieve this?

   A. Click Start, Programs, Control Panel, Network.

   B. Select TCP/IP, Properties, Gateway tab.

   C. Click Start, Settings, Control Panel, Network.

   D. Select TCP/IP, Properties, IP Properties, Gateway tab.

   E. None of the above.

6. You are responsible for connecting Windows 95 to a heterogeneous network. You're running a number of different network operating systems on this large network, and you want to be sure Windows 95 is compatible with them. Windows 95 includes software to support which three of the following networks?

   A. TCP/IP

   B. NetBEUI

   C. Novell NetWare

   D. Apple AppleShare

7. A user installs a network adapter card on a computer running Windows 95. When he does this, Windows 95 automatically installs two protocols for this card. Which two protocols are installed by default when the first network adapter driver is installed?

   A. AppleTalk

   B. NetBEUI

   C. TCP/IP

   D. IPX/SPX-compatible

8. **Required Result:** Share your local printer with the Windows 95 clients in your domain.

   Option One: Share your local printer with DOS clients in your domain.

   Option Two: Secure your printer through assigned permissions.

   Action: Install and configure Client for Microsoft Networks to log on to a Windows NT domain. Install File and Printer Sharing for Microsoft Networks. Assign a share name of *hplaserjet* to your local printer. Select user-level access control. Install the TCP/IP protocol.

   Evaluation: Which of the following statements is true of the suggested action?

   A. It fulfills the required result and all options.

   B. It fulfills the required result and option one only.

   C. It fulfills the required result and option two only.

   D. It fulfills the required result only.

   E. None of the above.

9. **Required Result:** Assign user rights to a local shared folder with Windows 95 clients on your NT domain.

   Option One: Connect to a shared printer.

   Option Two: Map a network drive to a Windows NT Server resource.

   Action: Install and configure Client for NetWare Networks to log on to a Windows NT domain. Install File and Printer Sharing for NetWare Networks. Open Windows 95 Explorer and select Tools, Map a Drive.

   Evaluation: Which of the following statements is true of the suggested action?

   A. It fulfills the required result and all options.

   B. It fulfills the required result and option one only.

   C. It fulfills the required result and option two only.

   D. It fulfills the required result only.

   E. None of the above.

10. In a training class you are teaching, you explain to end users how to use UNC to access resources on the network. You provide this example to the class: What is the full UNC path for a file named test.bat in a directory named BATCH located in a share named PUBLIC on a server named FREDSPC? Select the correct answer.

    A. \\PUBLIC\BATCH\test.bat

    B. \\FREDSPC\BATCH\test.bat

    C. \\FREDSPC\PUBLIC\BATCH\ test.bat

    D. None of the above

11. Susan prepares for a presentation describing the Windows 95 network architecture. One of the bullet points is this: A __________ maps network names used by an application to a physical network device name. Pick the appropriate answer to fill in the blank.

    A. Device driver

    B. Redirector

    C. Requestor

    D. Transport interface

12. Which three of the following are layers in the Windows 95 networking architecture?

    A. Transport Programming Interface

    B. Internal File System Manager

    C. Device Driver Interface

    D. Network Providers

13. You have Windows 95 installed on a computer connected to a network running only one network operating system (NOS). A user calls and says she cannot browse network resources using Network Neighborhood. Which NOS could you be running that does not support browser services?

    A. Novell NetWare 3.12

    B. Banyan VINES

    C. Windows NT

    D. None of the above

14. Stuart is attaching his Windows 95 computer directly to another Windows 95 computer using Microsoft Networking. He wants to set them up so that each computer has access to files and printers on either machine. Which of the following must he do to enable this in Windows 95?

    A. Set up user-level security.

    B. Install File and Printer Sharing for Microsoft Networks on both computers.

    C. Set up share-level security.

    D. All of the above.

15. As you instruct a user on how to configure a peer-to-peer network with five connected Windows 95 computers, you use the term "Windows 95 server" several times. After you finish, he asks you what a Windows 95 server is. What do you tell him?

    A. A computer that is the Primary Domain Controller (PDC) on the LAN.

    B. A computer running Windows 95 that has the Enable Windows 95 Server Registry option turned on.

    C. A Windows 95 computer that has the File and Printer Sharing Service enabled.

    D. A computer running Windows 95 that performs as an application and database server for the LAN.

16. Windows 95's modular architecture includes the Installable File Service (IFS) Manager. The IFS Manager manages communication between three of the following. Pick the three best answers.

    A. The miniport driver

    B. The various installable file systems

    C. The network provider

    D. The network redirectors and services

17. **Required Result:** Assign user permissions to a secure folder located on a Windows 95 client in an NT domain.

    Option One: Access a resource using a UNC path.

    Option Two: Enable connectivity between users running TCP/IP only.

    Action: Install and configure Client for Microsoft Networks to log on to a Windows NT domain. Install TCP/IP protocol.

    Evaluation: Which of the following statements is true of the proposed action?

    A. It fulfills the required result and all options.

    B. It fulfills the required result and option one only.

    C. It fulfills the required result and option two only.

    D. It fulfills the required result only.

    E. None of the above.

18. What command-line utility enables you to connect to a network-shared folder using a drive letter? Select the best answer.

    A. Map

    B. Net

    C. Redirect

    D. Connect

19. A user's Windows 95 machine is a member of a peer-to-peer workgroup. What security level options are available?

    A. Domain-level

    B. Share-level

    C. Group-level

    D. Workgroup-level

20. To enable sharing of resources on a Windows NT network, which of the following components is mandatory?

    A. NETREDIR.VXD

    B. NWREDIR.VXD

    C. VREDIR.VXD

    D. NETREDIR. EXE

5.1.14 Answers and Explanations

1. **B, D** NetBIOS names are limited to 15 characters and cannot contain spaces.

2. **A, C** Read and Full are the two options in share-level access control. You combine additional security with passwords.

3. **B** You can use the Add Printer Wizard.

4. **B** You need to install File and Printer Sharing for Microsoft Networks in order to fulfill the other options.

5. **B, C** You must add an IP address in the Gateway properties of the TCP/IP protocol.

6. **A, B, C** AppleShare is not a standard in Windows 95.

7. **B, D** NetBEUI and IPX/SPX-compatible protocols are installed as defaults.

8. **A** Because Client for Microsoft Networks is installed, you can connect to an NT domain and set user-level access control.

9. **E** You must install Client for Microsoft Networks in order to connect to an NT domain.

10. **C** \\FREDSPC\PUBLIC\BATCH\ test.bat follows the correct UNC format of *computer_name**share_name**directory**file*.

11. **B** The redirector in Windows 95 architecture provides this capability for the Workstation service.

12. **A, C, D** Windows 95 network architecture closely matches the seven layers of the OSI model.

13. **B** Banyan VINES does not support the Windows browse service.

14. **B, C** Both machines must be configured with File and Printer Sharing for Microsoft Networks. Share-level access control is the default setting.

15. **C** By enabling File and Printer Sharing for Microsoft Networks, you can use a Windows 95 machine as a central source for file and printer sharing in a workgroup.

16. **B, C, D** The IFS manager acts as a mediator between other various IFS, the network provider, and the network redirector and services.

17. **E** Both options can be achieved through the actions described. However, without installing File and Printer Sharing for Microsoft Networks, you cannot complete the required result.

18. **B**   The Net command provides several command-line capabilities. For a listing of Net commands, type **NET /?** at the command line.

19. **B**   User-level security is available only when a system is authenticated in an NT domain or a NetWare environment.

20. **C**   VREDIR.VXD is the virtual redirector for Microsoft Networks. NWREDIR.VXD is the virtual redirector for NetWare networks.

5.1.15   Key Words and Definitions

Config.pol   A policy file that is used to create a specific environment for a Windows 95 or Windows NT client. Windows 95 is set to automatically look in the domain controller's NetLogon share or the NetWare server's public directory for the default Config.pol file.

MAC address   The unique hexadecimal number assigned to each network interface card. The number is used to identify the individual card (much like a social security number is used to identify individuals).

NDIS (Network Driver Interface Specification)   The layer that wraps itself around the network device driver to allow communication with the protocol layers and the hardware. NDIS 3.1 adds Plug and Play capabilities.

NetBIOS (Network Basic Input/Output System)   An application program interface that provides application programs, such as Windows Explorer, with a set of rules. These rules are used as a guideline to conduct communication between nodes on a network.

NIC (Network Interface Card)   The peripheral hardware device that provides transport access for network packets.

Server Message Block (SMB)   A file sharing protocol. Its main function is to allow a user, or more specifically a system, to access a remote file transparently.

5.2   Configuring Windows 95 for a NetWare Network

Microsoft Windows 95 includes an IPX/SPX-compatible protocol that allows integration into existing NetWare LANs. For interoperability with NetWare 2.x and 3.x networks and NetWare 4.x networks with servers using bindery emulation, the retail and OEM versions of Windows 95 include the following:

- The 32-bit Client for NetWare Networks, using the NWREDIR.VXD driver

- Support for older 16-bit NetWare clients

- A NetWare logon script processor

- The IPX/SPX-compatible protocol

- The IPX ODI protocol for compatibility with older NetWare networks

- File and Printer Sharing for NetWare Networks service

In later versions of Windows 95, the OSR2 release, and service-packed earlier versions, a NetWare Directory Services (NDS) service is also available. When assigned a valid user object and password, NDS allows Windows 95 computers to authenticate to a NetWare 4.x network and access shared resources.

The File and Printer Sharing for NetWare Networks service allows Windows 95 to act as a peer-to-peer server on a NetWare network. This allows sharing of resources such as printers that may be attached to the Windows 95 computer.

Windows 95's capability to use multiple network providers allows Windows 95 workstations to be integrated into mixed NetWare and Windows NT networks.

5.2.1   Configure Windows 95 to Access a NetWare Bindery

To take advantage of the IPX/SPX-compatible protocol and allow connections to NetWare servers with binderies, your Windows 95 workstation can be configured with the Client for NetWare Networks.

5.2.2   Configure Windows 95 to Access an NDS Tree

The OSR2 version of Windows 95 comes with a NetWare Directory Services (NDS) service to allow access to NetWare 4.x NDS "trees." Earlier versions of Windows 95 can run the NDS service only if the Windows 95 version has been upgraded to at least Service Pack 1.

The options on the Directory Services property sheet are described in the following list.

- **Preferred Tree.** This is the NDS tree where the user will want to access shared resources.

- **Workstation Default Context.** The default context where the user's NDS user object can be found.

> **This service can be configured on only Windows 95 workstations that *already* have the IPX/SPX-compatible protocol and the Client for NetWare Networks installed.**

5.2.3   File and Printer Sharing with NetWare Networks

File and Printer Sharing for NetWare Networks allows directories and printers to be shared with other NetWare users. There are two very important points to keep in mind if you're considering using File and Printer Sharing for NetWare:

- You can't simultaneously have File and Printer Sharing for NetWare Networks and File and Printer Sharing for Microsoft Networks installed. Only one can be configured on a particular Windows 95 workstation.

- File and Printer Sharing for NetWare Networks must use the user-level security model. The account list must be on a NetWare server bindery or in the bindery context of a NetWare 4.x server using bindery emulation.

User-level security with NetWare Networks is similar to user-level security for Microsoft Networks. A server is queried anytime a shared resource access is attempted. The username or group membership must be on the NetWare server's account list and must have the necessary rights to gain access to the resource.

Windows 95 doesn't normally make a distinction between Microsoft shares and Novell volumes: Both appear as directories, also called folders, on the network to a Windows 95 computer.

You can use the Net command from a DOS prompt to control connections to either type of network resource, using either Microsoft networking UNC paths or NetWare *server/volume* paths. This could be useful in the creation of batch files or logon scripts. At the DOS prompt, type **NET /?** for a listing of Net commands.

5.2.4   IPX/SPX Configuration

The IPX/SPX-compatible protocol is installed automatically when the Client for NetWare Networks is installed. You can also install this protocol to support different network clients, including the built-in Client for Microsoft Networks.

NetBIOS over IPX is also included with Windows 95 and can be enabled by selecting the I Want to Enable NetBIOS over IPX/SPX check box in the IPX/SPX-compatible properties sheet. Once that's enabled, name resolution can be obtained over an IPX network.

Usually, the IPX/SPX-compatible protocol is self-configuring. By default, when a Windows 95 computer with IPX/SPX-compatible protocol is started, it determines by responses from routers which frame type is most prevalent on the local network. Network addresses are also determined automatically.

In a mixed Windows NT and NetWare network, client to transport protocol bindings may need to be changed. This can improve your networking performance and can eliminate problems with older 16-bit network applications that may require a certain client-protocol configuration.

5.2.5   Exercise

Exercise 1: Install the Client for NetWare Networks

In this exercise, you will install and configure the Client for NetWare Networks.

1. Click Start, Settings, Control Panel, and then double-click the Network icon.

2. Click the Add button in the Network properties sheet. The Select Network Component Type dialog box appears (see Figure 5.5).

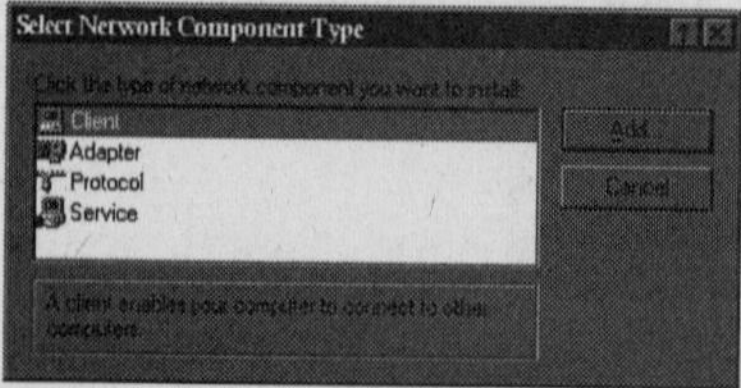

Figure 5.5   The Select Network Component Type dialog box.

3. Double-click Client, and the Select Network Client dialog box opens.

4. In the Manufacturers column, click Microsoft.

5. In the Network Clients column, click Client for NetWare Networks (see Figure 5.6).

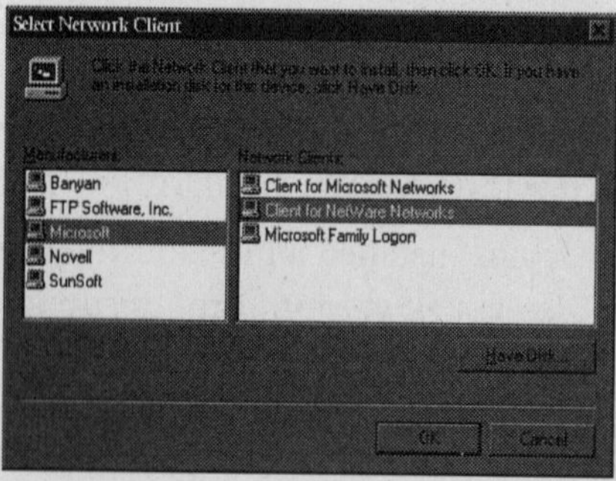

Figure 5.6   The Select Network Client dialog box showing Microsoft's network clients.

6. Click OK. The Client for NetWare Networks is installed. When the installation is complete, you're returned to the Network properties sheet.

7. On the Network properties sheet, click the Configuration tab.

8. Double-click Client for NetWare Networks. The Client for NetWare Networks Properties sheet opens (see Figure 5.7). Configure the following options on this properties sheet:

    - **Preferred Server.** Specify the NetWare server to be used for logon and authentication.

    - **First Network Drive.** Indicate the first drive that will be allowed by Windows 95 to be mapped to a network volume on a NetWare server. Drives F through Z are allowed for NetWare, but you might need to alter this list depending on your Windows 95 configuration.

    - **Enable Logon Script Processing.** Choose whether you want to enable logon scripts. Logon scripts are often stored on the preferred NetWare server.

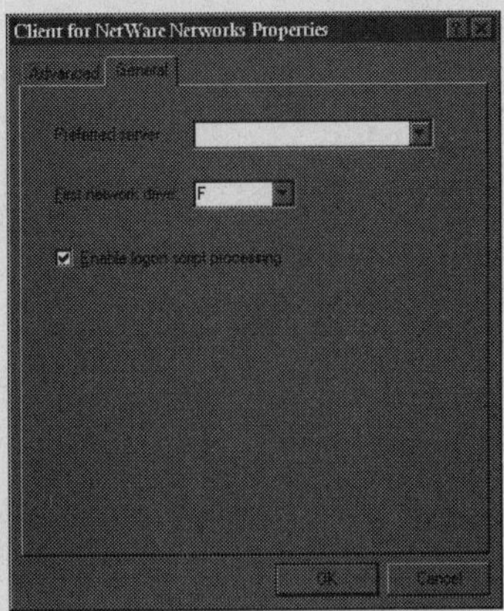

Figure 5.7   The Client for NetWare Networks Properties sheet needs to be configured.

9. Click OK to close the Network properties sheet.

10. If needed, specify the location of any necessary files Windows 95 asks about, and then restart the computer to make the Client for NetWare Networks accessible.

5.2.6   Practice Problems

1. You configure a Windows 95 workstation to connect to a NetWare network. When you install Client for NetWare Networks, which protocol is installed?

   A. TCP/IP

   B. NetBEUI

   C. IPX/SPX-compatible

   D. DLC

2. Steve is connecting his Windows 95 computer to a network running Novell NetWare. He wants to share files and a printer with other users. What type of security must he use?

   A. NetWare-level

   B. Share-level

   C. User-level

   D. Group-level

3. You want to install a Windows 95 client on a Novell NetWare network that includes NetWare 4.*x* servers. Which two of the following network components might you need?

   A. Microsoft Client for NetWare Networks

   B. Microsoft NDS service

   C. File and Printer Sharing for Microsoft Networks

   D. NetBEUI

4. Chuck is setting up a network to use user-level security. From the following list, pick the two places where the user list can be selected.

   A. Windows NT domain

   B. Window 95 home directory

   C. NetWare bindery server

   D. Banyan VINES server

5. You are asked to connect ten Windows 95 computers to a Novell NetWare network. From the following list, pick the two components or features that Windows 95 has for NetWare networks.

   A. Capability to run File and Printer Sharing for NetWare Networks with File and Printer Sharing for Microsoft Networks at the same time.

   B. Share-level security support of File and Printer Sharing for NetWare Networks.

   C. IPX/SPX-compatible protocol.

   D. 32-bit Client for NetWare Networks.

6. Martina has been told that she can run multiple network clients under Windows 95, but she is having problems getting this feature to work on her system. She calls you and asks you to help her. From the following list, what would be the best question to ask her to start diagnosing her problem?

   A. Does she have protocols for IPX/SPX set up?

   B. Is Windows 95 set up to handle user profiles?

   C. Is there a Primary Domain Controller (PDC) established on a Windows 95 Server?

   D. Are all the network clients 32-bit clients?

7. **Required Result:** Share your local printer with NetWare clients.

   Option One: Share your local printer with DOS clients in your domain.

   Option Two: Secure your printer through assigned permissions.

   Action: Install and configure Client for NetWare Networks to log on to an NDS tree. Install File and Printer Sharing for

Microsoft Networks. Assign a share name of *hplaserjet* to your local printer. Select User Level Access control. Install the IPX/SPX protocol.

Evaluation: Which of the following statements is true of the suggested action?

A. It fulfills the required result and all options.

B. It fulfills the required result and option one only.

C. It fulfills the required result and option two only.

D. It fulfills the required result only.

E. None of the above.

8. **Required Result:** Assign user rights to a local shared folder with NetWare clients.

Option One: Connect to a shared printer.

Option Two: Map a network drive to a Windows NT server resource.

Action: Install and configure Client for Microsoft Networks to log on to a Windows NT domain. Install and configure Client for NetWare Networks to log on to a NetWare NDS tree. Install File and Printer Sharing for NetWare Networks. Open Windows 95 Explorer and select Tools, Map a Drive.

Evaluation: Which of the following statements is true of the suggested action?

A. It fulfills the required result and all options.

B. It fulfills the required result and option one only.

C. It fulfills the required result and option two only.

D. It fulfills the required result only.

E. None of the above.

9. What is the full UNC path required to access the "syscon" utility located on the "Sales" NetWare server in a share named PUBLIC on a NetWare volume named SYS?

A. \\PUBLIC\Syscon

B. \\Server\Syscon

C. \\Sys\PUBLIC\Syscon

D. None of the above

10. You are the administrator of a NetWare network environment. A user contacts you and requests help connecting her Windows 95 client to a printer located on the NetWare server. What steps would you use to guide the user?

A. Click Start, Run and type *//server/printer_name*.

B. Click Start, Settings, Printers, Add Printer, Network, and then type *//server/share_name*.

C. Click Start, Control Panel, Printers, Add Printer, Network, and then type *//server/printer_name*.

D. Click Start, Settings, Printers, Add Printer, Network, and then type *\\server\share_name*.

E. Click Start, Settings, Printers, Add Printer, Network, and then type *\\server\print_queue*.

11. You are connecting a Windows 95 client to a NetWare 4.*x* NDS tree. What three components are necessary?

A. Client for Microsoft Networks

B. Client for NetWare Networks

C. Microsoft NDS Service

D. IPX/SPX-compatible protocol

E. File and Printer Sharing for NetWare Networks

12. A user contacts you and states that he can log on to the Microsoft network, but his system is unable to access files from the NetWare server. You check his permissions, and they are in order. What other option would you check?

   A. IPX/SPX-compatible protocol

   B. Client for Microsoft Networks

   C. Client for NetWare Networks

   D. File and Printer Sharing for NetWare Networks

13. You are connecting a Windows 95 client to a NetWare 4.*x* NDS tree. What settings have you configured for Microsoft NDS Service? Select all that apply.

   A. Preferred Login

   B. Preferred Tree

   C. Preferred Logon

   D. Preferred Server

14. **Required Result:** Share a local folder with NetWare clients.

   Option One: Secure your folder through assigned permissions.

   Option Two: Log on and be authenticated by a Windows NT domain.

   Action: Install and configure Client for NetWare Networks to log on to an NDS tree. Install File and Printer Sharing for NetWare Networks. Install the IPX/SPX protocol.

   Evaluation: Which of the following statements if true of the suggested action?

   A. It fulfills the required result and all options.

   B. It fulfills the required result and option one only.

   C. It fulfills the required result and option two only.

   D. It fulfills the required result only.

   E. None of the above.

15. You upgrade a Windows 95 client on a NetWare network. The user contacts you and says he can log on, but he cannot see drive M: as he did before. What configuration setting is missing?

   A. Client for NetWare Networks

   B. Enable Logon Script Processing

   C. Preferred Server

   D. Client for Microsoft Networks

16. Which files are necessary in order to connect a Windows 95 client to a NetWare network with Client for NetWare Networks?

   A. LSL

   B. IPXODI

   C. VLM

   D. MLID

   E. IPX/SPX-compatible protocol

17. Which options are found in the Configuration tab of the NetWare Directory Services properties sheet?

   A. Preferred Logon

   B. Preferred Tree

   C. Preferred Context

   D. Default Context

18. Which two services cannot be installed at the same time?

   A. Client for Microsoft Networks

   B. File and Printer Sharing for NetWare Networks

   C. Client for NetWare Networks

   D. File and Printer Sharing for Microsoft Networks

19. **Required Result:** Connect a Windows 95 system as a client on a NetWare network.

    Option One: Provide automated drive mappings for shared resources.

    Option Two: Define Preferred Server and Default Context properties.

    Action: Install and configure Client for NetWare Networks to log on to an NDS tree. Install File and Printer Sharing for NetWare Networks. Install NetWare Directory Services (NDS) service. Enable Login Script Processing.

    Evaluation: Which of the following statements is true of the suggested action?

    A. It fulfills the required result and all options.

    B. It fulfills the required result and option one only.

    C. It fulfills the required result and option two only.

    D. It fulfills the required result only.

    E. None of the above.

20. Which option is available with Windows 95 OSR2 or by installing the Windows 95 Service Pack 1?

    A. Banyan Network Services

    B. NetWare Directory Services (NDS) service

    C. NTFS

    D. FAT64

5.2.7 Answers and Explanations

1. **C** The IPX/SPX-compatible protocol is installed automatically when Client for NetWare Networks is installed.

2. **C** User-level access is required when connecting and sharing files and printers on a NetWare network.

3. **A, B** Client for NetWare Networks is mandatory to connect to a NetWare 4.*x* server. If you want to connect to a 4.*x* server's NDS, Microsoft NDS service can be used.

4. **A, C** User-level security can be used with both a Windows NT domain and a NetWare server in bindery emulation.

5. **C, D** Client for NetWare Networks is necessary, along with the IPX/SPX-compatible protocol for communication.

6. **D** Using Novell's 16-bit network client can cause problems when combining multiple network clients.

7. **E** The required result has not been met. By installing File and Printer Sharing for Microsoft Networks, you are unable to share resources with NetWare clients.

8. **C** Installing both clients allows you to access resources on a Microsoft and a NetWare network. In addition, the installation of File and Printer Sharing for NetWare Networks not only allows you to share a resource with NetWare clients, it also allows you to assign user-specific permissions to the shared resource.

9. **D** The correct UNC path to a NetWare volume follows the format *Server*\ *Volume:\path*.

10. **D** You can use the Add Printer Wizard and reference the printer with the UNC path referencing the print queue.

11. **B, C, D** These items are necessary. File and Printer Sharing for NetWare Networks is necessary only if you are wanting to share local resources with NetWare clients.

12. **C** The term "logon" indicates the user has been authenticated by an NT domain. Check Client for NetWare Networks to verify a connection to a NetWare server.

13. **B, D**   The Microsoft NDS service allows you to configure a preferred tree, preferred server, default context, and first network drive letter.

14. **B**   You must install Client for Microsoft Networks to log on to an NT domain.

15. **B**   The user most likely had a logon script on the NetWare server that mapped drive M:. Enabling Logon Script Processing should correct the problem.

16. **E**   Client for NetWare Networks installs the Microsoft 32-bit IPX/SPX-compatible protocol. The other options will install the real mode 16-bit client.

17. **B, D**   The Microsoft NDS service allows you to configure a preferred tree, preferred server, default context, and first network drive letter.

18. **B, D**   You can install both Clients for Microsoft and NetWare Networks. Because they cannot be installed at the same time, you must select between File and Printer Sharing for NetWare Networks or File and Printer Sharing for Microsoft Networks.

19. **A**   Installing client services for NetWare NDS fulfills the required result and all options.

20. **B**   Microsoft NetWare Directory Service (NDS) service is available with the OSR2 version of Windows 95.

5.2.8   Key Words and Definitions

Context   Defines your position in relation to the NDS tree. For example, Jim is the Sales Manager for the Eastern Division of the Widget Company.

IPX/SPX (Internetwork Packet Exchange/ Sequenced Packet Exchange)   The protocol designed by NetWare for communication in a NetWare network environment. NWLink is the Windows NT–compatible version of the protocol.

NetWare Directory Services (NDS)   A user database designed by Novell. It allows a single point of network administration for users, computers, and other objects.

Tree   In the NDS structure, a tree provides a focal starting point, or encapsulation, much like a company name provides recognition for an employee.

5.3 Configuring Windows 95 to Access the Internet: TCP/IP

Windows 95 comes with the Microsoft 32-bit TCP/IP protocol, related utilities, and an SNMP client. TCP/IP gives Windows 95 an industry standard routeable enterprise-level networking protocol. TCP/IP is the transport protocol of the Internet, and with the included TCP/IP utilities, Windows 95 can access its rapidly growing resources.

After you install TCP/IP, the TCP/IP Properties sheet appears. It offers the following tabs of options:

- IP Address
- Gateway
- DNS Configuration
- WINS Configuration
- Advanced
- Bindings

5.3.1 Choosing Manual or DHCP IP Configuration

The IP Address tab of the TCP/IP Properties sheet (see Figure 5.8) contains two radio buttons from which to choose:

- Obtain an IP Address Automatically
- Specify an IP Address

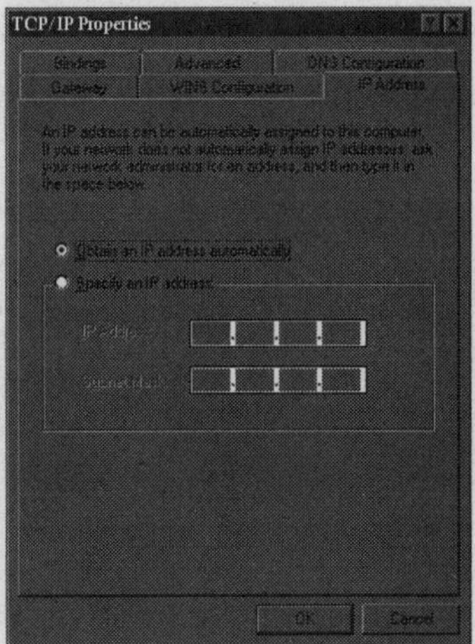

Figure 5.8 The IP Address sheet configured to use DHCP.

Dynamic Host Control Protocol (DHCP) allows automatic IP address assignment. When Windows 95 is configured as a DHCP client and then restarted, it broadcasts a message looking for a DHCP server. The DHCP server provides the client with an IP address to use for a pre-determined length of time.

A DHCP server can be configured to pass all the necessary IP address information to a DHCP client. This includes the IP address leased to the client, as well as the IP addresses of the default gateway, subnet mask, DNS servers, and WINS servers.

> **While this information probably isn't hit very heavy on the exam, it's useful context information for the topic.**

5.3.2 Subnet Masking

Along with the IP address, a subnet mask is required for every TCP/IP device. A subnet mask is used to determine if a destination address is located on the local subnet or on a remote network. Subnet masks can be configured manually, along with the IP address, by network administrators. A DHCP server can also assign a subnet mask automatically. See Table 5.1 for a listing of IP address classes and the default subnet mask.

Table 5.1   IP Address Classes and Subnet Masks

Class	First Octet Range	Default Subnet Mask
Class A	1–126	255.0.0.0
Class B	128–191	255.255.0.0
Class C	192–223	255.255.255.0

5.3.3 Configuring a Gateway

When you have an IP address and subnet mask, your Windows 95 computer is ready to talk to other workstations on the local network, but it still has no way to reach a wide area network or the Internet. A default gateway provides that connectivity to the rest of the networked world.

5.3.4 Using Name Resolution

Name resolution is the process of turning a host or computer name into an IP address. You can configure Windows 95 to attempt name resolution using any of the following methods:

- Domain Name Service (DNS)
- Windows Internet Name Service (WINS)
- LMHosts file
- Hosts file
- Broadcasts

Configuring Windows 95 to Use DNS

DNS provides a static, centrally administrated database for resolving domain names to IP addresses. A fully qualified DNS name consists of a host name appended to an Internet or intranet domain name. Keep in mind that this is different from a Windows NT domain name. For example, the host www could be appended to microsoft.com to give the fully qualified domain name www.microsoft.com.

You configure Windows 95 to use DNS by using the options on the DNS Configuration tab of the TCP/IP Properties sheet (see Figure 5.9).

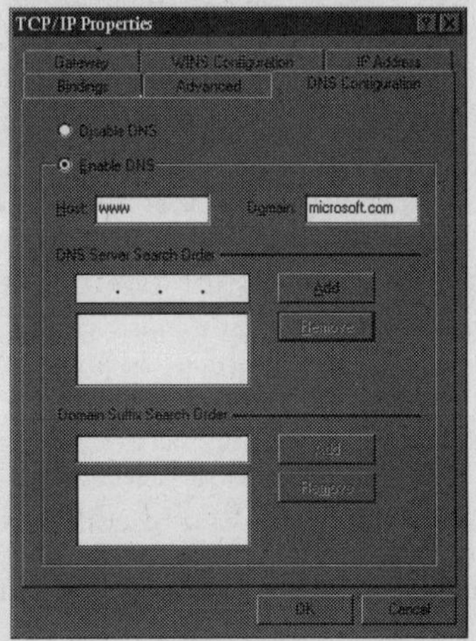

Figure 5.9 Enabling DNS through the TCP/IP Properties sheet.

The Enable DNS fields on the DNS Configuration tab allow Windows 95 to take advantage of several DNS services. Configure the following options:

- **Host.** Is the local computer's registered DNS name.

- **Domain.** Is the organization's InterNIC registered domain name.

- **DNS Server Search Order.** Allows backup DNS servers to be configured in case the primary fails.

- **Domain Suffix Search Order.** Tells TCP/IP utilities what domains to append and search if only a hostname is given to the utility.

Configuring Windows 95 to Use WINS

WINS allows a Windows 95 user to use a human-friendly NetBIOS name in network utilities, such as to use a UNC path to access a share. Then Windows 95 can query the WINS server to resolve the NetBIOS name to an IP address, allowing a TCP/IP communication to take place.

You configure Windows 95 to use a WINS server by using the options on the WINS Configuration tab of the TCP/IP Properties sheet (see Figure 5.10).

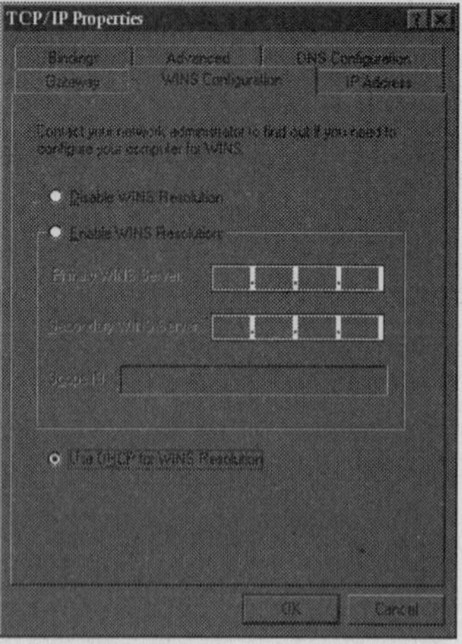

Figure 5.10　Enabling WINS through the TCP/IP Properties sheet.

You have three choices of WINS configuration for a Windows 95 TCP/IP client:

- **Disable WINS Resolution.** If WINS is disabled, an alternate form of NetBIOS name resolution, such as an LMHosts file, is necessary.

- **Enable WINS Resolution.** If WINS resolution is enabled, the IP address of a primary WINS server is required. A secondary WINS server can be configured to provide backup.

- **Use DHCP for WINS Resolution.** If the Windows 95 client is using DHCP to configure IP numbers, you can select this option to use the WINS servers specified by the DHCP server.

It is important to keep in mind the differences between WINS and DNS:

- WINS uses a dynamic registration system; DNS relies on static tables.

- DNS resolves fully qualified domain names into IP addresses; WINS resolves NetBIOS computer names into IP addresses.

- DNS is a hierarchical system; WINS uses the flat NetBIOS name space.

Configuring Static Name Resolution: Hosts and LMHosts

If WINS is unavailable, the Hosts and LMHosts files provide local, static lists that allow name resolution.

- The Hosts file is used as a local DNS equivalent to resolve host names to IP numbers.

- The LMHosts file is used as a local WINS equivalent to resolve NetBIOS computer names to IP addresses.

Broadcast Name Resolution

Computers running Microsoft TCP/IP can use broadcast NetBIOS name resolution, a NetBIOS over TCP/IP mode of operation that involves the client computer making an IP-level broadcast to register its name by announcing it on the network.

5.3.5   Troubleshooting Windows 95 TCP/IP

You can solve common TCP/IP problems by using Windows 95's built-in TCP/IP diagnostic utilities (see Table 5.2).

Table 5.2   Windows 95 TCP/IP Utilities

Utility	Description
WINIPCFG	Displays all TCP/IP addressing information, including DHCP lease status
NetStat	Indicates network status
Ping	Tests connections
Route	Allows you to configure a route
Tracert	Checks and displays the route to a remote computer
Nbtstat	Checks the state of NetBIOS over TCP/IP connections
Arp	Checks the local ARP table

5.3.6   Exercise

Exercise 1: Installing the TCP/IP Protocol

In this exercise, you will install TCP/IP and configure your system to connect to the Internet. You need to install TCP/IP because Windows 95 does not have it installed by default.

1. Click Start, Settings, Control Panel, and then double-click on the Network icon.

2. Click the Add button in the Network Properties sheet. The Select Network Component Type dialog box appears.

3. Select Protocol, and then choose Add to open the Select Network Protocol dialog box.

4. Select Microsoft from the Manufacturers list and select TCP/IP from the Network Protocols list.

5. Choose OK to return to the Network Properties sheet.

To manually configure or change an IP address and subnet mask, follow these steps:

1. Click Start, Settings, Control Panel, and then double-click on the Network icon.

2. Double-click on the TCP/IP protocol in the installed network components window. The TCP/IP Properties sheet appears (see Figure 5.11).

3. Click the Specify an IP Address radio button.

4. Fill in the IP Address and Subnet Mask fields.

5. Click OK to close this Properties sheet, and then click OK again. Windows 95 will restart using your new IP information.

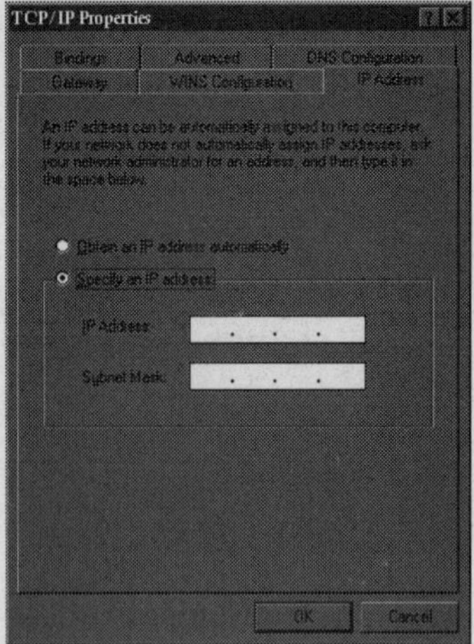

Figure 5.11   The TCP/IP Properties sheet.

Follow these steps to configure a default gateway:

1.   Click Start, Settings, Control Panel, and then double-click the Network icon.

2.   Double-click the TCP/IP protocol in the installed network components window.

3.   Select the Gateway tab (see Figure 5.12) on the TCP/IP Properties sheet.

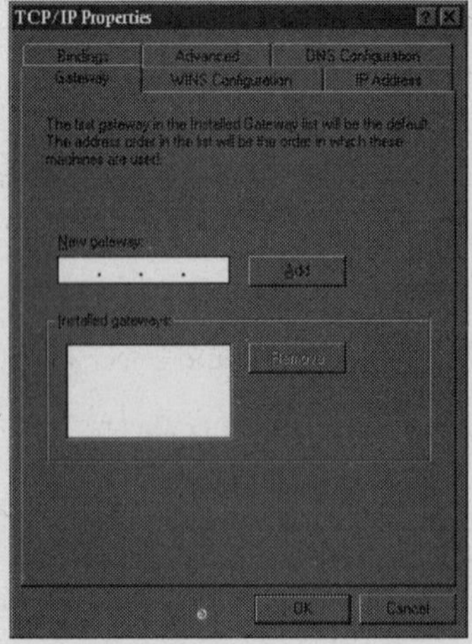

Figure 5.12   The Gateway tab of the TCP/IP Properties sheet.

4.   Enter your default gateway's IP address in the New Gateway box.

5.   Click Add, and the new default gateway appears in the Installed Gateways window.

6.   Click OK to close this Properties sheet, and then click OK again. Windows 95 will prompt you to restart with your new gateway information.

To pinpoint IP configuration connection difficulties or the reason for no connection, follow these steps:

1. From a DOS prompt, use WINIPCFG to make sure there are no errors in your TCP/IP configuration.

2. Ping 127.0.0.1 (the loopback address) to check basic TCP/IP functionality.

3. Then ping the IP address of your computer, your default gateway, and a remote host.

4. If your connection difficulty occurs only with a remote host, use Tracert to determine where along the route the connection is failing.

5.3.7   Practice Problems

1. With Windows 95, what methods can you use to resolve host names?

    A. DNS

    B. LMHosts file

    C. Hosts file

    D. WINS

2. While setting up Windows 95 to access the Internet, you find that connections over TCP/IP by host don't work, but connections by IP number do. What could be wrong?

    A. No WINS server is available.

    B. IPX/SPX-compatible protocol is not installed.

    C. No DNS server is available.

    D. No TCP/IP server is available.

3. Isabel is configuring her Windows 95 computer with the TCP/IP protocol. As she fills out the properties for the protocol, she comes across a blank for the DNS entry. What does DNS stand for?

    A. Downloadable Network Share

    B. DOS-Node Server

    C. Domain Name Service

    D. Domain Network Server

4. You run a network using NetBIOS. The _______ registers and resolves NetBIOS names to IP addresses.

    A. DNS server

    B. IFS Manager

    C. Network Adapter Card

    D. WINS server

5. While stationed at the company help desk, you receive a call from a user accessing the Internet. He asks what a fully qualified domain name is. From the following list, pick the one entry that would not meet the criteria of a fully qualified domain name.

    A. `www.microsoft.com`

    B. `www3.iquest.net`

    C. `www.microsoft_com`

    D. `www.mcp.com\newriders`

6. You are configuring TCP/IP on Windows 95 and have just put in the IP address 135.33.45.5. What is the default subnet mask?

    A. 255.0.0.0

    B. 255.255.0.0

    C. 255.255.255.0

    D. 255.255.255.255

7. Which of the following two utilities are most useful for tracking down TCP/IP connection problems on a Windows 95 client?

    A. Ping

    B. Arp

    C. WINIPCFG

    D. IPCONFIG

8. You're installing TCP/IP to configure a subnet mask for the Windows 95 client. What steps must you take to achieve this?

    A. Click Start, Programs, Control Panel, Network.

    B. Select TCP/IP, Properties, IP Address.

    C. Click Start, Settings, Control Panel, Network.

    D. Select TCP/IP, Programs, IP Properties.

    E. None of the above.

9. You are responsible for connecting Windows 95 to a TCP/IP network. You're running a number of different network operating systems on this large network, and you want to be sure Windows 95 is compatible with them. Which additional protocols must be installed?

   A. DNS

   B. NetBEUI

   C. WINS

   D. AppleShare

   E. None of the above

10. You are the administrator of an NT network. You install a network adapter card in a computer running Windows 95. You configure the adapter on the Network Properties sheet with the default settings. However, when you try to connect to the Internet, the connection fails. What would you check?

    A. Installed Client for Microsoft Network

    B. Installed NetBEUI

    C. Installed TCP/IP

    D. Installed IPX/SPX-compatible

11. **Situation:** As a member of the corporate MIS team, it is your responsibility to fulfill the needs of the Help Desk department. The Help Desk department has requested access to resources available on the Internet. Your company currently has Internet access, but only the Sales department is properly configured.

    Required Result: Provide the Help Desk department with access to the Internet.

    Option One: Download support files from the Internet.

    Option Two: Order books from www.mcp.com using Internet Explorer.

Action: Install and configure TCP/IP protocol. Install Client for Microsoft Networks. Configure TCP/IP properties with a static IP address and subnet mask. Configure an external DNS server to resolve IP addresses.

Evaluation: Which of the following statements is true of the proposed action?

   A. It fulfills the required result and all options.

   B. It fulfills the required result and option one only.

   C. It fulfills the required result and option two only.

   D. It fulfills the required result only.

   E. None of the above.

12. You sign up to access an Internet service provider from your Windows 95 computer at home. The instructions say to select "Obtain an IP Address Automatically." When you connect, you have access and are able to locate the www.mcp.com Web site using Internet Explorer. What did the ISP provide in order for this to happen? Select the best answer.

   A. DNS server

   B. WINS server

   C. DHCP server

   D. Primary Domain Controller

   E. Backup Domain Controller

13. You have connected to the Internet. While browsing Web sites using Internet Explorer, you notice that one site takes a longer time to respond. What command-line utility can tell you the path to the site?

   A. DNS

   B. WINIPCFG

   C. HOSTS

   D. TRACERT

14. Which applications are TCP/IP socket-based?

   A. Outlook Express

   B. Internet Explorer

   C. Word 5.0

   D. Excel 5.0

15. You have Windows 95 installed on a computer connected to an intranet. You receive a message stating An IP address conflict has occurred. What could be causing this error?

   A. Two DHCP servers with overlapping scopes

   B. Internet Explorer

   C. A static IP configured incorrectly

   D. A cached IP address from a different subnet

16. Which utility would allow you to view the NetBIOS over TCP/IP information?

   A. WINIPCFG

   B. NETSTAT

   C. PING

   D. NBTSTAT

17. A user contacts you and wants to see if a remote system is available. Which of the following commands can she use to test it?

   A. ping *remotehost*

   B. ping 194.264.45.19

   C. ping *IP_address*

   D. ping *computer_name*

18. You have just loaded Personal Web Server on your Windows 95 client and created a Web site. You tell a colleague to connect to your FQDN of allen.company.com. He cannot connect to your computer. What file can be quickly modified to enable such a connection?

   A. User.dat

   B. Hosts

   C. LMHosts

   D. System.dat

19. **Required Result:** Log on to an FTP server as anonymous.

   Option One: Resolve the FTP server name to an IP address.

   Option Two: Download a file.

   Action: Install the TCP/IP protocol. Obtain an IP address automatically. Modify the Hosts file to reference the FTP server. At the FTP prompt, type **get** *filename*.

   Evaluation: Which of the following statements is true of the proposed action?

   A. It fulfills the required result and all options.

   B. It fulfills the required result and option one only.

   C. It fulfills the required result and option two only.

   D. It fulfills the required result only.

   E. None of the above.

20. You are the administrator of a Windows NT domain. A user contacts you and says he has finished his FTP session but cannot return to the DOS prompt. What FTP commands will help?

   A. Stop

   B. End

   C. Quit

   D. Leave

5.3.8 Answers and Explanations

1. **A, C** The Hosts file, located in the Windows 95 directory, resolves host names to IP addresses. A Domain Name Server (DNS) located on an NT server also resolves host names when they are registered in the database.

2. **C** Although you have Internet connectivity, there is no Domain Name Server (DNS) available to resolve the host name with an IP address.

3. **C** A Domain Name Server (DNS) located on a UNIX machine or NT server resolves host names when they are registered in the database.

4. **D** A Windows Internet Name Server resolves a computer's NetBIOS name to an IP address. This is a dynamic database, as opposed to DNS, which is a static database.

5. **C** A fully qualified domain name (FQDN) lists the host name, followed by a period and the DNS domain name.

6. **B** The first octet of the IP address defines the class network. In the example, 135 is a Class B network with a default subnet mask of 255.255.0.0.

7. **A, C** The WINIPCFG and PING utilities are the two most useful TCP/IP utilities for tracking down TCP/IP troubleshooting issues.

8. **B, C** You must modify the Subnet Mask entry on the IP Address tab of the TCP/IP Properties sheet in order to specify and complete an IP address.

9. **E** If you are connecting a Windows 95 client to a TCP/IP network, only access to the Internet and the TCP/IP protocol is necessary.

10. **C** TCP/IP is not installed by default, so it would be necessary to install the TCP/IP protocol.

11. **E** Because no default gateway was defined, access to the Internet is not possible. External DNS resolution isn't available without access to the Internet.

12. **C** Installing a DHCP server allows you to set parameters for DNS servers, WINS servers, default gateways, and more.

13. **D** The TRACERT utility allows you to trace the path of the IP packet to the destination IP address.

14. **A, B** Outlook 97 and Internet Explorer are TCP/IP socket-based applications. Both use the Winsock.dll.

15. **A, C** It is possible that two DHCP servers have overlapping scopes and the same IP address may have been manually configured.

16. **D** Type **NBTSTAT** at the command line to display the NetBIOS name table. Type **NBTSTAT /?** at the command line for additional information about the command.

17. **C** Pinging the IP address of the host would allow you to quickly determine if the host is up and running.

18. **B** The Hosts file can be modified to resolve the FQDN to an IP address.

19. **A** The **get** command in FTP retrieves a file from the FTP server. An example is **get** *filename*.

20. **B, C** End and Quit will enable the user to finish the FTP session and return to the DOS prompt.

5.3.9 Key Words and Definitions

Class A network address Category for all the IP addresses that start with a particular first octet; for example, they might be assigned 107.0.0.0. This means that a class A address might have as many as 16,777,216 IP hosts.

Class B network address   Category for the first two octets of an IP address such as 145.170.0.0. This would allow 65,536 hosts.

Class C network address   Category for the first three octets such as 208.192.235.0. This allows a maximum of 256 hosts on a class C network.

PING   A command-line utility that is the most widely used utility for simple trouble-shooting. It sends a network packet to the destination host in search of a response.

TRACERT   A utility you use to manually define the path in which an IP packet travels in order to reach its destination.

WINIPCFG   A utility that provides a graphical display of current TCP/IP settings for all currently installed adapters on your Windows 95 client.

5.4 Setting Up Dial-Up Networking (DUN)

Windows 95 includes the Dial-Up Adapter, which you can set up to connect to not only an Internet service provider (ISP) but also a Windows NT server configured as a Remote Access Server (RAS). After the adapter is installed, Windows 95 will automatically bind any previously installed protocols to your new adapter. You might want to confirm the installation of the TCP/IP protocol, dial into your ISP (using the Dial-Up Networking [DUN] feature), and communicate over the Internet.

IPX/SPX-compatible and NetBEUI are automatically installed when the Dial-Up Adapter is installed. However, TCP/IP has to be installed as an option.

5.4.1 Configuring DUN Options

Dial-Up Networking supports many configuration options and can be a client for several different dial-up servers. This flexibility allows Windows 95 to connect into most dial-up environments.

Windows 95 can be a client for a Windows NT RAS server, can use the Serial Line Internet Protocol (SLIP) or PPP line protocol, and can function with Novell NetWare Connect. Windows 95 can authenticate passwords using Password Authentication Protocol (PAP), Shiva Password Authentication Protocol (SPAP), and Microsoft's version of Challenge Handshake Authentication Protocol (CHAP), and it provides terminal dial-up window and scripting capabilities if none of the standard password authentication schemes are being used. DUN can use the following three network protocols:

- NetBEUI
- IPX/SPX-compatible
- TCP/IP

> **NetBEUI, IPX/SPX-compatible, and TCP/IP are supported by DUN only in their 32-bit implementations (as provided with Windows 95). Therefore, you cannot use DUN with a real-mode IPX protocol, such as that provided by Novell and installed through a batch file.**

5.4.2 Password Authentication Schemes

PPP supports several password authentication schemes, which are used by different servers and have different features. The DUN connection automatically negotiates which of the following authentication protocol schemes to use.

- **Password Authentication Protocol (PAP).** Uses a two-way handshake to establish identity. This handshake occurs only when the link is originally established. Passwords are sent over the media in text format, which offers no protection from playback attacks.

- **Challenge-Handshake Authentication Protocol (CHAP).** Periodically verifies the identity of the peer by using a three-way handshake. CHAP provides protection from playback attack, and the password is never sent over the media, which also prevents illicit snooping. Windows 95 and NT don't support ongoing challenges with CHAP, but they do implement Microsoft's version of CHAP, called MS-CHAP.

- **Shiva Password Authentication Protocol (SPAP).** Offers encryption of PAP passwords and Novell NetWare bindery access for user account information.

5.4.3   Choosing Line Protocols

Line protocols provide the means by which network protocols are transported over communication media for which they were not originally intended. The line protocol provides a "wrapping" for the network protocol packet, which allows it to be transmitted over the unfamiliar media. When the line protocol packet reaches the dial-up server, the packet is "unwrapped," and the normal network protocol packet is sent on to the network.

The most common line protocol—and the default protocol that Windows 95 installs—is PPP. PPP was originally designed for the TCP/IP environment, but it is capable of transporting all three network protocols DUN supports and connecting to a wide variety of dial-up servers. PPP supports the following features:

- Multiplexing of sessions across a single serial link, allowing multiple network applications to appear to communicate simultaneously

- Transportation of multiple network protocols simultaneously over a single link

- Software compression to increase throughput

- Automatic negotiation of addressing, which allows DHCP to assign a dynamic IP address to Windows 95

- Error detection

SLIP, an older line protocol, is not installed by default with Windows 95. Rather, it must be installed separately from the Windows 95 disk or CD. Unfortunately, SLIP has the following limitations:

- It does not support dynamic IP addressing.

- It does not support multiple protocols.

- It provides no error detection or correction.

- It lacks data compression support (although you can compress the IP header information).

5.4.4   Configuring Network Protocols Through DUN

Three network protocols are supported by Windows 95 DUN: NetBEUI, IPX/SPX-compatible, and TCP/IP. These three protocols are configured through the Server Types properties sheet. To enable or disable NetBEUI and IPX/SPX-compatible you simply select the appropriate check boxes. In order to increase the speed of your connection, having only the necessary protocols enabled is a good idea.

For TCP/IP, however, you must also configure the IP address the ISP assigns, DNS information, and WINS information, in the TCP/IP Properties sheet. This allows you to have multiple sets of IP address information—one for each DUN connection icon you create. There are also two other check boxes on the TCP/IP Properties sheet. One allows higher throughput by enabling IP header compression, and the other uses the default gateway on the remote network.

5.4.5   Enhancements with DUN 1.2 Upgrade

The Microsoft Dial-Up Networking 1.2 upgrade fixes bugs and replaces several parts of the original DUN. The following new features come with the DUN 1.2 upgrade:

- Client support for PPTP
- Support for internal ISDN adapters
- Multilink capabilities
- Connection-time scripting

All the improvements to Microsoft's DUN included in the OSR2 release of Windows 95 and the ISDN 1.1 Accelerator Pack have been included in DUN 1.2.

The Microsoft Dial-Up Networking 1.2 upgrade client supports the Point-to-Point Tunneling Protocol (PPTP). PPTP allows the Windows 95 user to establish a Virtual Private Network (VPN) over the Internet. Your VPN connection allows PPTP to encapsulate its data stream in the PPP protocol and send the information over the public Internet. PPTP can encrypt the data, preventing others from easily accessing your sensitive information.

5.4.6   Setting Up DUN with Windows NT Remote Access Services

Windows NT has a built-in Remote Access Server (RAS) that allows Windows NT Workstation or Server to act as a connection to a network. Windows NT Workstation allows only one in-bound dial-in connection at a time, so is not suitable as a large-scale gateway to your institutional network.

A RAS server can automatically provide a Windows 95 client with an IP address because the RAS server is configured with a reserved pool from which to draw. RAS can also allow NetBEUI or IPX/SPX-compatible connections.

The DUN setup for dialing into a RAS server is identical to the setup with any other PPP server; however, a RAS server can support Microsoft-encrypted logons. And if you log on to your Windows 95 machine with the correct username and password for a Windows NT domain you want to use, that information will be passed through the RAS server to allow you access to domain resources.

If you're using RAS and the DUN 1.2 upgrade, you might want to configure Dial-Up Networking with DNS and WINS information to allow name resolution. To do so, open the DUN Properties sheet, select the Server Types tab, and click the TCP/IP Settings button.

5.4.7   Exercise

Exercise 1: Setting Up Windows 95 for Dial-Up Connections

The following steps show you how to set up Windows 95 to access the Internet through a dial-up connection. Before you begin, you need to make sure your system meets the following requirements:

- A modem is installed and works properly with Windows 95.

- You have an Internet account set up with an ISP. You need a username, IP information (see the "TCP/IP" section earlier in the chapter), telephone number of the ISP, password, email address, and DNS server name. Your ISP can provide you with this information.

- Internet software is installed on your computer. The software can vary, but users usually have a WWW browser (such as Microsoft Internet Explorer), an email application, and a newsgroup reader. Windows 95 clients for the common TCP/IP communications utilities FTP and Telnet are included with the operating system.

Knowing that your system meets these requirements, follow these steps:

1. Click the Start button, choose Settings, and open the Control Panel. In the Control Panel, double-click the Network icon.

2. On the Configuration tab of the Network Properties sheet, click the Add button. The Select Network Component Type dialog box appears.

3. Select Adapter and click the Add button. The Select Network Adapters dialog box appears.

4. Scroll down the Manufacturers list and click Microsoft. This displays Dial-Up Adapter in the Network Adapters list (see Figure 5.13).

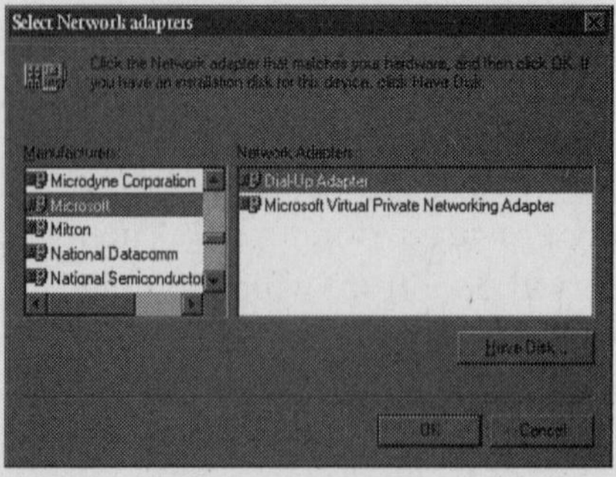

Figure 5.13   The Select Network Adapters dialog box.

5. Click OK. The Dial-Up Adapter component and a network protocol are added to the list of components shown on the Configuration tab. The default protocol added is NetBEUI.

    If you do not have the TCP/IP protocol installed yet, you'll need to add it as the protocol for Dial-Up Networking.

6. Click the Add button on the Configuration tab of the Network Properties sheet and select Protocol from the Select Network Component Type dialog box.

7. Click Add again. The Select Network Protocol dialog box appears.

8. Select Microsoft in the Manufacturers list and click the TCP/IP item in the Network Protocols list. Click OK. You're returned to the Configuration tab.

9. Select the TCP/IP Dial-Up Adapter component and click the Properties button. The TCP/IP Properties sheet appears.

10. On the IP Address tab, specify how your IP address is set up (see Figure 5.14). If you have a dynamic IP address, choose the Obtain an IP Address Automatically option. If your ISP assigned you a permanent IP address, choose the Specify an IP Address option and fill in the IP Address field. If your ISP also assigned you a subnet mask, enter it in the Subnet Mask field.

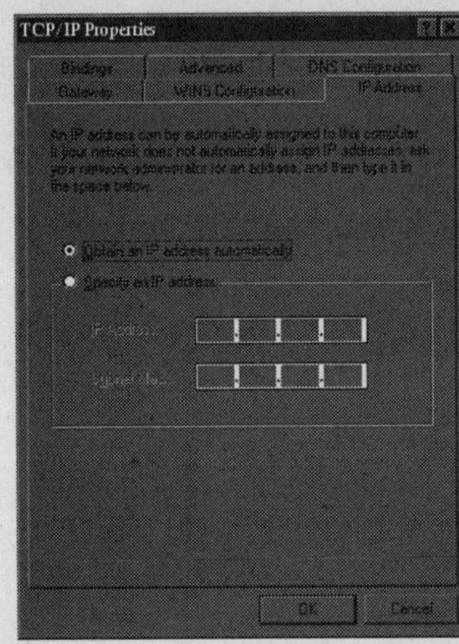

Figure 5.14   The TCP/IP Properties dialog box.

11. Click the DNS Configuration tab to set the Domain Name Service information. Choose the Enable DNS option and fill in the options.

12. Click OK to save your settings and to return to the Network properties sheet. Click OK again.

13. When you're prompted to restart Windows 95, click Yes to shut down and restart Windows 95.

Follow these steps to configure a dial-up connection:

1. Double-click the My Computer icon on the client computer.

2. Double-click the Dial-Up Networking icon to display the Dial-Up Networking folder.

3. Double-click the Make New Connection icon to start the Make New Connection Wizard (see Figure 5.15). Enter a name for the connection—such as the name of your ISP—in the Type a Name for the Computer You Are Dialing field.

4. In the Select a Device drop-down list, pick the modem you want to use to dial out when you use the new Dial-Up Networking connection. Click the Next button.

5. In the next Make New Connection screen, enter the area code and telephone number for the host computer. Click the Next button.

6. Click Finish to create a new Dial-Up Networking connection. An icon for the connection is added to the Dial-Up Networking folder. See the section "Configuring DUN Options" for more on configuring DUN.

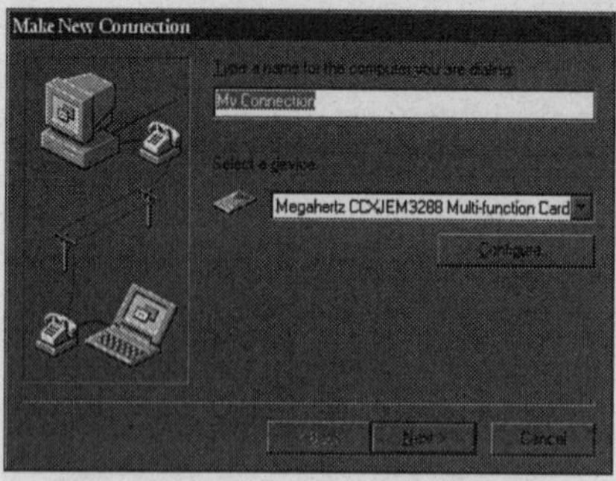

Figure 5.15   The Make New Connection Wizard showing a Megahertz modem.

5.4.8 Practice Problems

1. To access the Internet, you need to use Windows 95 Dial-Up Adapter and associated software. Pick two items from the following list that you must have in order to set up Windows 95 to access the Internet via Dial-Up Networking.

   A. ISP account

   B. modem

   C. gateway information

   D. DNS information

2. With Windows 95, what methods can you use to resolve fully qualified domain names over a Dial-Up Networking connection to the Internet?

   A. Hosts file

   B. LMHosts file

   C. DNS

   D. WINS

3. You want to configure a dial-up connection to a server that allows simultaneous applications to be run using multiple network protocols. Assuming the server is capable, what line protocol do you have to use to connect?

   A. SLIP

   B. NRN

   C. PPP

   D. RAS (Asynchronous NetBEUI)

4. Which of the following password authentication protocols protect against a playback-type attack and are supported by DUN?

   A. PAP

   B. CHAP

   C. MS-CHAP

   D. DUN terminal pop-up windows

5. Jenny wants to gain access to the Internet, but her company does not have Internet connectivity. Using Windows 95, how can she connect to the Internet with her phone line?

   A. Install File and Printer Sharing for Microsoft Networks.

   B. Install Dial-Up Networking.

   C. Configure her Web browser to access a proxy server.

   D. Install a modem.

   E. None of the above.

6. When installing TCP/IP, you should configure a default gateway for the Windows 95 client. What steps must be taken to achieve this?

   A. Click Start, Programs, Control Panel, Network.

   B. Select TCP/IP, Properties, Gateway tab.

   C. Click Start, Settings, Control Panel, Network.

   D. Select TCP/IP, Properties, IP Properties, Gateway tab.

   E. None of the above.

7. You are working the help desk at your company. A user calls and tells you he has set up Dial-Up Networking. What protocols are available to the user?

   A. TCP/IP

   B. NetBEUI

   C. IPX/SPX-compatible

   D. AppleTalk

8. You have called and connected to your Internet service provider, and now you want to access a Web site. What information was given to you by your ISP?

   A. Web site address

   B. IP address

C. Computer name

D. Default gateway

E. Subnet mask

9. **Situation:** Your company CEO has just received his new laptop computer. He is enjoying his newfound mobility, but he has one request. He would like to get to the same files he has access to while he is at his desk in the office.

Required Result: Give your CEO access to the company network from home.

Option One: Access a shared printer and print a document.

Option Two: Copy a file from the user's directory on the server to his home computer.

Action: Install and configure Dial-Up Networking to call and log on to the company RAS server. Install File and Printer Sharing for Microsoft Networks. select user-level access control.

Evaluation: Which of the following statements is true of the proposed action?

A. It fulfills the required result and all options.

B. It fulfills the required result and option one only.

C. It fulfills the required result and option two only.

D. It fulfills the required result only.

E. None of the above.

10. You are the administrator of a NetWare network with Windows 95 clients. Sarah, from accounting, calls and needs help installing Dial-Up Networking. She has already installed a modem. How would you walk her through? Select all that apply.

A. Click Start, Programs, Accessories, Dial-Up Networking.

B. Double-click Network Neighborhood and click Dial-Up Networking.

C. Use the Dial-Up Connection Wizard.

D. Use the Make New Connection Wizard.

5.4.9 Answers and Explanations

1. **A, B** You must have an ISP account and a modem.

2. **A, C** You can resolve FQDN over a dial-up connection using either the Hosts file or a DNS server.

3. **C** Point-to-Point Protocol (PPP) allows you to run simultaneous applications on multiple protocols through your dial-up connection.

4. **B, C** Challenge-Handshake Authentication Protocol (CHAP) and MS-CHAP provide protection against playback attack because the challenge value changes in every message.

5. **B, D** Along with having an Internet account, she must install a modem and Dial-Up Networking.

6. **B, C** You must add an IP address in the Gateway properties of the TCP/IP protocol.

7. **A, B, C** TCP/IP, NetBEUI, and IPX/SPX-compatible protocols are available to use with Dial-Up Networking.

8. **B, D, E** An ISP must provide an IP address, subnet mask, and default gateway to access the Internet.

9. **A** By installing and configuring Dial-Up Networking to allow access to the company RAS server, you have given him the ability to do the same things he can do from his computer located at work.

10. **A, C** You can get started by method A. Once you activate Dial-Up Networking (assuming no previous connection exists), the Make New Connection Wizard appears.

5.4.10   Key Words and Definitions

Internet service provider (ISP)   Provides users with access to the Internet through a direct line. The ISP is responsible for assigning the IP address, a subnet mask, a default gateway, and in most cases, a DNS server.

Point-to-Point Tunneling Protocol (PPTP)   An advanced method of networking that allows secure access, via a Virtual Private Network (VPN), to remote networks across the Internet.

Virtual Private Network (VPN)   Allows communication from a remote client already configured with secure access. It accepts network packets only from its PPTP clients and discards all others.

5

Practice Exam: Integration and Interoperability

1. Your company has decided to upgrade all user machines from Windows 3.11 to Windows 95. The powers that be want to allow for Internet access. Your network currently consists of 25 clients accessing a Windows NT server. You upgrade everyone's system to Windows 95 with the default settings. You then configure a router to access the Internet through your company's Internet service provider.

   When you test the connection to the Internet, it fails. You can see everyone on the network, as well as the NT servers. You can even access all the same files that you could before. Which of the following is the best solution?

   A. You must first install and configure a modem on all clients, and then enable Dial-Up Networking to access the Internet service provider.

   B. You must install Client for Microsoft Networks and configure user-level security to access the Internet Service Provider.

   C. You must install TCP/IP on all clients and configure an IP address, subnet mask, and default gateway.

   D. You must run WINIPCFG to configure the IP settings to access the Internet service provider and assign a NetBIOS identification.

2. **SITUATION:**

   John, an employee in the shipping department, has a request to share information regarding packages that have been shipped. He wants to make the shipping information, located on his computer, available to all other employees to reduce the number of phone calls and inquiries he receives. Your network currently consists of 65 Windows 95 clients and 25 DOS/NetWare clients, all connected to a NetWare 4.11 server in bindery emulation.

PRIMARY OBJECTIVES:

- Configure John's machine to be a file server for all the Windows 95 clients and NetWare clients on the network.

- On John's machine, share the folder that contains the shipping information.

SECONDARY OBJECTIVES:

- Assign Read-Only rights to all users.

- Assign Full Control rights to Peter, John's assistant, so that he can update the files and information in John's absence.

PROPOSED SOLUTION:

Install File and Printer Sharing for Microsoft Networks on John's machine. Configure his machine for user-level security. On the Access Control tab of the Network Properties sheet, type the NetWare server name in the Obtain a List of Users and Groups From box. Share and assign the default permissions to the folder containing the shipping information. Assign user rights to Peter's account on the NetWare server.

EVALUATION OF PROPOSED SOLUTION:

Choose the most correct answer.

A. The proposed solution meets all objectives; it is an outstanding solution.

B. The proposed solution meets the primary objectives and most of the secondary objectives; it is a good solution.

C. The proposed solution does not meet the primary objectives, but it meets all the secondary objectives; it is a good solution.

D. The proposed solution does not meet the primary objectives and meets only some of the secondary objectives; it is an adequate solution.

E. The proposed solution does not meet the primary objectives or any of the secondary objectives; it is not adequate.

3. You are responsible for managing a Windows NT 4.0 domain network consisting of 25 workstations running Windows NT Workstation 4.0 and 75 workstations running Windows 95. Those employees on the Windows NT machines are having no problems with their system policies. However, the 95 workstations are not successfully loading them from the server. What might be the problem?

A. The policy file has been saved in the netlogon share as config.pol.

B. The policy file is configured to Hide Network Neighborhood.

C. The policy file has been saved in the netlogon share as Ntconfig.pol.

D. The policy file is configured for Windows 95 clients only.

4. You are the administrator of a mixed network environment. Your clients consist of 45 Windows 95 machines, 16 NetWare machines, and 5 Windows NT Workstation machines. You need to connect each client to both NetWare and Windows NT servers. On the Windows 95 clients, you install both the Client for Microsoft Networks and the Client for NetWare Networks with the default settings. On the NetWare clients, you install and connect with the default NetWare DOS configuration. You have also installed the NWLink protocol on the Windows NT Servers. What statements below are incorrect?

A. Each Windows 95 client can share files with the Windows NT servers.

B. Each Windows 95 client can share files with the NetWare servers.

C. Each Windows 95 client can share files with other Windows 95 clients.

D. Each Windows 95 client can access files from the Windows NT servers.

E. Each Windows 95 client can access files from the NetWare servers.

5. **SITUATION:**

Bob, a member of the Human Resources group, has been working on an Access database, that will include the entire company's employees. Each listing will contain the employee's name, address, phone number, email address, title, and some family information. He has been saving the database to his Windows 95 client and saving a copy on his domain's NT server to ensure that a backup is made each night.

Close to finishing the database, he shares the folder on his Windows 95 client with the default settings. He places the database in the newly shared folder. He then posts a note in the company newsgroup, informing people of its location and asking everyone to look at it and provide feedback.

PRIMARY OBJECTIVE:

- Allow the Human Resources group access to the database.

SECONDARY OBJECTIVES:

- Allow the company employees to view all the information in the database.

- Under no circumstances should anyone outside the company have access to the database.

PROPOSED SOLUTION:

Configure Bob's machine for user-level security.

EVALUATION OF PROPOSED SOLUTION:

Choose the most correct answer.

A. The proposed solution meets all objectives; it is an outstanding solution.

B.   The proposed solution meets the primary objective and most of the secondary objectives; it is a good solution.

C.   The proposed solution does not meet the primary objective but meets all the secondary objectives; it is a good solution.

D.   The proposed solution does not meet the primary objective and meets only some of the secondary objectives; it is adequate.

E.   The proposed solution does not meet the primary objective and meets only some of the secondary objectives; it is not adequate.

F.   The proposed solution does not meet any objectives.

6.   Because you have proven your abilities, you have been promoted to Network Administrator. Your responsibilities now include system administration of three Windows NT servers in the company domain and five NetWare 3.12 servers. Before your promotion, the company was connected and given Internet access for each employee using static IP addresses. A support call comes in, and the user is requesting help accessing the www.yahoo.com site. Every time he opens Internet Explorer, it connects to the default page, which is the company web site, located on the same network ID. You ping the default gateway and receive a reply.

What steps would you take to diagnose this problem?

A.   Click Start, Settings, Control Panel, Add/Remove Programs, and then remove Internet Explorer and reinstall.

B.   Click Start, Settings, Control Panel, Add New Hardware, and then let Windows redetect the network card.

C.   Click Start, Settings, Control Panel, Network, and then remove the TCP/IP protocol. Reboot the machine and add the TCP/IP protocol.

D.   Click Start, Run, type **WINIPCFG**, and click OK.

E.   Click Start, Settings, Control Panel, Network, and then configure the TCP/IP settings to include a default gateway.

7.   **SITUATION:**

Mary has been working with Frank and Joe on an important project for the Sales department. Her machine has been updated to Windows 95 over the weekend. As the administrator of a mixed network environment, she calls you and tells you that, although she can see Joe's and Frank's machines on the network, she can no longer see or access the shared folder to update the sales project files.

Your network is connected to a NetWare 4.11 server in bindery emulation.

PRIMARY OBJECTIVE:

- Connect Mary's machine to the shared folder containing the sales project files.

SECONDARY OBJECTIVES:

- Automatically connect Mary to the shared folder containing the sales project files each time she logs in.

- Give Mary the rights to share folders on her machine with other Windows 95 clients.

PROPOSED SOLUTION:

Install File and Printer Sharing for Microsoft Networks on Mary's machine. Configure her machine for user-level security. On the Access Control tab of the Network Properties sheet, type the NetWare server name in the Obtain a List of Users and Groups From box. Install

Client Services for Microsoft Networks. Install Client Services for NetWare Networks.

EVALUATION OF PROPOSED SOLUTION:

Choose the most correct answer.

A. The proposed solution meets all objectives; it is an outstanding solution.

B. The proposed solution meets the primary objective and most of the secondary objectives; it is a good solution.

C. The proposed solution does not meet the primary objective but meets all the secondary objectives; it is a good solution.

D. The proposed solution does not meet the primary objective and meets only some of the secondary objectives; it is an adequate solution.

E. The proposed solution does not meet the primary objective or any of the secondary objectives; it is not adequate.

8. Patricia has recently had surgery on her right foot. Although she is capable of proofreading documents for her company, she cannot drive a car to get her to the office. The files she proofreads are stored on a Windows NT server and a Novell NetWare 3.12 server. She has a computer with Windows 95, a modem, and Internet access at home. You configure her account on the NT domain and grant her permission to dial-in to your company's Windows NT RAS server. What additional steps must you take to allow her to access the company network from her home? Select all that apply.

A. On her Windows 95 machine at home, you guide her to type in the RAS server access phone number.

B. On her Windows 95 machine at home, you guide her to click Start, Programs, Accessories, Dial-Up Networking, and Make New Connection.

C. On her Windows 95 machine at home, you guide her to double-click My Computer and select Dial-Up Scripting Tools.

D. On her Windows 95 machine at home, you guide her to install File and Printer Sharing for Microsoft Networks.

9. **SITUATION:**

Harry works in the Accounting Department on the third floor. You are the administrator of a Windows NT domain, of which he is a member. He wants to save a document to a folder located on a coworker's machine. Both machines are running Windows 95. You instruct the coworker to create a folder and share it with user-level security. After creating the folder and assigning the proper rights to Harry, you go on your way. Harry contacts you in a few minutes and explains he cannot find the newly created resource in Network Neighborhood.

PRIMARY OBJECTIVE:

- Connect Harry to the shared folder located on the coworker's Windows 95 client.

SECONDARY OBJECTIVES:

- Allow Harry to continually connect to the shared folder automatically.

- Assign the coworker Full Control over the shared folder.

PROPOSED SOLUTION:

Have Harry right-click on Network Neighborhood, select Map a Network Drive, and type **//computer_name/ share_name** in the Path box.

EVALUATION OF PROPOSED SOLUTION:

Choose the most correct answer.

A. The proposed solution meets all objectives; it is an outstanding solution.

B. The proposed solution meets the primary objective and most of the secondary objectives; it is a good solution.

C. The proposed solution does not meet the primary objective but meets all the secondary objectives; it is a good solution.

D. The proposed solution does not meet the primary objective and meets only some of the secondary objectives; it is adequate.

E. The proposed solution does not meet any of the objectives; it is, therefore, inadequate.

10. As the network administrator of a company, you must sometimes access your network from a remote location. Recently, you decided to set up access to your Windows NT domain through the Internet. You set up a RAS server and make it accessible over the Internet. To enable a secure channel of communication, you decide to create a Virtual Private Network (VPN). What protocol would you select in your Windows 95 client machine's Network Properties sheet to access the VPN?

A. TCP/IP

B. PPTP

C. NWLink

D. NetBEUI

E. Secure TCP/IP

Practice Exam Answers and Explanations

1. **C**   The original network configuration settings for the Windows 3.11 clients did not include TCP/IP as a protocol. After upgrading the systems, you must add and configure the TCP/IP protocol to access the Internet. The default upgrade does not add TCP/IP automatically.

2. **E**   The proposed solution would allow John to share the shipping information with the Windows 95 clients only. The DOS/NetWare clients would not gain access to the resource. You may assign user-level security to an NT domain given the proposed solution. To complete John's request, you should install File and Printer Sharing for Novell Networks on John's client. Then you can configure the Obtain a List of Users and Groups From setting to use the NetWare server as a security authority.

3. **A**   The policy file must be configured for Windows 95 clients only. NT clients have their own policy file (Ntconfig.pol). The default policy file for Windows is Config.pol and should be located in the netlogon share.

4. **A, B, C**   The default settings for installing the Clients for Microsoft and NetWare networks consist of the NetBEUI and IPX/SPX-compatible protocols being installed. This would allow the Windows 95 clients to access the NT servers as well as the NetWare servers. By default, Windows NT server installs the NWLink protocol, allowing connectivity from the Windows 95 and NetWare clients. Because File and Printer Sharing for either network was not installed, no file-sharing capabilities are currently present.

5. **B**   The proposed solution would allow Bob to assign specific user rights to his shared folder containing the database. Although this is a good solution, an outstanding solution would be for Bob to store the database on the NT server and assign user permissions to the new folder.

6. **D, E**   The first step is to see what configuration item is missing or mistyped. Using the WINIPCFG utility would allow you to quickly see the TCP/IP configuration settings. Given the information above, you can conclude that the default gateway is either incorrectly configured or not configured at all. Because you were able to ping the default gateway successfully, you can assume it is up.

7. **B**   Installing Client for NetWare Networks would provide Mary with access to the folder with the sales project files, located on the NetWare server. Installing File and Printer Sharing for Microsoft Networks on Mary's machine would allow her to share resources with other Windows 95 clients. Without configuring Enable Logon Scripts in the Client for NetWare Networks or mapping a network drive and reconnecting to the sales project folder, her connectivity would not be automated.

8. **A, B**   Patricia already has Internet access on her Windows 95 machine at home, so Dial-Up Networking is already installed. After allowing her the proper permissions on the NT RAS server, you must guide her through setting up a new dial-up connection. Dial-Up Scripting Tool is not used to configure a new dial-up connection. Installing File and Printer Sharing for Microsoft Networks would not be necessary to give her access to the files located on either the NT server or the NetWare server.

9. **E**   Harry should use the correct UNC path of *computer_name**share_name* and check the Reconnect at Logon box.

10. **B**   Point-to-Point Tunneling Protocol would allow you to set up a secure communication channel with your RAS server's VPN. The RAS server's VPN would accept PPTP requests from your client machine, unwrap them, and process them on the company network. You can use NetBEUI, IPX/SPX, or TCP/IP with PPTP.

CHAPTER 6

Monitoring and Optimization

This chapter will help you prepare for the exam by covering the following objectives:

- Monitor system performance. Tools include Net Watcher and System Monitor

- Tune and optimize the system. Tools include:

  - Disk Defragmenter

  - ScanDisk

  - Compression Utility

Monitoring a computer system is an important part of administration, which can prevent errors from occurring. This chapter discusses tools which will help you monitor, optimize, and troubleshoot problems in a Windows 95 environment. Some of these tools, such as the Disk Defragmenter and ScanDisk, should be run on a regular basis (for example, weekly for a heavily used computer) to provide a proactive approach to problems. Other tools, such as the Net Watcher and the System Monitor, will be used when you make changes to your environment, or when you suspect trouble.

In addition to their usefulness in troubleshooting, these tools can also be used to provide information about your environment. Some tell you what resources (that is, disk space, memory, and the like) are available. Other provide information about your network, and allow an administrator to monitor and maintain other computers. The first tool this chapter covers is Net Watcher.

6.1   Using Net Watcher

Net Watcher enables a user to manage shared resources on a local or remote computer. A user can create or delete a shared resource on a remote computer and monitor access to the shared resources.

The Net Watcher is included in the Accessories group and can be used to view connections to the local computer or to remote computers if Remote Administration is enabled on the remote computer. Net Watcher is primarily used to display the status of connections to shared folders. The features of Net Watcher enable an administrator to remotely perform the following tasks:

- Create a new shared folder.

- List the shared folders on a server.

- Stop the sharing of a folder.

- Show which users are connected to a shared folder.

- Show how long a user has been connected to a shared folder and how long the user has been idle.

- Close files a user has opened (only on Microsoft networks).

- Disconnect a user from a shared resource.

Net Watcher also can be accessed through the Network Neighborhood by right-clicking on a computer and selecting Properties from the context-sensitive menu. Choose Net Watcher from the Tools tab to view the shared folders and the users accessing those folders on the selected computer.

To use Net Watcher, the following characteristics must apply:

- File and Print Sharing must be enabled on the remote computer.

- You can only access remote systems that use the same access control that you are using on your computer; that is, both computers must be set to user-level access control or share-level access control.

- You can only access remote systems using the same type of file and print sharing (Microsoft or NetWare).

Net Watcher is useful as an administration tool in a peer-to-peer network because it allows one administrator to manage the resources on all computers in the workgroup.

When connecting to a remote computer using share-level access control, the password used is the one specified in the Remote Administration dialog box.

When connecting to a remote computer using user-level access control, the password is the Administrator's account password.

6.1.1 Exercise

Exercise 1: Monitoring Remote Computers with the Net Watcher

In this exercise you will monitor another Windows 95 computer using the Net Watcher program. The following exercise shows how to monitor a remote computer by using Net Watcher.

1. Start Net Watcher as previously described. You also can select the Start menu, and choose Programs, Accessories, System Tools, Net Watcher.

2. Choose Administer, Select Server. The Select Server dialog box appears.

3. Enter the name of the server (the remote computer) you want to view. Choose the Browse button to see a list of the computers to which you can connect.

4. Click OK. A view of the remote computer appears in Net Watcher.

5. Click the Show Users button to see the users connected to the selected computer. On the left, you see the username, computer name, number of shares, number of open files, time of connection, and idle time. On the right, you see the shared folders and the files that are opened.

6. Click the Show Shared Folders button to see the names of the shared folders on the selected computer. On the left, you see the shared folder, the name it is shared as, the access type, and a comment associated with the folder. On the right, you see the connections to the share and the files that are opened.

7. Click the Show Files button to see files that are opened by other users. You see the name of the file, the share it is using, the person accessing it, and the open mode.

8. Press F5 to refresh the display.

9. Choose Administer and exit to Net Watcher.

6.1.2 Practice Problems

1. Net Watcher requires that you use File and Printer Sharing Services.

   A. True

   B. False

2. Which of the following can you do with Net Watcher?

   A. Show all connected users.

   B. Connect to a remote computer.

   C. Disconnect a user.

   D. Close files that users have opened.

3. To connect to a remote computer using the Net Watcher utility, you must enter a password for the remote computer. What are the two types of security that can be used?

   A. Share-level

   B. Group-level

   C. User-level

   D. Resource-level

4. Your computer is using share-level security. What types of computers can you connect to?

   A. Any computer

   B. Any computer that uses File and Printer Sharing

   C. Computers that use user-level security and File and Printer Sharing

   D. Computers that use share-level security and File and Printer Sharing

5. On a NetWare network, which of the following can you do with Net Watcher?

   A. Close documents on remote computers.

   B. Disconnect users.

   C. Both of the above.

   D. None of the above.

6. Jack wants to use Net Watcher to view connections to his local computer. He wants to see the users connected to your computer. Which toolbar button do you click to allow this?

   A. View Users

   B. Show Connected Users

   C. View Connected Users

   D. Show Users

7. You would like to use the Net Watcher administration tool to present a graphical presentation of your network usage. Is this possible using Net Watcher?

   A. Yes

   B. No

8. Using Net Watcher, you discover that your users are sharing a large number of resources, including sensitive data. Can you alter these shares and reduce the number of shares on your network by using Net Watcher?

   A. No. The shares can only be changed at the local computer by the user who created the share.

   B. No. You must alter the shares at the local computer.

   C. Yes. You may control and remove the shares of remote computers.

   D. No. After the resource is shared, users have that level of access until the shared resource is removed and then re-added with the appropriate share permissions.

9. Where would Larry find the installation files for Net Watcher on the Windows 95 CD?

   A. ADMIN\APPTOOLS\ NETWATCH

   B. NETTOOLS\ADMIN\ NETWATCH

    C. NETTOOLS\REMOTE\
       NETWATCH

    D. None of the above

10. To create a shared folder on a remote computer using the Net Watcher administration tool, you would select which of the following choices to initiate the process of creating the shared resource?

    A. Select the Administer menu and then select Add Shared Folder.

    B. Select Administer menu and then select Add Shared Local Resource.

    C. You must connect to the computer prior to creating shares on the remote computer.

    D. After connecting to the remote computer, you should select the Administer menu and then select Add Shared Folder.

11. You may only use the remote Net Watcher administration tool to administer remote computers if you are a member of the Domain Admins group on an NT domain or a Supervisory equivalent on an NetWare server.

    A. This is only true if you are using user-level security.

    B. This is only true if the user's computer you want to monitor has user-level security enabled.

    C. This is not true in a Windows NT domain, but true in a NetWare environment.

    D. None of the above is accurate.

12. You are unable to connect to the ADMIN$ share on several computers using the Net Watcher administration tool. Which of the following choices best indicates what the problem might be?

    A. The computer you are attempting to connect to is not sharing resources.

    B. The remote computer does not have remote administration enabled.

    C. You do not have access to the special share.

    D. None of the above.

6.1.3 Answers and Explanations

1. **A** File and Printer Services must be installed before you can use the Net Watcher utility.

2. **A, B, C, D** Net Watcher can be used to show all users connected to a computer, to connect to a remote computer, to disconnect a user, and to close files and resources which another user has open.

3. **A, C** The two types of security that Windows 95 uses are share-level and user-level security.

4. **D** If you are using share-level security, you can only connect to other computers which are also using share-level security, and which have File and Printer Sharing enabled.

5. **B** If you are on a NetWare network, you can disconnect other users with Net Watcher, but you cannot close documents on remote computers.

6. **D** Show Users will show the user name, computer name, connection time, open files, idle time, and number of shares he is using.

7. **A** You can select the parameters you want to present from Category and Item.

8. **C** Net Watcher enables you to create new shares and stop existing shares.

9. **D** Net Watcher is contained in the .cab files and can be installed from Add/Remove, Windows Setup, Accessories.

6

10. **D** You must be connected to the remote computer before you can add shared folders.

11. **D** You may use Net Watcher to administer remote computers as long as you are granted remote administration privileges.

12. **C** This is a special share created when Net Watcher is installed and it is not accessible.

6.1.4 Key Words and Definitions

File and Printer Sharing A network setting that, when enabled, allows you to share your resources with others, and allows you to use any of their resources for which you have authority to access.

Net Watcher A Windows 95 utility which allows the monitoring and administration of remote computers across a network.

Share-level security A type of security in which a password is assigned to a resource. Anyone who knows the password can access the resource.

Shared resource A computer resource, such as a file, folder, or printer, for which you are providing access for other users.

User-level security A type of security in which rights to resources are granted on a user-by-user basis. No additional passwords are assigned to the resource.

6.2   Using the System Monitor

The System Monitor is a Windows 95 accessory used to display data on various performance counters in Windows 95. With System Monitor and Remote Administration enabled, you can connect to remote computers to view their system performance through the System Monitor.

You also can quickly enable monitoring of a remote computer by right-clicking on that computer in Network Neighborhood and selecting Properties from the context-sensitive menu. Choose System Monitor to start the applet and connect to the selected computer.

System Monitor can be used to monitor the performance of a Windows 95 computer. System Monitor can be used to provide real-time tracking of system activities on local or remote computers.

System Monitor is useful for viewing the effects of configuration or hardware changes on the computer's performance. It can also be used to identify bottlenecks that can affect the computer's performance.

Performance information including processor usage, the number of reads per second, or the amount of dirty data can be viewed over time as a line chart, bar chart, or as values.

The following system activities can be monitored:

- File system
- IPX/SPX–compatible protocol
- Kernel
- Memory Manager
- Microsoft Client for NetWare Networks
- Microsoft Network Client
- Microsoft Network Server

To view the effect of a configuration or hardware change on a Windows 95 computer:

- Determine which items in System Monitor are to be tracked.
- Run System Monitor before the change is made to establish the baseline and record the information.
- Make the desired configuration change.
- Run System Monitor after the change and view the results of the change.

The results of the change can then be compared to the baseline to see if the change has had a positive or negative effect on system performance.

When establishing the baseline, make sure you run System Monitor during "average" usage. Monitoring the computer's performance while performing abnormal system-intensive tasks will affect System Monitor's values and may not give a true baseline.

In order to monitor a remote computer, Remote Administration must be enabled on the other computer and the password must be known.

System Monitor results cannot be saved to a log file.

6.2.1   Exercises

Exercise 1: Viewing Kernel Information with the System Monitor

In this exercise, you will use the System Monitor utility to view information about the Kernel. You will walk through the steps required to set up the System Monitor, and see how actions you perform on your computer affect resources. To run System Monitor, execute the following steps:

1. Start the System Monitor. From the Start button, select Programs, Accessories, System Tools, System Monitor.

2. Once the System Monitor is running, you have to tell it what you want to monitor. From the menu, select Edit, and the Add Item. This will give you a dialog of all the System Monitor options.

3. Select Kernel from the Category list. This will display all the items associated with the Kernel.

4. Select all the items in the Item list. These should be Processor Usage, Threads, and Virtual Machines. Click the OK button.

5. You should now see three graphs on your System Monitor window. As you watch, you should see the graphs move over time.

6. While the System Monitor is running, start several other programs and watch how the graphs change.

7. From the View menu, select Always On Top. This will keep the System Monitor window on top of all other windows so that you can watch performance over time.

8. Now you will remove all of the items being graphed. From the Edit menu, select Remove Item. From the dialog, select all of the items, and click the OK button. You should now have an empty window, and can start over.

Exercise 2: Options of the System Monitor

In this exercise, you will see and use some of the different options of the System Monitor. You will monitor some items from the Memory Manager, and see how you can change the appearance of the System Monitor.

1. If the System Monitor is not running, start it as you did above.

2. Add some items that you will be monitoring. From the Add Item dialog, select Memory Manager as the category, and then select Allocated Memory, Free Memory, Disk Cache Size, and Page Faults as items.

3. After you click on the OK button, watch the graphs change.

4. Run some additional programs, such as WordPad, Explorer, to see how the graphs change over time.

5. Next, you will change the appearance of the graphs. From the View menu, try changing the appearance of the graphs using the three options available, Line Charts, Bar Charts, and Numeric Charts.

6. If you want to reset the graphs, you could select Clear Window from the Edit menu. This will clear all graphs, and you can start with new data.

7. With the System Monitor, you can increase and decrease the speed at which it updates the charts. From the Options menu, select Chart. A dialog appears that will allow you to change the speed of refreshes. Change the interval to 1 second, and see what effect this has on the charts.

8. Finally, you can edit properties of individual charts. From the Edit menu, select Edit Item. Then from the dialog which appears, select one of the items you are monitoring. A Chart Options dialog is displayed. This will allow you to change the colors used for charts, and to change the scale method.

6

6.2.2 Practice Problems

1. Before you can use the System Monitor to monitor a remote computer, which tool must be installed on your computer and the remote computer?

   A. Net Watcher

   B. System Policy Editor

   C. Microsoft Remote Registry

   D. Registry Editor

2. System Monitor can be used to do which of the following?

   A. Determine hardware performance

   B. View connected users

   C. Find performance bottlenecks

   D. Measure the effects of system configuration changes

3. The System Monitor can be used to compare historical performance over a period of time.

   A. True

   B. False

4. Which of the following is a category of the System Monitor?

   A. Kernel

   B. User

   C. GDI

   D. Usage

5. Which System Monitor category is used to view items such as bytes read per second, the amount of dirty data in cache, and the number of write operations per second?

   A. Memory Manager

   B. File system

   C. IPX/SPX–compatible protocol

   D. Kernel

6. Which of the following categories of the System Monitor allow you to see performance over a network?

   A. Microsoft Client for NetWare Networks

   B. Microsoft Network Client

   C. Microsoft Network Server

   D. Net Watcher

   E. Network Manager

7. The System Monitor results can be written to a log file.

   A. True

   B. False

8. System Monitor cannot be used to monitor which of the following activities?

   A. The number of bytes read per second

   B. The number of virtual machines currently running

   C. The size of the disk cache

   D. The number of users connected to a shared directory

9. When connecting to a remote computer in System Monitor, what must you specify?

   A. The MAC address of the remote computer's network card

   B. The name of the user currently using the remote computer

   C. The NetBIOS name of the remote computer

   D. The name of the domain in which the remote computer is a member

10. What is dirty data in System Monitor?

   A. Data that is trying to be read from a bad sector on the disk

   B. Data that is trying to be written to a bad sector on the disk

C. Data waiting in cache to be written to disk

D. Bad data that cannot be written to disk

E. Data that cannot be saved to disk due to illegal filenames

11. Which of the following system options cannot be monitored? Select all that apply.

A. File system

B. IPX/SPX protocol

C. Memory

D. Microsoft Client for NetWare Networks

E. TCP/IP protocol

6.2.3 Answers and Explanations

1. **C** To use the System Monitor to monitor a remote computer, you must first install Microsoft Remote Registry.

2. **A, C, D** The System Monitor can be used to view hardware performance, look for bottlenecks, and measure the changes to a system configuration. It cannot be used to view connected users. That is a job of the Net Watcher.

3. **A** You can run the System Monitor before and after a configuration change to determine the impact of that change.

4. **A** Kernel is a category of the System Monitor that provides a view into memory and related functions.

5. **B** The File System category can be used to view information about disk activity.

6. **A, B, C** Three categories of the System Monitor allow you to view performance in relation to a network. They are Microsoft Client for NetWare Networks, Microsoft Network Client, and Microsoft Network Server.

7. **B** The System Monitor does not write to log files.

8. **D** To monitor the number of users connected to a shared directory, use Net Watcher.

9. **C** When connecting to a remote computer through Net Watcher, the NetBIOS name of the remote computer is entered.

10. **C** Dirty data is data held in cache waiting to be written to hard disk.

11. **E** System Monitor cannot monitor TCP/IP protocol options.

6.2.4 Key Terms and Definitions

File system The organization of files and folders on a drive. For Windows 95 computers, the file system is either FAT16 or FAT32. For NT, it is either FAT16 or NTFS.

IPX/SPX A networking protocol used primarily by Novell NetWare.

Kernel The part of the Windows 95 operating system that handles memory management.

Remote Administration The ability of administrators to view and maintain Windows 95 system configurations across a network.

System Monitor A utility which allows you to view various Windows 95 resources, both on a local machine and on remote computers across a network.

TCP/IP Transmission Control Protocol/Internet Protocol, a widely used networking protocol, popular because of the Internet.

6.3   Tuning and Optimizing the System

Three key disk-management utilities are included with Windows 95. Each is intended to address particular file system issues or problems. Table 6.1 provides a summary of the disk-management utilities and the issues they address.

Table 6.1   Windows 95 Utilities for Various File System Issues

Utility	Issue
Disk Defragmenter	Prevention of file system performance degradation due to inefficient hard-disk access
ScanDisk	Correction of cross-linked files, lost clusters, and other hard-disk errors
Disk Compression	Maximization of available hard-disk space

To select the appropriate disk-management tool, you must examine the symptoms displayed in a given situation. Table 6.2 matches symptoms to the appropriate disk-management tool to be used to correct them.

Table 6.2   Selecting the Appropriate Tool for Various File System Symptoms

Utility	Symptom
Disk Defragmenter	Applications open, read, or write to files slowly.
ScanDisk	Applications report corruption of data or are unable to open files.
Disk Compression	Applications report insufficient available hard-disk space.

The use of one utility often leads to the use of another. For example, while you're correcting slow hard-disk access by running Disk Defragmenter, the utility may report an error. In this case, you should run ScanDisk and specify a physical surface scan.

6.3.1   The Disk Defragmenter

One of the most common performance issues related to the FAT file system, which is native to both MS-DOS and Windows 95, is disk fragmentation. When a hard drive is new and contains no information, it is possible for the file system to write all the data for a new file to a contiguous area of the hard drive. As the hard drive fills up and files are deleted and copied numerous times, the space available to new files no longer is contiguous. The file system is forced to put part of the new file in one location, part at another location, and so on. When a request is made to read the file, the hard disk must access all these different locations to reconstitute the file. This requires much more mechanical activity and takes longer than reading the whole file from one location on the hard disk.

Windows 95 includes a utility called *Disk Defragmenter* that is designed to address this issue. It does so by rewriting all the files on the hard drive to contiguous locations, thus enhancing file system performance for that drive. This procedure can be time-consuming because, as the drive becomes full, there is less room to temporarily store the different parts of a file before it is rewritten to a new location.

The Disk Defragmenter can be run against compressed and uncompressed drives. If you want to use it against compressed drives, those drives must have been compressed in a format recognizable by Windows 95. These formats include drives compressed with the MS-DOS utilities DoubleSpace and DriveSpace, programs which came with versions of MS-DOS 6.*x*.

Although the Disk Defragmenter existed in MS-DOS 6.2 and is still a 16-bit application, the Windows 95 Disk Defragmenter utility has the following enhancements:

- It is much faster at optimizing drives compressesd in MS-DOS 6.*x* using DoubleSpace or DriveSpace.

- The utility no longer requires any INI files because all settings are stored in the Registry.

- The utility now has a Windows 95 GUI interface.

- The Windows 95 Disk Defragmenter is capable of running as a background application, freeing the user to perform other tasks.

Certain types of files are not handled by Disk Defragmenter in the normal fashion:

- Files with both Hidden and System attributes are not moved.

- Files with either Hidden or System attributes are moved.

- Mounted DriveSpace or DoubleSpace volumes are not moved.

The following points should also be noted when using the Disk Defragmenter:

- If Disk Defragmenter reports errors (usually at the beginning of the process), you should run ScanDisk (including a surface scan).

- This utility should not be run on Stacker drives, because the compression scheme on such drives is different from that of DriveSpace and DoubleSpace.

Over time, hard disks tend to become fragmented. When that happens, files are spread out over the disk's free space instead of being stored in contiguous sectors on the hard disk. This increases the amount of time necessary to read and write files to the hard disk.

Disk Defragmenter can defrag compressed and uncompressed disks. When running Disk Defragmenter, the user can select three defragment options:

- Full defragmentation

- Defragment files only

- Consolidate free space only

Disk Defragmenter will not defrag most drives compressed using non-Microsoft compression utilities, network drives, CD-ROM drives, or drives created using the DOS ASSIGN, SUBST, or JOIN commands.

Disk Defragment will not move files that have both the System and Hidden attributes assigned to them nor will it move mounted CVFs.

6.3.2   Exercise

Exercise 1: Using The Disk Defragmenter

In this exercise, you will use the Disk Defragmenter to defragment files and free space on a hard drive. You will be able to see the different options available to you, and watch to see how the Defragmenter works.

1. Run the Disk Defragmenter. From the Start button, select Programs, Accessories, System Tools, and then Disk Defragmenter.

2. From the drop-down list, choose a hard drive on your computer and click the OK button. You may get a dialog telling you that defragmenting this drive is not necessary.

3. Click the Advanced button. A dialog of advanced options appears. This allows you to select the type of defragmentation (files, free space, or both) and whether or not you want to do error-checking at the same time. Select Full Defragmentation, and click OK.

4. Click the Start button. A dialog will appear showing you the progress of the utility.

5. Click the Show Details button. This will show you a mapping of your hard drive that shows how each cluster on the hard drive is being used. This may take several seconds to appear.

6. If you want to see a legend describing what the different colors mean for each cluster, click the Legend button.

7. Depending on the size of your hard drive, and the speed of your computer, disk defragmentation can take a considerable amount of time. If you want to stop the process, click the Stop button and exit the application.

6.3.3 Practice Problems

1. Which of the following is a benefit of using the Disk Defragmenter?

    A. Fixing corrupt files

    B. Increasing memory

    C. Repairing bad sectors

    D. Improving file-access time

2. Disk Defragmenter allows you to defragment which types of drives?

    A. Uncompressed drives

    B. Drives compressed with DriveSpace

    C. Drives compressed with DoubleSpace

    D. Network drives

3. Disk Defragmenter allows you to do which of the following?

    A. Defragment files

    B. Defragment free space

    C. Both of the above

    D. None of the above

4. Which of the following will improve the performance of the Disk Defragmenter?

    A. Defragmenting files and free space at the same time

    B. Showing details while running

    C. Minimizing the Defragmenter while running

    D. Checking the drive for errors while defragmenting

5. Which types of files will the Disk Defragmenter move during operation?

    A. Files marked as Hidden and System

    B. Files marked as Hidden and non-System

    C. Files marked as non-Hidden and System

    D. Files marked as both non-Hidden and non-System

6. The Disk Defragmenter can run as a background application (that is, while other applications are running). True or false?

    A. True

    B. False

7. Many of your users run Disk Defragmenter in the background while running other applications. Some grow aggravated, however, when Disk Defragmenter restarts the defragmentation process during this time. At what times does Defragmenter restart?

    A. When an application is inactive for 30 minutes

    B. After an application opens a document

    C. When Defragmenter finds lost clusters

    D. When an application is writing to disk

8. For maximum efficiency, files should be located on the hard disk in what way?

    A. From the center toward the outside of the disk

    B. In the order in which they were saved

    C. In contiguous space

    D. In interleaved clusters

9. Juli is running Disk Defragmenter on her hard drive. Which of the following is *not* an option she will find on the Advanced dialog box?

    A. Full defragmentation

    B. Defragment directories only

    C. Defragment files only

    D. Consolidate free space only

10. Jamie has never run Disk Defragmenter on his PC. Which two advanced options should he choose?

    A. Full defragmentation

    B. Check drive for errors

    C. Defragment files only

    D. Consolidate free space only

6.3.4 Answers and Explanations

1. **D** The Disk Defragmenter can be used to improve file access time. Fixing corrupt files and repairing bad sectors are functions of ScanDisk.

2. **A, B, C** Disk Defragmenter cannot be used on Network drives.

3. **C** Disk Defragmenter options allow you to defragment files, free space, or both.

4. **C** The performance of the Disk Defragmenter can be increased slightly if it is minimized while running.

5. **B, C, D** The Disk Defragmenter will not move files that are marked as both Hidden and System files.

6. **A** Other applications can be run while the Disk Defragmenter is operating.

7. **D** When an application writes to the hard disk, it has, in effect, changed the location of data on the disk. This could cause Disk Defragmenter to have to start the defragmentation process over again to ensure that the data is in contiguous space.

8. **C** Files located in contiguous space are read from the disk most efficiently.

9. **B** Options on the Advanced dialog box are Full Defragmentation, Defragment Files Only, and Consolidate Free Space Only.

10. **A, B** If Disk Defragmenter has never been run on a machine, having it check the disk for errors before starting the defragmentation process is a good idea. The first time you run Disk Defragmenter, the disk probably is badly fragmented and a full defragmentation should be run.

6.3.5 Key Words and Definitions

Cluster The minimum amount of space on a drive that can be allocated to a file.

CVF Compressed Volume File, a file that stores data and the structure of a compressed drive.

Disk Defragmenter A utility which moves files and free space to contiguous clusters on a drive.

DoubleSpace A disk compression utility that came with MS-DOS 6.0.

DriveSpace A disk compression utility that came with MS-DOS 6.2.

Fragmentation When pieces of files are scattered across a drive in non-contiguous clusters, increasing the time required to read and write to a disk.

Free space Clusters on a drive which have not been assigned to a file, or have not been allocated for system use.

6.4 Using ScanDisk

ScanDisk is used to check a disk for physical errors (such as bad sectors) and logical errors (such as cross-linked file) and repair the problem areas. ScanDisk also checks and repairs DMF-formatted floppy disks.

Any time a disk is shut down improperly, or physical problems exist with the media, ScanDisk should be run.

ScanDisk can be configured to run in the background while other applications are run.

ScanDisk can also be run from a command prompt by using the following parameters:

- **/a.** Checks all local, nonremovable drives

- **/n.** Starts and closes ScanDisk when complete

- **/p.** Does not correct errors encountered

Another file system issue that pertains to both performance and data integrity is that of cross-linked files and lost clusters. If either of these problems is suspected or if the user wants to ensure that they do not impact the integrity or performance of the computer's drives, ScanDisk should be used regularly.

When you run the Windows 95 Setup program to install Windows 95, ScanDisk runs automatically. The following are areas on which ScanDisk checks and fixes errors:

- File system structure, including lost clusters and cross-linked files

- Long filenames

- File allocation table

- Physical surface of the drive

- Directory tree structure

- DriveSpace or DoubleSpace volumes

Under a FAT file system, the clusters for a specific file are often scattered throughout the drive. Each cluster for a file contains both data and a pointer to the location of the next cluster in the chain. When a file is requested, the file system looks up the name of the file in the directory tree (which tells where the first cluster for the file is located) and begins to read through the various clusters, collecting the file's data.

Problems can occur when the pointer to the next cluster becomes corrupted. If, for example, file A has a cluster with some data and a pointer to cluster 12, and file B has a cluster that also points to cluster 12, these files are said to be *cross-linked*. The data at cluster 12 cannot belong to both files; therefore, there is a logical inconsistency in the file structure of the drive. ScanDisk is able to detect such inconsistencies, but it cannot determine to which file the cluster truly belongs. ScanDisk defaults to making a copy of the cluster so that each file can make use of the information in the cluster. This increases the chance that at least one of the two files in question can be salvaged.

Another associated problem is that now the clusters that should have been in the chain after the corrupted cluster are not referenced by any file, and are thus "orphaned" or lost. These clusters may still contain valid data, but they no longer are part of any file on the drive. ScanDisk is able to find these clusters and either save them as files to be examined later, or mark the clusters as available to the file system, thus freeing up space on the drive.

6.4.1   Operation Modes

ScanDisk can perform two levels of testing on hard drives: Standard and Thorough. Standard mode is best used on a daily basis, whereas Thorough mode is best used when you suspect a problem with the hard drive.

In *Standard* mode, ScanDisk performs logical tests against the file allocation table (FAT) of the file system, checking for the logical inconsistencies outlined earlier. In addition, the Standard scan checks for various other potential problems, such as invalid filenames and invalid date and time stamps.

In *Thorough* mode, ScanDisk not only performs all the tests included in Standard mode, but also performs a surface scan. Each cluster on the drive is checked for physical defects that would make the cluster in question unsafe for data storage. A surface scan is performed by reading the information from the cluster and rewriting it back to the same cluster. If the information matches what ScanDisk read the first time, the cluster is likely to be safe. If the data is different, a media problem might exist, in which case ScanDisk marks the cluster as bad.

> **ScanDisk does not test clusters that have been marked as bad in the FAT by other programs. You must use other programs to fix those clusters.**

6.4.2   Other Features of ScanDisk

ScanDisk contains a number of additional features, such as the following:

- ScanDisk can be run from the command line, with parameters to specify how it will run, or from the Windows 95 graphical interface.

- ScanDisk can fix problems on hard drives, floppy disk drives, RAM drives, and removable media (such as PCMCIA hard cards and Bernoulli drives).

- ScanDisk can detect and repair errors in long file names.

- ScanDisk can be used to test and maintain the integrity of DoubleSpace and DriveSpace volumes.

- ScanDisk can log its activities. The results of the scan are stored in the file SCANDISK.LOG in the root of the drive that has been examined.

- ScanDisk cannot fix errors on CD-ROMs, network drives, drives created by the DOS command INTERLNK, or drives referenced via MS-DOS commands (such as ASSIGN, JOIN, or SUBST).

- As with the Disk Defragmenter, it is possible to multitask with ScanDisk, but if any disk write activity occurs, ScanDisk may be forced to restart the testing process.

6.4.3   Exercise

Exercise 1: Running ScanDisk on a Hard Drive

In this exercise, you will run the ScanDisk utility against a hard drive to check it for errors. You will see the different options available to you as part of the utility, and see the results of the process.

1. Run the ScanDisk utility. Click the Start button, and select Programs, Accessories, System Tools, ScanDisk.

2. The ScanDisk dialog will appear, giving you the choice of a drive to scan for errors. Select a hard drive on your computer.

3. There are other options you can select from this window. The first is whether you want to do a Standard or a Thorough scan. Thorough scans will check for all errors that a Standard scan will, in addition to a scan of the physical surface of the drive. Thorough scans take substantially longer to perform. Select Standard.

4. Click on the Advanced button to see other options that are available to you. Select Always Display Summary. This will give you a report of ScanDisk's findings. Click the OK button.

5. Click the Start button to begin the scan. It is important to know that you should not do other work while ScanDisk is running. If the work you are doing writes information to the drive that is being scanned, ScanDisk may have to start over from the beginning.

6. Wait for ScanDisk to finish, and look at the results that are displayed to you.

6.4.4   Practice Problems

1. ScanDisk can be run against uncompressed drives only.

   A. True

   B. False

2. ScanDisk can be used to check which of the following?

   A. Hard drives

   B. Floppy drives

   C. Memory cards

   D. A and B

   E. A, B and C

3. ScanDisk can be used to detect errors on network drives.

   A. True

   B. False

4. ScanDisk cannot be used to detect which of the following?

   A. Errors in the File Allocation Table

   B. Errors on a CD-ROM

   C. Errors in the directory tree structure

   D. Physical errors on a hard drive

5. When running ScanDisk, what are the two options for handling lost file fragments?

   A. Free

   B. Ignore

   C. Make copies

   D. Convert to files

6. Which option do you use when running ScanDisk from a command prompt, to check all local non-removable drives?

   A. /n

   B. /a

   C. /p

   D. /x

7. What type(s) of errors does ScanDisk detect and correct?

   A. Lost clusters

   B. Cross-linked files

   C. Long filename errors

   D. Physical surface errors

8. Two files, File A and File B, can erroneously reference the same cluster. This problem is referred to as what?

   A. Lost clustering.

   B. Fragmented data.

   C. Cross-linking.

   D. None of the above; it can't happen in Windows 95.

9. When ScanDisk encounters cross-linked files, how are they repaired?

   A. The cluster and references to it are removed from both files.

   B. A copy of the cluster is made so that each file references a different copy of the cluster.

   C. Only one file keeps a reference to the cluster; the other reference is removed.

   D. The cross-link is not repaired.

10. Which type(s) of problems are found only during a "thorough" ScanDisk?

    A. Cross-linking

    B. Lost clusters

    C. Directory tree structure errors

    D. Physical surface errors

11. ScanDisk may be forced to restart if

   A. Disk writes occur during the testing process.

   B. It detects errors on the disk.

   C. Lost clusters cannot be saved to files.

   D. Auto-restart is selected.

12. Where would you look for the results of a ScanDisk operation after running ScanDisk on drive C?

   A. In the file C:\SCAN.LOG

   B. In the file C:\Windows\SCANDISK.LOG

   C. In the file C:\SCANDISK.LOG

   D. In the file C:\SCANLOG.TXT

6.4.5   Answers and Explanations

1. **B**   ScanDisk can be run against both compressed and uncompressed drives.

2. **E**   ScanDisk can be used to check hard drives, floppy drives, and memory cards.

3. **B**   ScanDisk will not detect errors on a network drive.

4. **B**   ScanDisk cannot detect errors on a CD-ROM drive. Some types of errors that can be detected are in the File Allocation Table, the directory tree structure, and physical errors on a drive.

5. **A, D**   When ScanDisk detects lost file fragments (fragments not associated with a file), they can either be freed (removed) or converted to files.

6. **B**   Using the /a parameter will cause ScanDisk to check all non-removable drives.

7. **A, B, C, D**   ScanDisk can detect and correct lost clusters, cross-linked files, long filename errors, and physical errors on a drive.

8. **C**   Cross-linking occurs when two files are linked to the same cluster on a drive.

9. **B**   ScanDisk will create a copy of a cross-linked cluster. A copy of each will be assigned to the cross-linked files so that the files are now referencing different clusters.

10. **D**   ScanDisk only performs a surface scan of a drive to detect physical errors when the Thorough option is selected.

11. **A**   If an application writes to the disk while ScanDisk is running, ScanDisk may need to reevaluate the state of the clusters which were written to by the application.

12. **C**   ScanDisk writes a Scandisk.log file in the root directory of the disk being analyzed.

6.4.6   Key Words and Definitions

Cross-linked files   Two or more files that erroneously reference the same cluster on a drive.

FAT   File Allocation Table, which maintains the structure of files and folders on a drive.

Logical errors   Problems with the data and organization of files stored on a drive.

Physical errors   Problems with the surface of an actual hardware device or floppy drive.

ScanDisk   A utility that checks hard drives and floppy drives for logical and physical errors, and then attempts to repair those errors.

6.5   The Compression Utility

Windows 95 implements a form of disk compression known as *on-the-fly compression*. On-the-fly compression is so named because the compression/decompression process occurs automatically in the background and is transparent to the user. On-the-fly compression is the process of intercepting normal MS-DOS read/write calls and compressing the data before writing it to the hard disk, so that the data consumes less space. Similarly, when the data is read back, it is automatically uncompressed before being transferred to the application or process that requested it.

Disk compression, as implemented in Windows 95 (and in the versions released with MS-DOS 6.*x*), consists of two processes:

- **Token Conversion.** A token, which takes up less space, replaces repetitive patterns that occur in a given piece of data.

- **Sector Allocation Granularity.** By circumventing the often large amounts of wasted space created under a normal FAT file system, disk compression changes the way data is stored on a hard drive.

Any FAT file system operates based on a cluster being the smallest traceable unit of measure. Therefore, if the cluster size is 4KB, for example, and a 2KB file is stored in that cluster, 2KB can be wasted. If 1,000 such files exist on a hard drive, $1,000 \times 2KB$ is wasted. With disk compression in place, the smallest allocation unit shrinks to one sector, or 512 bytes, which can greatly reduce the amount of wasted space on a drive.

6.5.1   DoubleSpace and DriveSpace Structure

Disk compression (called *DoubleSpace*) was first introduced in version 6.0 of MS-DOS. It was later re-released as *DriveSpace* in version 6.2, with some changes to the compression routines and with a new feature: the capability to uncompress a drive. The compression structure has remained fairly consistent.

After disk compression is installed and the files initially compressed, the files are stored in the *Compressed Volume File* (CVF), a large hidden file that sits on the physical drive C. When the system boots up, however, the CVF is assigned the drive letter C and is known as the *compressed drive*. The physical C drive, which now contains only a few files because everything else is in a compressed state inside the CVF, is assigned a higher drive letter, typically H, and is known as the *host drive*. The process of switching the drive letters and making the CVF available for viewing in MS-DOS and Windows is called *mounting*. From this point on, any file operation is handled through the disk compression routines, which are responsible for compressing and uncompressing files as disk I/O requests are made by the operating system.

6.5.2   Advantages of Windows 95 Disk Compression

Windows 95 disk compression contains many features that have been specifically optimized. The main advantages to using Windows 95 disk compression are as follows:

- Disk compression is implemented with 32-bit code for better performance.

- It does not use conventional memory.

- It is integrated with the operating system for ease of use and better performance.

> **When a floppy is compressed, the DriveSpace drivers load only when the floppy is in the drive. In general, the DriveSpace drivers load only when compressed media (hard drive or floppy) is detected.**

6.5.3 Further Notes on Windows 95 Disk Compression

The following information should be noted whenever a user is considering Windows 95 disk compression:

- Windows 95 is compatible with third-party compression software such as Stacker versions 2.*x*, 3.*x*, and 4.*x*, and with all versions of SuperStore, but these use real-mode compression and thus take up conventional memory and usually are slower.

- The maximum size of a compressed volume is 512MB when you are using DriveSpace 2.0, which comes with Windows 95. If you use Microsoft Plus!, which includes DriveSpace 3.0, the maximum size of a compressed volume is 2GB.

- The best compression ratio of a compressed volume is 2:1 (using DriveSpace 2.0, which comes with Windows 95). If you use Microsoft Plus!, which includes DriveSpace 3.0, this improves to approximately 2.4:1.

- Using compression slows down system performance because of the processing required by the operating system to interpret compressed data. With the continuing drop in prices for storage devices, disk compression is less important today than in the past, and should be avoided.

- A compressed drive, or CVF, is just a file stored on a hard drive or floppy. It is just as susceptible to disk errors as any other file, but any error in the CVF can cause the loss of all data in the CVF.

6.5.4 Practice Problems

1. If you have a DBLSPACE.BIN or DRVSPACE.BIN file in the root directory when you install Windows 95, they will be replaced by which file?

   A. DBLSPACX.VXD

   B. DBLSPACX.BIN

   C. DRVSPACX.BIN

   D. None of the above. The files are left unchanged.

2. Which of the following is a property of a compressed volume file?

   A. Read-only

   B. Hidden

   C. System

   D. All of the above

3. Which of the following relationships is true?

   A. A compressed drive is a file on a host drive.

   B. A host drive is a file on a compressed drive.

   C. A compressed drive is a partition of a host drive.

   D. Compressed and host drives are separate, unrelated items.

4. DriveSpace can be used to compress floppy drives.

   A. True

   B. False

5. What is the maximum size of a compressed drive that can be created using DriveSpace included with Windows 95?

   A. 256MB

   B. 512MB

   C. 1GB

   D. 2GB

6. What will the DIR /c command do on a disk drive?

   A. Compress the drive

   B. Display CVFs on a host drive

   C. Display the compression ratio for files

   D. Give a syntax error

7. What is the best compression ratio that you can obtain by using DriveSpace 2.0, which comes with Windows 95?

   A. 1.5 : 1

   B. 2 : 1

   C. 2.5 : 1

   D. 3 : 1

8. When John runs Disk Compression under Windows 95, he calls asking you how files are compressed. You tell him which two of the following are ways in which disk compression maximizes disk space.

   A. Cluster conversion

   B. Token conversion

   C. ASCII collapse

   D. Sector allocation granularity

9. Windows 95 implements which form of disk compression?

   A. On-the-fly compression

   B. Read/write compression

   C. Token conversion

   D. LZ compression

10. What is the smallest measure of disk allocation under Windows 95 compression?

   A. One byte

   B. One cluster

C. One sector

D. One cylinder

11. Which is *not* a benefit of DriveSpace compression?

   A. DriveSpace is integrated into the operating system.

   B. DriveSpace uses no conventional memory.

   C. DriveSpace uses all 32-bit code.

   D. DriveSpace drivers stay loaded at all times.

6.5.5 Answers and Explanations

1. **A**   DBLSPACE.BIN and DRVSPACE.BIN, files from older versions of compression utilities, will be replaced by a newer DBLSPACX.VXD file.

2. **D**   A compressed volume file (CVF) is marked as Read-Only, System, and Hidden.

3. **A**   A CVF is simply a file that resides on a host (physical) drive.

4. **A**   DriveSpace will compress floppy drives as well as hard drives.

5. **B**   The maximum size of a compressed file using the version of DriveSpace packaged with Windows 95 is 512MB.

6. **C**   Using the DIR /c command will show you the compression ratio for files.

7. **B**   The best compression ratio you can get with DriveSpace 2.0 is 2 : 1.

8. **B, D**   Token conversion replaces repetitive data patterns with tokens. Sector allocation granularity allocates file space by sector, not by cluster, reducing wasted disk space.

9. **A**   DriveSpace performs compression on-the-fly, transparently and in the background.

10. **C**   Sector allocation granularity enables file space to be allocated sector by sector instead of cluster by cluster.

11. **D**   DriveSpace drivers are loaded only when compressed media is detected and mounted.

6.5.6 Key Words and Definitions

Disk Compression   The process of increasing available space on a drive by storing data in packed format, reducing the space required by a file.

DoubleSpace   A disk compression utility that came with MS-DOS 6.0.

DriveSpace   A disk compression utility that came with MS-DOS 6.2.

Host drive   A drive which contains a compressed volume file (CVF).

On-the-fly compression   Compression and expansion of files by the operating system which is transparent to the user.

Practice Exam: Monitoring and Optimization

1. This is a scenario question. First, you must review the situation, then review the objectives. Following that is a proposed solution. You must pick the best evaluation of that solution.

SITUATION:

As an administrator, you want to use Net Watcher to monitor activity in your network. Your network consists of Windows 95 and Windows NT Workstation clients, and a Windows NT Server.

PRIMARY OBJECTIVES:

- Monitor file sharing in the network.

- Monitor printer services in the network.

- Limit file sharing for "classified" data in the network.

SECONDARY OBJECTIVES:

- View users who are connected to your workstation.

- Close resources shared by other users.

PROPOSED SOLUTION:

You install share-level security on your workstation and the NT Server, and user-level security on all of the other workstations which you want to monitor. In addition, you install File and Printer Sharing services on all of the machines.

EVALUATION OF PROPOSED SOLUTION (Choose the most correct answer):

A. The proposed solution meets all objectives.

B. The proposed solution meets all the primary objectives and most of the secondary objectives.

C. The proposed solution meets only one of the primary objectives and all the secondary objectives.

D. The proposed solution meets none of the primary objectives and all of the secondary objectives.

E. The proposed solution meets none of the primary objectives and only some of the secondary objectives.

F. The proposed solution meets none of the primary objectives and none of the secondary objectives.

2. This is a scenario question. First, you must review the situation, then review the objectives. Following that is a proposed solution. You must pick the best evaluation of that solution.

SITUATION:

You need to install a tool or tools that will allow you to view and control various aspects of your environment, including system performance, changes to your workstation, and disk and network activity.

PRIMARY OBJECTIVES:

- Monitor hardware performance.

- Find performance bottlenecks in the system.

- Determine when other users are connected to your workstation.

SECONDARY OBJECTIVES:

- View and log changes to your system configuration.

- Monitor system page faults to reduce disk activity.

PROPOSED SOLUTION:

You install the Windows 95 System Monitor software on your system and use that as the tool to perform the above objectives.

EVALUATION OF PROPOSED SOLUTION (Choose the most correct answer):

A. The proposed solution meets all objectives.

B. The proposed solution meets all the primary objectives and most of the secondary objectives.

C. The proposed solution meets only one of the primary objectives and all of the secondary objectives.

D. The proposed solution meets none of the primary objectives and all the secondary objectives.

E. The proposed solution meets some of the primary objectives and some of the secondary objectives.

F. The proposed solution meets none of the primary objectives and none of the secondary objectives.

3. What are advantages of using the Disk Defragmenter to optimize contiguous space on a hard drive?

A. Preventing fragmentation of new files stored on the drive.

B. Reducing the number of physical drive errors that can occur.

C. Improving disk performance.

D. Reducing dirty data in cache.

4. If ScanDisk detects a cross-linked file error during operation, what can ScanDisk do to address the problem?

A. Repair both files to their proper content.

B. Repair one file, and give you the option of how to re-link the second file.

C. Repair one file, but not the other.

D. Repair neither file.

5. Occasionally, when you are at your workstation, but not doing anything, you notice that there is hard disk activity. You want to use the System Monitor to see what is causing this to happen. Which item should you monitor?

A. Page Faults

B. Disk Activity

C. Dirty Data

D. None of the above

6. Within your network, you have several workstations that contain sensitive information that should not be available to the general user population. Which tool can you use to monitor and control the availability of that data across the network?

A. Net Watcher

B. System Monitor

C. Network Administrator

D. Security Administrator

7. This is a scenario question. First, you must review the situation, then review the objectives. Following that is a proposed solution. You must pick the best evaluation of that solution.

SITUATION:

You have several users who are complaining about performance on their computers. They are saying that it is taking them longer and longer to open and save files, and that files are getting corrupted on a regular basis.

PRIMARY OBJECTIVES:

• Improve disk access to speed performance.

• Reduce the occurrences of corrupt files.

SECONDARY OBJECTIVES:

- Scan hard drives for viruses.

- Increase available memory.

- Repair corrupt files.

PROPOSED SOLUTION:

You install the ScanDisk and Disk Defragmenter utilities on the users' machines, and then run a thorough scandisk before defragmenting their hard drives.

EVALUATION OF PROPOSED SOLUTION (Choose the most correct answer):

A. The proposed solution meets all objectives.

B. The proposed solution meets all the primary objectives and one of the secondary objectives.

C. The proposed solution meets only one of the primary objectives and all the secondary objectives.

D. The proposed solution meets none of the primary objectives and all the secondary objectives.

E. The proposed solution meets none of the primary objectives and only some of the secondary objectives.

F. The proposed solution meets none of the primary objectives and none of the secondary objectives.

Practice Exam Answers and Explanations

1. **F**   Computers using share-level security can only connect to other computers using share-level security. If you have chosen user-level security, you will not be able to see the other workstations in the environment. When you switch your workstation to user-level security, you will meet all of the objectives, assuming you have the proper authorization as the network administrator.

2. **E**   System monitor will not be able to tell you if other users are connected to your workstation, and it cannot be used to log changes to your system configuration. To monitor connected users, you will need to use Net Watcher.

3. **A, C**   Optimizing contiguous free space on a hard drive provides more room for large files to be stored without fragmentation occurring. These large files can be placed in large amounts of contiguous free space, which in turn improves disk performance since the new files aren't fragmented.

4. **C**   Most likely, ScanDisk can repair one of the two (or more) files involved in the cross-linking. Cross-linked files are caused by two files referencing the same cluster on a drive, when, in reality, only one file should reference it.

5. **C**   Disk activity can be caused by dirty data. Dirty data is data in cache that is written to disk when the system is idle. You can see the amount of dirty data in cache by using the System Monitor.

6. **A**   Net Watcher can be used to monitor the sharing of files across the network. With Net Watcher, you can also control how files are shared, and limit access within the network.

7. **B**   Performing a thorough scandisk on a drive will search that drive for physical problems that may be causing slow performance. Disk performance may be slow due to a highly fragmented drive. The Disk Defragmenter can repair this. Neither the ScanDisk nor the Defragmenter utilities will check a drive for viruses, or improve memory on a workstation.

CHAPTER 7

Troubleshooting

This chapter helps you prepare for the exam by covering the following objectives:

- Diagnose and resolve installation failures

- Diagnose and resolve connectivity problems in a Microsoft environment and a mixed Microsoft and NetWare environment, covering these tools:

    - WinIPCfg

    - Net Watcher

    - Troubleshooting wizards

- Diagnose and resolve printing problems in a Microsoft environment and a mixed Microsoft and NetWare environment

- Diagnose and resolve file system problems

- Diagnose and resolve resource access problems in a Microsoft environment and a mixed Microsoft and NetWare environment

- Diagnose and resolve hardware device and device driver problems, discussing these tools:

    - MSD

    - Add Hardware Wizard

- Perform direct modification of the Registry as appropriate by using Regedit

7.1   Installation Failures

Although Windows 95 has been designed to install without problems, hardware and software can cause problems during a Windows 95 installation. Microsoft has built-in mechanisms for the Windows 95 Setup program to detect failure and to recover automatically.

The Windows 95 Setup program maintains a setup log (SETUPLOG.TXT) during the installation and can determine where failures have occurred. The most likely place for failure is during hardware detection. A detection log (DETLOG.TXT) keeps track of what the Windows 95

Setup program discovers during the hardware detection phase. The following are basic Safe Recovery rules for you to know in case you have a failure:

- Before hardware detection begins, the Windows 95 Setup program uses SETUPLOG.TXT to determine the point of failure when you restart.

- During hardware detection, a DETCRASH.LOG is created. When the Windows 95 Setup program is restarted, it finds this file and uses it to determine which detection module was running at the point of failure.

- After completion of the hardware detection phase, the Windows 95 Setup program recognizes that hardware detection was successfully completed and skips past this point.

To continue if Windows 95 Setup stops during hardware detection, execute the following steps:

1. Press F3 or click the Cancel button to quit Setup.

   If the computer does not respond to the Cancel button, restart the computer by turning it off and then back on again. Do not just warm-boot using the Ctl+Alt+Del key sequence.

2. Run Setup again. The Windows 95 Setup program prompts you to use Safe Recovery to recover the failed Windows 95 installation.

3. Choose Use Safe Recovery (should be the default) and then click the Next button.

4. Repeat your installation choices. Hardware detection then runs again, but the Windows 95 Setup program skips the portion that caused the initial failure.

5. If the computer stops again during the hardware detection process, repeat this procedure until the hardware detection portion of Setup completes successfully.

The Windows 95 Setup program creates several log files (SETUPLOG.TXT, DETLOG.TXT, DETCRASH.LOG) during hardware detection failure, and others (NETLOG.TXT and BOOTLOG.TXT) as Windows 95 starts up the first time.

- **SETUPLOG.TXT.** This ASCII text file contains the Windows 95 Setup information created during installation.

  The Windows 95 Setup program uses the information contained in SETUPLOG.TXT to ensure that the Windows 95 installation program does not fail twice on the same problem. When you restart the Windows 95 Setup program after a failure, the contents are reviewed to see which process started but did not complete successfully. These processes are skipped, and the next process in sequence is run. The DETLOG.TXT and DETCRASH.LOG files are used to skip any hardware detection modules that failed.

- **DETLOG.TXT.** This ASCII text file contains a record of all devices found during the hardware detection phase of installation.

- **DETCRASH.LOG.** This binary file exists only during the hardware detection phase.

- **NETLOG.TXT.** This ASCII text file contains a record of all detected network components found during installation.

- **BOOTLOG.TXT.** This ASCII text file contains a record of the current startup process when starting Windows 95.

Installing Windows 95 should be a simple and trouble-free process. Sometimes, however, Windows 95 crashes during the hardware detection phase of the installation process. To aid the troubleshooting process, Windows 95 creates log files during the hardware detection process and when Windows 95 is started successfully.

If Windows 95 crashes during hardware detect, the binary file DETCRASH.LOG is created. When the setup process is restarted, this file is used by Windows 95 to bypass the device that crashed the hardware detection phase.

After Windows 95 has been installed, the file DETLOG.TXT is created. This file is a text file that contains a record of all devices found during the hardware detection phase. This file can be reviewed by the user using any text editor to determine which device was undetected by Windows 95 and crashed the installation process.

DETLOG.TXT is stored as a hidden file in the root directory of the hard drive.

Another file created when Windows 95 has been installed is SETUPLOG.TXT, which contains a list of Windows 95 Setup information created during the installation process. Each step of the installation process is written to the text file in sequence.

Windows 95 uses SETUPLOG.TXT to bypass problems. When Setup is restarted, Windows 95 bypasses processes that were started but failed to complete successfully.

Any network components detected during installation are recorded in the file NETLOG.TXT. The file is divided into four classes: network clients, network protocols, network adapters, and network services.

NETLOG.TXT is also stored on the hard disk's root directory, but it is not hidden.

BOOTLOG.TXT is another text file created during Windows 95 startup that lists all startup processes including components and drivers. This information is also written in sequence during startup. This file can be created at any time by selecting option 2 Logged Mode in the Boot menu.

7.1.1   Installed Components Verification

Windows 95 provides an option for verification of installed components when the Windows 95 Setup program detects an existing Windows 95 installation. When you run the Verify option, the Windows 95 Setup program reads SETUPLOG.TXT for the installed components and then reruns the setup process to verify all system components. If Verify finds a missing or damaged file, the Windows 95 Setup program reinstalls that file. As part of the verification, VMM32.VXD also gets rebuilt.

If the user suspects the Registry or some system files have become corrupted, he can choose to reinstall Windows 95. If Setup is run after installation, Setup prompts the user whether the installation should be rerun or whether to check the integrity of the installed components. If the user selects to check the integrity of the installed components, he should expect three things:

- Each installed component is checked. If the validity check fails for a specific file, the file is re-installed.

- The VMM32.VXD file is rebuilt.

- The Registry is rebuilt.

7.1.2   Exercise

Exercise 1: Downloading the Hardware Compatibility List

This exercise demonstrates how to use the Internet to download Windows 95 technical files by using Microsoft Internet Explorer version 3.0.

1. From your computer, start Internet Explorer.

2. Specify `http://www.microsoft.com` as the address.

3. Click Search from the Microsoft Web page toolbar.

4. In the I want to search for text box, type **hardware compatibility list**.

5. Click Search Now.

6. Scroll through the list and find the Windows 95 Hardware Compatibility List.

7. Click the title for the Windows 95 Hardware Compatibility List.

8. Scroll through the document.

9. Locate the section titled More Information.

10. Click the displayed link to download the HCL95.EXE file.

11. Select Save it to disk.

12. Save the file to a new folder named HCL in the root folder of your hard drive.

13. Close Internet Explorer when you finish.

14. Start Windows 95 Explorer and double-click the file HCL95.EXE located in the HCL folder.

15. Type y to expand the files.

16. When completed, double-click the file HCL95.HLP and view the file.

17. When you finish, close the application.

7.1.3   Practice Problems

1. Installation fails while Setup is detecting hardware devices. Which file can you check to help determine the cause of the failure?

   A. SYSTEM.INI

   B. SETUP.LOG

   C. DETLOG.TXT

   D. HARDWARE.INI

2. Which file does Windows 95 use if installation is interrupted (that is, by a failure) before hardware detection and then restarted?

   A. STARTUP.LOG

   B. SETUP.LOG

   C. SETUPLOG.TXT

   D. DETLOG.TXT

3. What is the purpose of the NETLOG.TXT file?

   A. Logging all invalid logon attempts

   B. Maintaining a list of all users that have made a network connection from the machine

   C. Keeping an encrypted list of Windows user IDs and passwords

   D. Tracking network component detection and installation

4. Which file does Windows 95 Setup use to bypass devices that previously caused a hardware detection failure?

   A. DETCRASH.LOG

   B. DETLOG.TXT

   C. BYPASS.LOG

   D. SETUPLOG.TXT

5. Where is the DETLOG.TXT file found?

   A. In the root directory

   B. \Windows

   C. \Windows\System

   D. \Windows\Setup

6. What classes of information are found in the NETLOG.TXT file?

   A. Network clients

   B. Network protocols

   C. Network adapters

   D. Network services

7. If you have already installed Windows 95 successfully and you try to run Setup again, what happens?

   A. The installed version is removed, and Windows 95 is reinstalled.

   B. Setup fails.

   C. You are prompted to either reinstall Windows or verify install components.

   D. Windows is uninstalled and the computer reverts to the previous operating system.

8. If you are reinstalling Windows 95 over an existing copy and Setup finds a corrupted system file, what happens?

   A. The name of the corrupt file is logged in SETUPLOG.TXT.

   B. The file is automatically reinstalled.

   C. You are prompted to replace the corrupt file.

   D. Nothing. Setup cannot detect corrupt files.

9. DETCRASH.LOG is an ASCII file that can be read with Notepad to troubleshoot installation problems if hardware detection fails.

   A. True

   B. False

10. Setup uses the DETLOG.TXT file to restart if installation fails during hardware detection.

    A. True

    B. False

11. If Setup fails during hardware detection, what should you do?

    A. Remove the hardware that is causing the failure.

    B. Uninstall Windows 95, remove all log files, and restart the process.

    C. Run Setup again, repeating the process until detection completes.

    D. Buy new hardware.

12. If Setup fails during hardware detection, which file(s) can you check for information on the problem?

    A. AUTOEXEC.BAT

    B. CONFIG.SYS

    C. SETUPLOG.TXT

    D. DETLOG.TXT

13. What does a B1 error indicate during the setup process?

    A. The processor is too old.

    B. You don't have a valid license to install Windows 95.

    C. Setup can't find the installation drive.

    D. The system doesn't have enough memory to run Windows 95.

14. If you receive a message about an incorrect MS-DOS version during setup, you should check to make sure you are running at least which version of MS-DOS?

    A. MS-DOS 2.0

    B. MS-DOS 3.1

    C. MS-DOS 5.0

    D. MS-DOS 6.2

15. When you run Setup and try to create a Startup disk, and the setup process fails, how should you resolve the problem?

    A. Don't create the Startup disk, you probably won't need it.

    B. Run SETUP /s to create the Startup disk before Windows 95 is installed.

    C. Run the SYSCOPY.EXE utility on the Window 95 CD to create the Startup disk.

    D. Set up Windows without making a Startup disk, and after installation is complete, make the Startup disk from the Control Panel.

16. What is the major cause of problems when you install Windows 95?

    A. Not enough RAM

    B. Bad media

    C. Drivers not available for Windows 95

    D. Hardware configuration

17. You have installed Windows 95, but continually receive error messages reporting bad or missing files. What should you do?

    A. Reinstall Windows 95.

    B. Always use Safe mode.

    C. Run Setup's verification of installed components option.

    D. Use the Emergency Repair Disk.

18. You are installing Windows 95 on a PC, and the Setup program fails to start. What do you suspect is the problem?

    A. You are installing from an unsupported version of DOS, such as DR DOS.

    B. You are installing from Windows 3.0.

    C. You do not have enough free RAM.

    D. You do not have enough hard disk space.

19. You are installing Windows 95, and the Setup program hangs during the file copy phase. What can be causing the problem? Choose the best answer.

    A. You do not have enough RAM.

    B. You do not have enough free space.

    C. You have virus detection software enabled.

    D. You have disk compression enabled.

20. The Setup program reports an error and states that it cannot find a valid boot partition. You are certain that there is a boot partition, as you are upgrading from Windows 3.1. What do you suspect is the problem?

    A. You have disk compression enabled.

    B. You have virus software running.

    C. You have formatted the drive, but have not marked a disk active.

    D. You probably have a dormant virus that has affected your Master Boot Record.

21. You have opted to remove Windows 95 from your system. What is the best way to do this?

    A. Use FDISK.

    B. Upgrade to Windows NT.

    C. Choose Remove Windows 95 from the Add/Remove Programs applet.

    D. Run Setup and choose Uninstall.

7.1.4 Answers and Explanations

1. **C** DETLOG.TXT is an ASCII file created by the setup process that contains information about hardware detection.

2. **C** If the setup process is interrupted, the SETUPLOG.TXT file will be used to restart from the point of interruption.

3. **D** NETLOG.TXT contains information about network detection and installation.

4. **A** If the hardware detection process fails, Setup uses DETCRASH.LOG to determine which device failed and bypass that device during the next setup attempt.

5. **A** DETLOG.TXT is created in the root directory.

6. **A, B, C, D** The NETLOG.TXT file contains information about network clients, protocols, adapters, and services detected during setup.

7. **C** If you run Setup on a machine that already has Windows 95 installed, Setup verifies the installed components.

8. **B** If Windows 95 finds a corrupt file, it automatically replaces it.

9. **B** The DETCRASH.LOG is a binary file that is used by the Setup program.

10. **B** DETLOG.TXT is an ASCII file created for the user and not read by the setup procedure.

11. **C** If Setup fails during hardware detection, rerun Setup. The hardware that caused the failure will be bypassed the second time.

12. **A, C, D** Information on hardware detection is stored in the AUTOEXEC.BAT, SETUPLOG.TXT, and DETLOG.TXT files.

13. **A** A B1 error indicates that the processor is too old, usually an early version of the 80386.

14. **B** MS-DOS 3.1 or higher is required.

15. **D** If Setup fails to create a Startup disk, create the disk from the Control Panel after Setup has completed.

16. **D** Hardware configuration. Due to Windows 95's attempt to dynamically assign system resources through Plug and Play, legacy hardware or hardware that has been assigned IRQs through jumpers or

setup-type programs typically introduces conflicts and problems with the Setup programs.

17. **C**   Run Setup's verification of installed components option. Through Setup you can run a verification that will ensure that Windows 95's system files are in working order. If they are found to be damaged or missing, Setup reinstalls the appropriate files.

18. **C**   You do not have enough free RAM. If you were trying to upgrade from DR DOS, Setup would have started but halted at the qualifying upgrade check. From Windows 3.0, Setup would also start. The hard disk space problem would not stop Setup from starting.

19. **C**   You have virus detection enabled. Virus detection software and other TSRs often cause problems during the file copy phase of Setup. These should be turned off before running Setup.

20. **A**   You have disk compression enabled. Some disk compression actually hides the boot partition through its compression mechanisms. Turn off compression and then run Setup again.

21. **C**   Use the Add/Remove Programs applet and remove Windows 95 from itself.

7.1.5   Key Words and Definitions

BOOTLOG.TXT   An ASCII file containing a log of the most recent startup process of Windows 95.

DETCRASH.LOG   A binary file created by Windows 95 if Setup fails during the hardware detection phase, and then subsequently used when Setup is rerun.

DETLOG.TXT   An ASCII file containing a list of hardware devices found by Windows 95 during the hardware detection phase of Setup.

NETLOG.TXT   An ASCII file containing a list of all network components found during the Windows 95 installation.

Safe Recovery   Restart of the Windows 95 Setup program after a failure, allowing Setup to use previous log files to continue installation.

SETUPLOG.TXT   An ASCII file containing setup information, created during Windows 95 installation.

Warm boot   Restarting a computer by using the Ctrl+Alt+Del keys.

7.2   Boot Process Failures

Windows 95 has many troubleshooting options when Windows will not boot properly. This problem might occur during the installation process while detecting hardware or after installing new drivers. At any time, the user can override the default settings and manually configure the startup process. This can be accomplished by using the following features:

- Safe Recovery mode

- Windows 95 Boot menu

- Reinstall Windows 95 to verify the installation process

- The Startup disk

- WIN.COM switches

7.2.1   Safe Recovery Mode

During the installation of Windows 95, a system crash automatically implements Safe Recovery mode, which will restart the installation process at the point the crash occurred. This prevents the user from reinstalling Windows 95 from the beginning.

7.2.2   The Boot Menu

The Boot menu contains a list of boot options the user can select during Windows 95 startup. Pressing F8 when Windows 95 is booting, when you see the message `Starting Windows 95`, can access the Boot menu. This menu is used to select the desired mode Windows 95 can be booted into. Each mode has a specific function:

- **Normal.** This is the default Windows 95 boot option and starts Windows 95 under normal conditions.

- **Logged.** This option boots Windows 95 under normal conditions but creates the file BOOTLOG.TXT, which documents all components and drivers that are loaded and initialized by the system.

- **Safe Mode.** This mode starts Windows 95 in a minimum configuration that does not load any device drivers except the keyboard, mouse, and standard VGA video drivers; the Registry, the Startup group, and CONFIG.SYS or AUTOEXEC.BAT; the [BOOT] and [386ENH] sections of SYSTEM.INI; and the LOAD and RUN command parameters of WIN.INI. This option is useful for recovering from GPFs, application hangs, device errors, and boot problems.

- **Safe Mode with Network Support.** This option is the same as Safe mode with Real mode NetBEUI networking support enabled.

- **Step-by-Step Confirmation.** This option enables the user to decide which parts of the boot process should or should not be completed.

- **Command Prompt Only Mode.** This option is similar to a normal DOS boot. AUTOEXEC.BAT, CONFIG.SYS, and the Registry are loaded.

- **Safe Mode Command Prompt.** This option is similar to Command Prompt Only Mode except that CONFIG.SYS and AUTOEXEC.BAT are not processed.

- **Previous Version of MS-DOS.** This option enables the user to boot to the previous operating system. It is often used to test the functionality of MS-DOS–based functions in both environments.

7.2.3   Reinstall Windows 95 to Verify the Installation Process

If the user suspects the Registry or some system files have become corrupted, he can choose to reinstall Windows 95. If Setup is run after installation, Setup prompts the user whether the installation should be rerun or whether to check the integrity of the installed components. If the user selects to check the integrity of the installed components, he should expect three things:

- Each installed component is checked. If the validity check fails for a specific file, the file is reinstalled.

- The VMM32.VXD file is rebuilt.

- The Registry is rebuilt.

7.2.4   Exercises

Exercise 1: Booting to Windows 95 Safe Mode

In this exercise, you start your computer in Safe mode and see the differences in options available to you.

1. Restart your computer. When you see the message `Starting Windows 95`, press the F8 function key.

2. You see the Windows Boot menu. From the menu, select Safe Mode (option 3).

3. While Windows is loading, you see a dialog box that indicates you started in Safe mode. After Windows 95 is loaded, notice the changes to the desktop. You see the words `Safe Mode` in the four corners of the screen.

4. Notice other changes as well. If you set up a resolution other than 640×480, you now see the resolution has changed.

5. Look for your network connections. Notice that the Network Neighborhood icon is missing from the desktop. This is because Safe mode doesn't provide support for networks.

Exercise 2: Booting to Logged Mode

In this exercise, you start your computer in Logged mode and see the steps that occur during normal Windows 95 startup.

1. Restart your computer. When you see the message `Starting Windows 95`, press the F8 function key.

2. You see the Windows Boot menu. From the menu, select Logged Mode (option 2).

3. Windows now starts normally. After it is finished, run WordPad. From the WordPad menu, open the file BOOTLOG.TXT, which will be in the root directory of your boot drive. BOOTLOG.TXT is a log of everything that occurred during Windows startup.

4. Browse through the file, and notice the different events that occurred during startup:

    - Loading devices

    - Loading successes (and failures if any)

    - Initialization loads

    - Dynamic loads

    You should recognize some information from your CONFIG.SYS or AUTOEXEC.BAT files.

5. You can continue your work normally now. Starting Windows 95 in Logged mode doesn't have any impact on your system except for creating the BOOTLOG.TXT file.

7.2.5   Practice Problems

1. When a system is booting and the message `Starting Windows 95` appears, you can choose how to start the system (that is, Normal, Safe Mode, Logged, and so on). Which function key invokes the Boot menu?

    A. F2

    B. F4

    C. F8

    D. F10

2. If you choose the Logged option from the Windows 95 Boot menu, which file will be created?

    A. BOOTLOG.TXT

    B. BOOT. LOG

    C. STARTUP.LOG

    D. LOG.TXT

3. If a system crash occurs during the boot process, how will Windows restart?

    A. In Normal mode

    B. In Logged mode

    C. In Safe mode

    D. In DOS mode

4. When starting in Safe mode, the CONFIG.SYS and AUTOEXEC.BAT files are loaded.

    A. True

    B. False

5. When starting Windows 95 in Safe mode with Network support, which network type is enabled?

    A. TCP/IP

    B. IPX/SPX

    C. NetBEUI

    D. All the above

6. Which of the following are loaded in Safe mode?

    A. The Registry

    B. Keyboard and mouse drivers

    C. VGA drivers

    D. The Startup group

7. If Windows doesn't find the SYSTEM.DAT Registry file during startup, what happens?

    A. SYSTEM.DAT is restored from SYSTEM.DA0.

    B. The system starts in DOS mode.

    C. You are prompted to reinstall Windows 95 because the Registry is missing or corrupt.

    D. Windows 95 starts in Safe mode.

8. You are trying to use dual boot to boot to an earlier version of DOS but get an error stating `Previous MS-DOS files not found`. What is the problem?

    A. You are trying to use MS-DOS 3.1.

    B. You are trying to use MS-DOS 5.0.

    C. You are trying to use MS-DOS 6.0.

    D. You are trying to use MS-DOS 6.2.

9. If you start a PC with a command prompt only and then decide to run Windows in Safe mode, which WIN.COM switch would you use?

    A. /d:m

    B. /d:s

    C. /d:x

    D. /d:f

10. Settings that were previously kept in the CONFIG.SYS and AUTOEXEC.BAT files in older versions of Windows are stored in which Windows 95 file(s)?

A. SYSTEM.INI

B. COMMAND.COM

C. IO.SYS

D. MSDOS.SYS

11. An option for startup under the Windows 95 menu is to start with a previous version of MS-DOS. Which setting is required in the MSDOS.SYS file for this option?

    A. DOSBoot=1

    B. BootMulti=1

    C. MultiBoot=2

    D. MSDOS=2

12. What is the first thing you should do if you try to start a computer in Safe mode and it fails?

    A. Reinstall Windows 95.

    B. Run the Disk Defragmenter.

    C. Run ScanDisk.

    D. Call a consultant.

13. You want to boot Windows 95 into Safe mode. How can you do this?

    A. Choose Shutdown and Restart in safe mode from the Start button.

    B. Press F8 when the message `Starting Windows 95` appears and then select Safe mode.

    C. Choose Shutdown and Restart while holding down the Shift key.

    D. You cannot force Windows 95 to go into Safe mode. It will automatically detect when a problem exists and reboot into Safe mode.

14. You have accessed the Windows 95 Boot menu during the boot phase. What does the option Step by Step do?

    A. Windows 95 checks the validity of each file as it loads the system file into memory.

    B. Requires users to verify each file loaded.

    C. Requires the Windows 95 media so that the SETUP.EXE file can test the validity of each system file.

    D. No such option exists.

15. You have chosen the option to reboot into Safe mode. You cannot access your network resources, however. Why is this?

    A. You do not have permission to the resources under Safe mode (for security reasons).

    B. The network card drivers have not been loaded.

    C. Safe mode does not support any network devices.

    D. You must add the network card and protocol through Control Panel, Networks. Then you must reboot back into Safe mode to have network support.

16. Which file is not copied to the Startup disk by Windows 95?

    A. COMMAND.COM

    B. FDISK.EXE

    C. FORMAT.COM

    D. SYSTEM.DAT

17. Which file is required on the Startup disk to enable the FAT32 file system?

    A. FDISK.EXE

    B. FAT32.EXE

    C. FAT32.COM

    D. FAT32.SYS

18. You just installed a new driver for your video adapter. When you restart Windows 95, it informs you the adapter did not load properly. In which mode should you start to install a different video driver?

A. Normal

B. Safe mode

C. Command Prompt

D. Previous Version of MS-DOS

19. You believe that some Windows 95 files were corrupted by a virus. What should you do to check their integrity?

  A. Start Windows 95 in MS-DOS mode and run Setup from the Windows 95 CD-ROM.

  B. Run Setup from within Windows 95 and select Verification.

  C. Reformat the hard driver and reinstall Windows 95.

  D. Copy the damaged files from the Windows 95 floppies to the WIN-DOWS folder on the hard disk.

20. The file IO.SYS was accidentally deleted from the boot drive and Windows 95 will not start properly. What can you do to solve the problem?

  A. Boot the computer using the Startup disk and copy IO.SYS from the floppy disk to the hard drive.

  B. Reinstall Windows 95.

  C. Boot the machine into Safe mode and run ScanDisk.

  D. None of the above.

21. In MSDOS.SYS, which command tells the boot process where to find the Windows 95 Startup files?

  A. WinBootDir

  B. WinDir

  C. HostBootWinDrv

  D. WinStart

7.2.6 Answers and Explanations

1. **C** F8 displays the Windows Boot menu.

2. **A** BOOTLOG.TXT displays the steps that Windows took to start.

3. **C** If the system crashed during startup, Windows starts in Safe mode.

4. **B** The AUTOEXEC.BAT and CONFIG.SYS files are not loaded if you start in Safe mode.

5. **C** When you start Windows in Safe mode with network support, Windows enables NetBEUI.

6. **B, C** Keyboard, mouse, and VGA drivers are loaded when Windows 95 starts in Safe mode.

7. **A, D** If Windows doesn't find the SYSTEM.DAT file during the boot process, it attempts to restore from SYSTEM.DA0 and start in Safe mode.

8. **A** To dual-boot MS-DOS and Windows 95, you must have MS-DOS version 5.0 or higher.

9. **A** Running Windows with the /d:m switch starts Windows 95 in Save mode.

10. **C, D** Older settings that were previously stored in the CONFIG.SYS and AUTOEXEC.BAT files are now stored in the IO.SYS and MSDOS.SYS files.

11. **B** The BootMulti=1 option must be set for dual-booting with Windows 95.

12. **C** Run ScanDisk to check the file system if Windows fails to start in Safe mode.

13. **B** Press F8 during startup and choose the Safe mode option.

14. **B** Requires the user to verify each file loaded. This is useful if you suspect one device or device driver is generating troubles.

15.   **B**   The network card drivers have not been loaded. To access network resources during Safe mode, you need to choose Safe Mode with Networking Support after you press F8.

16.   **D**   SYSTEM.DAT forms part of the Registry files and is not part of the Startup disk by default.

17.   **A**   FDISK.EXE available with OSR2 provides support for the FAT32 file system.

18.   **B**   Safe mode loads the default VGA driver. The proper driver can then be installed in Safe mode.

19.   **B**   Corrupted Windows 95 files can be automatically checked and reinstalled if necessary by running Setup again from within Windows and selecting Verification.

20.   **A**   IO.SYS is available on any bootable Windows 95 disk. It is marked as Hidden and Read-only.

21.   **A**   The WinBootDir is used to specify the location of the Windows 95 Startup files.

7.2.7   Key Words and Definitions

Boot menu   A menu that enables a choice of Windows 95 startup modes, available when pressing F8 after the message Starting Windows 95 appears.

Logged   A Windows 95 startup option that creates the BOOTLOG.TXT file.

Safe Mode   A Windows 95 startup option that loads a minimum configuration, with few device drivers or other options.

Safe Mode with Network Support   A startup option, similar to Safe Mode, but with the added capability of NetBEUI networking.

Step-by-Step Confirmation   A startup option that enables you to decide which parts of the boot process occur.

7.3   Connectivity Problems Failures

Various problems can occur when you use Dial-Up Networking to connect to remote computers. It is increasingly important these days to be aware of where problems can occur and how to fix them. Because of the growing popularity of the Internet, more and more people are using Dial-Up Networking.

The majority of the problems described in this section are common the first time a user attempts to establish a connection to a remote server. Problems such as using the wrong phone number or not having the proper protocol installed usually occur once. These are typically easy to fix if you know what to look for and how to go about correcting the problem.

7.3.1   Dial-Up Networking

Dial-Up Networking problems can be divided into six categories:

- **Modem problems.** Ensure the modem is installed properly. Check to see that the phone line is plugged into the modem and that the modem is turned on (if it is an external modem).

- **Phone numbers.** Ensure the phone number being dialed is the correct number. If you share your modem with the phone line, disable call-waiting. When dialing a long-distance number, ensure the entire number, including 1 + area code, is being used.

- **Protocol.** Ensure the same protocol (such as NetBEUI or IPX/SPX) is installed on the client and server. If TCP/IP is used, ensure it is configured.

- **Access rights.** Ensure you have the appropriate rights to connect to the remote server. If a password is used, check to see that the correct password is being typed.

- **Server problems.** If the client computer is configured properly, the problem might be with the server computer. Ensure the server is configured to allow client to dial-in. Check the modem and the phone line as well.

- **Application problems.** If the problem occurs when connected to the remote server, the connection might be bad or the application might not support remote access.

7.3.2   Modem Diagnostics

During installation of a modem, or when troubleshooting problems with a modem, you need to use the Modems properties sheet and the Diagnostics tab of this sheet. The Modems properties sheet is available by clicking the Modems icon in the Control Panel.

The Diagnostics tab on the Modems properties sheet displays information about your modem, including the port it uses, resources, highest speed, and command set configured for it. You cannot run this utility while you are using the modem.

7.3.3   Using Log Files to Diagnose Connection Problems

Modem command logging is available only when you use Windows 95 TAPI-compliant communication software. Because Windows 3.1 communication software does not use the same software layers to communicate with the modem, Windows 95 cannot trap the AT commands that these applications send to the modem.

To diagnose connection problems when using Dial-Up Networking, Windows 95 provides two log files:

- PPPLOG.TXT
- MODEMLOG.TXT

PPPLOG.TXT

The PPPLOG.TXT file contains information on how the software layers of PPP have processed a Dial-Up Networking call. This logging feature is disabled by default.

MODEMLOG.TXT

Although the MODEMLOG.TXT log file is not specific to Dial-Up Networking, it is nonetheless useful in troubleshooting connection difficulties. It records all AT-type commands sent to the modem and logs responses from the modem. This logging feature is disabled by default.

To enable modem command logging, select the modem in the Modems control panel applet, select the Connection tab of the properties sheet, choose Advanced, and then choose Record a log file.

A log file can be used to troubleshoot connection problems such as modem initialization problems and slow baud rate connections, and to determine which computer (the host or the guest) is dropping the connection.

7.3.4   Using the Startup Disk to Repair a Faulty Network Setup

During the installation of Windows 95, the user is asked whether he wants to create a Startup disk. This Startup disk can also be created at a later time using the Add/Remove Program option in the Control Panel.

The Startup disk serves two primary functions:

- It functions as an emergency boot disk for Windows 95.
- It contains useful MS-DOS–based commands and utilities for troubleshooting purposes.

In addition, other files should be copied to the Startup disk for troubleshooting purposes. These include the following:

- A copy of SYSTEM.DAT
- A copy of the computer's AUTOEXEC.BAT and CONFIG.SYS
- Any CD-ROM drivers

The Startup disk also serves an additional function in a shared network installation: It contains real-mode software that is required to boot the computer and attach to the shared Windows folder located on the server. A copy of the mini-Registry used to start the computer is also stored on the Startup disk. In a network situation, the Startup disk can be a local drive or a disk image on the server.

7.3.5 WIN.COM Switches

The user can specify how Windows 95 is started by adding a switch(es) to the WIN.COM file in the format

```
win /d:switch
```

The following switches are valid:

- **f.** Disables the 32-bit file system drivers. This is useful if you experience problems with the hard drive.

- **m.** Starts Windows 95 in Safe mode. This is the same as pressing F8 when Windows 95 starts and selecting Safe mode.

- **n.** Starts Windows 95 in Safe mode with networking. This is the same as pressing F8 when Windows 95 starts and selecting Safe mode with Network Support.

- **s.** Excludes the ROM address space between F000 and 1MB from use by Windows 95.

- **v.** Disables the virtualization of hardware disk interrupts.

- **x.** Disables use of upper memory by Windows 95.

7.3.6 WinIPCfg

WinIPCfg is a utility that comes with Windows 95 that lets you view information about your IP configuration. You can use this tool to view information about the following:

- Installed adapters

- The IP address assigned to your computer

- Subnet mask

- Host name

- DNS information

- Lease information for an IP address

WINIPCFG.EXE is available in the \WINDOWS directory.

7.3.7 Net Watcher

Another tool for troubleshooting, available with Windows 95, is the Net Watcher. Net Watcher enables a user to manage shared resources on a local or remote computer. A user can create or delete a shared resource on a remote computer and monitor access to the shared resources.

The following characteristics must apply in order to use Net Watcher:

- File and Printer Sharing must be enabled on the remote computer.

- You can only access remote systems that use the same access control that you use on your computer; that is, both computers must be set to user-level access control or share-level access control.

- You can only access remote systems using the same type of file and print sharing (Microsoft or NetWare).

Using Net Watcher, a user might perform the following tasks on the local or remote computer:

- List all shared resources and connected users.

- Create a new shared resource.

- Close files a user has opened (only on Microsoft networks).

- Disconnect a user from a shared resource.

Net Watcher is useful as an administration tool in a peer-to-peer network because it enables one administrator to manage the resources on all computers in the workgroup.

When connecting to a remote computer using share-level access control, the password used is the one specified in the Remote Administration dialog box.

When connecting to a remote computer using user-level access control, the password is the Administrator's account password.

7.3.8 Troubleshooting Wizards

Windows provides numerous troubleshooting wizards that can help you resolve problems in Windows 95. These wizards are available as part of the help system. Simply click Start and Help, and from the Windows 95 Help dialog box, click the Contents tab. One of the books in the Contents is the Troubleshooting book. From here, you can get help for the following items:

- Printing

- Hardware conflicts

- Networking

- Modem and dial-up problems

These wizards walk you through a series of questions to help you determine the cause of problems you are having with Windows 95.

7.3.9 Exercises

Exercise 1: Running a Troubleshooting Wizard

In this exercise, you see how to use a Windows 95 troubleshooting wizard to help you resolve a problem connecting to a network.

1. From the Start Button, click Help. This opens the Windows 95 Help dialog box.

2. Click the Contents tab and then expand the Troubleshooting book by double-clicking it.

3. Select the option that says If you are having trouble using the network. This opens a new help dialog box that asks you a series of questions to help you resolve a network problem.

4. Read through the questions and then select I can't log onto the network. A new set of questions appears asking what type of network you use.

5. Click on the response that says I don't know. You see a new set of questions, along with a button that displays the Network properties. If you click this button, the Network Properties window opens.

6. Walk through some of the questions in the wizard, selecting different answers to see how the wizard responds to the scenario.

Exercise 2: Monitoring a Computer Using Net Watcher

In this exercise, you monitor another Windows 95 computer using the Net Watcher program. The following exercise shows how to monitor a remote computer using Net Watcher.

1. Start Net Watcher as previously described. You also can select the Start menu, and choose Programs, Accessories, System Tools, Net Watcher.

2. Choose Administer, Select Server. The Select Server dialog box appears.

3. Enter the name of the server (the remote computer) you want to view. Choose the Browse button to see a list of the computers to which you can connect.

4. Click OK. A view of the remote computer appears in Net Watcher.

5. Click the Show Users button to see the users connected to the selected computer. On the left, you see the username, computer name, number of shares, number of open files, time of connection, and idle time. On the right, you see the shared folders and the files that are opened.

6. Click the Show Shared Folders button to see the names of the shared folders on the selected computer. On the left, you see the shared folder, the name it is shared as, the access type, and a comment associated with the folder. On the right, you see the connections to the share and the files that are opened.

7. Click the Show Files button to see files that are opened by other users. You see the name of the file, the share it is using, the person accessing it, and the open mode.

8. Press F5 to refresh the display.

9. Choose Administer, Exit to exit Net Watcher.

7.3.10   Practice Problems

1. Which utility enables you to examine the IP address assigned to your computer?

    A. Net Watcher

    B. System Monitor

    C. WinIPCfg

    D. TCP/IP

2. WINIPCfg enables you to view configuration values for computers running which protocol?

    A. TCP/IP

    B. NetBEUI

    C. IPX/SPX

    D. NetWare

3. WINIPCfg helps you determine which values have been configured by DHCP.

    A. True

    B. False

4. Which of the following can explain why you are having problems connecting a client machine to a server?

    A. The two machines are running different operating systems.

    B. The two machines are running different protocols.

    C. The client user doesn't have sufficient rights.

    D. None of the above.

5. In which situations can Dial-Up Networking be used?

    A. To connect to a Banyan VINES server running SLIP

    B. To connect a remote laptop to a Windows 95 computer using an ISDN line

    C. To connect to the Internet

    D. To connect to a Windows NT server using DLC

6. Dial-Up Networking supports which two protocols to connect to a Windows NT server?

    A. PPP

    B. SLIP

    C. CSLIP

    D. RAS

7. Which network transport protocols does PPP support?

    A. NetBEUI

    B. IPX/SPX

    C. TCP/IP

    D. DLC

8. Which protocol must be used to connect to the Internet?

    A. NetBEUI

    B. IPX/SPX

    C. TCP/IP

    D. None of the above

9. SLIP is used with which protocol?

    A. NetBEUI

    B. IPX/SPX

    C. TCP/IP

    D. All the above

10. Which system can Windows 95 Dial-Up Networking *not* be used to connect to?

    A. Windows NT

    B. Windows for Workgroups

    C. NetWare Connect

    D. OS/2

11. In which file are dialing properties for a modem stored?

    A. The Registry in HKEY_LOCAL_MACHINE

    B. TELEPHON.INI

    C. DIALUP.INI

    D. TELEPHONY.INI

12. Which protocol(s) does not support encrypted passwords?

    A. SLIP

    B. PPP

    C. RAS

    D. All the above

13. If enabled, a log file of all modem AT commands sent to the modem is stored in which file?

    A. MODEM.LOG.

    B. MODEMLOG.TXT.

    C. AT.TXT.

    D. No such file exists.

14. In a network situation, what can the Startup disk *not* be?

    A. An image file on a network drive

    B. A floppy disk

    C. A hard disk

    D. A CD-ROM drive

7.3.11 Answers and Explanations

1. **C** WinIPCfg is a utility that enables you to examine IP addresses.

2. **A** WinIPCfg lets you view computers running TCP/IP.

3. **A** WinIPCFG can be used to determine which values have been set by DHCP.

4. **B, C** If you cannot connect to a server, it might mean that the client and server are using different network protocols or that the client doesn't have the required privileges.

5. **A, B, C** Dial-Up Networking is most often used to connect to a network from offsite or to connect to the Internet by using a modem or IDSN line. DUN can connect to any server that supports SLIP. In all cases, the modem acts as a network card to provide connectivity.

6. **A, D** SLIP and CSLIP are used to connect to UNIX servers.

7. **A, C** NetBEUI and TCP/IP are supported by PPP.

8. **C** TCP/IP is the only protocol that provides Internet access.

9. **C** SLIP is used with TCP/IP under UNIX.

10. **E, F** Windows 95 can use Dial-Up Networking to connect only to Windows NT, Windows for Workgroups, and NetWare connect systems.

11. **B** Modem properties are stored in the TELEPHON.INI text file in the \WINDOWS folder.

12. **A** SLIP transmits passwords in clear text; therefore, it is not as secure as PPP or RAS. CSLIP does support encryption.

13. **B** MODEMLOG.TXT stores all AT commands sent by the modem. This file is used for troubleshooting purposes.

14. **D** CD-ROMs are not supported in a network environment as a Startup disk.

7.3.12 Key Words and Definitions

Dial-Up Networking Connecting to remote servers by using a modem and telephone lines; used to access files, printers, and other resources; increasingly popular for users accessing the Internet.

MODEMLOG.TXT   A log file of all modem commands sent and responses received over a phone line.

NetBEUI   A small, fast networking protocol used in LANs.

PPPLOG.TXT   A log file containing information on how the software layers of PPP have processed a Dial-Up Networking call.

TAPI   Telephony Application Program Interface, a standard set of procedures used for modem communications.

Troubleshooting wizards   Wizards, available through Windows Help, that will walk you step-by-step through the procedures to correct common system problems.

WinIPCfg   An IP-configuration utility that displays IP settings and enables a user to change some of those settings.

7.4   Printing Problems and Printer Optimization

This section addresses the issues of printer optimization and troubleshooting printer problems. To optimize printer performance, you typically adjust spool settings for the printer. When dealing with printer performance, you must also remember "perceived speed"—how the user perceives the speed of the printer and how quickly control returns to the application. This section also provides recommended steps to use when approaching printer problems.

7.4.1   Printer Optimization

Each Windows 95 computer's printer spool can be configured for EMF printing or RAW printing.

- EMF uses a proprietary internal page-description format called Enhanced Metafile for printing. EMF is printer-independent with most of the processing of the print job to RAW format occurring in the background. This returns control to the application sooner than printing in RAW format.

- RAW printing is printer-dependent format with the processing occurring in the foreground. This results in a long wait for control to return to the application.

On a local Windows 95 computer, both processes occur at the local computer. In a Microsoft networked environment, the process of converting the EMF format to the printer's RAW format occurs on the server.

Each Windows 95 computer can also be configured to return control to the user after the print job is submitted. Print jobs can be configured to start printing after the last page has been spooled or after the first page has been spooled. The printer can also be configured to print directly to the printer on a local computer; however, this method is the slowest.

These options can be configured in the Spool Settings (from the Device Options tab of the Printer Properties dialog box).

7.4.2   Printer Problems

Use the following guidelines to solve printing problems:

- Ensure the printer is turned on, is online, and has paper in the paper tray.

- Ensure the printer cable is attached to the printer and to the computer. If using a serial cable, ensure it is plugged into the correct serial port on the Windows 95 computer (if it has multiple serial ports).

- Ensure the printer properties are correct by right-clicking the printer and selecting Properties. Ensure the correct print driver is installed and that paper options are set correctly.

- Ensure the latest driver is being used. Download an upgraded 32-bit driver from the printer manufacturer's Web page if necessary.

- Ensure that print spooling has enough free disk space. If necessary, delete unnecessary files or compress the drive.

- Try printing from another application. If you can print, the original application might have to be reconfigured. If you cannot print, reinstall the printer.

- Print to a file instead of the printer. Copy the file to the printer port in DOS. If the file prints correctly, the spooler might be corrupt.

- Restart Windows 95. Try turning the printer on and off to clear its buffer.

- Document all printing problems and their solutions. Have these document available to all users in the workgroup via an intranet or email.

7.4.3   Exercises

Exercise 1: Optimizing Printing

Printing will be optimized by printing EMF files and ensuring that control is returned to the application as soon as possible.

1. Click the Start button and select Settings, Printers.

2. Right-click the printer and select Properties.

3. Click the Details tab and select Spool Settings.

4. Select Spool print jobs so program finishes printing faster.

5. Select Start printing after first page is spooled.

6. Select EMF as the spool data format.

7. Select OK twice and close the Printers window.

Exercise 2: Running the Print Troubleshooting Wizard

In this exercise, you use the Windows 95 wizard for print troubleshooting. This is a wizard that walks you through a series of questions to help you determine the cause of a problem.

1. From the Start Button, click Help. This open the Windows 95 Help dialog box.

2. Click the Contents tab and then expand the Troubleshooting book by double-clicking it.

3. Select the option that says If you are having trouble printing. This opens a new Help dialog box that asks you a series of questions to help you resolve a printing problem.

4. Click Printing is unusually slow.

5. Select It takes a long time for the document to come out of the printer.

6. You will then be presented with the option to open the Print folder. If you do this, you are given a few steps to follow that help improve printer performance. Do not change any options unless you are having trouble printing.

7.4.4 Practice Problems

1. Which file is a built-in list of printer models and manufacturers?

    A. PRINTERS.DAT

    B. PRTUPD.DAT

    C. PRTUPD.INF

    D. PRINTERS.INF

2. How can you start a printer wizard to help you troubleshoot printing problems?

    A. Click Start, Help, and then open the Troubleshooting book.

    B. Right-click the Printer icon in the Control Panel and select Wizard.

    C. Click Start, Programs, Accessories, and Troubleshooters.

    D. Run the Enhanced Print troubleshooter from the Windows 95 CD.

3. If you have print problems due to the spooler, how do you disable the spooler?

    A. From the Device Manager.

    B. From the printer's properties.

    C. From the printer itself.

    D. The spooler cannot be disabled.

4. You try to install a new printer, but no printers are listed in the print dialog box. Why might this happen?

    A. You don't have a network connection.

    B. The PRTUPD.INF file is missing.

    C. Your printer is not supported.

    D. File and Printer Sharing has not been enabled.

5. How can you clear the print buffer?

    A. Right-click the Printer icon and select the clear buffer option.

    B. Reinstall the print drivers.

    C. Turn the printer off and on.

    D. Disconnect the printer from the PC and then reconnect it.

6. If you set up a new printer and Setup cannot find a print driver, which utility can help load the driver?

    A. Add Print Wizard

    B. Net Watcher

    C. System Monitor

    D. Driver Loader

7. What are possible causes for slow printer?

    A. Low hard disk space

    B. Low system resources

    C. A clogged print head

    D. A loose connection to the printer

8. The Print Troubleshooter is a wizard that helps you fix printer problems. How do you run the Troubleshooter?

    A. From the Windows 95 CD-ROM

    B. By right-clicking the Printer icon and selecting Print Wizard

    C. From the Programs, Accessories, System Tools menu

    D. By opening the Troubleshooting book from Windows Help

9. Which of the following improves printer performance?

    A. Adding more RAM to the computer

    B. Increasing printer memory

    C. Running the Disk Defragmenter

    D. Printing with lower resolutions

10. Which of the following is not a typical cause when only partial pages are being printed?

A. The font being used isn't supported by the printer.

B. Insufficient printer memory.

C. A corrupt UNIDRV.DLL file.

D. None of the above.

11. A user calls informing you that he is having problems printing to a local printer. What should be your first question?

 A. Are you logged on to the network?

 B. Are you printing to EMF format?

 C. Is the printer turned on?

 D. Do you have a bi-directional parallel cable?

12. Another user calls informing you that she cannot print to a network printer. What should you check?

 A. Check the user permissions for the shared printer.

 B. Check whether the user has logged on to the network properly.

 C. Check to see whether the printer is shared.

 D. All the above.

13. A user can print from a Windows 32-bit application but cannot print from an MS-DOS application. What should you do to enable printing?

 A. Reinstall the print driver.

 B. Redirect the print job to a network printer.

 C. Enable spooling for MS-DOS applications.

 D. Capture the printer port in the printer's Properties dialog box.

14. When printing many files to a printer, it takes too long for the print jobs to spool and return control to the application. What should you enable to speed up the process?

A. Free up additional disk space on his computer.

B. Set the jobs to print directly to the printer.

C. Set the spool option to print after the last page is spooled.

D. Set the spool option to print after the first page is spooled.

15. A user printed a memo but the print job does not reach the desired printer. No print errors were displayed and the job is not listed in the print queue. What is the most likely cause?

 A. The wrong print driver was installed.

 B. The user is not logged on to the network.

 C. The print job was sent to another printer.

 D. The printer was paused.

16. You are printing many documents to your local printer. You need to send a financial report to the printer but are worried that it will not print in time for the meeting in 10 minutes. What is the best method to ensure the financial budget prints next?

 A. Purge the printer and then send the financial budget.

 B. Delete all print jobs from the print queue that came before the financial budget.

 C. Pause all individual print jobs except the financial budget.

 D. Reorder the print jobs by dragging the financial budget print job to the top of the list after the currently printing print job.

17. When printing a document to a local printer, the print job goes to the print queue but nothing prints. The printer is turned on and connected to the computer.

You cannot find anything wrong with the printer setup. What would be your next step before reinstalling the printer?

A. Shut down and restart your computer.

B. Try printing from another application.

C. Try another printer cable.

D. Turn the printer off and then back on again.

18. Your computer is running Windows 95 and you want to share your printer on the Windows NT network. You only want valid NT users to access the printer. Which access control should you select in the network properties?

A. Share-level

B. User-level

C. Domain-level

D. Admin-level

7.4.5 Answers and Explanations

1. **C** The PRTUPD.INF file is a list of supported printers and manufacturers.

2. **A** The Print Troubleshooter is available from the Help window.

3. **B** The spooler can be disabled from the printer's properties page.

4. **B** If you don't see any printers listed in the Printer dialog box, it probably means that the PRTUPD.INF file is missing.

5. **C** Turning the printer off and on clears the print buffer.

6. **A** The Add Print Wizard can help you install new printers.

7. **A, B** Slow printing can be caused by low system resources, or low hard disk space that is required for spooling.

8. **D** The Print Troubleshooter is run from Windows Help.

9. **A, B, C, D** All these improve printer performance in Windows 95. Adding memory to the computer and the printer reduces the need to access the hard drive. Running the Defragmenter opens more contiguous space for spooling.

10. **D** None of these are typical causes of partial pages being printed.

11. **C** The first step should be to check the obvious. Check whether the printer is turned on and plugged into the correct port, and that there are no paper jams.

12. **D** All the options affect printing to a shared printer.

13. **D** Most MS-DOS applications require the printer to be physically attached to a printer port. This can be done by capturing the printer port in the Details tab of the printer's Properties dialog box.

14. **D** Setting the spool option to print after the first page has spooled enables the printer to print while the other pages are spooling. This is enabled by default.

15. **C** The most likely cause is that the wrong printer was selected as the default printer. Ensure that the desired printer is selected.

16. **D** Reordering the print jobs is the simplest and fastest method. Be sure to place the print job in the list after the currently printing print job.

17. **C** The next step should be to try a different printer cable. A pin might have been bent attaching it to the computer.

18. **B** User-level security enables the user to select valid users from the NT domain. The name of the domain from which the users are members must be provided as the security provider.

7.4.6 Key Words and Definitions

EMF Enhanced Metafile, an internal page-description format for printing that typically returns control to the user more quickly than RAW format. EMF is printer-independent.

Printer spool Storage of data to be printed, can be configured for RAW or EMF format.

RAW printing A printer-dependent print format in which processing occurs in the foreground keeping control from the user or application.

7.5   File System Problems

Generally speaking, most applications work with Windows 95 with little, if any, user intervention. However, some older MS-DOS and Windows 16-bit applications might not run properly under Windows 95's file system. To solve this problem, some advanced features of Windows 95 can be disabled to provide support for older applications. The following features can be enabled or disabled using the Performance tab of the My Computer Properties sheet:

- **Disable new file sharing and locking semantics.** Some older applications do not work properly using Windows 95's file sharing. Disable this option until the application is updated and will work properly with Windows 95.

- **Disable long filename preservation for old programs.** Some older applications, especially Windows 16-bit applications do not support long filenames and will destroy the long filenames of files saved with the application. Disable this feature to provide compatibility with short filenames.

- **Disable protected-mode hard disk interrupt handling.** Some applications have disk access problems using Windows 95's 32-bit virtual disk driver. Disable this feature to provide compatibility but with a performance penalty.

- **Disable all 32-bit protected-mode disk drivers.** Some older disk drives do not work properly with Windows 95's disk drivers when reading or writing to the hard disk. Disable this feature to enable real-mode drivers that are supported. This degrades disk performance, however.

- **Disable write-behind caching.** Windows 95 uses write-behind caching to enhance disk performance by storing writes to the hard disk in cache temporarily until the processor can commit the cache to disk. Disabling this feature writes the data immediately to disk. This slows down disk performance but ensures the data is written to disk in the event of a power failure.

7.5.1   Selecting the Appropriate Disk-Management Tool

Four key disk-management utilities are included with Windows 95. Each is intended to address particular file system issues or problems. Table 7.1 provides a summary of the disk-management utilities and the issues they address.

Table 7.1   Windows 95 Utilities for Various File System Issues

Utility	Issue
Disk Defragmenter	Prevention of file system performance degradation due to inefficient hard disk access
ScanDisk	Correction of cross-linked files, lost clusters, and other hard disk errors
Backup	Prevention of data loss due to power failures, corruption, hard disk failures
Disk Compression	Maximization of available hard disk space

To select the appropriate disk-management tool, you must examine the symptoms displayed in a given situation. Table 7.2 matches symptoms to the appropriate disk-management tools to be used to correct them.

Table 7.2 Selecting the Appropriate Tool for Various File System Symptoms

Utility	Symptom
Disk Defragmenter	Applications open, read, or write to files slowly.
ScanDisk	Applications report corruption of data or are unable to open files.
Backup	Valuable data is considered to be at risk of loss.
Disk Compression	Applications report insufficient available hard disk space.

The use of one utility often leads to the use of another. For example, while you're correcting slow hard disk access by running Disk Defragmenter, the utility might report an error. In this case, run ScanDisk and specify a physical surface scan.

7.5.2 Exercises

Exercise 1: Optimizing the Computer's File System

The file system will be optimized by running Disk Defragmenter to speed up disk reads and writes.

1. Double-click My Computer and right-click drive C. Select Properties and select the Tools tab.

2. Select Defragment Now. Windows 95 now checks the amount of fragmentation on the hard drive. A message appears informing you how fragmented the drive is.

3. Select Advanced. Select Full Defragmentation. Also select the Save these options and use them every time radio button. Select OK.

4. Select Start. Click Show Details. A visual representation of the defragmenting process appears. Click Legend to display the color legend. Notice how free space is moved to the end of the drive and that some files cannot be moved.

5. When prompted to quit Disk Defragmenter, select Yes. Select OK to close the Properties dialog box. Close My Computer.

Exercise 2: The File System Dialog Box

In this exercise, you will explore the File System dialog box. This shows you the options that are available to you and where to change them.

1. From the Control Panel, double-click the System icon.

2. When the System dialog box opens, select the Performance tab.

3. At the bottom of the Performance tab is a button that reads File System. Click this button to open up the File System dialog box.

4. The File System dialog box has three tabs. The first displays the role of the computer and read-ahead optimization. Look at how your computer is set up.

5. Click the second tab (CD-ROM). This tab shows you information about how your CD-ROM is set up.

6. Click the third tab (Troubleshooting). This tab presents options that can be used to troubleshoot problems you have with the file system. You shouldn't change any of these selections unless you fully understand the impact the changes will have on your system.

7.5.3   Practice Problems

1. Disabling write-behind caching will

    A. Cause data to be saved immediately.

    B. Cause files to be stored when the system is idle.

    C. Improve disk performance.

    D. Degrade disk performance.

2. If you suspect that problems you are having with corrupt files are related to physical problems on your hard drive, which utility should you run?

    A. Disk Defragmenter

    B. ScanDisk

    C. System Monitor

    D. Net Watcher

3. What are the typical roles that can be selected for a computer from the System Performance tab?

    A. Desktop computer

    B. Net PC

    C. Mobile computer

    D. Network server

4. CD-ROM cache is the same cache used for disk and network access.

    A. True

    B. False

5. Enabling file system troubleshooting options will improve system performance.

    A. True

    B. False

6. If a system doesn't start because of disk I/O problems, which troubleshooting options should you select?

    A. Disable write-behind caching for all drives.

    B. Disable protected-mode hard disk interrupt handling.

    C. Disable new file sharing and locking semantics.

    D. Disable all 32-bit protected-mode disk drivers.

7. If you have older disk drives improperly reading or writing under Windows 95, which of the following can you do?

    A. Disable real-mode drivers.

    B. Disable protected-mode drivers.

    C. Disable FAT16 drivers.

    D. Disable FAT32 drivers.

8. Long filenames take up more directory entries than 8.3 filenames.

    A. True

    B. False

9. How many directory entries are allowed in the root of a drive using FAT16?

    A. 128

    B. 256

    C. 512

    D. 1024

10. How many spaces are allocated to a directory entry?

    A. 8

    B. 11

    C. 12

    D. 16

11. Long filenames can be temporarily disabled if you need to run an application that doesn't support them.

    A. True

    B. False

12. Which utility is used to remove and restore long filenames?

    A. LongFN

    B. SwapLFN

    C. LFNBK

    D. BackLFN

13. If you back up and delete long filenames, how does Windows 95 store the information to restore the names?

    A. In the system Registry.

    B. In LFNBK.DAT.

    C. In the SYSTEM.INI.

    D. It doesn't; they have to be restored manually.

14. How do you permanently disable long filenames?

    A. LFNBK /b.

    B. From the File System icon in the Control Panel.

    C. ScanDskw /o.

    D. You can't permanently disable long filenames.

15. Which applications do not support long filenames?

    A. MS-DOS applications

    B. Windows 16-bit applications

    C. Windows 32-bit applications

    D. All the above

16. Long filenames are preserved for older applications using which technique?

    A. LFN conversion

    B. Thunking

    C. Tunneling

    D. Thonking

17. You are experiencing intermittent problems with your older 240MB hard disk while running Windows 95. Which feature(s) should you disable?

    A. File sharing

    B. Long filename preservation

    C. Protected-mode hard disk interrupt handling

    D. All 32-bit protected-mode disk drivers

18. Which two features affect Windows 16-bit applications?

    A. Disabling file sharing

    B. Disabling write-behind caching

    C. Disabling long filename preservation for old programs

    D. None of the above

19. You want to increase the performance of a dual-speed CD-ROM drive by setting the CD-ROM as a quad speed in the CD-ROM Settings tab of the File System Properties dialog box. You notice, however, that the system is even slower than it was before you made the change. Why is the CD-ROM drive slower?

    A. Changing the setting set the cache size to 0.

    B. You do not have enough RAM to support the new setting.

    C. Windows 95 detected that the CD-ROM is not a quad speed.

    D. None of the above.

7.5.4 Answers and Explanations

1. **A, D**   Disabling write-behind caching causes data to be saved immediately instead of being placed in cache. This degrades disk performance.

2. **B**   A thorough ScanDisk detects physical problems on a hard drive.

3. **A, C, D**   You can identify your computer as a desktop, mobile, or network server through the System Performance tab.

4. **B**   CD-ROM and disk access use separate cache.

5. **B**   Enabling file system troubleshooting options degrades system performance.

6. **A, B, C, D**   All these options can be used to troubleshoot problems with the file system.

7. **B**   Disabling protected-mode drives might help you access older disk devices.

8. **A**   Long filenames take up more room in the directory structure than standard 8.3 filenames.

9. **C**   The limit on directory entries is 512 for the root directory.

10. **B**   Eleven spaces are allocated for a directory entry, one for each character of an 8.3 filename.

11. **A**   Long filenames can be disabled if necessary to run older applications.

12. **C**   LFNBK is the utility that can be used to disable and enable long filenames.

13. **B**   When you disable long filenames, the information is stored in LFNBK.DAT and is used when long filenames are restored.

14. **A, C**   Both LFNBK and ScanDskw can be used to permanently disable long filenames.

15. **A, B**   MS-DOS and most Windows 16-bit applications do not support long filenames.

16. **C**   Tunneling is used by Windows 95 to preserve long filenames with older applications.

17. **C, D**   Older drives might not support the newer 32-bit drivers. Also, Windows 95's protected-mode hard disk interrupt handling might cause problems with older drives for the same reason.

18. **A, C**   Disabling file sharing and long filename preservation can affect older 16-bit applications. Long filenames are not supported under most 16-bit applications, and the Windows 95 file sharing might not be compatible with older 16-bit applications.

19. **B**   Changing the CD-ROM setting increases the amount of cache available to the CD-ROM. This can negatively affect system performance if RAM is limited.

7.5.5   Key Terms and Definitions

Backup   A Windows 95 utility that stores data in a compressed format to be used as a backup.

Disk compression   The process of increasing available space on a drive by storing data in packed format, reducing the space required by a file.

Disk Defragmenter   A utility that moves files and free space to contiguous clusters on a drive.

Protected mode   An operating-system processing mode in which address spaces are protected from each other; 32-bit Windows applications run in protected mode.

Real mode   An operating-system processing mode in which address spaces of applications are not protected from each other; 16-bit applications run in real mode.

Restore   A Windows 95 utility that restores compressed data, created by the Backup utility, to its original format.

ScanDisk   A utility that checks hard drives and floppy drives for logical and physical errors, and then attempts to repair those errors.

Write-behind caching   A process by which data isn't written immediately to disk but is written when the processor is otherwise idle. Write-behind caching improves disk performance by writing data to cache until the processor can commit the cache to disk.

7.6   Resource Access Problems

On a network, a user must often share resources (files or printers) with others and decide whether, and how, he will prevent unauthorized access to these resources.

Windows 95 enables you to leverage security access to users by utilizing either share-level or user-level security. Share-level security is used by default when File and Printer Sharing for Microsoft Networks is installed.

> **File and Printer Sharing for NetWare Networks must use user-level security. The share-level security option is unavailable if File and Printer Sharing for NetWare Networks is installed.**

7.6.1   Share-Level Security

With share-level security, passwords are assigned to each individual share to permit access. To access the share, a user must supply the correct password. This can become difficult to manage in even small workgroups. If no password is used, any user will have full or read-only access to the directory, depending on which option was specified when the shared directory was created. When creating a shared directory using share-level security, one of three types of access can be granted: Read, Full, or Depends on Password. Print queues also can be shared with other network users using share-level security. Printers are either shared or not shared in Windows 95.

Because share-level security relies on access passwords, this form of security has the following disadvantages:

- To access different shares, a network user must know numerous passwords.

- Passwords can easily be forgotten. Windows 95 can cache passwords so that a user must enter them each time. If the creator of the share forgets the password, however, the password has to be changed to allow another user to access the share.

- Nothing prevents an authorized user from disclosing the password to an unauthorized user.

7.6.2   User-Level Security

With user-level security, specific user accounts or group accounts can be granted access to a shared directory or printer. Instead of relying on a password that can be used by anyone, the user account accessing a shared resource must be authenticated to ensure that the account has been granted access.

Windows 95 does not manage user accounts by itself. User-level security enables you to create a list of users who have access to a particular resource; you can store that list on a server (called the *central server*). Before a user can gain access to a resource, he must be on this list of users. When a user logs on to the server, he must use pass-through authentication to have a Windows NT or NetWare server authenticate the user who is trying to access the resource.

You can use user-level security for a variety of services beyond network access, such as network management, Backup agents, and Dial-Up Networking.

To use user-level security, the Windows 95 computer must obtain a copy of the accounts list from one of the following sources:

- Windows NT Server or Workstation 3.5 (or later) computer

- NetWare 3.*x* or 4.*x*

With user-level security, when a directory is shared, the users or groups that have access to the share are assigned privileges allowing the appropriate levels of access to the resource. When sharing a printer, users or groups can be added to a list of users with access to that printer.

Although you can change from user-level to share-level security, or from share-level to user-level security, you probably should not. When you switch from one to the other, you lose all the current security settings. You must re-create all security settings on each individual share.

7.6.3   The Resource Meter

Occasionally, resource access problems occur when attempting to access local resources, such as memory. The System Resource Meter is a utility that enables you to view local resources. The System Resource Meter is an application that monitors dynamic changes in the operating system, including the following changes:

- System resources

- User resources

- GDI resources

System resources include I/O services and virtual memory management to provide applications with the necessary resources. If this number continues to fall as applications are started and closed, it indicates that some applications are not releasing their allocated resources when the application is closed, causing the resource pool to decrease in size. Eventually, Windows 95 must be restarted to reclaim the resources.

User resources include input devices such as the keyboard and mouse.

Graphical Device Interface resources are used to manage the appearance of the screen and other output devices such as printers.

Anytime these numbers become low, it is necessary to close unused applications or restart Windows 95 to reclaim resources.

7.6.4   Exercises

Exercise 1: Running the System Monitor

The System Monitor is a tool you can use to monitor resources on your system. This exercise walks you through the processing of running the System Monitor, and selecting several resources to display.

1. From the Start menu, select Programs, Accessories, System Tools.

2. From the list of System Tools, select System Monitor.

3. If the System Monitor is currently set up to monitor any aspect of your system, click the Edit menu and then Remove Item. Clear any selections that have been made previously.

4. From the Edit menu, click Add Item. A dialog box listing the properties of the system that the System Monitor will display appears.

5. In the Category list box, select Kernel. This lists three items in the right list box: Processor Usage, Threads, and Virtual Machines.

6. Select all three of the items and click OK. This will bring you back to the main window and show you, over time, how these Kernel properties change.

7. With System Monitor running, start some other programs such as Explorer or WordPad to see the effect on system resources.

8. Run the MS-DOS prompt in the window and see the effect this has on Virtual Machines.

Exercise 2: Using Resource Meter to Monitor System Resources

This exercise demonstrates how Resource Meter can be used to monitor the amount of free resources on your computer.

1. From the Start menu, choose Programs, Accessories, System Tools, Resource Meter. A message appears stating that Resource Meter requires system resources and might cause your computer to run more slowly. Click OK.

2. Double-click the Resource Meter icon on the Tray (the portion of the Taskbar that displays the time and specialized functions). The System Monitor window appears.

3. Write down the current settings for

    - System Resources

    - User Resources

    - GDI Resources

4. From the Start menu, choose Programs, Accessories, WordPad. Minimize the window. What are the settings in Resource Meter now?

5. Start an MS-DOS prompt and minimize the DOS window. What are the settings for Resource Meter now?

6. Close the MS-DOS prompt. Were its resources reclaimed by Windows 95?

7. Close WordPad. What are the Resource Meter settings now?

8. Close Resource Meter.

7.6.5 Practice Problems

1. If other users cannot connect to your shared resources, what should you do?

    A. Verify that File and Printer Sharing is installed.

    B. Make sure you are running TCP/IP.

    C. Check to see if the other users are running a common protocol.

    D. Be sure to configure your computer as a server.

2. If File and Printer Sharing for NetWare Networks is installed, which security option must be used?

    A. Share-level

    B. User-level

3. Under which security option are passwords assigned to each resource?

    A. Share-level

    B. User-level

4. What access option(s) can be assigned to share-level resources?

    A. Read

    B. Read/Write

    C. Full

    D. Depends on Password

5. Under user-level security, a person must know a password for a shared directory.

    A. True

    B. False

6. When implementing user-level security, where can a Windows 95 machine obtain an accounts list for resources?

    A. A Windows NT Server

    B. A Windows 95 client

    C. A NetWare 3.*x* server

    D. A NetWare 4.*x* server

7. What happens when you change from share-level security to user-level security or vice versa?

    A. Access rights are converted when changing from one to the other.

    B. Access rights are converted only when changing to share-level.

    C. Access rights are converted only when changing to user-level.

    D. Access rights are not converted and must be set up again.

8. Which of the following resources controls input devices?

    A. System

    B. User

    C. GDI

    D. All the above

    E. None of the above

9. Which of the following resources control output devices and services?

    A. System

    B. User

    C. GDI

    D. All the above

    E. None of the above

10. Which utility will continually show an updated measure of system resources?

    A. Net Watcher

    B. System Monitor

    C. Sysmeter

    D. Resource Meter

11. What is the process of translating between 16- and 32-bit code called?

    A. Parsing

    B. Banging

C. Slow

D. Thunking

12. Which resource(s) does the Resource Meter display?

A. GDI

B. Swap space

C. Paging

D. Kernel

13. GDI is approximately half 16-bit code and half 32-bit code.

A. True

B. False

14. The user interface is completely written in 32-bit code.

A. True

B. False

15. Which level of security is used by default when Microsoft File and Printer Sharing is installed?

A. Group-level

B. User-level

C. Share-level

D. Resource-level

16. If no password is assigned a resource in share-level security, what rights will a remote user have to the directory?

A. Full

B. Read-only

C. Depends on which option was specified when the shared directory was created

D. Modify

17. Print queues also can be shared with other network users using ________________.

A. Group-level

B. User-level

C. Share-level

D. Resource-level

18. With which level of security can specific user accounts or group accounts be granted access to a shared directory or printer?

A. Group-level

B. User-level

C. Share-level

D. Resource-level

19. You are running three applications simultaneously. You want to start a fourth application but notice in Resource Meter that your system resources are under 50%. What can you do to free up some system resources? Select all that apply.

A. Restart Windows 95.

B. Run each application in a separate VM.

C. Close applications not currently being used.

D. Start the applications in real-mode at an MS-DOS prompt instead of from a menu.

20. You suspect that an older 16-bit application is not releasing all its resources when you exit the application. Which utility will tell you if system resources are not being released?

A. Net Watcher

B. System Monitor

C. System Resource Meter

D. Device Manager

21. Which two of the following resources are not monitored by System Resource Meter?

    A. User resources

    B. Free disk space

    C. User environment variables

    D. GDI resources

    E. System resources

7.6.6 Answers and Explanations

1. **A, C** File and Printer Sharing must be enabled and common protocols must be used to allow sharing of resources.

2. **B** If you use File and Printer Sharing for NetWare, you must also use user-level security.

3. **A** Passwords are assigned to resources under share-level security.

4. **A, C, D** Read/write is not an option of share-level security.

5. **B** With user-level security, passwords are not set up for individual resources.

6. **A, C, D** Windows 95 can get an account list of resources from a Windows NT server, or NetWare 3.*x* and 4.*x* servers, but not a Windows 95 client.

7. **D** Access rights are not converted when security is switched between share-level and user-level.

8. **B** User resources control input devices connected to a computer.

9. **A, C** Output devices are controlled by both the system and GDI.

10. **B, D** You can monitor system resources by using either the System Monitor or the Resource Meter. The Resource Meter only shows System, User, and Kernel resources.

11. **D** The translation that occurs between 16- and 32-bit code is called thunking.

12. **A, D** The Resource Meter shows measurements of GDI, Kernel, and User resources.

13. **A** The code behind the GDI is composed of 16- and 32-bit code, almost equally split.

14. **B** The User interface is written almost entirely in 16-bit code to improve performance.

15. **C** Share-level security is used by default when File and Printer Sharing for Microsoft Networks is installed.

16. **C** If no password is used, any user will have full or read-only access to the directory, depending on which option was specified when the shared directory was created.

17. **C** Print queues can be shared with other network users using share-level security.

18. **B** With user-level security, specific user accounts or group accounts can be granted access to a shared directory or printer.

19. **A, C** Closing applications that are not being used should free up resources. If the applications were poorly written and do not release their allocated resources upon closure, however, Windows 95 must be restarted to reclaim all system resources.

20. **C** System Resource Meter indicates whether an application is not releasing its resources when it is closed.

21. **B, C** System Resource Meter consists of system resources, user resources, and GDI resources.

7.6.7 Key Words and Definitions

File and Printer Sharing A network setting that, when enabled, allows you to share your resources with others and allows you to use any of their resources for which you have authority to access.

GDI resources   Graphical Device Interface resources, related to the management of the screen, printer, and other output devices.

Kernel resources   Also called system resources, manage memory, and I/O services. The Kernel manages the distribution of other resources to applications.

Share-level security   A type of security in which a password is assigned to a resource. Anyone who knows the password can access the resource.

System Resource Meter   A Windows 95 utility that shows available resources for User, GDI, and Kernel (or System) resources.

User resources   System resources related to input devices, such as the keyboard or mouse.

User-level security   A type of security in which rights to resources are granted on a user-by-user basis. No additional passwords are assigned to the resource.

7.7 Hardware Device and Device Driver Problems

In this section, you examine several tools that enable you to troubleshoot hardware device and device driver problems. You look at several Windows 95 features (the hardware compatibility list and the Add/Remove Hardware Wizard), as well as a utility that can be run from MS-DOS (MSD). These utilities enable you to view hardware settings to look for potential problems and give you the opportunity to make changes to the system configuration.

7.7.1 Hardware/Software Compatibility List

Microsoft publishes a list of supported hardware and software that has been tested with Windows 95. Items not on the list might work with Windows 95; however, they have not been tested and certified by Microsoft. As such, technical help might not be available from Microsoft. These lists are available from the Microsoft Web site or from TechNet.

7.7.2 MSD

Microsoft Diagnostics, or MSD, is a DOS utility that can help you troubleshoot problems with hardware and devices. Although MSD does not come packaged on the Windows 95 installation disks or CD-ROM, it is available on computers that were upgraded from MS-DOS and Windows 3.*x*.

MSD is most helpful when you cannot start Windows 95 because of hardware problems. If you cannot start Windows 95, you can't get to the Device Manager to troubleshoot the problems. MSD can help when your only boot option is the command prompt.

MSD provides information about the following:

- Computer (manufacturer, BIOS information, processor, keyboard, and other hardware)
- Memory (conventional, extended, and expanded)
- Video (manufacturer, drivers, and resolution)
- Network information
- OS Version (MS-DOS version, AUTOEXEC.BAT settings, and Windows version)
- Mouse information
- Drive information (floppy and hard drives, total size, and free space)
- LPT and COM port information
- IRQ settings and status
- TSR programs
- Device drivers

MSD also provides various utilities for viewing the contents of memory, testing printers, and printing reports on the information found in MSD.

7.7.3   Add/Remove Hardware Wizard

With Windows 95, many of the complications with installing hardware are minimized. The key to minimizing hardware installation is the Add New Hardware Wizard. This wizard walks users through the process of detecting the new hardware and then installing the proper device driver for it.

To install new hardware under Windows 95, use the following steps:

1. From the Start menu, choose Settings, Control Panel to open the Control Panel window.

2. Double-click the Add New Hardware icon to open the Add New Hardware Wizard.

3. Choose the Next button to begin the wizard. A new wizard screen appears.

4. To have Windows search for your new hardware, keep the Yes option clicked. To specify the type and name of the device you are installing, choose No. The following steps assume you choose the No option.

5. Choose Next. On the next screen, select the type of hardware to install. The next wizard screen that displays depends on the device type you select here.

6. Choose Next. A screen displays showing you manufacturer and model names. If your manufacturer and model name appear, click them. If not, click the Have Disk button and select the path for the hardware installation disk that comes with your device. Choose OK after entering this information.

7. Choose Next. The final wizard screen appears.

8. Choose Finish to have Windows install your new hardware.

After Windows installs the hardware drivers, you might need to shut down and restart Windows for the new device to be active.

7.7.4   Exercises

Exercise 1: Using MSD

In this exercise, you use Microsoft Diagnostics (MSD) to look at various features of your system. If you are running Windows 95 on a machine that never had an older version of MS-DOS or Windows 3.x installed, you might not have MSD.EXE.

1. From the Start menu, select Programs and then MS-DOS Prompt.

2. In the DOS window, type **MSD**. If MSD.EXE is in the DOS path, you probably don't need to specify a path name with MSD.

3. When you run MSD, it takes a few seconds to scan your system for information. When it is done, you have a menu of options to look at. Select the Computer option and look at the information that MSD presents for your computer, processor, and so on.

4. Click OK to close the Computer dialog box and then select the Disk Drives button. This shows a dialog box of all your floppy and hard drives, along with information about the size of the drive and remaining space.

5. Close the Disk Drive dialog box and then select Device Drivers to look at installed drivers.

6. If you want a report of the information displayed by MSD, click the File menu and select Print Report. A dialog box appears that gives you the option of what to include in the report. It might be a good idea to keep a hard copy printout of the information on hand for future reference.

Exercise 2: Adding New Hardware to a System

This exercise walks you part of the way through the process of adding new hardware to your computer. If you really do have hardware to install, you can continue through the process to complete the installation.

1. You will be adding new hardware to your system and you want Windows 95 to recognize it. From the Start menu, select Settings and open the Control Panel.

2. In the Control Panel, double-click the Add New Hardware icon. This opens up a wizard that guides you through the installation process.

3. The first dialog box that appears is informational. Click the Next button until you are prompted to select whether you want Windows to detect new hardware or if you are going to tell Windows what you are installing.

4. Letting Windows detect new hardware is usually what you want to do. This might take several minutes, but it is usually the safest way to install new hardware that Windows 95 recognizes.

5. For this exercise, you select No and then click the Next button. Now you see a dialog box listing the different types of hardware that you can install.

6. Select CD-ROM from the list and click the Next button.

7. You are now presented with a list of manufacturers and models of CD-ROM drives that Windows 95 recognizes. At this point, you can select the make and model of your new CD-ROM drive and click Next. If your hardware is not in the list, click the Have Disk button and Windows reads information from a floppy disk about the new hardware.

8. At this point, unless you are really installing new hardware, click the Cancel button. If you are installing new hardware, click the Next button and continue walking through the Add New Hardware Wizard.

7.7.5   Practice Problems

1. MSD can be found on the Windows 95 CD-ROM.

   A. True

   B. False

2. Which of the following can you view through MSD?

   A. BIOS information

   B. COM and serial port status

   C. Plug and Play devices

   D. Windows version

3. How do you get access to the Device Manager?

   A. From the Windows 95 CD-ROM

   B. Through the Troubleshooting tab in Help

   C. From the System dialog box of the Control Panel

   D. From the Device Manager icon in My Computer

4. When would you use MSD instead of the Device Manager?

   A. When you are having trouble with an older DOS device

   B. When you can't start Windows

   C. When the Device Manager refers you to MSD

   D. If your computer never had a version of DOS installed

5. Through the Device Manager, what information can you obtain from the device's properties page?

   A. Manufacturer

   B. Supporting drivers

   C. Driver version

   D. Hardware version

6. Which utility enables you to view and change multiple system files (such as CONFIG.SYS, AUTOEXEC.BAT, and so on) without opening each one individually?

   A. SYSEDIT.COM

   B. SYSTEMED.COM

   C. SYSCONFG.EXE

   D. None of the above

7. In Safe mode, you can use the Device Manager to troubleshoot hardware problems.

   A. True

   B. False

8. You need to manually reallocate resources in your computer. Before you do, you wants to look at the current allocations. Where can you display, by resource type, lists of all the devices on your computer?

   A. In Device Manager, click My Computer in the device type list and choose Properties.

   B. In the Registry Editor, click the plus sign (+) next to HKEY_LOCAL_MACHINE.

   C. In Device Manager, double-click Computer in the device type list.

   D. In the Registry Editor, click the + next to HARDWARE.

9. You just downloaded an updated driver for your display adapter. What are two ways you can install the new driver?

   A. Use the Change Driver button in the Driver tab of the device's properties sheet.

   B. Copy the file to the Drivers directory.

C. Use the Network applet in the Control Panel.

D. Use the Add New Hardware applet in the Control Panel.

10. You need to manually reconfigure one of your Plug and Play devices. What's the first thing you need to do to change the device's settings in the Resource tab of the device's properties sheet?

A. Double-click the resource type you want to change.

B. Turn on the Allow Manual Settings check box.

C. Click the resource type you want to change and then choose Change Settings.

D. Turn off the Use Automatic Settings check box.

11. What are the two drawbacks of manually reconfiguring a Plug and Play device?

A. You must set jumpers or switches on the device.

B. The settings become fixed so that Windows 95 will have less flexibility when configuring other devices.

C. Doing so can cause hardware conflicts, making some devices unavailable on the system.

D. To do so, you must install the Configuration Manager from the Windows 95 CD-ROM.

12. Name two ways to open Device Manager.

A. Run the Device Manager applet in the Control Panel.

B. Right-click the My Computer icon on the desktop, choose Properties, and select the Device Manager tab.

C. Run the System applet in the Control Panel and choose the Device Manager tab.

D. Run the Add New Hardware applet in the Control Panel and choose the Device Manager tab.

13. Adding a new card to your computer created a conflict between two devices. A Plug and Play card is using IRQ 5, but a legacy card also needs this same IRQ. Which is the best strategy for you to use to resolve the conflict?

A. Use Device Manager to manually change the IRQ settings for each device.

B. Remove the Plug and Play device from the current configuration, manually change the IRQ setting for the legacy device, add the Plug and Play device back to the configuration, and then let Windows 95 dynamically assign an available IRQ to the Plug and Play device.

C. Physically remove the Plug and Play device from the computer, manually change the IRQ setting for the legacy device, insert the Plug and Play device back into the computer, and then let Windows 95 dynamically assign an available IRQ to the Plug and Play device.

D. Change the jumper switch on the legacy device.

14. When Windows 95 is allocating resources to the various devices on a computer, how does it prioritize resource allocation?

A. Legacy devices get first priority.

B. Plug and Play devices get first priority.

C.   Legacy and Plug and Play devices get equal priority.

D.   Resources are allocated on a first-come, first-served basis.

15. You install a new sound card and the next time you starts Windows 95, the operating system detects the new device. Windows 95 is unable to find the appropriate driver, however. What happens?

A.   Startup is unable to continue; you must restart the system in Safe mode.

B.   Windows 95 prompts you to insert a disk with the driver; you can install the driver at this time.

C.   The Driver tab in Device Manager displays so that you can choose a driver file.

D.   Windows 95 warns you that it cannot find the driver and instructs you to use Device Manager to choose a driver file.

16. John, part of the technical support team in the MIS department, will be setting up a computer training room at his company. He needs to put together five Windows 95 computers by using previously used (but working) components (such as mouse devices, keyboards, and modems) removed from employees' computers when they upgraded to newer devices. Which are two ways John can install and configure drivers for these legacy devices?

A.   Use Device Manager to add each device.

B.   Run the appropriate applet (such as Modems, Mouse, or Keyboard) in the Control Panel.

C.   Run the Add New Hardware Wizard in the Control Panel.

D.   Use the Registry Editor to add the device to the current configuration.

17. You have a 486 computer that runs Windows 95 on a legacy system BIOS. How does Windows 95 handle the configuration of devices that were added after initial installation of the operating system? Which two of the following answers are correct?

A.   For legacy devices, you must run the Add New Hardware Wizard.

B.   For Plug and Play devices, you must run the Add New Hardware Wizard.

C.   Windows 95 polls legacy devices at boot time and configures them dynamically.

D.   Windows 95 polls Plug and Play devices at boot time and configures them dynamically.

7.7.6   Answers and Explanations

1.   **B**   MSD does not come with Windows 95, only with MS-DOS.

2.   **A, B, C**   MSD shows information about things that were available before Windows 95 was released, so newer features, such as Plug and Play, don't show in MSD.

3.   **C**   The Device Manager can be accessed through the Control Panel's System icon.

4.   **B**   MSD is the most beneficial when you cannot start Windows 95 and run the Device Manager.

5.   **A, B, C**   The Device Manager shows the manufacturer of a device, the supporting drivers, and the version of the device, but not the version of the drivers.

6.   **A**   SYSEDIT.COM opens multiple configuration files.

7.   **A**   After you can start a computer in Safe mode, you can use the Device Manager to troubleshoot hardware problems.

8. **C**   To view system resources, go to Device Manager and double-click Computer.

9. **A., D**   One place to install a new driver is in the Driver tab of the device's properties sheet. (To display the display adapter's properties sheet, go to Device Manager, double-click Display Adapter, and then double-click the adapter name.) The other way to install a new driver is by using the Add New Hardware applet.

10. **D**   Sheldon will be unable to change the settings until he turns off the Use Automatic Settings check box.

11. **B, C**   When you manually reconfigure a device, the resource settings become fixed, restricting Windows 95's capability to configure other devices. Also, some settings might make one or more devices unavailable.

12. **B, C**   Device Manager is a tab in the System Properties dialog box. To display this dialog box, you can either right-click the My Computer icon and choose Properties, or run the System applet in the Control Panel.

13. **B**   Option B is the best answer because only one of the devices will have fixed settings; this allows for more flexibility in the future. Furthermore, with this option, you don't need to open the computer and remove any devices.

14. **A**   Legacy devices are given first priority in resource allocation because unlike Plug and Play devices, they cannot be dynamically configured.

15. **B**   When Windows 95 detects a Plug and Play–compliant device, it looks for the driver on the system. If it cannot locate the driver, it will prompt you to insert a driver disk.

16. **B, C**   You can install a legacy device in the Add New Hardware applet or use one of the other applets to install a particular type of device.

17. **A, D**   Legacy devices must be configured with the Add New Hardware Wizard; Plug and Play devices are configured dynamically at boot time.

7.7.7   Key Words and Definitions

Add/Remove Hardware Wizard   A Windows utility, or help wizard, that walks you step by step through the process of adding or removing hardware from a system.

Device Manager   A Windows 95 utility that enables you to view and change a system's hardware configuration.

Hardware/Software Compatibility List   A list of hardware and software supported by and tested with Windows 95.

MSD   Microsoft Diagnostics, an MS-DOS utility that provides information about hardware configuration.

SYSEDIT.COM   A program that opens multiple configuration files, such as the AUTOEXEC.BAT and CONFIG.SYS, for you in a text editor similar to Notepad.

7.8   Modification of the Registry

The Windows 95 Registry was designed with the following purposes:

- To centralize all the configuration information

- To utilize a tree-structured, hierarchical database structure

- To provide a means to store user-, application-, and computer-specific information

- To simplify the support burden and allow both local and remote access to configuration information

The Windows 95 Registry is stored in two files. The SYSTEM.DAT file contains the computer hardware configurations, and the USER.DAT file contains user-specific settings. Together, these two files are the central repository of information for the Windows 95 operating system. After each successful boot of Windows 95, copies of both files are saved as SYSTEM.DA0 and USER.DA0.

Some Windows 95 references include a third file, CONFIG.POL, that stores administrative policies that are set up on a network server.

> **Microsoft provides the REGEDIT utility to view and change the contents of the Windows 95 Registry. Before you make changes to the Windows 95 Registry, first make a backup copy of the two Registry files, SYSTEM.DAT and USER.DAT. Both of these files are hidden in the Windows folder.**

For backward compatibility, the older Windows 3.*x* configuration files, such as CONFIG.SYS, AUTOEXEC.BAT, WIN.INI, SYSTEM.INI, PROGMAN.INI, CONTROL.INI, and PROTOCOL.INI, still exist. The 16-bit Windows APIs used to update the INI files also still exist.

The Windows 95 Registry is a database created during Windows 95 startup. The actual files in which this configuration information is stored are called USER.DAT, SYSTEM.DAT, and, optionally, CONFIG.POL. To view and change your current user and system configurations, you need to run REGEDIT.EXE, the Windows 95 Registry Editor.

The Windows 95 Registry is made up of six root keys. The following sections describe the six root keys.

7.8.1   HKEY_CLASSES_ROOT

This key contains the same type of data as the simple REG.DAT Registry file in Windows 3.*x* and provides backward-compatibility for OLE and DDE support. It also contains OLE and association mapping information to support drag-and-drop operations, Windows 95 shortcuts (that are, in fact, OLE links), and core aspects of the Windows 95 user interface. The association mappings allow Windows 95 to run or print from an application when a specific file type is selected.

This key merely points to the Registry branch within another root key, HKEY_LOCAL_MACHINE\SOFTWARE\Classes. The three basic key types within HKEY_CLASSES_ROOT are file extensions, file associations, and OLE2 objects.

7.8.2 HKEY_CURRENT_USER

This key contains user-specific settings for applications, desktop configurations, and user preferences. This key is created at runtime (when the user logs on to Windows 95) from information stored in the user's entry under HKEY_USERS. If the user does not already exist, the .DEFAULT information is used.

These user-specific settings are copied back into the HKEY_USERS branch when you shut down Windows 95. There are several different key types: events, schemes, user-specific Control Panel settings, most recently used (MRU) location of installation files, keyboard layout, network, Dial-Up Networking settings, and software settings.

7.8.3 HKEY_LOCAL_MACHINE

This key contains computer-specific information about the type of hardware installed, drivers, and other system settings. It is the same information stored within the SYSTEM.DAT configuration file.

Multiple hardware configurations are listed under the Config key, in the case of a laptop computer with a docking station and both docked and undocked configurations. Much of the device manager information can be found under the Enum key, though this information is easier to view through the System icon in the Control Panel. There are several different key types: hardware configurations (usually only one), device manager information, network-specific security information, installed software information, and system settings.

7.8.4 HKEY_USERS

This key contains information about all users who log on to the computer, including the .DEFAULT generic user settings. The generic program and system settings act as a template for any new users on the computer. It is the same information stored within the USER.DAT configuration file and is required to properly run the system.

7.8.5 HKEY_CURRENT_CONFIG

This key contains information about the current running hardware configuration. It is used when multiple hardware configurations are available to the computer. The prime example of multiple hardware configurations is a laptop computer that can be either docked or undocked in a docking station. The information for this key is directly copied from the various configuration information contained in the HKEY_LOCAL_MACHINE key.

7.8.6 HKEY_DYN_DATA

This key contains the dynamic status information for various devices as part of the Plug and Play configuration. It is regenerated every time the system starts up. This information can change as hardware devices are added to or removed from the computer. The information kept for each hardware device includes the associated hardware key, any problems, and current status. This key also contains information on system monitoring being performed using the System Monitor tool. This key is not part of either Registry file and is always dynamically created.

7.8.7   Determining Where the Registry Is Stored

The Windows 95 Registry contains all the Windows 95 system and user information. It is an ASCII database that pulls information from the three files listed in Table 7.3. These files are not in readable form, so you can view or change their contents only by using a Windows application, such as the Windows 95 Registry Editor program, the Control Panel icons, or the System Policies Editor (for the optional CONFIG.POL file). The USER.DAT and SYSTEM.DAT files are stored on the local computer's hard drive. If the CONFIG.POL file exists, it is stored on a network file server to be downloaded when a user logs on to the network.

Table 7.3   Files in the Windows 95 Registry

Registry File	Description
SYSTEM.DAT	Contains hardware-related and computer-specific settings.
USER.DAT	Contains user-specific information found in user profiles, such as user rights, desktop settings, and so on.
CONFIG.POL (Optional)	Contains policy information related to the system and user settings. The information in the system policies file can override information in both SYSTEM.DAT and USER.DAT files. This is an optional file.

Always make backup copies of your Windows 95 Registry files before you make any changes. In the Windows 95 Registry Editor program, choose Registry, Export Registry file to create a REG file. This exported REG file represents the contents of the DAT files at a given point in time. The Windows 95 CD-ROM includes two other useful utilities, found in the Other\Misc subdirectory. The first is an Emergency Recovery Utility (ERU.EXE), which saves key Windows 95 files to either a floppy drive, a local drive, or a network drive. The second is a Configuration Backup (CFGBACK.EXE) utility that can save and restore up to nine configurations of your Windows 95 Registry.

Most of the configuration information you can modify in the Windows 95 Registry can be changed using a GUI front-end; however, some configuration information cannot. Only in certain situations is it appropriate to modify the Registry using the Registry Editor program.

The following are some of these situations:

- You might need to edit the Registry via the Registry Editor because of data not deleted from the Registry from an application or device you have removed.

- You might read about a bug fix from Microsoft that you need to use the Registry Editor to fix.

- You might want to enhance a feature using the Registry Editor.

7.8.8   System Policy Editor

Windows 95 policies enable an administrator to set various Registry entries and control whether a user can change such settings:

- Computer-specific (HKEY_LOCAL_MACHINE) Registry entries can be enforced through a computer policy.

- User-specific Registry entries can be enforced through user policies.

- Group policies can be created to enforce user-specific settings for groups of user accounts defined on a Windows NT or NetWare server.

System policies are more inclusive than mandatory user profiles in that they allow an administrator to restrict user-specific and computer-specific settings. User profiles allow control over user-specific settings only.

Computer, user, and group system policies are created using the System Policy Editor, POLEDIT.EXE.

The System Policy Editor uses a template that defines which keys in the Registry can be affected by the system policy. The template ADMIN.ADM, which is included with the System Policy Editor, allows many standard policies to be enforced.

In addition to creating system policies, the System Policy Editor can be used to perform the following functions:

- Access the local Registry settings defined in the system policy template being used

- Access the Registry settings on a remote Windows 95 computer to change the settings defined in the template

Policies created with the System Policy Editor are saved with the filename extension .pol. The system policy to be used should be given the name CONFIG.POL and must be placed in the default location:

- For computers using share-level security, CONFIG.POL should be placed in the *systemroot* directory, for example, C:\WINDOWS.

- For computers using user-level security, CONFIG.POL should be placed in the NETLOGON directory on the Windows NT Server or in the PUBLIC directory on a NetWare server.

The default location for the CONFIG.POL file can be changed later using a specific policy setting.

Registry information in the CONFIG.POL file can overwrite existing information in the computer's Registry. The policy setting also can be configured so that it will not change the Registry setting if it already exists; therefore, even if a Registry on a computer has a certain setting, that setting can be changed to the setting in the CONFIG.POL policy file.

A group policy might be used to enforce a user policy for a group of users. The group must be defined on the Windows NT or NetWare server, and each computer in the group using the group policy must have the GROUPPOL.DLL copied to its *systemroot*\system directory.

To create a group policy, choose Edit, Add Group in the System Policy Editor and enter the name of the group.

A user policy is processed after a group policy and therefore overrides any policies set by the group policy. If multiple group policies are defined and a user belongs to more than one group, the order in which the group policies are processed can be defined in the Group Priorities option of the Options menu. Group policies with a higher precedence override policies with a lower precedence.

7.8.9   Exercise

Exercise 1: Examining the Windows 95 Registry

In this exercise, you walk through the process of running the Regedit utility and looking at the Windows Registry. It's never a good idea to make changes to the Registry unless you are sure of what you are doing, and only then if you have made a backup of the SYSTEM.DAT and USER.DAT files.

1.   From the Start button, click Run.

2.   In the Run dialog box, type **REGEDIT.EXE** (or just **REGEDIT**) and click OK.

3.   You will now see the Registry editor with the six Registry keys displayed.

4.   Expand the HKEY_CLASSES_ROOT key. This shows you a list of all registered file extensions on your machine along with other OLE objects.

5.   Next, expand the HKEY_LOCAL_MACHINE key. Then expand the Software subdirectory. You see a list of some of the software installed on your system. (Not all software applications place information in the Registry.)

6.   Spend a few minutes browsing through the Registry. See if there are other things you recognize. Be sure not to make any changes before you exit.

7.8.10   Practice Problems

1. Which files make up the Windows Registry?

   A.   SYSTEM.DAT

   B.   USER.DAT

   C.   WINDOWS.REG

   D.   REG.DAT

2. Windows automatically creates backups of the Registry files each time the system boots successfully.

   A.   True

   B.   False

3. Before making changes to the Windows Registry, what should you do?

   A.   Back up the CONFIG.SYS and AUTOEXEC.BAT files.

   B.   Boot your computer in Safe mode.

   C.   Back up the SYSTEM.DAT and USER.DAT files.

4. If you accidentally delete things that you shouldn't have when editing the Registry, which two files can be used to restore the Registry before rebooting the system?

   A.   SYSTEM.BAK and USER.BAK

   B.   SYSTEM.DA0 and USER.DA0

   C.   SYSTEM.000 and USER.000

   D.   REGSVR32.EXE and REG.DAT

5. What is the utility that you use to edit the Registry?

   A.   REGSVR.EXE

   B.   REGSVR32.EXE

   C.   REGEDIT.EXE

   D.   REGEDT32.EXE

6. What are three basic types of information stored under the HKEY_CLASSES_ROOT?

   A.   User information

   B.   File extensions

   C.   File associations

   D.   OLE2 objects

7. The HKEY_CURRENT_USER key is created at runtime.

   A.   True

   B.   False

8. Which Registry key can contain multiple hardware configurations?

   A.   HKEY_CLASSES_ROOT

   B.   HKEY_LOCAL_MACHINE

   C.   HKEY_CURRENT_CONFG

   D.   HKEY_DYN_DATA

9. Which is not a key of the Registry?

   A.   HKEY_DYN_CONFIG

   B.   HKEY_CURRENT_CONFIG

   C.   HKEY_USERS

   D.   HKEY_LOCAL_MACHINE

10. How can you make changes to the Registry?

    A.   Using REGEDIT.EXE

    B.   Changing Control Panel settings

    C.   Editing SYSTEM.DAT and USER.DAT with Notepad

    D.   Using the System Policy Editor

11. CONFIG.POL is a required part of the system Registry.

    A.   True

    B.   False

12. The Windows Registry replaces the DOS SYSTEM.INI and WINDOWS.INI files.

    A. True

    B. False

13. The Registry editor is installed

    A. When Windows is installed from floppy disk

    B. When Windows is installed from CD-ROM

    C. Both of the above

    D. None of the above

14. What program file in Windows 95 can save and restore the Windows 95 Registry?

    A. REGIBACK.EXE

    B. BACKUP.EXE

    C. CFGREG.EXE

    D. GFGBACK.EXE

    E. CFGBACK.EXE

15. The Configuration Backup can save multiple configurations of the Windows 95 Registry. How many configurations can it save?

    A. 16

    B. 8

    C. 64

    D. 9

16. In HKEY_CURRENT_CONFIG, the information for this key is copied directly from the information in which of the following Registry keys?

    A. HKEY_DYN_DATA

    B. HKEY_CLASSES_ROOT

    C. HKEY_CURRENT_USER

    D. HKEY_LOCAL_MACHINE

    E. HKEY_USERS

17. Windows 95 contains how many root keys?

    A. 6

    B. 8

    C. 1

    D. 4

    E. 5

18. Similar to configuring user profiles, to use system policies, your workstations must have ____________ for policy settings to be established.

    A. User profiles enabled

    B. A computer account on the domain

    C. Local user profiles

    D. None of the above

19. Which of the following scenarios would best be suited for system policies?

    A. An environment in which users require similar settings and use similar workstations

    B. An environment in which users are not connecting to a logon server

    C. An environment in which users require a high degree of variation in the levels of system access required

    D. All the above

20. The Windows 95 System Policy Editor can be opened in one of two modes. Select the modes that apply.

    A. User mode

    B. Policy File mode

    C. Computer mode

    D. Registry mode

21. In what mode should you use the System Policy Editor if you want to make changes directly to the Registry?

    A. User mode

    B. Computer mode

    C. Policy File mode

    D. Registry mode

22. What should you use instead of the System Policy Editor to make direct changes to a computer's Registry?

    A. Registry Editor

    B. Object Properties

    C. Control Panel

    D. User Profile Editor

23. You can use system policies for computers to enforce greater security on Windows 95 by requiring validation by a network server prior to allowing access to Windows 95. Where would you enable such a setting using the System Policy Editor?

    A. Default User

    B. Default Group

    C. Default Computer

    D. Default Policy

7.8.11 Answers and Explanations

1. **A, B** The Registry is made up of SYSTEM.DAT and USER.DAT. Sometimes there is also a CONFIG.POL file.

2. **A** Each time the system boots successfully, backups are made of the SYSTEM.DAT and USER.DAT files in SYSTEM.DA0 and USER.DA0.

3. **C** You should always back up the Registry files before changing them manually.

4. **B** Backups of the Registry are stored in SYSTEM.DA0 and USER.DA0.

5. **C** REGEDIT.EXE can be used to change the Registry manually.

6. **B, C, D** The HKEY_CLASSES_ ROOT contains information about file extensions and associations, and OLE2 objects.

7. **A** HKEY_CURRENT_USER is created at runtime from HKEY_USERS.

8. **B** Multiple configurations for a machine are stored in the HKEY_LOCAL_MACHINE key.

9. **A** There is no HKEY_DYN_CONFIG key.

10. **A, B, D** The Registry can be changed directly with REGEDIT.EXE, or indirectly through the Control Panel or the System Policy Editor.

11. **B** CONFIG.POL is an optional part of the Registry.

12. **B** The Registry contains some information that used to be stored in the SYSTEM.INI and WINDOWS.INI files but doesn't replace them completely.

13. **B** REGEDIT.EXE is only installed when Window 95 is installed from CD-ROM.

14. **E** The CFGBACK.EXE file can be found on the Windows 95 CD-ROM and can back up and restore the Registry.

15. **D** CFGBACK.EXE is the program filename for configuration backup. It can back up nine instances of the Registry.

16. **D** HKEY_LOCAL_MACHINE should be considered the static configuration for the system, whereas HKEY_CURRENT_ CONFIG is used while the system is running.

17. **A** There are six root keys.

18. **A** Profiles must be manually turned on.

19. **A** Similar settings and similar workstations provide consistency for administration.

20. **B, D** Both modes are possible ways of opening the System Policy Editor.

21. **D**   The Registry mode enables you to make direct changes to the Registry.

22. **C**   The Control Panel is the preferred method of changing your system.

23. **C**   The Default Computer properties sheet contains the option Logon, Requires Validation by Network for Windows Access.

7.8.12   Key Words and Definitions

CONFIG.POL   An optional part of the Registry that contains policy information related to the system and user settings.

POLEDIT.EXE   The System Policy Editor, which allows an administrator to edit system policies that are stored in the CONFIG.POL file.

REGEDIT.EXE   A utility that provides the capability to view and edit the system Registry.

Registry   A database containing settings for Windows 95 and other installed applications. Made up of the SYSTEM.DAT and USER.DAT files.

SYSTEM.DA0   A backup of the SYSTEM.DAT file created by Windows 95 after the last successful startup.

SYSTEM.DAT   A Registry file containing information about the system configuration.

USER.DA0   A backup of the USER.DAT file created by Windows 95 after the last successful startup.

USER.DAT   A Registry file containing information about the users of a computer and their individual settings.

Practice Exam: Troubleshooting

1. This is a scenario question. First, you must review the situation and then review the objectives. Following that is a proposed solution. You must pick the best evaluation of that solution.

   SITUATION:

   A user calls to tell you that a large number of General Protection Faults are occurring on his system and that Windows frequently fails during startup. You suspect that Windows DLLs or the Registry is corrupt.

   PRIMARY OBJECTIVES:

   - Eliminate the frequent occurrence of General Protection Faults

   - Have Windows 95 start cleanly each time the user starts the computer

   SECONDARY OBJECTIVES:

   - Create a boot-up log each time the user starts Windows 95

   - Log any GPF messages when they occur

   PROPOSED SOLUTION:

   You decide to run the Windows 95 Setup program again to replace any corrupt files and repair the system Registry.

   EVALUATION OF PROPOSED SOLUTION: (Choose the most correct answer.)

   A. The proposed solution meets all objectives.

   B. The proposed solution meets all of the primary objectives and most of the secondary objectives.

   C. The proposed solution meets only one of the primary objectives and all of the secondary objectives.

   D. The proposed solution meets all of the primary objectives and none of the secondary objectives.

   E. The proposed solution meets none of the primary objectives and only some of the secondary objectives.

   F. The proposed solution meets none of the primary objectives and none of the secondary objectives.

2. You recently installed some new hardware devices in your computer and you suspect that it has something to do with the problems you are having starting Windows 95. What is the first thing you should do to fix any hardware conflicts? Choose the best answer.

   A. Start the computer in Safe mode.

   B. Boot in DOS mode from a floppy disk.

   C. Start Windows 95 in Logged mode.

   D. Reinstall Windows 95.

3. One of your users is calling you to say that he is having trouble saving files in his root directory. He says that he has only about 200 files in the root, but the system won't let him save any more. What could the problem be? Choose the best answer.

   A. The disk is formatted for NTFS.

   B. Long filenames are disabled.

   C. He has accidentally "write-protected" the drive.

   D. He is using long filenames and has exceeded the limit of directory entries.

4. During installation of Windows 95, Setup fails while copying necessary files to the computer. What should you do to correct the problem? Choose the best answer.

   A. Delete the \Windows directory and start Setup again.

   B. Reinstall the previous operating system (that is, MS-DOS or Windows 3.x) and then run Windows 95 Setup again.

   C.   Rerun Windows 95 Setup.

   D.   Boot the system from a floppy, re-format the hard drive, and then rerun Windows 95 Setup.

5. You are configuring a new notebook computer that will be used by a salesman. This person will be traveling extensively and using the computer on the road, dialing up to remote servers when necessary. How should you configure this computer? Choose the best answer.

   A.   Select Notebook Computer as the role in the System Performance tab in the Control Panel.

   B.   Select Mobile Computer as the role in the System Performance tab in the Control Panel.

   C.   Select Mobile Computer as the role in Network Setup in the Control Panel.

   D.   Select Network Client as the role in Network Setup in the Control Panel and install TCP/IP.

6. This is a scenario question. First, you must review the situation and then review the objectives. Following that is a proposed solution. You must pick the best evaluation of that solution.

SITUATION:

One of your users is going to be connecting to various servers using Dial-Up Networking. You have to install the various networking protocols so that the computer can connect to each of the desired servers.

PRIMARY OBJECTIVES:

- Use Dial-Up Networking to connect to remote servers

- Connect to Windows NT servers

- Connect to UNIX servers

SECONDARY OBJECTIVES:

- Connect to the Internet

- Connect to NetWare servers

PROPOSED SOLUTION:

You install TCP/IP with PPP and RAS protocols for your user so that she can remotely connect to servers using Dial-Up Networking.

EVALUATION OF PROPOSED SOLUTION: (Choose the most correct answer.)

   A.   The proposed solution meets all objectives.

   B.   The proposed solution meets all of the primary objectives and most of the secondary objectives.

   C.   The proposed solution meets only two of the primary objectives and all of the secondary objectives.

   D.   The proposed solution meets none of the primary objectives and all of the secondary objectives.

   E.   The proposed solution meets none of the primary objectives and only some of the secondary objectives.

   F.   The proposed solution meets none of the primary objectives and none of the secondary objectives.

7. You have installed a printer on a network, and you have shared it so that your users can print remotely to that printer. One of the users call to tell you that he's trying to print but isn't receiving any output and isn't getting any error messages. What is the most likely cause of the problem? Choose two correct answers.

   A.   The user isn't logged on to the network.

   B.   The user is printing to a different printer.

    C. The printer is paused.

    D. The user's machine doesn't have File and Printer Sharing.

8. One of your users calls to tell you that he is constantly getting `Out of Memory` messages. Which tools can you use to check the available resources on the user's machine? Choose two correct answers.

    A. Net Watcher

    B. Resource Meter

    C. System Monitor

    D. Memory Manager

9. When your computer was running Windows 3.*x*, you were able to customize some features by changing setting in the CONFIG.SYS and AUTOEXEC.BAT files. After you install Windows 95, you can't find these settings any more. Where did they go? Choose two correct answers.

    A. IO.SYS

    B. WIN.INI

    C. MSDOS.SYS

    D. AUTOEXEC.OLD

10. For what is the SYSEDIT.COM file used? Choose the best answer.

    A. Making changes to the system Registry.

    B. Editing system files such as AUTOEXEC.BAT and CONFIG.SYS.

    C. It is an MS-DOS version of Notepad.

    D. Nothing; there is no such file.

11. This is a scenario question. First, you must review the situation and then review the objectives. Following that is a proposed solution. You must pick the best evaluation of that solution.

SITUATION:

In your user environment, there are a number of older computers that the users are saying are too slow to shut down. You notice that some of the users don't wait for Windows 95 to shut down before turning the power off because it is taking too long. Some of these users are also complaining about losing data that they have saved.

PRIMARY OBJECTIVES:

- Prevent the problem of lost data

- Improve disk performance

SECONDARY OBJECTIVES:

- Speed up Windows Shutdown

- Improve the system response when saving data

PROPOSED SOLUTION:

To handle this situation, you disable write-behind caching on the users' machines.

EVALUATION OF PROPOSED SOLUTION: (Choose the most correct answer.)

    A. The proposed solution meets all objectives.

    B. The proposed solution meets all of the primary objectives and most of the secondary objectives.

    C. The proposed solution meets only one of the primary objectives and one of the secondary objectives.

    D. The proposed solution meets none of the primary objectives and all of the secondary objectives.

    E. The proposed solution meets none of the primary objectives and only some of the secondary objectives.

    F. The proposed solution meets none of the primary objectives and none of the secondary objectives.

12. You have just installed a new modem and the supporting device drivers, and it appears that this has corrupted your system Registry. How can you recover from this problem? Choose the best answer.

    A. Rerun Windows 95 Setup and let it re-create the system Registry.

    B. Restore the Registry from the backup you made immediately before installing the modem and drivers.

    C. Get a copy of the system Registry files from a friend.

    D. Restore the system Registry from backups that Windows created the last time it successfully started.

13. Which file does Windows 95 use to help you install new printers, by presenting you with a list of manufacturers and models? Choose the best answer.

    A. PRINTER.INI

    B. SYSTEM.INI

    C. SYSTEM.DAT

    D. PRTUPD.INF

14. In your networked environment, you have sensitive files for which you want to restrict access. You want to allow some users the ability to update these files, some to be able to read the files, and others no rights at all. How should you implement this? Choose two correct answers.

    A. Implement share-level security with a read/write password and a read password. Give users the appropriate password.

    B. Implement user-level security with a read/write password and a read password. Give users the appropriate password.

    C. Implement share-level security and set up the user IDs with appropriate rights so that users don't need to know a password.

    D. Implement user-level security and set up the user IDs with appropriate rights so that users don't need to know a password.

15. Within your network, you need to use secure passwords to ensure that data is protected from outside parties. You allow dial-up access to your network so that users can work from home. Which protocols can you use to enable password encryption? Choose two correct answers.

    A. PPP

    B. SLIP

    C. RAS

    D. XCOM

Practice Exam Answers and Explanations

1. **D** Rerunning the Windows 95 Setup program replaces corrupted Windows files and repairs errors it finds in the system Registry. You can create a boot-up log during Windows 95 startup, but it is not a setting you can use during Windows 95 installation. Windows 95 doesn't have a utility that logs GPF messages and information.

2. **A** From Safe mode, you can look at hardware devices and see which ones have conflicts.

3. **D** The most likely problem is that he is using long filenames that have filled up all the directory entries. Under the 8.3 filenaming convention, 512 directory entries were allowed. Long filenames, if the names exceed 11 characters, take up additional directory entries.

4. **C** When Windows 95 setup fails, especially before hardware detection, you can rerun Setup, and the program will know where to restart the process. The SETUPLOG.TXT file is used by Setup to determine where the failure occurred.

5. **B**   The notebook computer should be set up as Mobile Computer from the System Performance tab. You also need to install any protocols and adapters required for Dial-Up Networking in your environment.

6. **C**   Using PPP and RAS, the user can connect to NT servers but not UNIX servers. You must install SLIP or CSLIP to use Dial-Up Networking to connect to UNIX servers.

7. **B, C**   If the user doesn't receive any error messages, it most likely means that data is being printed, but to a printer other than the one desired. It can also mean that the printer is paused and that the print job is simply waiting in the queue.

8. **B, C**   The Resource Meter shows you the percentage of available User, GDI, and Kernel resources. The System Monitor shows you much more detail but can be used to monitor resource usage.

9. **A, C**   Windows 95 moves some settings from CONFIG.SYS and AUTOEXEC.BAT into the IO.SYS and MSDOS.SYS files during setup.

10. **B**   SYSEDIT.COM opens and allows you to edit multiple system files, such as CONFIG.SYS, AUTOEXEC.COM, and other system INI files.

11. **C**   Disabling write-behind caching eliminates the problem of lost data, which is caused when the user shuts off the system power before Windows 95 shuts down. Disabling write-behind caching causes data to be written to disk immediately, instead of during idle time or shutdown, thus improving the shutdown response time. Disabling write-behind caching does not improve general system response though, and causes the saving of information in an application to take longer.

12. **D**   B might also be correct, but most people don't back up the Registry when installing hardware or software. Windows 95 creates backups of the System Registry (SYSTEM.DA0 and USER.DA0) each time it starts successfully.

13. **D**   A list of printers and drivers that Windows 95 recognizes is stored in the PRTUPD.INF file.

14. **A or D**   If you use share-level security, the users need to know a password for a particular resource. For user-level security, you have to give each individual user the appropriate rights to a resource.

15. **A, C**   SLIP doesn't support encrypted passwords, and XCOM isn't a Dial-Up Networking protocol.

7

Practice Exam #1

Exam 70-64: Implementing and Supporting Microsoft Windows 95

1. What is the maximum path length under Windows 95?

   A. 32 characters

   B. 64 characters

   C. 256 characters

   D. 260 characters

2. You are installing Windows 95 on your PC at work. There are 12 other computers on your company network, each of which is running Windows for Workgroups. Which configuration should you select when installing Windows 95?

   A. Domain

   B. Workgroup

   C. Stand Alone

   D. Portable

3. You are installing Windows 95 on 50 computers connected to your company's Windows NT network. Which configuration should you choose when installing Windows 95?

   A. Domain

   B. Workgroup

   C. Stand Alone

   D. Portable

4. Jane is setting up six Windows 95 computers in the Sales department of her company. The computers will be connected to the corporate LAN, but they do not need to access any of the resources on the Windows NT server. Which configuration should Jane choose when installing Windows 95?

   A. Domain

   B. Workgroup

   C. Stand Alone

   D. Portable

5. David is planning to install 100 Windows 95 computers on a corporate LAN. Most applications and data are stored on the company's Windows NT servers, and administration of user accounts is centralized. Which configuration should David choose when installing Windows 95?

   A. Domain

   B. Workgroup

   C. Stand Alone

   D. Portable

6. You are charged with setting up 15 Windows 95 computers in a small workgroup. You want to be able to allow users to access data on one another's computers. How can you accomplish this?

A. Enable network logon.

B. Set up a domain.

C. Enable File and Printer Sharing.

D. Allow all users to log on to each computer.

7. Sharon wants to configure a Windows 95 computer to allow multiple users of that computer to customize their own desktop settings. How can she accomplish this?

A. Enable File and Printer Sharing.

B. Have each user log on to a Windows NT domain.

C. Enable user profiles.

D. Have each user log on with the same username.

8. You want to be able to enforce a standard desktop configuration for all your Windows 95 computers. How can you accomplish this?

A. Set up system policies.

B. Enable user profiles.

C. Enable share-level security.

D. Set up a Windows NT domain.

9. You have enabled user profiles for your Windows 95 users on the company NetWare LAN. Where is the USER.DAT file stored?

A. In the user's MAIL directory

B. In the SYS:PUBLIC directory

C. In the C:\Windows directory

D. In the SYS:SYSTEM directory

10. You have enabled user profiles for your Windows 95 users on the company's Windows NT LAN. Where is the USER.DAT file stored?

A. In the user's MAIL directory

B. In the user's HOME directory

C. In the NETLOGON directory

D. In the SYSTEM_ROOT directory

11. You want to enable your Windows 95 computers to access files on your Novell NetWare file server. What must you install to accomplish this?

A. File and Printer Sharing for NetWare Networks

B. Microsoft Client for NetWare Networks

C. Microsoft Client for Microsoft Networks

D. File and Printer Sharing for Microsoft Networks

12. Carol is planning to upgrade her Windows 3.1 computer to Windows 95. How much hard disk space must she have available?

A. 40MB

B. 30MB

C. 20MB

D. 10MB

13. Sheryl wants to uninstall Windows 95 from her computer. What must she have done to be successful with this procedure?

A. Format her C: drive prior to installing Windows 95.

B. Retain her original MS-DOS files when installing Windows 95.

C. Create an uninstall disk when setting up Windows 95.

D. Windows 95 can not be uninstalled.

14. David installs Windows NT on his computer, which already contains an installation of Windows 95. When he restarts his computer, he is presented with a menu from which to select an operating system. Why is he presented with this menu?

A. Windows NT has damaged his boot sector.

B. Windows 95 is no longer sure where the boot sector resides.

C. Windows NT has installed a boot loader.

D. His system BIOS needs to know where the master boot record resides.

15. Which file provides information necessary to perform an automated installation of Windows 95?

A. MSBATCH.INF

B. SETUPLOG.TXT

C. SETUPLOG.INF

D. BATCH.EXE

16. Kevin wants to upgrade his Windows 3.1 system to Windows 95. How can he do this and keep his existing Program Manager groups?

A. Install Windows 95 in its own unique directory.

B. Install Windows 95 into the existing Windows directory.

C. Copy all his .GRP files into the Windows 95 system directory.

D. Create a new partition just for Windows 95.

17. During an automated installation of Windows 95, how can you specify which protocols are to be installed?

A. Install each protocol manually after the operating system is installed.

B. Specify each protocol in the APPS.INF file.

C. Specify each protocol in the MSBATCH.INF file.

D. Windows 95 installs all protocols by default.

18. You are installing Windows 95 on your computer, and Setup stalls during the hardware detection phase. Where can you look to determine why this happened?

A. The SETUPLOG.TXT file

B. The DETCRASH.LOG file

C. The DETLOG.TXT file

D. The SETUP.TXT file

19. Windows 95 Setup stalls during the hardware detection phase. You examine the DETCRASH.LOG file to troubleshoot the situation and find that the file is unreadable. Why?

A. The DETCRASH.LOG file can only be read by Setup.

B. The file became damaged during the failed setup.

C. The file must be debugged.

D. The system contains a virus.

20. What information is stored in the NETLOG.TXT file?

A. A list of file servers detected on the network.

B. Detection results for network components found during setup.

C. A log of a user's network connections at Windows 95 startup.

D. The correct load order for Windows 95 network drivers.

21. Which protocol is required for connecting Windows 95 computers to Novell NetWare file servers?

A. NetBEUI

B. IPX/SPX

C. TCP/IP

D. DLC

22. Your company wishes to connect two corporate sights across the public Internet. Which protocol allows them to do this?

A. NetBEUI

B. IPX/SPX

C. TCP/IP

D. PPTP

23. Which protocol supports autodetection of frame type under Windows 95?

    A. NetBEUI

    B. IPX/SPX

    C. TCP/IP

    D. PPTP

24. Which protocol is required for connecting a Windows 95 computer to the Internet?

    A. NetBEUI

    B. IPX/SPX

    C. TCP/IP

    D. PPTP

25. You are installing TCP/IP onto your Windows 95 computer. You are not implementing static routing and are not using a HOSTS file. Your computer must be able to communicate with computers outside your local subnet. What information is required to properly configure this protocol?

    A. IP address

    B. MAC address

    C. Subnet mask

    D. Default gateway

26. You have connected your Windows 95 computer to an existing TCP/IP network. Using the PING utility to test your connection, you can successfully ping hosts by IP address but not by name. How can you resolve this?

    A. Create an LMHOSTS file.

    B. Verify that the IP address for your DNS server is correct.

    C. Install the WINS service.

    D. Flush the ARP cache.

27. You are attempting to connect your Windows 95 computer to a NetWare file server but are unsuccessful. Other Windows 95 computers on the same network are able to connect to the file server, though. What can you check to troubleshoot this situation?

    A. Verify that TCP/IP has been installed.

    B. Verify that NetBEUI has been installed.

    C. Verify the correct IPX/SPX frame type.

    D. Verify that the DLC protocol is configured for NetWare.

The next two questions both present the same scenario, required results, and optional results. Analyze each proposed solution and determine the best answer.

28. You are installing Windows 95 on your computer, and Windows 95 Setup hangs during the hardware detection phase. You suspect a hardware conflict and want to resolve it so that Setup will continue. Optionally, you would like to determine which device caused the system to hang.

    Solution:

    Turn off the computer, wait a few seconds, and turn it back on. When the operating system begins to load, press F8 and choose Command Prompt. Delete the DETCRASH.LOG file and restart the system. Resume Windows 95 Setup.

    A. The proposed solution meets all of the required results and all of the optional results.

    B. The proposed solution meets all of the required results and some of the optional results.

    C. The proposed solution meets all of the required results but none of the optional results.

    D. The proposed solution does not meet the required results.

29. You are installing Windows 95 on your computer, and Windows 95 Setup hangs during the hardware detection phase. You suspect a hardware conflict and want to

resolve it so that Setup will continue. Optionally, you would like to determine which device caused the system to hang.

Solution:

Turn off the computer, wait a few seconds, and turn it back on. Resume Windows 95 Setup. When Setup is complete, examine the DETCRASH.LOG file to determine which device caused Setup to hang.

- A. The proposed solution meets all of the required results and all of the optional results.
- B. The proposed solution meets all of the required results and some of the optional results.
- C. The proposed solution meets all of the required results but none of the optional results.
- D. The proposed solution does not meet the required results.

30. Derrick is configuring a Windows 95 computer to connect to a Novell NetWare file server on a token-ring LAN. What feature might he be required to configure?

- A. Name resolution
- B. Source routing
- C. Token-ring bridging
- D. MAC broadcasting

31. Which Registry key contains information about system hardware?

- A. HKEY_DYN_DATA
- B. HKEY_LOCAL_MACHINE
- C. HKEY_CURRENT_USER
- D. HKEY_USERS

32. Which Registry key is actually stored in memory and not on the hard disk?

- A. HKEY_DYN_DATA
- B. HKEY_LOCAL_MACHINE
- C. HKEY_CURRENT_USER
- D. HKEY_USERS

33. Which files comprise the Windows 95 Registry?

- A. USER.EXE
- B. USER.DAT
- C. SYSTEM.DAT
- D. SYSTEM.INI

34. Which Windows 95 utility can be used to directly edit the Registry?

- A. SYSEDIT
- B. ScanDisk
- C. REGEDIT
- D. Notepad

35. Which Windows 95 utility can be used to repair cross-linked files?

- A. Disk Defragmenter
- B. ScanDisk
- C. SYSEDIT
- D. REGEDIT

36. Roxanne wants to copy the contents of her hard drive to a safe location in case of system failure. Which utility should she use to do this?

- A. Disk Defragmenter
- B. ScanDisk
- C. Windows 95 Backup
- D. Net Watcher

37. What component is required for connecting the Windows 95 computer to a Windows NT network?

- A. Microsoft Client for Microsoft Networks
- B. Microsoft Client for NetWare Networks
- C. File and Printer Sharing for Microsoft Networks
- D. File and Printer Sharing for NetWare Networks

38. What component is required for connecting the Windows 95 computer to a Novell NetWare network?

    A. Microsoft Client for Microsoft Networks

    B. Microsoft Client for NetWare Networks

    C. File and Printer Sharing for Microsoft Networks

    D. File and Printer Sharing for Netware Networks

39. You want to enable users in your workgroup to access files on your Windows 95 computer. What security model can you select?

    A. Password security

    B. User-level security

    C. Clear text security

    D. Share-level security

40. You want to enable users of your Windows NT network to access files on your Windows 95 computer. What security model should you choose?

    A. Password security

    B. User-level security

    C. Clear text security

    D. Share-level security

41. Which utility can you use to create a new partition on your hard disk?

    A. DISKEDIT

    B. ScanDisk

    C. Disk Defragmenter

    D. FDISK

42. You want to create an additional partition in unpartitioned space on your hard disk. How can you accomplish this?

    A. Use the FDISK utility to create a new partition.

    B. Use the FDISK utility to remove the existing partition and create two new partitions.

    C. Use the FDISK utility to format the hard disk.

    D. Use the FDISK utility to create a non-DOS partition.

43. Your hard disk is set up as one large partition, and you want to split the disk into two separate partitions. How can you accomplish this?

    A. Use the FDISK utility to create a new partition.

    B. Use the FDISK utility to remove the existing partition and create two new partitions.

    C. Use the FDISK utility to format the hard disk.

    D. Use the FDISK utility to create two non-DOS partitions.

44. Which utility is used to create and modify system policies?

    A. SYSEDIT

    B. REGEDIT

    C. POLEDIT

    D. Notepad

45. You have exported a portion of the Registry to a file, and you want to modify the file. Which utility should you use?

    A. SYSEDIT

    B. REGEDIT

    C. POLEDIT

    D. Notepad

46. Which utility is used to connect your Windows 95 computer to an Internet service provider's network?

    A. HyperTerminal

    B. Net Watcher

    C. Dial-Up Networking

    D. System Monitor

47. Which protocols are supported by Windows 95 Dial-Up Networking?
    - A. NetBEUI
    - B. IPX/SPX
    - C. TCP/IP
    - D. DLC

48. Which protocol is required for using Dial-Up Networking to connect to the Internet?
    - A. NetBEUI
    - B. IPX/SPX
    - C. TCP/IP
    - D. PPTP

49. Which Windows 95 utility would you use to determine your TCP/IP configuration?
    - A. Net Watcher
    - B. NETCONFIG
    - C. IPCONFIG
    - D. WINIPCFG

50. You are unable to save files with long filenames to a NetWare file server. What is causing this?
    - A. The file server has not been configured with the OS/2 name space.
    - B. The file server has not been configured with the WIN/NT name space.
    - C. The file server has not been configured with the HPFS name space.
    - D. The file server has not been configured with the NTFS name space.

51. When using long filenames, how many characters are you allowed under Windows 95?
    - A. 255
    - B. 256
    - C. 260
    - D. 32

52. Your Windows 95 system has been configured to use DriveSpace 2.0 for disk compression. What is the best compression ratio that you can expect?
    - A. 1.5:1
    - B. 22:1
    - C. 2.5:1
    - D. 3:1

53. Which utility can be used to speed hard disk access?
    - A. ScanDisk
    - B. System Monitor
    - C. DriveSpace
    - D. Disk Defragmenter

54. How does the Windows 95 Backup utility restore the system Registry?
    - A. It replaces the existing Registry files with the restored versions.
    - B. It uses time stamps to update only the newest entries in the Registry.
    - C. It merges the restored Registry files into the existing Registry.
    - D. Windows 95 Backup cannot backup or restore the Registry files.

55. How can you enable user profiles on a Windows 95 system?
    - A. Use the POLEDIT utility.
    - B. Use the Passwords icon in Control Panel.
    - C. Right-click the My Computer icon and select users.
    - D. Double-click the Network Neighborhood icon, and then select Profiles from the Users menu.

56. Sharon is setting up a computer for a new user on your company's 500-user Windows NT network. The user of this computer will need to access enterprise network

resources and will need to share new files. You should set up this PC to

A. Join an existing domain.

B. Join an existing workgroup.

C. Be a member of a new workgroup.

D. Be a member of a new domain.

57. You're using a Windows 95 computer, and you need to run an MS-DOS application that requires specific memory configurations as well as exclusive use of system resources. How can you accommodate this application?

A. You cannot run this application on a Windows 95 computer.

B. You must run this application in customized MS-DOS mode.

C. You must reconfigure your system each time you run this application.

D. You must run this application as a virtual machine.

58. What command can you use to perform an automated installation of Windows 95?

A. SETUP.EXE /A

B. SETUP.EXE /N

C. NETSETUP.EXE

D. MSBATCH.EXE

59. David wants to maximize the available storage space on his Windows 95 computer. What Windows 95 utility will help him do this?

A. Disk Defragmenter

B. ScanDisk

C. DriveSpace

D. Backup

60. Which of the following is not a Windows 95 Registry root key?

A. HKEY_CLASSES_ROOT

B. HKEY_LOCAL_USER

C. HKEY_CURRENT_CONFIG

D. HKEY_DYN_DATA

61. What is the protected-mode file system driver that Windows 95 uses for CD-ROM access?

A. MSCDEX

B. CDFS

C. VFAT

D. NTFS

62. What is the smallest unit of allocation for data on a hard disk used by Windows 95 disk compression?

A. 1 bit

B. 1 byte

C. 1 sector

D. 1 cluster

63. Under Windows 95, one sector of hard disk space contains how many bytes?

A. 8

B. 64

C. 256

D. 512

64. Which is not a benefit of running an MS-DOS application in VM mode?

A. Protected-mode driver support

B. Increased conventional memory

C. Preemptive multitasking

D. Exclusive use of system resources

65. What is the default mode in which MS-DOS applications run under Windows 95?

A. MS-DOS mode

B. VM mode

C. Customized MS-DOS mode

D. Preemptive mode

66. Kevin wants to install Windows 95 on several remote boot workstations. What line must be included in the [Network] section of his setup script?

A. RemoteBoot=Yes

B. RPLSetup=1

C. Boot=RPL

D. RPLInstall=1

67. Which of the following networks support group policies?

    A. Windows NT

    B. Novell NetWare

    C. Banyan VINES

    D. LANtastic

68. Shirley wants to establish complete administrative control over user desktop settings. What sample policy file that's included with Windows 95 can she use to accomplish this?

    A. CONFIG.POL

    B. STANDARD.POL

    C. MAXIMUM.POL

    D. SECURE.POL

69. Fred is setting up system policies for his Windows 95 users. He wants to establish only typical administrative control over user desktop settings. What sample policy file that's included with Windows 95 could he use to accomplish this?

    A. CONFIG.POL

    B. STANDARD.POL

    C. MINIMUM.POL

    D. TYPICAL.POL

70. Which of the following is a valid computer name under Windows 95?

    A. myhost.pcsystem.com

    B. myhost!

    C. my_machine

    D. more$$$

71. How many characters are allowed in Windows 95 computer names?

    A. 8

    B. 15

C. 255

D. 260

72. You are running Windows 95 on your desktop computer, and you need to access shared directories on another Windows 95 computer on the network. How can you do this?

    A. Ping the computer from a command prompt.

    B. Double-click the computer in Network Neighborhood.

    C. Connect to the computer using FTP.

    D. Right-click the My Computer icon and choose Connect.

73. Alfredo is using Windows 95 Dial-Up Networking with PPP. What authentication protocols can Dial-Up Networking use to negotiate with?

    A. PAP

    B. CHAP

    C. SPAP

    D. TCPAP

74. You need to configure Dial-Up Networking to display a terminal window after dialing. How can you accomplish this?

    A. Select the appropriate check box in the connection icon's properties sheet.

    B. Use the Modems icon in Control Panel.

    C. Right-click the Network Neighborhood icon and choose Terminal Window.

    D. Right-click the Dial-Up Networking icon and choose Terminal Window.

75. Which statement about an MS-DOS application suggests that it should be run in MS-DOS mode?

A. The application requires a minimum of 4,096KB of XMS memory.

B. The application does not support long filenames.

C. The application uses the Ctrl+Esc key combination.

D. The application accesses system hardware directly.

The next three questions all present the same scenario, required results, and optional results. Analyze each proposed solution and determine the best answer.

76. Donald is setting up Windows 95 on 15 computers in the accounting department. Nine of the computers are currently running Windows for Workgroups 3.11, and the remaining six are running MS-DOS. The users need to share files with one another, and they need to share the three printers in the department. Optionally, the managers would also like to be able to access the Internet using modems connected to their computers.

Solution:

Upgrade all 15 computers to Windows 95 and configure them as a workgroup called "Accounting." Install and configure the IPX/SPX protocol on each computer. Connect the three printers to three users' workstations, and then enable File and Printer Sharing for Microsoft Networks on those computers. Connect a modem to each manager's computer.

A. The proposed solution meets all of the required results and all of the optional results.

B. The proposed solution meets all of the required results and some of the optional results.

C. The proposed solution meets all of the required results but none of the optional results.

D. The proposed solution does not meet the required results.

77. Donald is setting up Windows 95 on 15 computers in the accounting department. Nine of the computers are currently running Windows for Workgroups 3.11, and the remaining six are running MS-DOS. The users need to share files with one another, and they need to share the three printers in the department. Optionally, the managers would also like to be able to access the Internet using modems connected to their computers.

Solution:

Upgrade all 15 computers to Windows 95 and configure them as a workgroup called "Accounting." Install and configure the IPX/SPX protocol on each computer. Connect the three printers to three users' workstations, and then enable File and Printer Sharing for Microsoft Networks on all computers in the workgroup. Connect a modem to each manager's computer.

A. The proposed solution meets all of the required results and all of the optional results.

B. The proposed solution meets all of the required results and some of the optional results.

C. The proposed solution meets all of the required results but none of the optional results.

D. The proposed solution does not meet the required results.

78. Donald is setting up Windows 95 on 15 computers in the accounting department. Nine of the computers are currently running Windows for Workgroups 3.11, and the remaining six are running MS-DOS. The users need to share files with one another, and they need to share the three printers in the department. Optionally, the managers would also like to be able to access the Internet using modems connected to their computers.

Solution:

Upgrade all 15 computers to Windows 95 and configure them as a workgroup called "Accounting." Install and configure the IPX/SPX protocol on each computer. Connect the three printers to three users' workstations, and then enable File and Printer Sharing for Microsoft Networks on all computers in the workgroup. Connect a modem to each manager's computer. Install and configure the TCP/IP protocol and Dial-Up Networking on each manager's computer.

A. The proposed solution meets all of the required results and all of the optional results.

B. The proposed solution meets all of the required results and some of the optional results.

C. The proposed solution meets all of the required results but none of the optional results.

D. The proposed solution does not meet the required results.

Answers and Explanations

1. **D** Under Windows 95, the complete path and filename is limited to 260 characters.

2. **B** This workstation should be configured to join the existing workgroup.

3. **A** This workstation should be configured to join the existing domain.

4. **B** Because this is a small group of users that do not need access to resources on the NT servers, a workgroup configuration is appropriate. If in the future they need to access data on the NT server or they need to implement user-level security, they should be reconfigured to join a Windows NT domain.

5. **A** Given the large number of users, the need to access server-based data, and the centralization of user accounts, these Windows 95 stations should be set up to join the existing Windows NT domain.

6. **C** Enabling File and Printer Sharing allows users to access shared folders and printers on other PCs on the network.

7. **C** User profiles allow each individual user on a shared PC to customize and save his own desktop settings.

8. **A** System policies allow administrators to control the user's desktop settings and enforce a company-standard desktop.

9. **A** When you enable user profiles on a NetWare network, the USER.DAT file is stored in the user's MAIL directory by default.

10. **B** When you enable user profiles on a Windows NT network, the USER.DAT file is stored in the user's HOME directory by default.

11. **B** The Microsoft Client for NetWare Networks enables Windows 95 users to log on to and access files on a Novell NetWare file server.

12. **B** To install Windows 95 on a computer as an upgrade to Windows 3.1, 30MB of hard disk space is required.

13. **B** In order to successfully use the Uninstall feature of Windows 95, you must opt to retain your original MS-DOS files during Windows 95 installation.

14. **C** Windows NT uses a boot loader, which presents a menu from which you select the operating system you want to boot with.

15. **A** The MSBATCH.INF file contains the necessary configuration information for an automated installation of Windows 95.

16. **B** When you install Windows 95 into an existing Windows directory, the existing Program Manager groups are retained.

17. **C** The MSBATCH.INF file contains protocols to be included during an automated setup and the required configuration parameters.

18. **C**　The DETLOG.TXT file is an ASCII text file that contains information regarding the hardware detection phase of Windows 95 Setup.

19. **A**　The DETCRASH.LOG file is a binary file used by the Windows 95 Setup program. It does not contain any human readable information. Instead, look in the DETLOG.TXT file for information regarding the hardware detection phase of Windows 95 Setup.

20. **C, D**　Host names should not contain spaces or the at character (@).

21. **B**　The NETLOG.TXT file contains information regarding network components detected during Windows 95 Setup.

22. **D**　Point-to-Point Tunneling Protocol, or PPTP, is used as a secure method of connecting two networks across a TCP/IP network, such as the public Internet.

23. **B**　The IPX/SPX protocol supports the 802.2 and 802.3 frame types. Under Windows 95, the IPX/SPX protocol supports autodetection to determine which of these frame types is in use on the network.

24. **C**　TCP/IP is the protocol suite used on the Internet.

25. **A, B, D**　In order to properly configure the TCP/IP protocol on a Windows 95 computer, the computer must be assigned an IP address and a subnet mask. Microsoft also considers the Default Gateway parameter to be a required portion of the basic TCP/IP configuration.

26. **B**　DNS is the service that resolves host names to IP addresses. In order to use this service, you must provide the correct IP address for the DNS server.

27. **C**　The IPX/SPX protocol supports both the 802.2 and the 802.3 frame type. You must use the same frame type as the NetWare file server in order to see that server on the network. Under Windows 95, the IPX/SPX protocol supports autodetection to determine which frame type is in use on the network. If you do not use this feature, you must specify the correct frame type to use.

28. **C**　Windows 95 will fill in the default subnet mask for the network class it detects when you enter the IP address. For a class C network, for example, it will default to a subnet mask of 255.255.255.0.

29. **C**　Windows 95 will fill in the default subnet mask for the network class it detects when you enter the IP address. For a class B network, for example, it will default to a subnet mask of 255.255.0.0.

30. **B**　If a token-ring network is configured to use source routing, this feature might need to be enabled on the Windows 95 workstation.

31. **B**　The HKEY_LOCAL_MACHINE Registry key contains information about system hardware.

32. **A**　The HKEY_DYN_DATA Registry key is created and modified dynamically and is stored in system memory for faster access, (instead of on the hard disk, which is relatively slow).

33. **B, C**　The Windows 95 Registry is made up of the SYSTEM.DAT and the USER.DAT files.

34. **C**　The REGEDIT program is used to directly edit the Windows 95 Registry.

35. **B**　The ScanDisk utility can be used to detect and repair cross-linked files.

36. **C**　Windows 95 Backup is a utility provided with Windows 95 to copy system data for archive storage and for restoration of the system in case of system failure.

37. **A**　The Microsoft Client for Microsoft Networks allows Windows 95 computers to access Windows NT networks.

38. **B**　The Microsoft Client for NetWare Networks allows Windows 95 computers to access Novell NetWare networks.

39. **D**　Share-level security is the security model available in a workgroup environment.

40. **B** In a Windows NT domain environment, the user-level security model is the most effective security model.

41. **D** The FDISK utility is used to create partitions on a hard disk.

42. **A** The FDISK utility can be used to create a new partition in the unpartitioned space on a hard disk.

43. **B** When an entire hard disk has been set up with one partition, the FDISK utility cannot create an additional partition on that disk. The existing partition must be removed before additional partitions can be created.

44. **C** The POLEDIT utility is used to create and edit system policies.

45. **D** Exported portions of the Registry are stored as ASCII text files. The Notepad utility is a simple ASCII text editor, which can be used to modify these files.

46. **C** Dial-Up Networking is the utility that allows a Windows 95 computer to connect to an ISP's network.

47. **A, B, C** Windows 95 Dial-Up Networking supports the NetBEUI, IPX/SPX, and TCP/IP protocols.

48. **C** TCP/IP is the protocol necessary for connecting to the Internet.

49. **D** The WINIPCFG utility is used to determine the TCP/IP configuration of a Windows 95 computer.

50. **A** A NetWare file server must be configured with the OS/2 name space in order for it to support long filenames.

51. **B** In Windows 95, long filenames are limited to 256 characters.

52. **B** DriveSpace 2.0 provides a compression ratio of approximately 2:1.

53. **D** Disk Defragmenter is used to defragment files on a hard disk, making access to those files faster.

54. **C** The Windows 95 Backup utility merges restored Registry files into the existing Windows 95 Registry.

55. **B** User profiles are enabled through the Passwords icon in the Windows 95 Control Panel.

56. **A** Because the user will need to access NT server–based data as well as share local files, the computer should be set up to join the existing domain.

57. **B** Because the application requires exclusive use of system resources, it must be run in MS-DOS mode. The application's memory requirements can be configured by running it in Customized MS-DOS mode.

58. **C** The NETSETUP.EXE program is used to perform an automated installation of Windows 95.

59. **C** DriveSpace is a utility used to maximize available hard disk space.

60. **B** The Windows 95 Registry contains these six root keys:

   HKEY_CLASSES_ROOT

   HKEY_CURRENT_USER

   HKEY_LOCAL_MACHINE

   HKEY_USERS

   HKEY_CURRENT_CONFIG

   HKEY_DYN_DATA

61. **B** Windows 95 uses the CDFS file system for CD-ROM access.

62. **C** Windows 95 disk compression can allocate data on a hard disk down to 1 sector.

63. **D** Under Windows 95, one sector contains 512 bytes of data.

64. **D** MS-DOS applications benefit from running in VM mode by gaining protected-mode driver support, increased conventional memory, and preemptive multitasking. Exclusive use of system resources is available only in MS-DOS mode.

65. **B**   Under Windows 95, MD-DOS applications run in VM mode by default.

66. **A**   The RemoteBoot=Yes line in the [Network] section of the setup script indicates that the workstations are to be set up as remote boot workstations.

67. **A, B**   Both Windows NT and Novell NetWare support the use of group policies.

68. **C**   The MAXIMUM.POL file is a sample policy file included with Windows 95 that can be used to establish maximum administrative control over user desktop settings.

69. **B**   The STANDARD.POL file is a sample policy file included with Windows 95 that can be used to establish typical administrative control over user desktop settings.

70. **B, C, D**   Windows 95 computer names are limited to 15 characters. They can contain the following special characters:

. ! @ # $ % ^ & ( ) - _ ' { } ~

71. **B**   Windows 95 computer names are limited to 15 characters.

72. **B**   To access files on another computer on the network, start by double-clicking on that computer's name in Network Neighborhood.

73. **A, B, C**   When using PPP, Dial-Up Networking supports the following authentication protocols: PAP, CHAP, and SPAP.

74. **A**   To configure an existing Dial-Up Networking connection to display a terminal window before or after dialing, right-click that connection's icon and select Properties. On the Properties sheet, select the appropriate check box.

75. **D**   MS-DOS applications that require exclusive use of system resources must be run in MS-DOS mode.

76. **D**   File and Printer Sharing must be enabled on all the computers because all users need to share files with other users.

77. **C**   In order for the managers to connect to the Internet via modem, the TCP/IP protocol and Dial-Up Networking must be installed and configured on their PCs.

78. **A**   The proposed solution meets all of the required results and all of the optional results.

Practice Exam #2

Exam 70-64: Implementing and Supporting Microsoft Windows 95

1. Print jobs on a Windows 95 computer can use which of the following data formats?

   A. EMF

   B. DLC

   C. RAW

   D. PCL

2. Dave is running Windows 95 Disk Defragmenter as a background task. When he saves a file he is working on in his foreground application, Disk Defragmenter will

   A. Fail.

   B. Restart.

   C. Stop.

   D. Do nothing.

3. You want to use Device Manager to troubleshoot hardware conflicts on a Windows 95 machine. How do you start this utility?

   A. Run DEVICEMAN.EXE from the Start menu.

   B. Right-click My Computer and choose Device Manager.

   C. Double-click the System icon in Control Panel and choose the Device Manager tab.

   D. Choose Manage Devices from the System menu in System Monitor.

4. Sheryl is an administrator of a NetWare network. She is preparing for a network installation of Windows 95 on 175 client computers. She wants to enable user-level security on the Windows 95 computers. What entry should she add to the [Network] section of the MSBATCH.INF file?

   A. Security = user_level

   B. Security = netware

   C. Security = novell_netware

   D. Security = nwserver

5. What TCP/IP utility can you use to verify that a remote host is connected to the network?

   A. TRACERT

   B. PING

   C. WINIPCFG

   D. IPCONFIG

6. You want to verify the IP address and subnet mask in use on your computer. What Windows 95 utility can you use to check the IP address and subnet mask?

   A. PING

   B. WINIPCFG

   C. TRACERT

   D. NBTSTAT

7. Which utility would you use to create a new partition on your hard disk?

   A. FDISK

   B. ScanDisk

   C. Disk Defragmenter

   D. Windows Explorer

8. Allen is connecting a new printer to his computer. When he installed the printer drivers, a file was copied to the WINDOWS\SYSTEM\COLOR directory. What feature might this file support?

   A. Image color matching

   B. WYSIWYG

   C. Color image scanning

   D. Advanced color configuration

9. You get an error message when you try to print to your local printer. What can you do to resolve this problem?

   A. Verify that there is free space on the hard disk.

   B. Reinstall the printer drivers.

   C. Verify that the TEMP variable is set correctly.

   D. Try to print the document from the command prompt.

10. Henry uses the ScanDisk utility frequently, and he has learned that it cannot detect certain kinds of errors. What types of errors cannot be detected by ScanDisk?

   A. Errors on volumes compressed by DriveSpace

   B. Errors on FAT volumes

   C. Errors on floppy disks

   D. Errors on network drives

11. Nancy wants to use Windows 95 Backup to back up the data on her C: drive. She wants to back up only those files that have changed since the last time she ran the Backup program. What type of backup should she perform?

   A. Incremental

   B. Partial

   C. Full

   D. System

12. Darryl has decided to implement system policies for Windows 95 computers on his Novell NetWare network. Where must he store the CONFIG.POL file?

   A. On each Windows 95 computer in the WINDOWS\SYSTEM directory.

   B. On the NetWare server in each user's MAIL directory.

   C. On each Windows 95 computer in the WINDOWS\PROFILES directory.

   D. On the NetWare server in the SYS\PUBLIC directory.

13. Cindy wants to restore some files to her hard disk from an MS-DOS 6.2 Backup set using Windows 95 Backup. How can she accomplish this?

   A. Enable MS-DOS backup set support on the Backup Set properties sheet.

   B. Do nothing. MS-DOS backup sets are supported by default.

   C. MS-DOS backup sets are not supported by the Windows 95 Backup utility.

   D. Specify MS-DOS Backup Set in the Restore From dialog box.

14. Which protocols can be used to connect to a local area network under Windows 95?

   A. TCP/IP

   B. PPP

   C. IPX/SPX

   D. NetBEUI

15. You have enabled the use of profiles and system policies for Windows 95 clients in your Windows NT network. Where are the USER.DAT files stored?

    A. In the user's MAIL directory

    B. In the user's HOME directory

    C. In the SYSTEM32 directory

    D. In the user's PERSONAL directory

16. Where are the locally stored user profiles kept on a Windows 95 computer?

    A. In the \WINDOWS\PROFILES\ *username* directory

    B. In the user's HOME directory

    C. In the user's MAIL directory

    D. In the \WINDOWS\SYSTEM32 directory

17. Which Registry key contains user profile information?

    A. HKEY_DYN_DATA

    B. HKEY_USER

    C. HKEY_LOCAL_MACHINE

    D. HKEY_CURRENT_USER

18. Susan is an administrator of a Windows NT network. She wants to enable system policies for Windows 95 users on her network. Where are system policies stored on a Windows NT server?

    A. In the NETLOGON directory

    B. In the WINDOWS\SYSTEM32 directory

    C. In the user's HOME directory

    D. In the user's MAIL directory

19. You need to set up system policies for Windows 95 users on your Novell NetWare network. Where are system policies stored on a Novell NetWare file server?

    A. In the SYS:PUBLIC directory

    B. In the SYS:LOGIN directory

    C. In the SYS:MAIL directory

    D. In the SYS:ETC directory

20. You want to configure an MS-DOS–based application to run under Windows 95. In which modes can it be configured to run?

    A. VM mode

    B. MS-DOS mode

    C. Full Control mode

    D. Customized MS-DOS mode

21. Kelly is having trouble connecting to a dial up service using her new modem. How can she create a log file to troubleshoot the connection process?

    A. Select Record a Log File from the Advanced Connection Settings dialog box.

    B. Select the Modems icon in Control Panel.

    C. Select the Modem icon in Device Manager.

    D. Select Properties.

22. Greg sometimes has trouble establishing connections with his fax modem, so he creates a log file to help him troubleshoot. What is the name of that file?

    A. CONNECT.LOG

    B. MODEMLOG.TXT

    C. MODEM.TXT

    D. DIALUP.LOG

23. IPX/SPX is the default protocol for connecting to

    A. Microsoft Windows NT networks

    B. Novell NetWare networks

    C. The Internet

    D. DEC Pathworks networks

24. TCP/IP is the default protocol for connecting to

    A. The Internet.

    B. Novell NetWare networks.

    C. Microsoft Windows NT networks.

    D. LANtastic networks.

25. What part of an IP address references a group of computers and devices located on the same logical network?

    A. The host portion

    B. The network portion

    C. The subnet mask

    D. The MAC address

26. What part of an IP address references the individual device on a specific network?

    A. The network portion

    B. The subnet mask

    C. The host portion

    D. The MAC address

The next three questions all present the same scenario, required results, and optional results. Analyze each proposed solution and determine the best answer.

27. Connie is an administrator of a large Novell NetWare LAN. She is planning to upgrade the PCs on her network to Windows 95, and she wants each Windows 95 user to be able to log on to any Windows 95 computer and see his or her own personal desktop settings. Optionally, she would like Windows 95 users to be able to make the files on their local C: drives available to other users on the network.

    Solution:

    Upgrade the PCs to Windows 95. Install and configure the IPX/SPX protocol. Install and configure the Client for NetWare Networks.

    A. The proposed solution meets all of the required results and all of the optional results.

    B. The proposed solution meets all of the required results and some of the optional results.

    C. The proposed solution meets all of the required results but none of the optional results.

    D. The proposed solution does not meet the required results.

28. Connie is an administrator of a large Novell NetWare LAN. She is planning to upgrade the PCs on her network to Windows 95, and she wants each Windows 95 user to be able to log on to any Windows 95 computer and see his or her own personal desktop settings. Optionally, she would like Windows 95 users to be able to make the files on their local C: drives available to other users on the network.

    Solution:

    Upgrade the PCs to Windows 95. Install and configure the IPX/SPX protocol. Install and configure the Client for NetWare Networks. Enable profiles on the Windows 95 PCs.

    A. The proposed solution meets all of the required results and all of the optional results.

    B. The proposed solution meets all of the required results and some of the optional results.

    C. The proposed solution meets all of the required results but none of the optional results.

    D. The proposed solution does not meet the required results.

29. Connie is an administrator of a large Novell NetWare LAN. She is planning to upgrade the PCs on her network to Windows 95, and she wants each Windows 95 user to be able to log on to any Windows 95 computer and see his or her own personal desktop settings. Optionally, she would like Windows 95 users to be able to make the files on their local C: drives available to other users on the network.

    Solution:

    Upgrade the PCs to Windows 95. Install and configure the IPX/SPX protocol. Install and configure the Client for NetWare Networks. Enable profiles on the Windows 95 PCs. Install and configure File and Printer Sharing for Novell Networks.

A. The proposed solution meets all of the required results and all of the optional results.

B. The proposed solution meets all of the required results and some of the optional results.

C. The proposed solution meets all of the required results but none of the optional results.

D. The proposed solution does not meet the required results.

30. You are preparing to install Windows 95 on several network client computers using an automated installation. What line should you put in the [Setup] section of the MSBATCH.INF file to prevent user input during the setup process?

A. Express=0

B. Input=0

C. Express=1

D. Input=Default

31. What applications or devices use the DLC protocol?

A. Printers with HP Jet Direct network interface cards

B. Novell NetWare 4.11 file servers

C. Software used for browsing the World Wide Web

D. Terminal Emulation programs that communicate directly with IBM mainframes

32. PPTP supports encapsulation of which of the following protocols?

A. X.25

B. IPX/SPX

C. TCP/IP

D. NetBEUI

33. Through which type of network would PPTP enable connection to corporate resources?

A. ISDN

B. PSTN

C. The Internet

D. X.25

34. Jeff needs to establish a VPN connection to his corporate network. Which Windows 95 utility would he use to establish a VPN connection?

A. Network Neighborhood

B. Dial-Up Networking

C. HyperTerminal

D. Control Panel

35. When setting up a Windows 95 computer to connect to a token-ring LAN using the IPX/SPX protocol, what Advanced parameter might you need to adjust for the IPX/SPX protocol?

A. Node Type

B. Source Routing

C. MAC Address

D. Nearest Active Upstream Neighbor (NAUN)

36. What frame types are supported by the IPX/SPX protocol under Windows 95?

A. Ethernet II

B. Ethernet III

C. 802.2

D. 802.3

37. Fritz uses a local printer connected to his Windows 95 computer. He wants to configure the printer so that control returns more quickly to applications after a print command has been issued. How can he accomplish this?

A. Use the RAW format for print spooling.

B. Use the EMF format for print spooling.

   C. Disable print spooling.

   D. Use the PCL format for print spooling.

38. Which Windows 95 driver provides support for NetBIOS services over the IPX/SPX protocol?

   A. NETBEUI.DRV

   B. VNETBIOS.DRV

   C. VNETBIOS.386

   D. NETBEUI.386

39. You have installed Windows 95 on five computers in your corporate test lab. You now need to connect them to the corporate LAN. How can you install and configure the IPX/SPX protocol if you did not do so during the initial installation of Windows 95?

   A. Using the Network icon in Control Panel.

   B. Using the Protocol icon in Control Panel.

   C. Edit the PROTOCOL.INI file.

   D. Reinstall Windows 95.

40. You want to enable users with File and Printer Sharing for NetWare Networks to browse for other Windows 95 computers that are sharing resources on a Novell NetWare network. What type of advertising should you enable on the Windows 95 computers?

   A. SAP Advertising

   B. RIP Advertising

   C. Workgroup Advertising

   D. IPX Advertising

41. Steve is reconfiguring a Windows 95 computer that uses real-mode drivers to connect to a Novell NetWare network. When he installs the 32-bit protected-mode drivers for the IPX/SPX protocol and the Client for NetWare Networks, what

happens to the parameters specified in the NET.CFG file?

   A. They are moved to the WIN.INI file.

   B. They are moved to the Registry.

   C. They are moved to the SYSTEM.INI file.

   D. They are not changed.

42. Windows 95 supports autodetection of IPX network addresses. How does Windows 95 detect the IPX network address in IPX packets?

   A. It checks for RIP packets and chooses the most likely address.

   B. It sends a GetIPXNetAddress packet to the nearest sever.

   C. It uses the address specified in the LMHOSTS file.

   D. It cannot detect the IPX address; the address must be specified in the IPX/SPX properties.

43. When you enable disk compression under Windows 95 with DriveSpace, compressed files on a hard disk are written to a large file called a:

   A. Compressed Disk Volume

   B. Compressed File Volume

   C. Compressed Volume File

   D. Compressed Disk File

44. DriveSpace 3 supports compressed disks up to what size?

   A. 512KB

   B. 512MB

   C. 2GB

   D. 2TB

45. A user on your LAN reports that she is having a problem accessing computers on the Internet. She can access hosts on the Internet when she specifies them by their IP addresses, but not when she uses their

hostnames. Which parameter would you check to resolve this problem?

A. The IP address of her workstation

B. The subnet mask of her workstation

C. The IP address of her Internet provider

D. The IP address of the DNS server

46. Which Remote Access Servers are supported by Windows 95 Dial-Up Networking?

A. NetWare Connect

B. Windows NT 4.0 RAS

C. UNIX server running PPP

D. MS-DOS server running NetBIOS

47. You are considering enabling disk compression on your Windows 95 computer using the DriveSpace utility. When will the DriveSpace utility hide the host drive by default?

A. When the host drive contains more than 2GB of free space.

B. When the host drive contains the same amount of free space as the compressed drive.

C. When the host drive contains less than 2MB of free space.

D. DriveSpace will not hide the host drive by default.

48. Your Windows 95 computer is connected to a Novell NetWare LAN. How can you connect to a print queue on a Novell NetWare file server and enable Point and Print printing?

A. Enable Point and Print from the Network icon in Control Panel.

B. Drag the printer queue icon from Network Neighborhood to the Printers folder.

C. Enable Point and Print on the File and Printer Sharing for NetWare Networks properties sheet.

D. You cannot enable Point and Print printing for Novell NetWare print queues.

49. With the automounting feature disabled on a Windows 95 computer, how can you manually mount a compressed floppy disk in drive A:?

A. Type **automount a:** at the command prompt.

B. In DriveSpace, select Mount from the Advanced menu.

C. Type **mount a: /floppy** at the command prompt.

D. In DriveSpace, select Mount from the Drive menu.

50. Which Windows 95 utility will enable you to access a directory on a remote Windows 95 computer and share that directory with other users on the network?

A. Device Manager

B. Windows Explorer

C. System Monitor

D. Net Watcher

51. How can you run the Windows 95 DriveSpace utility from the command line?

A. Type **DRIVESPACE** at the command prompt.

B. Type **DBLSPACE** at the command prompt.

C. Type **DRVSPACE** at the command prompt.

D. Type **DRIVESPC** at the command prompt.

52. Mark is configuring disk compression on his Windows 95 computer. What types of compression are offered by DriveSpace version 3?

A. UltraPack

B. SuperPack

C. HiPack

D. Standard

53. What line can you add to the MSDOS.SYS file to prevent the use of the Windows 95 Boot menu?

    A. BootKeys=0

    B. BootMenu=1

    C. BootOptions=0

    D. BootDelay=1

54. After installing Windows 95, how can you turn off the animated Windows 95 banner that is displayed at startup?

    A. Set Banner=0 in the MSDOS.SYS file.

    B. Set Logo=0 in the MSDOS.SYS file.

    C. Set Banner-0 in the SYSTEM.INI file.

    D. The Windows 95 startup banner cannot be disabled.

55. Cathy is upgrading to Windows 95 from Windows for Workgroups. Where will Windows 95 get information about the network protocols to install?

    A. SYSTEM.INI

    B. PROTOCOL.INI

    C. NETWORKS.INI

    D. WIN.INI

56. When Cathy upgrades from Windows 3.1 to Windows 95, what will happen to her Program Manager program groups?

    A. They will remain unchanged.

    B. They will be converted to icons on the desktop.

    C. They will be converted to folders in the Programs directory.

    D. They will be deleted from the system.

57. Ralph has installed Windows 95 to dual boot with his existing Windows NT installation. However, when the machine starts under Windows 95, he cannot see his NTFS partitions in Windows 95 Explorer.

How can he configure Windows 95 to solve this problem?

    A. Enable NTFS file access in the MSDOS.SYS file.

    B. Right-click the My Computer icon and choose Enable NTFS from the Advanced tab.

    C. Load the NTFS file system drivers in Device Manager.

    D. Windows 95 cannot read NTFS partitions.

58. How much conventional memory must be available in order for Windows 95 Setup to run?

    A. 640KB

    B. 1024KB

    C. 417KB

    D. 512KB

59. How much hard disk space is required for a new Windows 95 installation using the Typical setup option?

    A. 40MB

    B. 50MB

    C. 30MB

    D. 90MB

60. Using the Compact setup option, how much hard disk space is required to upgrade to Windows 95 from Windows 3.1?

    A. 10MB

    B. 20MB

    C. 30MB

    D. 40MB

61. You are setting up Windows 95 on a computer for the first time. What different types of Windows 95 installations are available through Windows 95 Setup?

    A. Typical

    B. Express

C. Custom

D. Compact

E. Portable

62. You are planning to run an automated installation of Windows 95 on several computers. Which Windows 95 utility can you use to create a setup script for the automated installation of Windows 95?

A. MSBATCH.EXE

B. BATCH.EXE

C. MSBATCH.INF

D. NETSETUP.EXE

63. Which of the following utilities can you use to determine which IRQs are in use on your system?

A. WINIPCFG

B. System Monitor

C. MSD

D. My Computer

64. You need to enable Remote Administration of your Windows 95 computer. Which icon in Control Panel would you use?

A. Network

B. System

C. Passwords

D. Services

65. You are setting up Windows 95 computers in a Novell NetWare network environment. You enable File and Printer Sharing for NetWare Networks on the Windows 95 computers, and you want to ensure that NeTX clients on the network will be able to access shared resources on these computers. What must you do to accomplish this?

A. Enable Workgroup Advertising on the Windows 95 computers.

B. Enable Workgroup Browsing on the NeTX client computers.

C. Upgrade the NeTX clients to Windows 95.

D. Enable SAP Advertising on the Windows 95 computers.

66. You are responsible for setting up new printers for the 60 computers in your office. Which utility would you use to install a new printer on a Windows 95 computer?

A. Device Manager

B. Windows 95 Setup

C. Add New Hardware Wizard

D. Add Printer Wizard

67. Which utility would you use to connect to an existing network printer from your Windows 95 computer?

A. Device Manager

B. Windows 95 Setup

C. Network Neighborhood

D. Add Printer Wizard

68. How can Windows 95 run an MS-DOS–based application that cannot operate in a Virtual Machine?

A. It runs the application in a window.

B. It runs the application full-screen.

C. It runs the application in MS-DOS mode.

D. It cannot run the application.

69. Lea is setting up Windows 95 on a laptop computer. What Windows 95 features are installed automatically when she chooses the Portable Setup option?

A. Briefcase

B. System Monitor

C. Dial-Up Networking

D. Net Watcher

Practice Exam 2

70. Which version of MS-DOS is required to install Windows 95 on an MS-DOS computer?

    A. Version 3.3 or higher

    B. Version 4.1 or higher

    C. Version 5.0 or higher

    D. Version 3.2 or higher

71. MaryAnn is running a Win16 application, a Win32 application, and three MS-DOS–based applications, each running in a separate window. How many applications are running in the System VM?

    A. 1

    B. 2

    C. 3

    D. 5

72. You want to verify that your system is fully Plug and Play–compatible. What are the components of a fully Plug and Play system?

    A. Plug and Play BIOS

    B. Plug and Play devices

    C. Plug and Play CMOS

    D. Plug and Play operating system

73. Where is the information referenced by the HKEY_DYN_DATA Registry key stored?

    A. SYSTEM.DAT

    B. USER.DAT

    C. CONFIG.POL

    D. system memory

74. After making some changes in his Registry as recommended by the vendor of an application he is using, Bill wants to save the new information to a text file. How can he do this?

    A. Copy and paste the information from the Registry Editor into Notepad.

    B. Choose Export Registry File from the Registry menu in the Registry Editor.

    C. Choose Import Registry File from the Registry menu in the Registry Editor.

    D. He cannot store the Registry information in a text file.

75. What is the best way to add hardware that is not Plug and Play–compatible to a Windows 95 computer?

    A. Load the necessary drivers in Device Manager.

    B. Start the Add New Hardware Wizard and manually configure the device.

    C. Start the Add New Hardware Wizard and automatically detect the device.

    D. Start the computer in MS-DOS mode and configure the device manually.

The next two questions both present the same scenario, required results, and optional results. Analyze each proposed solution and determine the best answer.

76. As administrator of a small Windows 95 workgroup, David has been given the responsibility of installing and configuring an MS-DOS application for use by the entire workgroup. The application requires 1MB of XMS memory in order to run properly. Users need to be able to switch between this application and their Windows-based email application. Optionally, users would like the application to run full-screen when it is started.

Solution:

Install the application on all computers in the workgroup. Place a shortcut to the application on each user's desktop.

    A. The proposed solution meets all of the required results and all of the optional results.

    B. The proposed solution meets all of the required results and some of the optional results.

C.   The proposed solution meets all of the required results but none of the optional results.

D.   The proposed solution does not meet the required results.

77. As administrator of a small Windows 95 workgroup, David has been given the responsibility of installing and configuring an MS-DOS application for use by the entire workgroup. The application requires 1MB of XMS memory in order to run properly. Users need to be able to switch between this application and their Windows-based email application. Option-ally, users would like the application to run full-screen when it is started.

Solution:

Install the application on all computers in the workgroup. Place a shortcut to the application on each user's desktop. Right-click the shortcut icon and choose Proper-ties. On the Properties sheet, specify that the application be run in MS-DOS mode.

A.   The proposed solution meets all of the required results and all of the optional results.

B.   The proposed solution meets all of the required results and some of the optional results.

C.   The proposed solution meets all of the required results but none of the optional results.

D.   The proposed solution does not meet the required results.

Answers and Explanations

1. **A, C**   Under Windows 95, print jobs can use either the EMF or RAW format.

2. **B**   Disk Defragmenter will restart if it detects data written to the disk while it is running.

3. **C**   To start the Device Manager utility, double-click the System icon in Control Panel and choose the Device Manager tab.

4. **D**   The line Security = nwserver should be added to the MSBATCH.INF file to enable user-level security with the NetWare server as the security provider for Windows 95 computers installed using NETSETUP.

5. **B**   PING is a TCP/IP utility that is used to verify connectivity to other hosts on an internetwork.

6. **B**   The WINIPCFG utility can tell you the IP address and subnet mask that are in use on your Windows 95 computer.

7. **A**   Use the FDISK utility to create or delete hard disk partitions.

8. **A**   Files in the WINDOWS\SYSTEM\COLOR directory are used by Windows 95 to support the image color matching feature.

9. **A, C**   Windows 95 local printing tempo-rarily writes files to the location on the hard disk specified by the TEMP variable. If this variable is not properly set or if there is no space available on the hard disk, printing will not be successful.

10. **D**   ScanDisk can detect errors on floppy disks, hard disks, or even volumes com-pressed by DriveSpace, but it cannot detect errors on network drives.

11. **A**   Using Windows 95 Backup, an incremental backup will copy only the files that have changed since the last full backup of the system.

12. **D**   In a Novell NetWare network environ-ment, the CONFIG.POL file should be stored on the NetWare server in the SYS\PUBLIC directory.

13. **C**   Windows 95 Backup does not support backup sets created with the MS-DOS 6.2 Backup utility.

14. **A, C, D**   Windows 95 supports TCP/IP, IPX/SPX, and NetBEUI for connection to a local area network (LAN). PPP is used for connection to a remote network using Dial-Up Networking.

15. **B**   The USER.DAT file is stored in the user's HOME directory on a Windows NT server.

16. **A** The locally stored profile is kept in the WINDOWS\PROFILES*username* directory.

17. **D** User profile information is stored in the HKEY_CURRENT_USER Registry key.

18. **A** System policies are stored in the NETLOGON directory on the Windows NT server.

19. **A** System policies are stored in the SYS:PUBLIC directory on a Novell NetWare file server.

20. **A, B, D** The three operating modes available for MS-DOS applications are VM mode, MS-DOS mode, and Customized MS-DOS mode.

21. **A, B, D** To create a log file for modem connections, select the Modems icon in the Control Panel, click the Properties button, choose Advanced, and select Record a Log File.

22. **B** When you select Record a Log File from the Advanced Connection Settings dialog box, Windows 95 creates a file called MODEMLOG.TXT.

23. **B** Novell NetWare networks use the IPX/SPX protocol by default.

24. **A, C** TCP/IP is the protocol used to connect to the Internet. Since version 4.0, Microsoft Windows NT networks use the TCP/IP protocol by default.

25. **B** The network portion of an IP address refers to a group of computers and devices located on the same logical network.

26. **C** The host portion of an IP address references the individual device on a specific network.

27. **D** The proposed solution does not meet the required results.

28. **C** The proposed solution meets all of the required results but none of the optional results.

29. **A** The proposed solution meets all of the required results and all of the optional results.

30. **C** The Express=1 line in the [Setup] section of the MSBATCH.INF file will prevent user input during the setup process.

31. **A, D** The DLC protocol is used mainly by terminal emulation programs that communicate directly with IBM mainframes, but it can also be used by printers with HP Jet Direct network interface cards.

32. **B, C, D** PPTP supports encapsulation of IPX/SPX, TCP/IP, or NetBEUI protocol packets inside a standard PPP packet.

33. **C** Point-to-Point Tunneling Protocol enables users to access corporate resources securely across a TCP/IP network such as the Internet.

34. **B** Virtual Private Network connections are established through Dial-Up Networking.

35. **B** On the Advanced tab of the IPX/SPX protocol properties sheet, Source Routing can be enabled. The value indicates the cache size, in number of entries, for source route information.

36. **A, C, D** Windows 95 supports the Ethernet II, 802.2, and 802.3 frame types, as well as the Token-Ring and Token-Ring SNAP frame types when using the IPX/SPX protocol.

37. **B** Using the Enhanced Metafile (EMF) Spooling feature of Windows 95 allows control to return to an application more quickly after a print command has been issued.

38. **C** Support for NetBIOS services over the IPX/SPX protocol is provided by the VNETBIOS.386 32-bit protected-mode driver.

39. **A** The Network icon in the Control Panel can be used to install and configure network components after the initial installation of Windows 95.

40. **C** Workgroup advertising should be enabled on large networks. SAP advertising should not be used due to the amount of network traffic it generates.

41. **B**   Parameters specified in the NET.CFG file, used by real-mode drivers to connect to Novell NetWare networks, are moved to the Registry during installation of the 32-bit protected-mode drivers for the IPX/SPX protocol and the Client for NetWare Networks.

42. **A**   Windows 95 checks the network for RIP packets and chooses the most likely address when detecting the IPX network address in IPX packets.

43. **C**   Compressed files on a hard disk are written to a large file called a Compressed Volume File.

44. **C**   DriveSpace version 3 supports compressed disks up to 2GB in size. Previous versions supported only volumes up to 512MB.

45. **D**   The IP address of the DNS server must be correct in order for the DNS server to resolve hostnames into IP addresses.

46. **A, B, C**   Windows 95 Dial-Up Networking can connect to many different types of remote access servers, including Novell NetWare Connect, Windows NT 4.0 RAS, and UNIX servers running PPP.

47. **C**   The DriveSpace utility hides the host drive by default if the host drive contains less than 2MB of free space.

48. **B**   Drag the printer queue icon from Network Neighborhood and drop it in the Printers folder to enable Point and Print printing to a printer on a Novell NetWare file server.

49. **B**   To manually mount a compressed disk floppy disk, highlight the disk in DriveSpace and select Mount from the Advanced menu.

50. **D**   Net Watcher allows you to access a directory on a remote Windows 95 computer and share that directory with other users on the network.

51. **C**   DRVSPACE is the command for controlling Windows 95 DriveSpace from the command line. It can accept many command-line arguments and options.

52. **A, C, D**   DriveSpace 3 offers Standard, HiPack, and UltraPack compression methods.

53. **A**   Setting the BootKeys line to 0 in the MSDOS.SYS file disables the use of all the Windows 95 startup option keys (F8, F5, and so on). The BootMenu line controls whether or not the user must press F8 to see the Boot menu, but it does not disable any startup option.

54. **B**   Setting Logo=0 in the [Options] section of the MSDOS.SYS file disables the Windows 95 animated banner so it won't be displayed at startup.

55. **B**   When you upgrade from Windows for Workgroups, Windows 95 reads the PROTOCOL.INI file to determine which network protocols to install and their appropriate settings.

56. **C**   When you upgrade from Windows 3.1 to Windows 95, program groups are converted to folders under the Programs folder so they can be displayed on the Start menu.

57. **D**   Windows 95 cannot read NTFS partitions. If you have NTFS and FAT partitions on your Windows NT machine, you can dual boot to Windows 95, but you will not be able to access the data on the NTFS partitions.

58. **C**   Windows 95 Setup requires at least 417KB of conventional memory to run.

59. **A**   The Typical setup option for a new installation of Windows 95 requires approximately 40MB of hard disk space.

60. **B**   Upgrading Windows 3.1 to Windows 95 using the Compact setup option requires approximately 20MB of hard disk space.

61. **A, C, D, E**   Windows 95 Setup allows for Typical, Portable, Compact, or Custom installations.

62. **A**   The BATCH.EXE utility creates a setup script in the MSBATCH.INF format for use in an automated installation of Windows 95.

63. **C, D**   The MSD utility can show the IRQs in use on the system. In addition, right-clicking the My Computer icon and selecting Properties allows you to view the Device Manager, which will also show which IRQs are in use and which devices are using them.

64. **C**   The PASSWORDS icon in the Control Panel is the place to start when you want to enable Remote Administration.

65. **D**   Enabling SAP Advertising on the Windows 95 computers will allow the NeTX clients on the network to access the shared resources on the Windows 95 computers.

66. **C**   The Add Printer Wizard in the Printers folder is used to install a new printer on a Windows 95 computer.

67. **D**   The Add Printer Wizard in the Printers folder is used to connect to existing printers on a network.

68. **C**   MS-DOS–based applications that cannot run in a Virtual Machine must be run in MS-DOS mode.

69. **A, C**   If you select the Portable setup option, the Briefcase and Dial-Up Networking applications will be installed automatically.

70. **D**   MS-DOS version 3.2 or higher is required for installation of Windows 95 on an MS-DOS computer.

71. **B**   The Win16 and the Win32 applications are running in the System VM, and all the MS-DOS applications are running in their own VM.

72. **A, B, D**   To fully take advantage of Plug and Play features, a system must have a Plug and Play BIOS, Plug and Play devices, and a Plug and Play operating system.

73. **D**   Dynamic information referenced by the HKEY_DYN_DATA Registry key is stored in system memory so that it can be accessed and changed quickly. This type of information is updated often, so it is not well suited to storage in the disk-based Registry files.

74. **B**   To save the entire Registry or selected parts of the Registry to a text file, you choose Export Registry File from the Registry menu in the Registry Editor.

75. **C**   The best way to add new hardware that is not Plug and Play–compliant is to start the Add New Hardware Wizard and let Windows 95 automatically detect the new device. If this fails, you can manually configure the device from within the Add New Hardware Wizard.

76. **D**   The proposed solution does not meet the required results. The XMS memory requirements must be specified on the shortcut icon's Properties sheet.

77. **D**   The proposed solution does not meet the required results. MS-DOS mode will not allow users to switch between applications (MS-DOS mode is not multitasking).

Glossary

32-Bit Operating System Architecture—The 32-bit, protected-mode subsystems built into Windows 95 are more crash-resistant. A bad application, whether 16-bit or 32-bit, is less likely to stop the operating system.

A

Active fax modem—The fax modem that will be used to send and receive faxes. It can be a modem connected to the user's computer or a shared fax modem on the network.

Add/Remove Programs—A Control Panel applet used to add and remove programs, install additional Windows 95 components, and create a Windows 95 Startup disk.

Address Resolution Protocol (ARP)—Used to map IP addresses to the MAC address layer of an NIC.

ADMIN.ADM—A system policy template used to define system policies.

Algorithm—A formula for performing a certain calculation. Windows 95 uses a particular algorithm to calculate an 8.3 alias for a long filename.

Alias—The 8.3 name associated with long filenames, so that long filenames may be accessible through DOS and Windows 3.*x*.

Application Program Interface (API)—Provides all applications with a common means of interacting with an application.

Archive—A stored copy of data files that is kept up to date over time.

Arrange Icons—Leads to another menu that enables the contents to be sorted alphabetically by name, size, type, or modification date.

Attributes—Properties of a file that indicate whether the file is a Hidden, Read-Only, or System file.

B

B1 error—This message appears when the user runs the installation program and the processor type is a stepping processor that is not supported under Windows 95.

Background—Use the Background tab to establish settings for the background pattern and wallpaper.

Backup set—A backed-up copy of data files along with the preferences that were set up for that backup session.

Bad clusters—Clusters on a hard disk that reside in an area where the surface magnetic media is defective.

Bad sectors—Sectors of the media that cannot hold a magnetic charge due to normal wear or physical damage.

Baseline—A snapshot of the performance settings for a computer during its normal day-to-day functions. It represents an average use of the computer and is used for comparisons.

BATCH.EXE—A Windows-based program called Batch Setup makes it easy to create custom scripts.

Bindery—NetWare's database of users and resources that is a means by which items are bound or linked.

Bindings—The process of associating a protocol with a network card or a service.

Bitmap (BMP)—Bitmap file is the standard Windows bitmap format.

Boot menu—A displayed text screen listing StartUp options when F8 is pressed during Windows 95 Startup.

BOOTLOG.TXT—An ASCII text file that contains a record of the current Startup process when starting Windows 95, including components and drivers.

Bottlenecks—Areas that can slow down a computer by creating a queue where processes or functions must wait to be processed or executed.

Briefcase—When the user updates files by using Briefcase, Windows 95 automatically replaces unmodified files with modified files. If both files have changed, Windows 95 calls the appropriate application (if available) to merge the disparate files.

Browse master—The master browse server is responsible for maintaining the master list of workgroups, domains, and computers in a given workgroup.

Browsing—Seeing that computers and resources are available across the network.

Bus enumerator—A software driver that communicates with the devices attached to a particular type of bus architecture.

C

Caching—The process of storing disk information in memory for faster access. Windows 95 can store information to be written to disk in memory and write it to disk at a later time when the system is not busy.

Cancel—To delete a print job from the queue.

CFGBACK.EXE—A Configuration Backup utility that can save and restore up to nine configurations of a Windows 95 Registry.

Chain—A series of clusters that make up a file. The first cluster in a chain contains a pointer to the location of the second, which contains a pointer to the location of the third, and so on.

Challenge-Handshake Authentication Protocol (CHAP)—Periodically verifies the identity of the peer, using a three-way handshake. The authenticator sends a challenge message to the peer, which responds with a value using a one-way encryption. The authenticator then checks this response and, if the values match, the authentication is acknowledged; otherwise, the connection is ended.

Cluster—A grouping of sectors that is the minimum amount of disk space that can be allocated to a file.

Cold-docking—A style of docking that requires the laptop to be turned off before it can be removed from or inserted into a docking station.

Command-line switches—Adds flexibility to the way a window or folder is viewed.

Compact—The option for users who have extremely limited disk space. Installs only the minimum files required to run Windows 95.

Compressed drive—Files that have been compressed are stored in a Compressed Volume File (CVF), which is assigned a drive letter. This drive letter refers to the compressed drive.

Compressed Volume File (CVF)—The CVF contains the contents of a compressed drive.

CompuServe—An online information service that offers email messaging, forums, and access to the Internet.

CONFIG.POL—The policy file, which contains policy information related to the system user settings, created with the System Policy Editor and which must be placed in the default location. Registry information in the CONFIG.POL file can overwrite any existing information in the computer's Registry when downloaded.

Configuration Manager—The Windows 95 component that is in charge of the entire Plug and Play configuration process.

Consolidate—To move together; Windows 95 can consolidate free space on a hard disk by moving all data together to the front of the disk.

Contiguous space—An uninterrupted stream of disk clusters. Files that occupy sequential clusters on a disk without empty clusters are said to reside in contiguous space.

Cooperative multitasking—Cooperative multitasking requires the application to periodically check the message queue and cooperatively release control of the system to other applications that are running. In a cooperatively multitasked environment, one application generally maintains control of the CPU until the application has completed its task. Once the task is completed, the CPU is released to the next application awaiting access to the CPU.

Corruption—Errors in the file system that result in unreadable data.

Cross-linked—If file A has a cluster with some data and a pointer to cluster 12, and file B has a cluster that also points to cluster 12, these files are said to be cross-linked.

Cross-linked files—This occurs when two or more files share the same sector on the storage media.

Custom—The option for users who want to select applications and network components to be installed, and confirm the configuration settings for devices.

Customized MS-DOS mode—MS-DOS mode can be customized so that an application can make use of specific system parameter settings that differ from those needed by most other MS-DOS applications.

D

DBLSPACE—This Windows 95 Setup program replaces the old DOS file compression program.

DEBUG.EXE—A utility used to evaluate binary files during troubleshooting.

Deferred printing—The capability to print to a print queue, even if the printer is currently unavailable.

Degradation—System performance loss due to conditions on the hard disk that are not optimal.

Destination—The intended location for the backed-up files.

Details—Shows the contents of the folder as a detailed list. The detailed list contains the name, size, type, and date of the most recent modification.

DETCRASH.LOG—A binary file that exists only during the hardware detection phase.

DETLOG.TXT—An ASCII text file that contains a record of all devices found during the hardware detection phase of installation.

Device—A physical component on a computer, such as the printer, mouse, monitor, and so on.

Device conflicts—Conflicts can occur if applications access hardware directly. For this reason, direct access is not allowed under Windows 95. Direct access to hardware is only supported in MS-DOS mode.

Device driver—A configuration file that specifies the settings for a hardware component.

Device Manager—Part of the System applet that enables the user to view and edit hardware settings.

Dial-Up Networking—A service used for remote access to network services such as File and Printer Sharing, electronic mail, scheduling, and SQL database access. It provides remote networking for telecommuters, mobile workers, and system administrators who monitor and manage servers at multiple branch offices.

Dial-Up Networking Client—A remote computer configured to access a Windows 95 dial-up server or other remote access servers. With Dial-Up Networking, the dial-up client, running the appropriate connection protocol, can connect to many types of remote access servers, including the following: Windows 95 dial-up server, Windows NT Workstation, Windows NT 3.1 or later, Windows for Workgroups 3.11, NetWare Connect, Shiva LanRover and other dial-up routers, and any UNIX server that runs SLIP or PPP.

Dial-Up Scripting—A scripting application can be used by Dial-Up Networking for connecting to remote servers using SLIP. With this application installed, a user can associate an existing dial-in connection with a text file (script) to be run after the modem dials the remote server.

Dialing Properties—A utility that has been integrated with Phone Dialer, HyperTerminal, Dial-Up Networking, and other communications applications created for Windows 95.

Direct access—Direct access to system hardware is not available under Windows 95. If an MS-DOS application requires this, it must be run in MS-DOS mode.

Direct Cable Connection—With Direct Cable Connection, the user can establish a direct serial or parallel cable connection between two computers so that the resources of the computer designated as the host can be shared. If the host is connected to a network, the guest computer can also access the network.

Directory entry—Each file in a FAT file system has an entry in the Directory entry table that points to the location of the file. Files with long filenames require additional Directory entries.

Disk cache—The disk cache is a memory on the hard drive that stores data to be written to the disk until the computer is less busy and able to write the data to the disk.

Disk Defragmenter—A Windows 95 utility that defragments the user's files so they are read from and written to in a more efficient and faster way.

Disk errors—Hard drives can contain defects in the surface magnetic media that result in loss of the data that the operating system attempts to store there. These areas are referred to as Disk Errors.

Distribution Media Format (DMF)—Enables more data to be stored on one disk.

Dithering—Controls how colors are blended for the output on a color printer.

Docking station—A desktop base unit into which a laptop computer can be inserted for the purpose of taking advantage of additional hardware devices (such as a monitor, a printer, or a network).

Domain controller—The server that keeps the master account database.

DriveSpace—Compresses the data on the computer's hard disk to make more space on the disk.

DRVSPACE.BIN—The driver that supports compressed drives under Windows 95.

Dual boot—The capability to boot between two or more operating systems on the same machine.

Dynamic Memory Access (DMA) channel—A channel that enables peripherals to access portions of the computer's RAM directly.

E

Elections—Choosing which computer will become the browse master.

End task—When an application is hung, the user can select it in the Close Programs dialog box and click the End Task button to terminate the program.

Enhanced Industry Standard Architecture (EISA)—A bus design by non-IBM companies in the late 1980s. It offers the same features as MCA. The bus supports 32-bit edge adapter cards, which are configured through software. To integrate with Plug and Play, an EISA bus enumerator must be present.

Enhanced Metafile (EMF)—A printer-independent printing format with most of the processing of the print job to RAW format occurring in the background.

Enumeration—The process by which each device is examined and assigned an ID that will be used to identify it.

Error control—Used to boost file transfer speeds by eliminating errors caused by noise on the telephone line. This feature is available on most new modems.

Error correction—ScanDisk is a Windows 95 disk management tool that can correct certain errors in the FAT file system.

ERU.EXE—Emergency Recovery Utility saves key Windows 95 files to either a floppy drive, a local drive, or a network drive.

Exclusive use—If an MS-DOS application must have exclusive use of system resources and cannot share them, it must be run in MS-DOS mode.

Explorer—Runs the desktop, and the Start menu launches programs. It is also the main file management program.

Extended Capabilities Port (ECP)—Enables Windows 95 to use data compression at both the computer and the printer if they are both compliant.

Extension—The three characters following the period in an 8.3 format filename.

F

FAT32—The file system provided by OEMs through the OSR2 release of Windows 95. Accessible only through Windows 95 OSR2.

Fax modem—A device attached to a computer that can send and receive text and images through telephone lines. It offers the functionality of a fax machine except that all documents are electronic.

FDISK—A utility used to create and delete partitions, mark drives as active, and retrieve disk configuration information.

File Allocation Table (FAT)—The file system used by MS-DOS and by Windows 95.

File and Printer Sharing services—A service that enables a Windows 95 machine to share resources on a network.

File set—A saved list of files to be backed up or restored.

File synchronization—Windows 95 provides a set of OLE interfaces that enable applications to bind reconciliation handlers to it, track the contents of Briefcase, and define the outcome of any reconciliation on a class-by-class basis.

File system integrity—Indicates that the file system is free of errors from lost clusters or cross-linked files.

Filtering—The process of specifying certain files for inclusion or exclusion from a backup set.

Flat memory—Unlike MS-DOS, which had conventional and extended memory, Windows 95 memory is linear with no breaks.

Forum—A discussion group in which a user can read information posted by other people regarding a specific subject. Additional ideas can be posted to the forum for other people to read and comment on.

Fragmentation—A situation in which the clusters that make up a file are spread across a wide area of the disk.

Full backup—A complete backup of all the files on a Windows 95 system, including the Registry files.

G

Gateway—When the network uses a gateway to communicate with a host computer, the client computer running Windows 95 communicates with the gateway computer just as it does with any other computer on the network. The gateway computer translates requests from the client into a form that can be understood by the host, then communicates with the host and returns the information to the client.

General Protection Fault (GPF)—Occurs when an application attempts to violate the integrity of the system by performing an illegal operation.

Graphical User Interface (GUI)—A generic term in the context of how an operating system is displayed.

GROUPPOL.DLL—The dynamic link library or application extension that must be present on Windows 95 computers for support to group policy files.

GRPCONV.EXE—The utility used to convert *.grp files into the Windows 95 Program menu when Windows 95 is installed in its own directory.

H

Hardware Compatibility List (HCL)—A list of hardware made available by Microsoft that has been demonstrated to be compatible with Windows 95.

Hardware profile—A named configuration of the hardware devices used in a system.

Hardware tree—A list, created from entries in the Windows Registry, of all the hardware devices installed on a computer.

High Performance File System (HPFS)—A file system, originally developed for IBM's OS/2, that supports long filenames.

HIMEM.SYS—Enables access to High Memory Area (HMA). Loads and runs the real-mode Memory Manager.

Host drive—The physical drive on which a CVF is stored. This drive is assigned a higher drive letter, typically H.

HOSTS—The file for mapping host names to IP addresses.

Hot-docking—A style of docking that enables the laptop to be inserted into or removed from the docking station while running at full power.

Hung—Applications that have stopped responding to the system are said to be hung.

I-K

I/O port—The Input/Output port is an area of the computer's memory that peripherals use to execute input and output functions.

IFSHLP.SYS—Installable File System (IFS) Helper, which loads device drivers that enable Windows 95 to make calls to the file system.

Illegal characters—Reserved characters used by the operating system that are not allowed in file names.

Image Color Matching (ICM)—A technology that was developed by a number of the industry leaders to get the video display to match the colors being printed.

Implicit connection—An implicit connection is a feature of Dial-Up Networking that remembers network connections in the event that the user tries to access a resource from a network when he is not connected.

Inbox—A built-in universal inbox used to send, receive, and organize email, hold a user's received messages, and fax items from online services.

Inbox icon—An icon on the desktop that launches the Exchange program.

Incremental backup—A partial backup of a disk that includes only the files that have changed since the last full backup.

Industry Standard Architecture (ISA)—The bus design of the 1984 IBM PC/AT computer. The bus supports the original 8-bit or 16-bit edge adapter cards, configured through the use of jumper pins and dip switches.

Inefficient—When files on a hard disk become badly fragmented, it takes much more mechanical activity of the disk and slows performance. This type of disk activity is inefficient. Disk Defragmenter is a Windows 95 tool that addresses this.

INF files—These are files that define what is needed for a particular application or operating system.

INI files—These files are text-based, are limited to 64KB in size, and use APIs that allow only simple get/write operations.

WIN16 applications use INI files to store their configuration information. They cannot access the Windows 95 Registry.

Install program—Certain MS-DOS applications use an install program that detects whether they are running in a multitasking environment. If the applications are running in a multitasking environment, they shut themselves down. In this case, they must be run in MS-DOS mode.

Installable File System (IFS)—A file system with which the operating system may work.

Integrated Drive Electronics (IDE)—A standard for communication with hard drives and CD-ROM drives that is not Plug and Play.

Internet—A global network of computers used to exchange information.

Internet Mail—An information service supported by Exchange that sends and receives email over the Internet.

Internet service provider (ISP)—A company that provides Internet access or Internet presence to individuals, businesses, and other groups for a monthly fee.

Interrupt—The process by which a hardware device communicates with the system CPU. Windows 95 traps these messages and passes them to the appropriate driver for handling.

Interrupt Request (IRQ) line—A communication line that peripherals use to notify a software process that a hardware event has occurred.

IPX/SPX—A routable protocol used primarily in Novell NetWare networks.

L

Legacy components—Devices and BIOS that were not designed with the Plug and Play technology.

Legacy hardware—Older computers and hardware devices that do not support Plug and Play.

Legend—A color-coded guide that Disk Defragmenter provides to define the graphical representation of its operation.

List—Displays the contents of a folders as a list.

LMHOSTS—A file for mapping NetBIOS names to IP addresses.

Local installation—Accomplished by installing Windows 95 on the local hard drive.

Local reboot—The process of terminating a stalled application without affecting the system or other applications. Pressing Ctrl+Alt+Del once while Windows 95 is running brings up a Close Program dialog box where you can select an application to terminate.

Long filenames—Windows 95 allows up to 255 characters in a filename and 258 characters maximum for both the path and filename.

Loss of data—Loss of data can occur due to power failure, hard drive failure, or other errors. Windows 95 Backup is a tool that addresses this problem.

Lost clusters—When two files are cross-linked, it means that one of the files has a pointer to the wrong cluster. The cluster to which it was supposed to point, and all subsequent clusters in the file, are no longer referenced by any file. These are lost clusters.

M

Mail and Fax—An applet in the Control Panel that enables a user to add information services, modify information service settings, and create and modify profiles.

Mailbox—A place where electronic messages (incoming, outgoing, pending, and deleted) are stored for a particular user. MAILBOX.PST is stored on the user's hard drive.

Memory region—A portion of the computer's memory that a device reserves for its own use.

Memory space—The region of memory into which an application is loaded.

Message queue—Applications use the message queue to pass messages between the application and the processor. Each MS-DOS and Windows 32-bit application has its own unique message queue, and Windows 16-bit applications share a common message queue.

MicroChannel Architecture (MCA)—A bus architecture originally developed by IBM for its PS/2 computers. To integrate with Plug and Play, a MCA bus enumerator must be present.

Microsoft Fax—An applet included with Windows 95 that enables a computer's fax modem to send and receive faxes.

Microsoft Mail Information Service—A messaging system that enables users to send and receive mail on a network.

Microsoft Mail Postoffice—An applet in the Control Panel that enables an administrator to create a Workgroup Postoffice, create mailboxes, reset passwords, and perform other Postoffice management.

Minidriver—The printer-specific code that the manufacturer provides.

Mounting—The process of assigning drive letters and making a CVF available for viewing.

MS-DOS mode—An environment in which the Windows 95 GUI unloads itself from memory and grants a single MS-DOS application exclusive use of system resources.

MSBATCH.INF—The default batch script filename for automating the Windows 95 installation process.

MSPSERV—The Microsoft Print Agent for NetWare Networks that enables a Windows 95 print server to despool print jobs at a NetWare print server.

Multipurpose Internet Mail Extensions (MIME)—A message format for outgoing messages that maintains attached files if the recipient is also using MIME.

Multitasking—The capability of a computer to process more than one thread at a time. This is done by dividing the processor's time into slices and enabling each thread to access the processor for a specific amount of time. Windows 95 uses cooperative multitasking as well as preemptive multitasking.

My Briefcase—Represents a briefcase object that contains files and folders the user wants to keep current.

My Computer—Represents the computer object and loosely corresponds to the File Manager in the previous version of Windows. It is a folder that gives the user quick access to her entire computer.

N

Name space—Software that enables a Novell NetWare file system to support filenames and file formats used by another operating system's native file systems.

NetBEUI NetBIOS (Network Basic Input/Output System) Extended User Interface—A local area network transport protocol provided with Windows 95 and used in LAN environments. It is small, fast, and not routable.

NETLOG.TXT—An ASCII text file that contains a record of all detected network components found during installation.

NETSETUP.EXE—A server-based setup program that enables the user to install source files and create machine directories for a shared network installation.

NetWare Core Protocol (NCP)—A client protocol for NetWare 3.*x* services.

Network adapter—A hardware device used to attach one computer to another to form a network.

Network client software—The software that Windows 95 uses to communicate over the network with other computers and the network server.

Network fax server—A fax modem that has been shared so that other users on the network can use it to send and receive faxes.

Network Neighborhood—A new concept in Windows 95 that shows the user the computers in the user's workgroup or any NetWare servers to which the user is connected.

Network protocol—The language a network uses so that all computers connected to that network can communicate with each other.

New Technology File System (NTFS)—The file system provided by Windows NT that provides local security and is accessible only through NT. It also supports long filenames.

Notification Area—The area on the Taskbar where you can see status information.

Novell's DR DOS—Novell's version of DOS. This operating system is no longer being developed.

NT Boot Loader (NTLDR)—A built-in multiboot capability in Windows.

NT Hardware Compatibility List (HCL)—This list refers to all hardware tested to operate with Windows NT. Available from Microsoft at www.microsoft.com.

NWLink—Microsoft's IPX/SPX–compatible protocol.

O

Object Link Extensions (OLE)—This information is stored in HKEY_LOCAL_MACHINE\SOFTWARE\Classes. Shortcuts in Windows 95 are OLE links. OLE enables the user to share data between OLE-compliant applications.

Offending application—An application that has attempted to violate system integrity in some way.

On-the-fly—A process that occurs automatically. Windows 95 compression/decompression is on-the-fly because it occurs automatically and is transparent to the user.

Online help—Help regarding the current task that the user can access by selecting the Help menu or by pressing F1.

Orphan file—A copied file that does not have a master file with which to synchronize. This could be due to the original file being deleted or the file being created inside Briefcase.

Orphaned clusters—Another name for lost clusters.

OSI Reference Model—A seven-layer architecture that standardizes levels of service and types of interaction for computers exchanging information through a communications network. It is used to describe the flow of data between the physical connection to the network and the end-user program.

P

Path—The fully specified location of a file including all subdirectories between a file and the root directory of the drive on which the file is stored.

Pause—To stop printing a document or stop the entire printer.

PC-DOS—IBM's version of DOS.

PCX—This format has become the de facto graphics file standard.

Performance—Overall performance of the system can be improved with proper use of Windows 95 disk management tools—Disk Defragmenter, ScanDisk, DriveSpace, and Backup.

Peripheral Component Interconnect (PCI)—A standard bus architecture that is compatible with Plug and Play. It is being promoted as the logical successor to VL. It enables high-speed connections to peripheral hardware devices.

Personal Computer Memory Card International Association (PCMCIA)—A specification that supports the key features of Plug and Play.

PING—Used to verify that an IP address can be reached.

Plug and Play (PnP)—The goal of Plug and Play is to enable changes to be made to the computer's configuration without requiring active intervention by the user.

Point and Print—The capability to point to a printer that is shared on the network and print to it.

Point-to-Point Protocol (PPP)—An industry standard that is part of Windows 95 Dial-Up Networking. It ensures interoperability with remote access software from other vendors.

Pointer—A piece of information in a file cluster that indicates the location of the next cluster in the chain.

POLEDIT.EXE—The System Policy Editor executable file. Computer, user, and group system policies are created using the System Policy Editor.

Portable—The recommended option for mobile users with portable computers. Installs the appropriate set of files for a portable computer. This includes installing Briefcase for file synchronization and the supporting software for direct cable connections to exchange files.

PostScript—PostScript is a device-independent page description language used commonly when printing graphics. This type of print code does not require rendering because it already has all the code provided.

Power failure—Power failure can result in loss of data. Run Windows 95 Backup at regular intervals to prevent loss of valuable data files.

Preemptive multitasking—In preemptive multitasking, applications are allocated time slices or periods of execution time in which the application has access to the CPU.

These time slices are managed in part based on the applications' thread priority levels.

Prevention—It's always best to try to prevent problems from happening. Regular use of Windows 95 disk management tools can prevent many known problems with hard disks and the FAT file system.

Primary Scheduler—A component of the task scheduler responsible for evaluating all thread priorities and allocating time slices of execution for threads. If two or more threads have the same priority, they're stacked. Each stacked thread is granted a time slice of execution in sequence until no threads have the same priority.

Process—A process performs a specific function and is comprised of an executable program, a memory address space, system resources, and at least one thread to perform the function.

Profile—A collection of settings (Start menu, network connections, shortcuts, desktop icons, and screen colors) that specify which information services are configured for a particular user and define what types of connections to use for each service.

Program groups—A collection of executables or files in Windows 3.*x* and Windows 95.

PROGRAM.EXE—Program Manager is included as an optional interface at installation time for Windows 95. This enables a user to maintain the same interface as in Windows 3.1.

Properties—The properties of the environment in which an application runs can be modified and customized under Windows 95.

Properties sheet—An object's properties (settings and parameters) are found on this sheet.

Protected mode—A processor operating mode in which memory address space assigned to a process can be protected from other processes. Windows 95 32-bit drivers are protected-mode drivers.

Protected-mode drivers—Protected-mode drivers are 32-bit drivers that store configuration information in the Windows 95 Registry. These devices are dynamically loaded in Windows 95 when they are needed and release their allocated memory when unloaded, thereby increasing the amount of memory available to the system. MS-DOS applications can take advantage of these drivers if they run in a VM.

Protocol—The language a computer speaks on the network and a defined standard for how to perform an operation.

PSERVER—The DOS equivalent of MSPSERV, which must be run from a dedicated DOS computer to run the NetWare print service.

Q

Quarter-Inch Cartridge (QIC)—The tape backup specification that is supported by Windows 95 Backup.

Queue—The documents waiting to be printed.

Queue Management Services (QMS)—An API that Microsoft Print Agent for NetWare Networks uses for queue services.

R

RAW—This is the code that is native to the printer. When a document is sent to the printer, it must be rendered to this format. RAW printing is a printer-dependent format with the processing occurring in the foreground.

Real-mode drivers—Real-mode drivers are 16-bit drivers that were designed for Microsoft Windows 3.*x*. Real-mode drivers are implemented in AUTOEXEC.BAT or CONFIG.SYS. These drivers were loaded during boot-up and tend to use more memory than their respective 32-bit drivers.

Recycle Bin—Represents a trash-bin object. Any folders and files the user deletes are automatically moved to this folder.

Reentrant code—Reentrant code can be accessed by multiple applications at the same time, whereas non-reentrant code can only be accessed by one application at a time.

Refresh—Refreshes the contents of the folder. Any changes made in a folder may not always be shown immediately. Refresh will update the display.

REGEDIT.EXE—The Registry Editor executable file, which is used to view and change the contents of the Windows 95 Registry.

Registry—A database in which Windows 95 stores configuration information for hardware and software.

REGSERVE.EXE—The Microsoft Remote Registry Service executable file.

Remote Access Server (RAS)—A computer that is accessed remotely by modem that runs administrative software and controls access to all or part of the network and its resources.

Remote computer—Any Windows 95 computer that the user can physically connect to using network cabling or Dial-Up Networking.

Resolution—The number of dots per inch (dpi) used for printing scalable fonts and graphics.

Resource arbitrator—A Windows 95 component that is responsible for keeping track of resource allocation to the installed devices on a computer. Each major resource type has an arbitrator.

Restore—The process of retrieving files from a backup set and copying them back to their original location.

Resume—To continue printing a document or have the printer continue printing all documents.

Ring 0—The most protected and privileged ring in the Intel chip architecture. Ring 0 enjoys hardware-level protection services and contains system-level components such as virtual device drivers.

Ring 3—The third ring in the Intel architecture which has software-level protection services and is used by Windows 95 for running all applications.

RLE—A compressed bitmap graphics format.

Roving User Profiles—User profiles available on a network. These files are located in the home directory of users in a Windows NT domain, or in the users' mail\user_id directory on a NetWare server.

Run—Enables the user to launch applications directly from the Start menu.

S

Safe mode—A method of starting Windows 95 when the system is having trouble. When the user starts Windows 95 in the Safe mode, only the mouse, keyboard, and VGA device drivers are loaded.

Salvaged data—Data from a file that can be recovered after the file has become cross-linked.

ScanDisk—A Windows 95 utility that checks and fixes data errors and physical surface problems in files and folders on the user's hard disk.

Script—Typically an .inf file that works as an "engine" to "assemble" executables, operating systems, drivers, and others.

Secondary scheduler—A component of the task scheduler responsible for priority inheritance boosting and for adjusting the priority of threads over time to smooth the execution of programs.

Sector—A unit of space on a floppy or hard disk.

Separator page—A header page that is printed before each document to indicate whose print job it is and other specific information.

Serial Line Internet Protocol (SLIP)—An industry standard that can be used with Windows 95 Dial-Up Networking to ensure interoperability with remote access software from other vendors.

Server Message Block (SMB)—A protocol developed by IBM for networking.

Server-based setup—The process of loading the source files on a server so that Windows 95 may be installed across the network.

SETUPLOG.TXT—An ASCII text file that contains the Windows 95 Setup information created during installation.

SETVER.EXE—Included for compatibility reasons. Some MS-DOS applications require specific versions of MS-DOS to be running. This TSR-type device responds to those applications that query for version number by responding directly from an internal table.

Share-level access—The process of protecting network resources through passwords only.

Share-level access control—In share-level access control, the user assigns a password to a specific resource. Depending on the password used, a user may have Read-Only or Full Control.

Share-level security—Rights based on the access that users have to a resource.

Shared fax modem—A fax modem to which a user has given permission to other users on the network to send and receive faxes.

Shared installation—Accomplished by installing Windows 95 on a server and then running the OS across the network.

Shiva Password Authentication Protocol (SPAP)—SPAP offers encryption of PAP passwords and Novell NetWare bindery access for user account information. When Windows 95 is set up for user-level security using a NetWare server account list, this is the security type used for remote access clients.

Shortcut—An icon created for an application which points to the location of the executable file and contains properties that tailor the application's environment.

Shut down—Offers the user the choice to shut down, restart, restart in MS-DOS mode, close all programs and, if the user is on a network, to log on as a different user.

Simple Mail Transfer Protocol (SMTP)—An ASCII message format that is commonly used for mail sent on the Internet.

Single tasking—When running in MS-DOS mode, the system becomes single tasking, enabling only one application to be run at a time.

Small Computer Standard Interface (SCSI)—A bus architecture that can chain a number of devices on one cable.

Software compression—Software compression specifies that the computer will try to compress information before sending it. Compression will occur only if the computer to which the user is connecting is using a compatible compression program.

Spool—This is the act of rendering a document to be printed. The RAW code is kept on disk and then sent to the printer.

Stacker—A disk compression product sold by STAC Electronics, Inc. Windows 95 is compatible with this product, but it cannot use protected-mode drivers to access Stacker drives and is consequently slower in performance.

Stacks—System resource stacks under Windows 95 are now 32-bit, decreasing the likelihood of running out of system resources.

Stall—An application is said to be stalled when it does not check its message queue. As a result, the application stops working.

Standard mode—One of the operating modes for ScanDisk in which it does not scan the physical surface of the disk for defects.

Start menu—The component of Windows 95 that provides fast access to various components of Windows 95, including applications.

Startup disk—A floppy disk created in the Add/Remove programs applet or during installation. Used to boot Windows 95 into a non-GUI mode for emergency repair.

Status bar—Adds a message bar at the bottom of the Windows Explorer. This bar displays information about the various parts and functions of a Windows Explorer session.

Status information—The items located in the Notification Area appear as small icons for programs running in the background.

Storage media—The particular type of storage used for a backup. Windows 95 backup supports floppy disks, hard disks, and QIC tapes as storage media.

Subnet—Division of the network into smaller networks.

Subnet mask—The means by which networks are divided.

Supervisor—The highest authority account on a NetWare network.

Suspended—When a WIN16 application creates a GPF, all other WIN16 applications are suspended until the offending application is shut down.

Swap file—The swap file is used by Windows 95 to provide Virtual Memory by swapping pages from RAM to the swap file.

Switches—Parameters specified at the end of the command that modify the way the command is executed. Each program file supports different switches.

Symptom—A careful analysis of problem symptoms can lead to the selection of the appropriate tool for problem resolution.

System integrity—Windows 95 maintains system integrity by separating application memory address space and processor privilege, and by virtualizing hardware devices.

System policies—Files used to control a user's environment and restrict privileges based on users, groups, or computers.

System Policy Editor—Use the System Policy Editor to create system policy users, groups of users, and computers.

System Virtual Machine—The Virtual Machine in which all 16-bit and 32-bit Windows applications run. The 16-bit applications share a common address space within the System Virtual Machine, and 32-bit applications each maintain separate address spaces.

SYSTEM.DAT—One of two files that make up the Registry, this is the Registry file that contains the hardware and computer-specific settings for a workstation. By default, this file is located in the Windows SYSTEM directory. SYSTEM.DAT contains machine-specific data.

T

Taskbar—A list of all active programs by maintaining a title button for each active program.

TechNet—A CD-ROM available from Microsoft as a subscription containing technical information and updates to Microsoft products.

Telephone Application Programming Interface (TAPI)—Arbitrates among applications that want to share the same communications ports and devices.

Terminated—Applications that attempt to violate system integrity are terminated to protect the system and other applications running concurrently.

Third party—Refers to manufacturers other than the manufacturer of the specific application or hardware.

Thorough mode—One of the operating modes for ScanDisk in which it scans the physical surface of the disk for defects.

Thread—The smallest unit of executable code contained in an application. 32-bit applications may have multiple threads executing concurrently.

Thunking—The process of translating a 16-bit API call to a 32-bit API call and vice versa.

Token—A small piece of code used to represent longer, repetitive bit patterns in a data file.

Toolbar—The toolbar provides a faster way to access menu items in Windows Explorer.

Tools—Windows 95 provides several tools, or utilities, for managing disk resources.

Transmission Control Protocol/Internet Protocol (TCP/IP)—A routable protocol used to access the Internet, provide functionality in WANs, and access UNIX resources.

TSR—Terminate and Stay Resident programs can be activated each time an application is started by specifying them in a batch file on the application's shortcut Properties sheet.

Typical—The default option, which Microsoft recommends for most users with desktop computers.

U

Unidriver—The universal driver is the code that Microsoft provides that works with most printers. The manufacturer then only has to supply a small amount of code that is specific to the printer.

Unified Logon—The capability to connect to all resources after a single logon.

UNINSTAL.EXE—A utility used to remove Windows 95 from a computer.

Universal Naming Convention (UNC)—Refers to a standard way of referencing an object on another computer on a network.

USER.DAT—The file that contains user configuration settings used to implement user profiles either locally or on a network. One of two files that make up the Registry.

User-level access—The process of protecting network resources through users' logon accounts.

User-level access control—In user-level access control, specific users are given rights to a specific resource. A network server (NetWare or Microsoft) is required as a security provider, which provides a list of authorized users.

User-level security—Security based on rights assigned to a specific user.

USER.MAN—The file that contains user configuration settings used to implement mandatory user profiles on a network.

Utility—A tool for maintenance and problem resolution. Windows 95 provides four disk management utilities—Disk Defragmenter, ScanDisk, DriveSpace, and Backup.

UUENCODE—A message format for incoming and outgoing messages that converts attached binary files into text format before they are sent over the Internet.

V

Video Electronics Standards Association (VESA)—A high-speed bus architecture that is not Plug and Play.

Video problems—Certain MS-DOS games experience video problems running under Windows 95. In this case, they should be run in MS-DOS mode.

Virtual DOS Machine (VDM)—The virtual machine created for each MS-DOS application running. Each MS-DOS application executed creates another VDM.

Virtual Machine (VM)—Applications in Windows 95 are designed to be run in a Virtual Machine that provides the application access to memory, resources, and the use of hardware using virtual drivers.

Virtual Machine Manager (VMM)—The VMM subsystem provides the resources needed for each application and system process running on the computer, including memory management and task scheduling.

Virtual memory—A combination of physical RAM and hard disk space that provides more memory than is actually installed on the computer.

W-Z

Warm-docking—A style of docking that enables the laptop to be inserted into or removed from the docking station while in a suspended state.

WIN16 MUTEX—The flag set for WIN16 processes when they make requests to 16-bit API functions. This prevents other WIN16 applications from attempting to use the same code simultaneously.

Windows 95 Registry—Stored in two files: the SYSTEM.DAT file and the USER.DAT file.

Windows 95 Taskbar—Provides quick access to all active programs by maintaining a set of buttons that represent the program's title boxes.

Windows Internet Naming Service (WINS)—Automatic NetBIOS resolution service.

WINIPCFG—Microsoft's utility used to retrieve IP information about a host.

WINNT32.EXE—The 32-bit Windows version of the Windows NT Setup program.

WINREG.DLL—The application extension used by the Microsoft Remote Registry Service executable file. The default location for the file is the *%systemroot%/*system folder. This file must be present on all machines for the Remote Registry Service to function.

Wizard—A type of utility developed by Microsoft to make it easier for the average user to set up his own computer and software.

Workgroup Postoffice—A folder that temporarily stores messages for members of a workgroup until users request delivery of their messages.

World Wide Web—A network of servers that uses hypertext links to find and access files. A browser enables users to view documents on servers around the world without having to manually type each location.

Write-behind caching—Also known as lazy writes, it is the process of storing data in cache until the processor can write the data to disk.

About the Exam

The exam will incorporate a variety of questions from a question bank intended to determine if you have mastered the subject. Following are tips to keep in mind as you prepare for your exam:

- Make sure you understand the material thoroughly.

- Go through all the practice problems. Reread those sections with which you were having trouble.

- Make sure you are comfortable with the style of the scenario questions. These will probably be the most challenging part of the exam.

- Review the exam objectives.

The Microsoft Certification Process

Microsoft has a variety of certifications available for their products. You can find out more about their certifications on the Web page `http://www.microsoft.com/train_cert/`.

How to Become a Microsoft Certified Product Specialist (MCPS)

The Microsoft Certified Product Specialist is the entry level for Microsoft's certifications, and it requires passing a minimal number of exams. Microsoft Certified Product Specialists are required to pass one operating system exam, proving their expertise with a current Microsoft Windows desktop or server operating system, and one or more elective exams from the MCSE or MCSD tracks. The eligible operating system exam choices are as follows:

- Exam 70-73: Implementing and Supporting Microsoft Windows NT Workstation 4.0
  or Exam 70-42: Implementing and Supporting Microsoft Windows NT Workstation 3.51

- Exam 70-67: Implementing and Supporting Microsoft Windows NT Server 4.0
  or Exam 70-43: Implementing and Supporting Microsoft Windows NT Server 3.51

- Exam 70-30: Microsoft Windows 3.1

- Exam 70-48: Microsoft Windows for Workgroups 3.11-Desktop

- Exam 70-63: Implementing and Supporting Microsoft Windows 95

- Exam 70-160: Microsoft Windows Architecture I

- Exam 70-161: Microsoft Windows Architecture II

All exams for Microsoft's premium certifications (Microsoft Certified Systems Engineer and Microsoft Certified Solution Developer) are available as electives and provide further verification of skills with Microsoft BackOffice products, development tools, or desktop applications.

How to Become a Microsoft Certified Systems Engineer (MCSE)

The Microsoft Certified Systems Engineer is probably the most rapidly growing certification in the world. It proves that you are knowledgeable in advanced operating systems such as Windows 95 and Windows NT, that you excel in networking-related skills, and that you have a broad enough background to understand some of the elective products.

MCSE candidates need to pass four operating system exams and two elective exams. The MCSE certification path is divided into two tracks: the Windows NT 3.51 track and the Windows NT 4.0 track.

Table B.1 shows the core requirements (four operating system exams) and the elective courses (two exams) for the Windows NT 3.51 track.

Table B.1   Windows NT 3.51 MCSE Track

Take These Three Required Exams (Core Requirements)	Also, Pick One Exam from the Following Operating System Exams (Core Requirement)	Also, Pick Two Exams from the Following Elective Exams (Elective Requirements)
Implementing and Supporting Microsoft Windows NT Server 3.51 #70-43	Implementing and Supporting Microsoft Windows 95 #70-63	Implementing and Supporting Microsoft SNA Server 3.0 #70-13
AND Implementing and Supporting Microsoft Windows NT Workstation 3.51 #70-42	*OR* Microsoft Windows for Workgroups 3.11-Desktop #70-48	*OR* Implementing and Supporting Microsoft Systems Management Server 1.2 #70-18
AND Networking Essentials #70-58	*OR* Microsoft Windows 3.1 #70-30	*OR* Microsoft SQL Server 4.2 Database Implementation #70-21
		OR Implementing a Database Design on Microsoft SQL Server 6.5 #70-27
		OR Microsoft SQL Server 4.2 Database Administration for Microsoft Windows NT #70-22
		OR System Administration for Microsoft SQL Server 6.5 #70-26
		OR Microsoft Mail 3.2 for PC Networks Enterprise #70-37

Take These Three Required Exams (Core Requirements)	Also, Pick One Exam from the Following Operating System Exams (Core Requirement)	Also, Pick Two Exams from the Following Elective Exams (Elective Requirements)
		OR Internetworking Microsoft TCP/IP on Microsoft Windows NT (3.5-3.51) #70-53
		OR Internetworking Microsoft TCP/IP on Microsoft Windows NT 4.0 #70-59
		OR Implementing and Supporting Microsoft Exchange Server 4.0 #70-75
		OR Implementing and Supporting Microsoft Internet Information Server 3.0 and Microsoft Index Server 1.1 #70-77
		OR Implementing and Supporting Microsoft Proxy Server 1.0 #70-78

Table B.2 shows the core requirements (four operating system exams) and elective courses (two exams) for the Windows NT 4.0 track. Tables B.1 and B.2 have many of the same exams listed, yet the two have distinct differences. Make sure you read each track's requirements carefully.

Table B.2   Windows NT 4.0 MCSE Track

Take These Two Required Exams (Core Requirements)	Also, Pick One Exam from the Following Operating System Exams (Core Requirement)	Also, Take the Following Networking Exam (Core Requirement)	Also, Pick Two Exams from the Following Elective Exams (Elective Requirements)
Implementing and Supporting Microsoft Windows NT Server 4.0 #70-67	Implementing and Supporting Microsoft Windows 95 #70-63	Networking Essentials #70-58	Implementing and Supporting Microsoft SNA Server 3.0 #70-13
AND Implementing and Supporting Microsoft Windows NT Server 4.0 in the Enterprise #70-68	*OR* Microsoft Windows for Workgroups 3.11-Desktop #70-48		*OR* Implementing Supporting Systems Management Server 1.2 #70-18
	OR Microsoft Windows 3.1 #70-30		*OR* Microsoft SQL Server 4.2 Database Implementation #70-21

continues

Table B.2   Continued

Take These Two Required Exams (Core Requirements)	Also, Pick One Exam from the Following Operating System Exams (Core Requirement)	Also, Take the Following Networking Exam (Core Requirement)	Also, Pick Two Exams from the Following Elective Exams (Elective Requirements)
	OR Implementing and Supporting Microsoft Windows NT Workstation 4.0 #70-73		*OR* Microsoft SQL Server 4.2 Database Administration for Microsoft Windows NT #70-22
			OR System Administration for Microsoft SQL Server 6.5 #70-26
			OR Implementing a Database Design on Microsoft SQL Server 6.5 #70-27
			OR Microsoft Mail 3.2 for PC Networks Enterprise #70-37
			OR Internetworking Microsoft TCP/IP on Microsoft Windows NT 3.5-3.51 #70-53
			OR Internetworking Microsoft TCP/IP on Microsoft Windows NT 4.0 #70-59
			OR Implementing and Supporting Microsoft Exchange Server 4.0 #70-75
			OR Implementing and Supporting Microsoft Internet Information Server 3.0 and Microsoft Index Server 1.1 #70-77
			OR Implementing and Supporting Microsoft Proxy Server 1.1 #70-78

How to Become a Microsoft Certified Solution Developer (MCSD)

The Microsoft Certified Solution Developer (MCSD) program is targeted toward people who use development tools and platforms to create business solutions. If you are a software developer or programmer working with Microsoft products, this is the certification for you.

Take These Two Required Exams (Core Requirements)	Also, Pick Two Exams from the Following Elective Exams (Elective Requirements)
Microsoft Windows Architecture I #70-160	Microsoft SQL Server 4.2 Database Implementation #70-21
AND Microsoft Windows Architecture II #70-161	*OR* Implementing a Database Design on Microsoft SQL Server 6.5 #70-27
	OR Developing Applications with C++ Using the Microsoft Foundation Class Library #70-24
	OR Programming with Microsoft Visual Basic 4.0 #70-65
	OR Microsoft Visual Basic 5.0 Programming #70-165
	OR Microsoft Access 2.0 for Windows-Application Development #70-51
	OR Microsoft Access for Windows 95 and Microsoft Access Developer's Toolkit #70-69
	OR Developing Applications with Microsoft Excel 5.0 Using Visual Basic for Applications #70-52
	OR Programming in Microsoft Visual FoxPro 3.0 for Windows #70-54
	OR Implementing OLE in Microsoft Foundation Class Library 4.0 Applications #70-25

Becoming a Microsoft Certified Trainer (MCT)

MCTs are product evangelists who teach Microsoft Official Curriculum (MOC) courses to computer professionals through one or more of Microsoft's authorized education channels. MCTs have special access to current Microsoft product information and invitations to Microsoft conferences and technical training events. This certification is designed for those who want to teach official Microsoft classes. The process for becoming a certified trainer is relatively simple and consists of both a general approval for the MCT program as well as an approval for each course you want to teach.

MCT Application Approval

The MCT application approval process involves three steps:

1. Read the MCT guide and the MCT application at `http://www.microsoft.com/train_cert/mct/`.

2. Send a completed MCT application to Microsoft, including proof of your instructional presentation skills.

3. Send proof of your MCP status to Microsoft.

After you have done these, you will have satisfied the general part of the MCT application process. You only have to do this the first time.

MCT Course Certification Approval

The second part of becoming an MCT is certification for each class you teach. Certification to teach a Microsoft Official Curriculum course requires four steps:

1. Pass any required prerequisite MCP exams to measure your knowledge.

2. Study the Official Microsoft Trainer Kit for the course for which you seek certification.

3. Attend the MOC course for which you seek certification.

4. Pass any additional exam requirement(s).

After you've completed both the MCT application and the MCT course certification, you'll be authorized to begin teaching that MOC class at an official Microsoft Authorized Technical Education Center (ATEC).

Registering and Taking the Exam

When you are ready to schedule your exam, use the following list to contact the Sylvan Prometric test registration center that will be most convenient for you.

Country	Telephone Number
Australia	1-800-808-657
Austria	0660-8582
Belgium	0800-1-7414
Canada	800-755-3926
China	10800-3538
France	1-4289-8749
Germany	0130-83-9708
Guam	001-61-800-277583
Hong Kong	800-6375
Indonesia	001-800-61571
Ireland	1-800-626-104

Country	Telephone Number
Italy	1-6787-8441
Japan	0120-347737
Korea	007-8611-3095
Malaysia	800-2122
Netherlands	06-022-7584
New Zealand	0800-044-1603
Philippines	1-800-1-611-0126
Puerto Rico	800-755-3926
Singapore	800-616-1120
Switzerland	155-6966
Taiwan	008-061-1142
Thailand	001-800-611-2283
U.K.	0800-592-873
United States	800-755-3926
Vietnam	+61-2-9414-3666

If this is your first time registering for a Sylvan Prometric exam, Sylvan will assign you an identification number. They will ask to use your Social Security or Social Insurance number as your identification number, which works well for most people because it's relatively easy to remember. You also have the option of having them assign you a Sylvan ID number if you prefer not to disclose your private information.

If this is not your first exam, be prepared to give Sylvan your identification number. It's important that you use the same identification number for all your tests—if you don't, your tests won't be credited to your certification appropriately.

You must provide Sylvan Prometric with the following additional information:

- Mailing address and phone number

- Email address

- Organization or company name

- Method of payment (credit card number or check)

Sylvan requires that you pay in advance. Microsoft Certification Exam prices are related to the currency exchange rates between countries. In the United States, exams are $100, but Certification Exam prices are subject to change, and in some countries, additional taxes may apply. Please verify the price with your local Sylvan Registration Center when registering.

You can generally schedule exams up to six weeks in advance, or as late as the day before.

You can always cancel or reschedule your exam if you contact Sylvan Prometric at least two working days before the exam, or by Friday if your test is scheduled on Monday. If you cancel, exams must be taken within one year of payment.

Same-day registration is available in some locations if space is available. You must register at least 30 minutes before test time.

The day of the test, plan to arrive a few minutes early so that you can sign in and begin promptly. You will be provided with something on which to write notes to yourself during the test, but you will not be allowed to take these notes with you after the test.

You are not allowed to take in books, notes, pagers, or anything else that could contain answers to any of the questions.

Hints and Tips for Doing Your Best on the Tests

The Microsoft Certification Exams are all 75–90 minutes long. The more familiar you are with the test material and style, the easier it will be for you to concentrate on the questions during the exam.

You can divide your time between the questions in any way you like. This exam is comprised of 70 questions. If you are unsure of the answers to a few questions, mark them in some way and come back to them later if you have time. You will have 75 minutes for the actual exam, but you will be scheduled for 90 minutes so that you can spend up to 15 minutes on a practice pre-test (on unrelated subjects) to enable you to become familiar with the way the test engine works. Make sure you think about whether you want to try out the practice test before you sit down to take it—some people find that the additional familiarity helps them, but other people find that it increases their stress level.

Things to Watch For

Make sure that you read each question and all of its possible answers thoroughly. This is especially important for the scenario questions. Many people lose points because they select the first answer that looks right to them when, in fact, a better answer is lurking right on their screens.

After you've made sure that you understand the question, eliminate those answers which you know to be wrong. If you still have two or three choices, consider which of them would be the *best* answer and select it.

Marking Answers for Return

In the event that you aren't quite sure of an answer, you have the option of marking it by selecting a box in the upper-left and returning to the question at the end when you are given the option of reviewing your answers. Pay particular attention to related questions you find later in the test in case you can learn enough from them to figure out the answer to the question of which you were unsure before.

If you pay close attention, you will probably find that other questions help to clarify questions of which you were uncertain.

Attaching Notes to Test Questions

When you finish a Microsoft exam, you will be allowed to enter comments on the individual questions as well as on the entire test. This feature allows you to give some feedback to the team that reviews Microsoft exams. If you find a question that is poorly worded or seems ambiguous, this is the place to let them know about it. Microsoft wants to have good tests, and this is your best opportunity to let them know how they're doing.

Index

L

O

P

S